Y0-EHZ-921

HENRY JAMES
THE CONQUEST OF LONDON
1870–1883

By Leon Edel

THE LIFE OF HENRY JAMES

The Untried Years, 1843–1870

The Conquest of London, 1870–1883

In preparation

The Middle Years, 1883–1894

The Master, 1895–1916

The Psychological Novel

Literary Biography

James Joyce: The Last Journey

Willa Cather: A Critical Biography (with E. K. Brown)

A Bibliography of Henry James (with Dan H. Laurence)

Editor of *The Complete Plays*, *The Complete Tales*, *The Selected Letters* and *The Ghostly Tales* of Henry James

FRANCIS BOOTT AND LIZZIE (ca. 1850)
IN ITALY

"Osmond and Pansy" from a photograph

HENRY JAMES

The Conquest of London

1870–1883

★ ★

By LEON EDEL

RUPERT HART-DAVIS
36 Soho Square London W1
1962

Printed in Great Britain
by Butler & Tanner Ltd,
Frome and London

The great thing is to be *saturated* with something—that is, in one way or another, with life; and I chose the form of my saturation.

HENRY JAMES

CONTENTS

BOOK FIVE: THE SIEGE OF PARIS 1875–1876

BOOK SIX: THE CONQUEST OF LONDON 1876–1878

BOOK SEVEN: A REASONABLE SHOW OF FAME 1878–1879

BOOK EIGHT: PORTRAIT OF A LADY 1879–1881

ILLUSTRATIONS

INTRODUCTION

In this volume I continue the story of Henry James's life from the time of his return to America in 1870, after his "passionate pilgrimage," to the moment of his definitive expatriation in 1883. My first volume, *Henry James: The Untried Years*, published in 1953, showed the formation of his character and personality and the cosmopolitanism of his temperament. The present volume reveals the mature man in the process of fashioning his career. In the remaining two volumes I shall deal with his later middle years and his final phase.

Those familiar with the legendary Henry James, the Johnsonian "Master" of Rye and Chelsea, will discover an unknown figure in these pages. In his thirties the novelist was much more ardent and much less circumspect than the later James: he met life eagerly and often with exuberance. He was in the fullest sense an "addicted artist," but one who was guided at every turn by his intellect. And he was a man of action and a man of the world as well. No novelist of his time addressed himself more assiduously to wooing fame and fortune.

In my introduction to *The Untried Years* I alluded to Boswell's boast that he had not "melted down" his materials. My materials impose a different course. I had read five thousand of James's letters when I wrote the first volume; I have read (in round figures) seven thousand more since then. My task therefore has been one of arriving at significant detail and essence, lest I bury the reader under epistolary documents, all eminently quotable. The documents themselves are therefore reserved for the edition of James's letters which I have in preparation.

Henry James once wrote to his friend Charles Eliot Norton that biography was a "questionable honour to men of tranquillity." He argued that such men, of "the chimneyside, even of the chair and the table," furnished poor material unless they had been involved in great public events. Without these the picture was foreshortened, a mere record of the "poverty of alarms and excursions, and ought, thereby, I think, to be preserved for men of action and movement—with whom alarms and excursions are the native air."

This is a strange statement from the "biographer" of Isabel Archer or of Lambert Strether—he who argued that the revelation of Isabel's thoughts, sitting by her chimneyside, could be made as exciting as pirates and the surprise of a caravan. Clearly James felt that the biographer, having no access to the consciousness of his subject in the large omniscient way of the novelist, could do little with a literary figure. By this token, I suppose, he would have confined us to the lives of generals and politicians, explorers and Lord Byrons. But, as I showed in my lectures on *Literary Biography*, it is possible, in our century, to write the stories of "quiet" lives, if we address ourselves to character and to personality, through the revelation of the works themselves. James knew that the literary art is one of the most personal of arts—even while it insists upon its impersonality. In spinning tales, in using words, in developing a style, a writer asserts his characteristic being as well as his genius. His work, in the end, becomes a kind of supreme biography.

This is the biography I have sought to read in Henry James. By consulting constantly the parallel columns of the novels, tales, criticism and fugitive pieces, and those of the documents fortuitously, though abundantly, preserved—names, places, dates, encounters, comings, goings, personal relations—I have found images of the lost figure, the writer in the middle span in full possession of his creativity and deliberately exposed to the saturation of experience. If we scrutinize this material with a healthy respect for the laws of evidence, and a recognition—which the old biographers in their search for consistency overlooked—of the ambiguities of existence, we arrive at a Henry James of much tougher fibre than the soft and talkative figure of legend, though not one bit less sensitive or "aware" than he has been pictured.

The Conquest of London deals thus with the "human stuff" in a hardy novelist and critic, one who had in him all the splendid egotism of art.

LEON EDEL

New York
30 *September* 1961

Book One

A Season in Cambridge 1870–1872

★

THE PRECIOUS WOUND

THE EXQUISITE PROVINCIALS

THE DISPOSSESSED

"THE GREAT AMERICAN NOVEL"

ALICE

THE ART OF SEEING

ESCAPE

THE PRECIOUS WOUND

In the spring of 1870, when he had returned from his "passionate pilgrimage" abroad, Henry James settled down to live at No. 20 Quincy Street in Cambridge, Massachusetts, with his elderly parents, his brother William and his sister Alice. He had spent fifteen months in the Old World; and the worst of such an adventure, for a constituted cosmopolitan, was the coming back. The novelist was to say in later years that it was a little like being born again. Henry looked anew at the Cambridge horizons—the Harvard elms, Mount Auburn and Brattle, the friendly verandahs of Kirkland Street, the horse-cars in Harvard Square, the large trough and pump for the horses, the cows grazing in the lot beyond the Common. To this he was reduced now, after his adult journey to the Europe of his boyhood—after the campaniles and cathedrals, the glimpses of pagan and papal Rome, the theatres of Paris, the studios of the Pre-Raphaelites. In Cambridge the scene had remained rural, even rustic. The detached houses were set on their lawns or in small fields: the Harvard Yard was fenced with granite posts sunk at intervals, with three rails between, as if to keep animals from straying in; it possessed none of the mystery or the beauty of the Oxford colleges with their thick walls and cloistered privacy. A row of plain wooden houses inhabited by members of the Harvard faculty stood on the opposite side of Quincy Street; facing No. 20 was President Eliot's residence, in awkward red brick, with a close-fitting, top-heavy, slate mansard roof.

For a young man whose only desire was to be "literary," and who had spent childhood years in London, Paris and Geneva, the parochialism of Cambridge and the sparseness of the New England scene represented intellectual and sensual starvation. He had little in common with his Cambridge coevals; they had had their grand tours and were happy to be starting their careers on American soil. His elder brother had completed his medical studies and mingled with "long-headed youths," who had founded a metaphysical club, in which they "wrangle grimly and stick to the question." It gave Henry a headache merely to know of it. "I belong to no club myself and have not great choice of company either to wrangle or agree with," he wrote to his friend, Charles Eliot Norton, who was abroad. In the next sentence he alludes to his loneliness in Cambridge, as artist, as well as gregarious human being: "If it didn't sound weak-mindedly plaintive and fastidious, I would say I lacked society. I know no 'nice men'—that is, passing few, to converse withal." John Fiske was giving a long course in town on Positivism; Wendell Holmes, for whom Henry predicted (even then) a rise to eminence "in a specialty, but to a high degree," was lecturing on jurisprudence. Henry Adams, whom he had recently met, was teaching history at Harvard and editing the *North American Review*. William Dean Howells and his old Newport friend T. S. Perry were his sole literary company; but Howells was now busy at the *Atlantic Monthly*, and could only occasionally resume his old walks and talks with his friends. Henry complained there was little to do and little for his eyes to rest upon—"in a hundred places there are some charming bits of the picturesque—the Yankee picturesque of course I mean—which I devour as I go; but the more I go, the larger grows my appetite, and my sense aches at times for richer fare. When I go to Europe again, it will be, I think, from inanition of the eyes."

The older generation offered him occasional distraction; Longfellow could be bland and mild and anecdotal; Lowell, who might have been a valuable resource in spite of their difference in years, he knew but slightly. Sometimes he would be bidden to feasts in honour of celebrities and find himself among the Cambridge and Boston worthies: as when Cambridge fêted Bret Harte, "a clever writer," Henry observed, "but with a monstrous newspaper-made reputation which vulgarizes him in spite of himself." For the rest, he spent certain hours at his writing-desk, and he gave himself over to the round of the seasons: autumns in which the crickets filled the nights, and yellow leaves announced the drifting snows; the spring with its deepening green in President Eliot's front yard; summers of idle wandering in the Waltham and Arlington Hills. "I lie there, often, on the grass, with a book in my pocket," Henry wrote to his friends in Europe, "thinking hungry eastward thoughts; but thinking too that we have very good things near us at home—witness these untrodden hills and woods—so utterly unhaunted that I can people them with what shapes I will, with this vast outlook into purple distances and nameless inland horizons fretted by superb undulations—which all simply means honest Massachusetts."

He could not wholly reconcile himself, however, to substituting honest unfurnished Massachusetts for the furnished scenes of Europe. "My year in Europe," he writes to Grace Norton in the autumn of 1870, "is fading more and more into an incredible past. The continuity of life and routine and sensation has long since so effectually re-established itself here, that I feel my European gains sinking gradually out of sight and sound and American experience closing *bunchily* over them as flesh over a bullet—the simile is apropos! But I have only to probe a little to hear the golden ring of that precious projectile."

He had received a lasting wound; and his ache was the ache of having been free on an old and picturesque continent, and now finding himself tethered once again in a little street, in a suburb of Boston, with only his memories to feed on. Sometimes he called his wound a virus; sometimes it became a poison. In a later and more American image, the bullet was a buried arrow, "one of those well-directed shafts from the European quiver to which, of old, tender American flesh was more helplessly and bleedingly exposed." His most characteristic image was that he had been fed "too prompt a mouthful" of the fruit of the Tree of Knowledge. Why, he was to ask himself, long afterwards, had it left "so queer a taste" in his mouth, during all the early years of travel with his family on the Continent? In old age, when he looked back, he wondered at the "infinitely greater queerness" which he had experienced on his return from his first adult journey abroad, between "the summer of '70 and that of '72, when it set me again in motion."

I

The "queerness" was the stark contrast between his two worlds, and his dilemma: for however much he belonged to New York and Boston, his "home" seemed even more now to be Europe. He passed many melancholy hours. When William, years later, after a term abroad, spoke of America's "scraggy aspects," Henry told him: "I tasted of that intensity once and forever when I returned from Europe in May 1870—and determined, in the deadly days, on my future life. I felt then, as I felt after subsequent returns, that the only way to live in America was to turn one's back on Europe; that the attempt to *mix* them is a terribly comfortless business."

The "deadly days," the episodes of his Cambridge life, took on a certain humorous aspect as he described them in 1870 to Grace Norton. "Mr J. T. Fields lectured here on Cheerfulness lately (as who should say: I know I'm a humbug and a fountain of depression, but grin and bear it) and Mr Longfellow feasted him afterwards at supper. Apropos of which Mr Longfellow is just issuing a new poem *The Divine Tragedy*, on the Passion and Crucifixion. I don't suppose it will be quite as strong a picture as the San Cassano Tintoretto; but it will have its points. Lowell seems to write nothing. I believe he is given over to the study of Low French—I use the term in a historic and not a moral sense." Howells, he told his friend, was making a good editor of the *Atlantic*; it was probably with him that James passed his most congenial Cambridge hours. The *Atlantic* editor was to remember the sort of things they talked about—"how we might eliminate the everlasting young man and young woman" from fiction. "I remember he had one very notable scheme for a novel whose interest should centre about a mother and a son." But Howells could not meet the exigent standards of Henry James. "He has been writing a series of articles descriptive of a western tour he made last summer—which have greater finish and beauty than any thing he ever wrote. But there is to me a somewhat pathetic discordance in his talent—the need of applying really first-class handling to subjects belonging to *la petite littérature*. The more

I think of it the more I deprecate the growing tendency—born of the very desperation of the writer—to transfer directly and bodily, without any intellectual transmutation, all the crude accidents of his life as they successively befall, into the subject-matter of literature. Before we are fairly launched here, we are being swamped by the dire vulgarity of it."

"We have over here the high natural light of chance and space and prosperity," he tells Norton. Looking about for himself he had concluded that "the face of nature and civilization in this our country is to a certain point a very sufficient literary field. But," he added, "it will yield its secrets only to a really *grasping* imagination. This I think Howells lacks. (Of course *I* don't!) To write well and worthily of American things one needs even more than elsewhere to be a *master*. But unfortunately one is less!"

II

During his two years in Cambridge Henry James wrote not only a series of tales, but a short novel, eight travel-sketches, two dramatic sketches, seven book-reviews and three art-notices—and counted himself "wantonly idle." Following the course of the Franco-Prussian war, he told Grace Norton that he was so busy reading newspapers "that I largely manage to forget that I am doing no work of consequence." He held a large part of his desire to return to Europe to be "morbid"; he reasoned that "I should be very much less subject to it, if I were engaged here in some regular and absorbing work."

This was a further element of the "queerness." The literary life, in a busy and preoccupied America, seemed to Henry an idle life. His fellow-citizens were creating industry and building railroads, or preoccupied with the law or even with metaphysics. In the Cambridge society, trying to live by his pen and earning his meagre supply of dollars, Henry seemed confined to his room with his blank sheets of paper, and largely to female society. The hero of "A Passionate Pilgrim" remarks that in England "my vulgar idleness would have been—don't laugh now!—would have been elegant leisure," and Rowland Mallet tells a young lady in *Roderick Hudson* "I have the misfortune to be a rather idle man, and in Europe the burden of idleness is less heavy than here." This was the repeated refrain of Henry's dreary Cambridge days; the profession of literature seemed out of harmony with his American environment.

He was to speak of this later in his study of Hawthorne. "The young man who has not, in a word, an office in the business quarter of the town, with his name painted on the door, has but a limited place in the social system, finds no particular bough to perch upon." If Henry could have felt less solitary in Cambridge, he might not have dwelt so recurrently on his "idleness." And he remarked that every individual works better when he has "companions working in the same line and yielding the stimulus of suggestion, comparison, emulation." He was distinctly, at this moment, a young man in the provinces, with his eyes on the shining cities.

III

"Cambridge society is a little arid," Henry remarked to his friends in Europe. "My dissipations have been in Boston chiefly." The translation from Cambridge to Boston could be accomplished almost at any time without undue violence, even if it meant a shift from gentle ruralism to a metropolitan "hub." Henry had but to board a plodding horse-car in Harvard Square—let us say on some afternoon of the long winter—a huge, low omnibus, brightly painted, and decorated with jangling bells, dragged by small horses along grooves in the pavement. The journey took him over the long, low bridge that seemed to crawl on staggering posts across the Charles River. If he looked back, his view was of "the desolate suburban horizon, peeled and made bald by the rigour of the season." It was all "hard, cold, void"—boards and tin and frozen earth, sheds and rotting piles and railway-lines across puddles. The picture was one of clutter—loose fences, vacant lots, mounds of refuse, yards bestrewn with iron pipes, telegraph-poles, and the bare wooden backs of places.

In the streets round Boston Common the scene was sufficiently animated: the shop-fronts glowed through frosty panes, the bells of the street-cars were heard in counterpoint with the cries of newsboys in the cold air; and behind large plate-glass windows the interiors of the hotels, with their marble-paved lobbies, revealed their particular life in the white gaslight glare. Western visitors sprawled on divans, stretching long legs in a particular kind of American angularity, while young bell-hops with old faces handed them periodicals and discussed the town's entertainments with them. The illuminated playhouses to which Henry resorted seemed seductive behind swinging doors of red leather or baize, flanked by posters and photographs of actresses. Or he might make his way to the central haven of culture, the Music Hall, where he was to set the final scene of *The Bostonians* a decade and a half later—high, dim, dignified, with its great and sombre organ overhanging the bronze statue of Beethoven. Henry James had long ago exhausted the city's nocturnal life.

He reached out in his "dissipations" for anything that might offer an evening's relief from ennui. He ventured into private meetings and seances, demonstrations of mesmerism, speeches by ardent young reformers or discourses by lady editors advocating new religions, listening attentively to their flow of ready-made oratory derived from "circus-tent" cultural evenings and lecture-halls, all reflecting Boston's spirit of good-doing which continued to animate the citizens in the wake of Abolition. Henry looked, as he rode through the streets, upon rows of red houses that seemed dusky in the lamplight, with "protuberant fronts, approached by ladders of stone;" or he gazed into the interiors of tenements, in dark streets with their narrow halls and human misery, and wandered into areas where new detached houses gave a fine show of ornament—all in wood. Freshly-painted cupolas and belvederes, bow-windows, pillared piazzas and flourishes, scallops, brackets, cornices, presided over by silvered house-numbers painted in high letters over the doorway designed to be visible to the passing horse-cars and all testifying to exuberant and ephemeral carpentry. Years later Henry could still describe minutely his exploration of the down-at-heels

South End. To a reader who wrote to him inquiring about the particular Boston house in which he had sketched the rooms of Miss Birdseye in *The Bostonians*, James gave a general answer and added "I can smell it still."

THE EXQUISITE PROVINCIALS

"IDLE" though he might seem, he did not allow himself to be crushed by his recurrent nostalgia for Europe, nor lulled into inaction by his melancholy. He was barely resettled in Quincy Street in the early summer of 1870 when he persuaded the *Nation* to accept a series of travel-articles from his pen—pictures of Rhode Island, Vermont, New York: a strange enterprise, this writing of sketches of familiar American scenes. The *Nation* was probably beguiled by his fluent descriptive prose; his invidious comparisons were made with a certain charm and good faith. It was an opportunity for him to earn some ready money; it was also a way of convincing the *Nation* how lively a travel-writer he could be—especially if he were in Europe.

There was, however, a deeper prompting of national loyalty. He told Grace Norton that he wanted time for his plans "to mature and accumulate beneath this Western sky." He would be "haunted and wracked," he said, if he returned to Europe with a "thankless ignorance and neglect" of America. If only in self-defence, it was necessary for him to make up "a little list of accomplished devotions and emotions." He would therefore "see all I can of America and *rub it in* with unfaltering zeal."

The words "rub it in" somehow diminished the piety of his devotions. They suggested that Henry would be taking his native land as if it were a stiff dose of medicine. Nevertheless he insisted that he enjoyed his homeland "with a poignancy that perpetually surprises me." His tour consisted of a month in Saratoga, where he drank the waters and "cunningly noted many of the idiosyncrasies of American civilization;" a week at Lake George; a fortnight at Pomfret, where his parents were on holiday; and a fortnight at Newport "where nature was perhaps more attractive, and man rather less so, than ever." At the end of this summary he remarked: "I spent lately a couple of days with Mr Emerson at Concord—pleasantly, but with slender profit."

I

The *Nation* articles offer us a fairly good account of what James saw and how he travelled. His article on Newport explores the difficulty of the life of leisure in America. The question haunts him. His article on Saratoga is a shrewd and witty appraisal of American manners. His view of the American landscape in all its wild richness contains in it neither Emerson's affection for nature nor the studied observation of Thoreau. It is that of a man who appreciates it only when it has been tamed. To have seen the Italian hillsides from Perugia to Narni, with their old walled towns, their churches, their vineyards, their domesticated landscapes, and then to be confronted with the undisciplined green mass of upper New York State was indeed a contrast for Henry's eyes to brood upon: not a little like trying to compare walled-in Oxford with fenced-in Harvard. James spoke of the "complete absence of detail" as he crossed Lake George and explored Burlington and Ticonderoga, which Hawthorne had painted before him. Or the surroundings of Saratoga, "no white villages gleaming in the distance, no spires of churches, no salient details. It is all green, lonely, and vacant." Around him, as he journeyed and strolled in the great American land, Henry felt "the eloquent silence of undedicated nature."

Occasionally he would stumble on what he called "the pure picturesque;" by this he meant "the presentation of a picture, self-informed and complete." A little unpainted dwelling, on a grassy slope, "leaden-grey in the shade, silver-grey in the sun. Against the darkness of the open doorway, from where I stood, I saw a white butterfly soar and sink—I almost heard in the noon-day stillness the soundless whirr of his wings." And he went on to give an idyllic account of milk-pans glittering in the sun, hollyhocks lifting their blooming stalks, the expanse of golden-rod, the crowded apples on the crowded trees of the orchard all set in an "emanation of reflected composite light and colour, of leafed and bladed and fruited green." Nevertheless the foreground, more often than not, was bleak and nondescript: a wooden building, a saw-mill, a high black chimney, all "as transient and accidental as the furniture of a dream." There spoke the traveller who had looked upon the stones of antiquity—the *historical* picturesque.

The describer of scenery however was also an observer of manners, and already in these articles the future novelist is absorbed in the study of the American character. As he sits on the large piazza of his hotel in Saratoga, he notices the overdressed mothers and their young daughters idly circling in the broad noonday. In Europe, he muses, young women might spend their time on needlework, or cultivate the art of conversation, but "here at Saratoga, at any hour of morning or evening, you may see a hundred rustling beauties whose rustle is their sole occupation." The men, lounging about the hotels, struck Henry as diagonals—tilted hats, tilted chairs, feet and cigars tilted up, "they are not the mellow fruit of a society which has walked hand-in-hand with tradition and culture; they are hard nuts, which have grown and ripened as they could. When they talk among themselves, I seem to hear the cracking of the shells." And the children, left asleep in the big leather chairs of the lobby at all hours of the night—Henry had had his glimpse of Daisy and Randolph Miller, in their home environment.

II

Henry's visit to Emerson was a private matter, not chronicled in the *Nation*. He was invited apparently because Emerson remembered Henry's letters written during his European wanderings, which the elder Henry James had brought to Concord and read to him. Howells had said of this correspondence that "you're in great danger of having your private letters stolen and published." Emerson had asked the elder Henry whether he mightn't keep some of them, so that he could re-read and study them. Paternal vanity was strong, however, and the father carried them to show them in other quarters. Emerson "does nothing but talk of your letters," William had reported to his brother, who expressed on his side some uneasiness at this public display of his private musings. Now that the gifted young man had returned, Emerson wanted to set eyes on him once more. He had known him after all from the cradle; and what more natural than that Henry, on his side, should pay his compliments to his distinguished Concord admirer?

Emerson's notebooks show no record of the visit: but then young Harry James came to him in all familiarity. We can, however, reconstitute the scene. The nearby woods were showing their autumn colours; an aroma of apples hung over the sleepy town. There stood the familiar houses—Alcott's "academy," the old Manse hard by the rude bridge, and there was Walden, under its New England sky, with the bird-sounds and the animal life Thoreau had commemorated. Henry saw his father's friend in his well-known and homely surroundings. If the young writer had been looking at characteristic American landscape in recent weeks, he found himself here in the one town outside the beaten path of American material triumph where the "landscape of the soul" had been contemplated no less steadily—and always in close harmony with nature. Hawthorne was but six years dead; Thoreau eight. It was as if they still lived, as if the great moment in the town's history had not yet passed—that moment when there resided at one end of Concord a sage whose utterances were "the most poetical, the most beautiful productions of the American mind" while at the other—with rows of tall New England elms between—there lived an exquisite teller of tales.

Again and again Henry was to use the word "exquisite" in speaking of Emerson and Hawthorne. They were both "exquisite geniuses." He spoke of them also as "exquisite provincials." Provincial, to be sure, was not used by Henry in a derogatory sense: the adjective "exquisite" testified to this. Henry was simply stating a fact; the two men remained foreign to city streets; the large cosmopolitan world that he possessed had not been theirs. He was to wander later with Emerson in the Louvre and the Vatican. "But his spirit, his moral taste, as it were, abode always within the undecorated walls of his youth." So too, Henry remarked, Hawthorne had spent fifty of his years in small American towns, Salem, parochial Boston of the early nineteenth century, Concord, Lenox, West Newton; he had led what might be called a "village life." He too had been "exquisitely and consistently provincial."

The meeting of Emerson and the young writer in that early autumn was a meeting of past and future. Henry always remembered Emerson's voice: it was "irresistible" and he had a "beautiful mild modest authority." He also had (and Henry was to remark on this again and again) "that ripe unconsciousness of evil which is one of the most beautiful signs by which we know him." The Emersonian innocence, the exquisite provinciality of it, touched Henry deeply. Life had never bribed Emerson to look at anything but the soul. And the young realist, busy looking at the visible things of life and at human behaviour around him, pondered this: one might make up poems about the soul, or write philosophical essays; one could hardly write a novel about it. However, it gave the future novelist food for thought—that Emerson had considered Hawthorne's novels "not worthy of him." This was a judgment extremely odd: "How strange that he should not have been eager to read almost anything that such a gifted being might have let fall." Emerson's insensibility to imaginative writers, from Shelley to Dickens, Dante to Jane Austen, Aristophanes to Cervantes—Henry enumerated them—was "a large allowance to have to make for a man of letters."

A day or two after Henry's visit, Emerson wrote to his transatlantic friend, Thomas Carlyle: "A multitude of young men are growing up here of high promise, and I compare gladly the social poverty of my youth with the power on which these draw."

III

In Cambridge, later, Henry read the newly-published French and Italian journals of Hawthorne. Reviewing them for the *Nation* early in 1872, Henry remarked that they "show us one of the gentlest, lightest and most leisurely of observers, strolling at his ease among foreign sights in blessed intellectual irresponsibility, and weaving his chance impressions into a tissue as smooth as fireside gossip." The words "intellectual irresponsibility" might have escaped the eye of a reader at that time: but they express James's vision of Hawthorne in Europe. Hawthorne had been an idle Yankee loiterer with an ineffable charm, "bending a puzzled, ineffective gaze at things, full of a mild genial desire to apprehend and penetrate." The word "ineffective" might also give us pause. The truth was that he looked at things "as little as possible in that composite historic light which forms the atmosphere of many imaginations." Hawthorne's observations betrayed "a childlike evenness and clearness." He assented to nothing he could not understand. He seemed wholly unreceptive to certain elements in the pictures and statues; he was "unreconciled" to the nudity of the marbles. Such a sentiment could only come, Henry remarked, from someone to whom sculpture was a sealed book. But then much of Europe was a sealed book to Hawthorne. "We seem to see him strolling through churches and galleries as the last pure American—attesting by his shy responses to dark canvas and cold marble his loyalty to a simpler and less encumbered civilization."

Henry James would never be able to stroll through the churches and galleries of Europe with quite the same purity, the same air of innocence—or of ignorance.

IV

During this time Henry had ample leisure in which to ponder his own ambiguous state. He could look at Europe with American eyes, and he knew that he looked at America often as if he were a European. He might speak with irony later of the "baleful spirit of the cosmopolite" and the "uncomfortable consequence of seeing many lands and feeling at home in none." Cosmopolitanism was a civilized state of being; yet it was hardly the ideal state. The ideal, Henry believed, "should be to be a concentrated patriot." The international mind seemed to him an accident of nature. When it did happen, one had to make the best of it. "There comes a time when one set of customs, wherever it may be found,"

Henry wrote, "grows to seem to you about as provincial as another; and then I suppose it may be said of you that you have become a cosmopolite. You have formed the habit of comparing, of looking for points of difference and of resemblance, for present and absent advantages, for the virtues that go with certain defects and the defects that go with certain virtues." One became an initiate "into the merits of all peoples." National virtues were numerous. They could be very different. "Downright preferences" were hard.

Such was the lesson of his summer's travels, of his Concord visit, of his hours in Quincy Street. Henry came to see himself in the ironic light of the story of Eden. America was his lost paradise and his had been the "fortunate fall." "Very special and very interesting," Henry was to write, "to catch in the fact the state of being of the American who has bitten deep into the apple of 'Europe' and then been obliged to take his lips from the fruit."

THE DISPOSSESSED

In a passage of reminiscence set down when he was fifty-five Henry James spoke of his Cambridge period as a time of "brooding exile." He imagined himself as having been like "dispossessed princes and wandering heirs" deprived alike of kingdom and of inheritance. The kingdom, he believed, was the Europe of his *Wanderjahr*—where he wanted to be; the inheritance was his matured vision of the transatlantic world, which he could contemplate now only from the ruralism of Quincy Street and the town-pump in Harvard Square. The princely palaces had shrunk to the life of the provinces, the domicile of his immaturity.

The passage of memory in which the middle-aged Henry James looked back on his twenty-seven-year-old self was prompted by his re-reading late in life certain of his early stories, and his selection of two of them for inclusion in the definitive edition of his novels and tales. He chose "A Passionate Pilgrim" which he wrote at the beginning of his Cambridge "exile," and "The Madonna of the Future" which he had written at the end, when he was once more in Europe. These tales marked two significant moments in his career. In resurrecting them he described himself as having been engaged in "sneaking attempts to substitute the American romantic for the American real." He had done more; he had used romantic fancy to probe the personal "real." In the end Henry admitted that he found the stories "in the highest degree documentary for myself." They are so for us as well.

I

Although Henry used the phrase about dispossessed princes and wandering heirs in speaking of himself, he was echoing a remark dropped by his narrator in "A Passionate Pilgrim." Speaking to the "pilgrim" of the story, as they wander in the grounds of his ancestral home in England, the narrator says: "Here you can wander all day like a proscribed and exiled prince, hovering about the dominion of the usurper." And in "The Madonna of the Future" the hero speaks of Americans as being the "disinherited" of art. Dispossession, disinheritance, exile, usurpation—James's heroes in these stories think of themselves as deprived of their birthright, turned into spiritual (and actual) wanderers, unable in their new strange state to enter into possession. James's tale of his American pilgrim in England is a sentimental and romantic rhapsody on this theme, amid English fields and country houses and the colleges of Oxford. The sensitive New Yorker, who makes the pilgrimage, has found himself out of place in America. "I came into the world an aristocrat," he says. "I was born with a soul for the picturesque. It condemns me, I confess; but in a measure, too, it absolves me. I found it nowhere. I found a world all hard lines and harsh lights, without shade, without composition, as they say of pictures, without the lovely mystery of colour. To furnish colour, I melted down the very substance of my own soul." Sitting in a park in England he is "on the misty verge of what might have been."

The pilgrim's name is Clement Searle, and he is one of those old-time "claimants," who believes he still has a right to his ancestral property in England, an Elizabethan manor house named Lockley Park. When the narrator and Clement arrive at the manor, they are received with cordiality by the pilgrim's remote English kin, until their host discovers Clement's design. They are then understandably ordered from the great house. The pilgrim recognizes that he has had a vain dream; he has wished to possess something that in reality belongs to others. He wanders into delusion; he even fancies that he has become his ancestor, living in an earlier time. And he dies at Oxford of a delirious fever. He has been killed by an excess of sensibility, of spiritual "dispossession."

In dying, Clement thinks of the homeland he has abandoned. He speaks of "a certain heroic strain in those young imaginations of the West, which find nothing made to their hands, which have to concoct their own mysteries, and raise high into our morning air, with a ringing hammer and nails, the castles in which they dwell." Clement's last act is to give his modest belongings to an impecunious Englishman who wants to emigrate to America. "My friend, there is to be one American the less. Let there be one the more." If he has replaced the present by a dream of the past, he makes this small concession to the future in America.

The future is in the title of James's second tale of an American, this time a painter, who has arrived in Florence and passed twenty years dreaming before a large canvas that his great work (as in Balzac's tale of an "unknown masterpiece") would be the epitome of all the madonnas that ever were, the very ideal of the maternal, in its highest spiritual form. He is eloquent, this little artist, with his red untidy hair emerging from beneath his *beretto*, his wide eyes, his shabby velvet tunic. It is he who proclaims that "we are the disinherited of Art," as he orates to the American stranger he has met in the moonlight beside the Palazzo Vecchio. "We are condemned to be superficial!" he says; "the soil of American perception is a poor little barren, artificial deposit," and he adds, "we are wedded to imperfection. An American, to excel, has just ten times as much to learn as a European. We lack the deeper sense. We have neither taste, nor tact, nor force." He continues: "Our crude and garish climate, our silent past, our deafening present, the constant pressure about us of unlovely circumstance, are as void of all that nourishes and prompts and inspires the artist, as my sad heart is void of bitterness in saying so."

This passage has often been quoted as indicating Henry James's feeling about his own future as an artist in his homeland. Up to a point he seems indeed to be doing some private pleading. What has been overlooked, however, has been the reply made by the narrator: "You seem fairly at home, in exile, and Florence seems to me a very pretty Siberia." And he goes on to say that "nothing is so idle as to talk about our want of a nutritive soil, of opportunity, of inspiration, and all the rest of it. The worthy part is to do something fine! There's no law in our glorious Constitution against that. Invent, create, achieve! No matter if you've to study fifty times as much as one of these. What else are you an artist for?"

Theobald discloses his dream of a "madonna of the future." He has met the Italian madonna-type; he has sketched her, studied her, loved her. The narrator is told by a member of the American colony that "the months passed by and the miracle hung fire: our master has never produced his masterpiece." When the narrator remarks to Theobold, quite casually, that his model has lost her youth, it is as if he gives the painter a mortal blow. Serafina is, in truth, middle-aged, and rather fat. She "had made twenty years pass as a twelvemonth." The artist turns his face to the wall. Like Clement he dies in a raging fever. His masterpiece is "a mere dead blank, cracked and discoloured by time." In his last moments he mutters: "While I fancied my creation was growing, it was dying." He knows now that he has wasted his life in preparation. He has lived with an obsession—and with it has clung to a sterile past.

II

Beyond their vividness as stories, these tales of the Cambridge period are a mirror of James's deepest feelings at the time. If we strip them of their outward garments we can discern within them two facets of the writer's experience. On the surface they embody the novelist's debate between America and Europe, which was highly active at this time and seeking resolution. On a deeper level they picture Henry's double exile—his sense of being an outsider at home, his fear of being an outsider in Europe. He knew himself to be a prince who had taken possession of his domains in Europe, and tasted the joys of personal freedom. But by the familiar hearth he was once again the Henry James Jr of his past, the wide-eyed little Harry James, observed and observant, who had to defend his status within the family. We are reminded in these tales of earlier episodes—and earlier stories—in the lives of Henry and his brother, in which they had played Jacob and Esau to one another, believing that each was a usurper of the other's birthright. In the United States, in a word, Henry was not in control of his destiny; there was a family past as unreachable—and as smothering—as Clement's in England. The prevailing anxiety in these tales is over this state of "dispossession." It seems to be a question whether "exile" abroad may not be a forsaking of the future embodied in America for a past embodied in Europe; and conversely, might not America—in the form of a past embodied in "family"—prove altogether too limiting for a young man who wanted to create great works of art in a personal and independent future, the future of his maturity?

In a word, Henry James in Quincy Street knew that he had outgrown his past and needed to be freed from it; he knew that he had lingered too long at the family hearth, and that he must escape. The silver cords however were still strong. If the story of the painter in Florence, worshipping an eternal mother, and the pilgrim clinging to an unattainable family past were told on a fanciful and imaginative plane, there were other tales which are cruder and less embellished documents. These were not resurrected half a century later, and when we read them we can understand why. They take us uncomfortably close to the inner life of No. 20 Quincy Street and the inner world of the young artist who was curbing his restless soul, or giving it relief in the perorations of his suffering heroes.

One of the tales was called "Master Eustace." It was probably the story "whose interest should centre about a mother and son" of which James had spoken to Howells. The mother in this tantrum-packed tale, a widow, has treated her only child as if he were a lover, and also as an "heir-apparent." She spoiled him in every way. She liked to lean her head on his shoulder, and "resting in this delicious contact, with her arm round his neck and her cheek on his hair, she would close her eyes in a kind of tremor of ecstasy." She also would stroll with him in the garden giving him occasionally a "compulsive hug." Small wonder that Master Eustace experiences ecstasy as well—a sense of complete possession. He leaves for his grand tour of Europe; and if he is not a passionate pilgrim, the passion is reserved for his homecoming. He returns to find that his mother has married an old and loyal friend, and his rage explodes in speeches such as Henry must have heard upon the New York stage during his childhood. "I'm like Hamlet," says Master Eustace; "I don't approve of mothers consoling themselves." And he is indeed a small-town Hamlet of the New World with a wooden house for his Elsinore. While he was wandering in far-away places a stranger had occupied the domestic throne. But Eustace is incapable of Hamlet's monologues:

> Did she hope to keep it a secret? Did she hope to hide away her husband in a cupboard? Her husband! And I—I—I—what has she done with me? Where am I in this devil's game? Standing here crying like a schoolboy for a cut finger—for the bitterest of disappointments! She has blighted my life—she has blasted my rights. She has insulted me—dishonoured me. Am I a man to treat in that fashion? Am I a man to be made light of? Brought up as a flower and trampled as a weed! Bound in cotton and steeped in vitriol!

Eustace's inconsolable grief and sense of outrage is that of a husband who has an unfaithful wife, rather than that of a son whose mother has sought happiness in a new marriage. From now on Eustace is only a pretender to a throne he believed to be his. The drama, like its speeches, is resolved in a pistol-flourish, and the mother's death of heart-failure. Dispossession is complete.

So Henry, returning from his grand tour, discovered distinct changes in the climate of Quincy Street. He might still be the preferred son of his mother, the old-time "angel" of the family, but Mary James had settled into late middle age, serene, matronly, queenly and vaguely indifferent. Her children were grown and her domestic empire had been extended, for the younger brothers were in the west. Quincy Street had become quite accustomed to Henry's absence. The elder brother had remained at home, and was in comfortable possession. Into a second tale Henry projected this pendant side of the familial situation, his old fraternal attachments and animosities. As "Master Eustace" is a story of mother and son, so "Guest's Confession" is a tale of two brothers, the elder a successful man who is also a hypochondriac with a vengeful disposition, and the younger a sensitive and artistic individual.

> The terms on which we stood were a perpetual source of irritation. We were utterly unlike in temper and taste and opinions, and yet, having a number

of common interests, we were obliged, after a fashion, to compromise with each other's idiosyncrasies. In fact the concessions were all on my side. He was altogether too much my superior in all that makes the man who counts in the world for me not to feel it, and it cost me less to let him take his way than to make a stand for my dignity . . . He was a miserable invalid, and was perpetually concerned with his stomach, his lungs, and his liver, and as he was both doctor and patient in one, they kept him very busy.

When we recall Mary James's description of William James's multiple symptoms at this time, his "morbid sympathy" with "every form" of physical trouble, we are led to feel that Henry is writing at uncomfortably close quarters. William, much more literally than the fictitious Edgar, was both "doctor and patient in one."

The crucial scene in the story is one of the most painful and awkward ever written by James. The younger brother has been courting a young woman he has met at a summer resort. Edgar, the elder brother, arrives and discovers that the girl's father is a man who once defrauded him in a shady business deal. He seizes this moment for his revenge: he forces the older man to kneel in public and confess his business sins. He gives no thought to the fact that he is ruining his brother's chances with the girl. In other words, the elder brother, by a crude revengeful impulse, limits his younger brother's freedom of action.

"Was I, after all, so excessively his younger brother?" the suitor muses. The story shows that he was. And while Edgar bears no resemblance to William James, the fraternal rivalry and fraternal animosity described in this tale are but another instance of Henry's submerged feelings in Quincy Street. William may have sensed some part of himself in the story, for he singled it out when it was published to emphasize certain of his chronic complaints against Henry's writings: his use of French phrases, his "note of literary reminiscence in the midst of what ought to be pure imagination." The two phrases William focused on for attack were *les indifférents* and "to whom I had dedicated a sentiment." What he said about them was valid enough. The manner in which he criticized the story shows an excessive sharpness of feeling:

Of the people who experience a personal dislike so to speak of your stories, the most I think will be repelled by the element which gets expression in these two phrases, something cold, thin-blooded and priggish suddenly popping in and freezing the genial current. And I think that is the principal defect you have now to guard against. In flexibility, ease and light power of style you clearly continue to gain. "Guest's Confession" and this last letter in the *Nation* are proofs of it . . . I meanwhile say nothing of the great delight which all your pieces give me by their insight into the shades of being, and their exquisite diction and sense of beauty and expression in the sights of the world.

In effect, William, for all his praise, was calling Henry "cold, thin-blooded and priggish." Moreover, he added words hardly edifying to an imaginative writer: "I still believe in your greatness as a critic."

"THE GREAT AMERICAN NOVEL"

For Henry, spending his days in Cambridge in what he deemed to be a state of sinful idleness, the logical solution seemed to be to write a novel which would establish his fame, earn him some money, make possible perhaps a return to Italy. Unmistakable hints had appeared in his *Nation* travel-sketches. Describing a group of houses in the Lake George region, he had written: "One of them there was—but of it I shall say nothing. I reserve it for its proper immortality in the first chapter of the great American novel." Arriving at Newport, which he found substantial and "civilized" after Saratoga, he reflected: "I can almost imagine a transient observer of the Newport spectacle dreaming momentarily of a great American novel." Henry's dream apparently was not momentary. The innocent *Nation* reader would hardly be blamed for inferring that their anonymous author was planning—perhaps even embarked upon—a novel which he hoped would be both distinctively American and "great." Even Henry James, who in later years would have found the cliché intolerable, had this youthful dream of literary glory.

I

By the time the Saratoga and Newport seasons of 1870 were at an end, the writer had submitted three parts of a five-part work of fiction to Mr Fields, Howells's superior at the *Atlantic Monthly*. A surviving letter shows Henry adroitly pressing for early publication, or, in lieu of that, early payment. He was never to be modest in writing to editors and publishers. On this occasion he hoped Fields would content himself "with my assurance that the story is one of the greatest works of 'this or any age.' " This may have been his little joke: it is of a piece with his day-dream of "the great American novel." To Norton he wrote in a less exuberant vein, saying that the subject was "something slight; but I have tried to make a work of art, and if you are good enough to read it I trust you will detect my intention. A certain form will be its chief merit."

The modern reader may wonder what this certain form was, for *Watch and Ward* emerged demurely in the pages of the *Atlantic* as the story of an effete young Bostonian, who wears lavender gloves and consoles himself for failure in love by adopting a twelve-year-old girl. His motive can hardly be said to be disinterested; he nourishes the private hope that Nora Lambert, on attaining womanhood, will marry him: he will have thus married, so to speak, his own carefully-raised daughter, without incurring the risk of incest. Moreover, by this Pygmalion act, he tries to remove himself from the competition of courtship. He is not wholly successful, for his cousin, the Rev. Hubert Lawrence, a rather worldly clergyman, shows unusual interest in the young lady; and Nora's own cousin, a penniless and rather shabby individual named Charles Fenton, also pursues her in the hope of a substantial dowry. We can see from this that Henry somehow has been unable to stray from picturing family relations: indeed everyone seems related to everyone in this novel. As Henry describes the two Lawrence cousins, we find ourselves listening to familiar words:

> He and Roger had been much together in early life and had formed an intimacy strangely compounded of harmony and discord. Utterly unlike in temper and tone, they neither thought nor felt nor acted together on any single point. Roger was constantly differing, mutely and profoundly, and Hubert frankly and sarcastically; but each, nevertheless, seemed to find in the other a welcome counterpart and complement to his own personality.[1]

Thus the brothers of "Guest's Confession" are converted in this novel into Roger, the man of sentiment, and Hubert, the religious-worldly type. In the end Hubert's insincerity and Fenton's opportunism are unmasked; and Roger wins his wife—after arousing her attention and her pity by a prolonged illness. Once again James has duplicated his old stories of a "heroine of the scene" surrounded by suitors who possess traits of the significant

[1] This was revised in 1878 to read "an irritating counterpart and complement."

figures in his childhood, with himself as the unassertive and self-doubting aspirant. But this time he gives himself the victory.

II

Conceived as a study of Boston manners, *Watch and Ward* deals rather with the *mœurs* of Quincy Street. Indeed there is no painting of the Boston scene: we are unaware that we are in that city until the middle of the book. At every turn we are aware, however, of the relationships among the characters. The book is of a piece with the tales of the "dispossessed;" Henry has moved into a further phase of dispossession. Where before he made tantrum-tales of it, he now writes a fairy-tale. The rejected Roger entertains Henry's dream of fair women: and the ideal woman, this time, will be secured from rivals by an act of previous possession. If in "Master Eustace" Henry's Hamlet-theme showed strong sensual feeling between a mother and a son, the relationship between Roger and Nora has a more overt element of sexuality but how conscious he was of this is a moot point. It must have seemed harmless in its day, since it escaped Mr Field's watchful eye, and that of his assistant, Howells, as well as the type-setters of the *Atlantic*. Both the serial and book versions—published eight years apart—contain a passage in which Roger wonders after adopting Nora whether at the worst a little precursory love-making would do any harm. "The ground might be gently tickled to receive his own sowing; the petals of the young girl's nature, playfully forced apart, would leave the golden heart of the flower but the more accessible to his own vertical rays." This is a curious passage to come from an inveterate reader of French novels. It may have been penned tongue-in-cheek; yet it may represent also a certain unconscious eroticism. Another and better-known passage in this novel describes Nora, in *déshabille* at bedtime, bringing her watch to be wound, with Roger's key proving a "misfit" and Hubert Lawrence's rather more successful even though "some rather intimate fumbling was needed to adjust it to Nora's diminutive timepiece." These passages survived the close revision of *Watch and Ward* in 1878, after William

James had found in the manuscript of *The American* certain phrases which, he wrote Henry, were so "shocking" as to make the "reader's flesh creep." William had no difficulty in inducing Howells to remove them from the copy, and when Henry was informed, he gave Howells *carte blanche* over any future "infelicities" of this kind.

Watch and Ward found a public in the magazine, but long before it had run its course Henry must have realized that his claims for it had been rather large. He was to republish it in book form in 1878 only because of expediency and for purposes of copyright. Yet his original strong feeling for the work is understandable. It contained certain personal emotions which were to yield him at least three of his best-known novels: *The Portrait of a Lady*, which has better claim to be judged a "great American novel;" its later and grandiose version, *The Wings of the Dove*, and the ever-popular story of a father, a daughter and a fortune-hunter, *Washington Square*. Henry's fault in this first novel was similar to that of most beginners: he tried to cram too much of his subject-matter into the single work; he achieved a fiction rich in potential material and overstuffed in performance. Yet we see the artist, working within a literary tradition, grasping his form, and in possession of the verbal ear that will help him fashion his later style. *Watch and Ward* is a harbinger of Henry's greatness, a glimpse into the beginning of his creative process. His verdict, when he finally brought it out as a book, was at the opposite pole to what he had said to Fields or to Norton. It was "pretty enough" he remarked after revising it; nevertheless it was "very thin and as 'cold' as an icicle."

ALICE

HENRY had written a novel about a young man of his own age, a maturing girl and her suitors. The suitors seemed to resemble figures in his own family. The young heroine reflected, to a considerable degree, Henry's discovery on his return from Europe that his only sister Alice, some four years his junior, had arrived at charming—if nervous and high-strung—womanhood. She had figured first in his life as a young and romping presence. When she was a quiet and troubled adolescent, Henry was going through his own tribulations of the Civil War years. Now, after his absence, he saw her with new eyes. At twenty-three she was gentle, almost sedate; her eyes were large and candid; she had a broad brow, a strong mouth, a straight nose. She was of medium height and combed her thick hair back tightly from her forehead. Photographs suggest a colleen of American growth, with a certain strong facial resemblance to her novelist-brother and her father.

I

Alice had grown up in a family circle wholly masculine, save for the presence of her mother and her aunt. Five men, four brothers and a father, loomed in her childhood and youth: the father and the two elder brothers had always bestowed upon her elaborate mocking gallantries. She was a much-teased child—that is a child exposed to more than a modicum of peculiar, and often aggressive adult behaviour. Even the great Thackeray, paying a call on the family one day in Paris, raised a laugh at her expense. Bending friendly eyes on her frock, he raised his voice in high and simulated shock: "Crinoline—I was suspecting it! So young and so depraved!"

One gathers that life in the nursery was an endless battle for

ALICE JAMES IN HER TEENS
From a photograph

Alice. When her two younger brothers, those closer to her own age—Wilky and Bob—did not ignore her, they subjected her to the usual petty indignities which small boys heap on sisters. At forty she wrote down her memories of a trip in an open carriage to the outskirts of Boulogne-sur-Mer, when she had been seven or eight, recording "the anguish, greater even than usual, of Wilky's and Bob's heels grinding into my shins." The phrase "greater even than usual" conveys a world of juvenile history. Outside the nursery the world proved deceptive and ambiguous. Certain female figures—Aunt Kate, her mother, governesses—hovered over her. They were admonitory, critical, disciplinary. In the front parlour, however, the elder Henry smothered her with affection, while the older and more distant brothers, Willie and Harry, petted—and teased.

The teasing seemed harmless enough. Its character may be judged from a letter written by William to Alice when he was eighteen and she was twelve. He sends his love to the "cherry-lipped, apricot-nosed, double-chinned" Alice, whom he saluted also as "sweetlington" and "sisterkin." He wishes that she would "sass" him, "as of yore." We thus have to do with a girl who "sassed." This is reflected also in a letter from Mary James to one of her sons, while Alice was away from home. "Father's greatest trial," she wrote, "is Alice's absence. She has become an immense comfort to him. Her sweet, loving chaffing does him more good than anything else."

Adolescence was scarcely better. "The ancient superstition as to spring and youth being the joyous periods is pretty well exploded," Alice was to write in her journal. "As the one is the most depressing moment of the year, so is the other the most difficult of life." She remembered "absorbing into the bone that the better part is to clothe one's self in neutral tints, walk by still waters and possess one's soul in silence." We may meditate on the implications of these words: the assumption by a young and spirited creature of an emotional neutrality, a nun-like withdrawal into inaction, quiet, silence. To be silent in the midst of ubiquitous and brilliantly talkative brothers, and a verbally imaginative father, was not however easy. In self-preservation she learned to emulate them. Imitation was protection. If they teased, she teased back. If they argued, she argued also. She cultivated the robust attitude of mind of her coevals, and she could write again in her journal after the words about neutral tints and still waters, that "the only thing which survives is the resistance we bring to life and not the strain life brings to us."

Alice brought a full measure of resistance by merging into her surroundings. Her voice chimed in with William's and Henry's as they in turn teased their father at the dinner-table; and it clashed in battles of wit during the fraternal crossfire. In Newport, T. S. Perry, their young contemporary, could speak of the "unhappy" James children, fighting "like cats and dogs." Alice's memories of Newport, when she was awakening to life, were of the "low, grey Newport sky in that winter of 62–63 as I used to wander about over the cliffs my young soul struggling out of its swaddling-clothes." One feels that she doffed her swaddling-clothes but to don a spiritual straitjacket.

The girl's attachment to her father was strong; and in the end it was transferred to her brother Henry. Since he was the quiet one, among the children, he probably constituted less of a threat to her individuality and selfhood than the lively William, or the boisterous shin-kicking younger brothers. The remembered ride in the carriage frames a picture of childhood hierarchies in the James family. The occasion had been an outing to the home of their French governess Marie Boningue at Boulogne. The American children were fed sundry items, including an enormous frosted cake, and then were turned into a sandy garden to play with their French friends. William did not accompany his brothers and sister. At fourteen he had his own resources. Henry, twelve or thirteen, was senior-in-charge. Alice remembered that her younger brothers "disappeared, not to my grief," with some of the French children, and she was left alone with Henry. He had taken possession of a swing and sat in it meditatively. She stood near by. The dreary minutes passed; the sun slanted, and Henry remained lost in thought. Then he remarked casually to his sister: "This might certainly be called pleasure under difficulties." Alice recorded "the stir of my whole being in response to the exquisite substance and original form of this remark." For the first time she obtained a glimpse of the imaginative process. Henry had put into words the essence of the afternoon's experience. This little passage of brother-and-sister history shows the early bonds of understanding that existed between them. They were to endure to the end.

II

"In our family group," Henry was to write, "girls seem scarcely to have had a chance." Alice had no chance in this group of vigorous and competing masculine egos. In our time she might have learned to play tennis, to swim, to row, to ski, to drive a car—to leave home and find her own way in life, expend some of the great store of vitality of which she gave, at first, abundant proof. Instead, the time came when she sat with folded hands and cultivated a Victorian composure, the mask of modest dress and quiet demeanour concealing intensities of feeling. She sat and waited—waited as the young women of her time did—for the liberation matrimony might bring. She grew up possessing all the social graces and the intellectual vigour of her elder brothers; she watched the younger ones go off to war—they disappeared from the family as they did from her presence that day in Boulogne. William and Henry were absorbed by their ailments and their careers. She was committed to the company of the ageing parents and, for a long time, to that of her beloved aunt. And she lapsed progressively into the familiar invalidism of so many of her Victorian sisters. Unlike some of them, she never recovered. "Her tragic health," Henry was to write, "was, in a manner, the only solution for her of the practical problem of life."

Her brother had discerned the truth. Alice's high spirits and her fund of energy could not be sufficiently discharged upon the world. She discharged them upon herself. In 1868—when she was twenty—she had a nervous prostration. During the next ten years she was recurrently ill, with periods of recovery during which she was able to be reasonably active, do charitable work and indulge in a moderate social life. During one of these she was able to travel abroad with Henry and her Aunt Kate. Her second nervous collapse occurred some years later, in 1878. After this she was ill more frequently. When she had her relapses, doctors treated her for ailments that seemed to them emotional and neurasthenic. They prescribed massage, cold water treatment, ice and electric therapy, "blistering," Turkish baths. This was the best that medicine could do for Alice James. Only during the last years of her life did she develop a diagnosable ailment. Like Henry during his early years, his sister had her "obscure hurt."

III

Her first illness is vividly remembered in her journal. She lets us see a person wishing to use to the full the energies of her body; however, "violent turns of hysteria" are substituted. Then she finds her mind "luminous and active and susceptible of the clearest, strongest impressions." Relief came in this way. She envisaged her fight as "simply between my body and my will." The will was worn out, she saw, by "the strains of its constabulary functions." She wrote:

> As I used to sit immovable reading in the library with waves of violent inclination suddenly invading my muscles, taking some one of their myriad forms such as throwing myself out of the window or knocking off the head of the benignant pater as he sat with his silver locks, writing at his table, it used to seem to me that the only difference between me and the insane was that I had not only all the horrors and suffering of insanity but the duties of doctor, nurse, and straitjacket imposed upon me too. Conceive of never being without the sense that if you let yourself go for a moment your mechanism will fall into pie and that at some given moment you must abandon it all, let the dykes break and the flood sweep in, acknowledging yourself abjectly impotent before the immutable laws. When all one's moral and natural stock-in-trade is a temperament forbidding the abandonment of an inch or the relaxation of a muscle, 'tis a never-ending fight.

The impulses recorded in these words, and the strong need for self-policing, could not be stated more clearly. Alice's desire to "knock off the head of the benignant pater," even though she loved him, must have been but one of the crowning assaults she would have liked to discharge upon any inhibiting figure. The straitjacket of such fantasies in Alice's mind seems to have taken forms of hysteria and fainting spells. By being ill she made herself powerless to execute the violence that she entertained and that normally might have found release in healthy activities; and by the same token she gave herself the power of the invalid—she created concern and exacted attention.

Her illness of a decade later was described as "an exaggerated recurrence of her old troubles" and as "a nervous breakdown of a very severe character." Alice's own memory of it, recorded in her journal, was of "that hideous summer of '78 when I went down to the deep sea, and its dark waters closed over me, and I knew neither hope nor peace." She told her parents at one point "I cannot hear anything that touches my feelings" and refused to be given news of her brothers.

When she was mending on this occasion, her mother wrote that "her periods of depression and feelings of inability to meet life are less frequent, and in the intervals she is quite cheerful and like herself." She added: "She is able now when driving to take the reins herself, and has done so for an hour and a half at a time. She always enjoyed this very much, and the country is so exquisitely lovely just now, that I am in hopes she will get great gain by being out in this way." The detail may be a small one, but Alice's pleasure in holding the reins was perhaps more than a return of strength during convalescence: it suggests with some vividness how much she would have relished some kind of driver's seat in her existence. This she was never to have: and when she did become independent, she no longer had the power to use her freedom.

There were times when she frankly talked to her father of suicide. The very fact that she chose to discuss it showed a hesitation to do away with herself: and perhaps it was again a way of engaging the elder Henry's sympathies. She was intelligent enough to know that such talk would deeply disturb him. Her father, however, was a match for his clever daughter. She put the question to him on religious ground. Was it a sin for her to feel "very strongly tempted" to suicide? He replied that he did not think it was. It might be, he philosophically said, "when a person from a mere love of pleasurable excitement indulged in drink or opium to the utter degradation of his faculties, and often to the ruin of the human form in him." But, he added, it was absurd to believe it sinful, if she wished to escape from suffering. And he gave Alice (as he wrote to his youngest son) his fatherly permission to "end her life whenever she pleased," exhorting her only to "do it in a perfectly gentle way in order not to distress her friends."

The elder Henry James had in this simple fashion made Alice aware that she sat in the driver's seat so far as her body was concerned. Alice told him, after pondering his answer, that "now she could perceive it to be her *right* to dispose of her own body when life had become intolerable, she could never do it; that when she felt tempted to it, it was with a view to break bonds, or to assert her freedom." After this talk the elder Henry told his family that he no longer felt she would do away with herself, "though she often tells me she is strongly tempted still." And indeed, although Alice was to undergo intolerable suffering, she never took the final step that would have brought her an earlier peace.

THE ART OF SEEING

William James had good reason for believing in his brother's "greatness" as a critic. A reader of Henry's early tales, with their blurred emotions and rage-filled soliloquies, might understandably show a preference for his book-reviews and art-notices. These bear no relation to the inner life of Quincy Street. They are the work of a cool, competent, disinterested and vigorous appreciator of the arts. In the periodicals at this time Henry deals adroitly with a group of light novels, among them Disraeli's *Lothair*; he discusses Taine's *Notes sur l'Angleterre* with the relish of one who has always been comparing French and English traits; and he is completely in his element in a long review of Taine's *English Literature*, then newly translated. He notices a work on Alpine climbing as one who has himself trudged—modestly—in Switzerland, and also as one who has been reading of Clarence King's exploits in the Rockies. And he casts his eye over Théophile Gautier's account of the Siege of Paris with the warmth and sympathy of an observer who has followed the vicissitudes of France from the catastrophe at Sedan to the end of the Commune, and who has been led, in the process, to appraise the historical rôle of the lately defunct Second Empire.

The touch is always light, and there is a tidiness of formulation, an orderliness of thought and yet a weight of authority in these reviews. He finds a "deplorable levity" in Disraeli, and a "great deal of small clevernesses." He muses on the author's sovereign opportunity for disenchantment, and how it is nullified by his "infantine joy" in being initiated into "the value and glory of dukes and ducal possessions." The fictions of Gustave Droz, one of the last novelists of the Second Empire, delight Henry. They have French precision of thought and statement, and the "old Gallic salt of humour." He is particularly struck by one which tells of the history of a watering-place. Its central character, a

Frenchman who tries to build his fortune by promoting a mineral spring, reminds him of "the Yankee type (not the best)," observes Henry, "self-made, sharp as a razor, 'genial,' ambitious, bent on finding an 'operation' in all things." For Taine's classic he has much admiration. He would rename it *A Comparative Survey of the English Mind in the Leading Works of its Literature.* The book is pictorial and critical; he cannot accept its philosophy, nor its theory of "the race, the milieu and the moment"—but it is in itself a "literary achievement." Taine, however, is "a stranger to what we may call the intellectual climate of our literature."

The reader of these reviews, which included Henry's important notice of Hawthorne's French and Italian notebooks, is constantly aware of being in touch with a curious, ranging, logical mind. Its point of view is empirical; its interest lies in places and persons, in generalizations about peoples, not in abstract ideas. Henry James is concerned above all with things his eyes can rest upon. By this process he shows himself, at every turn, the novelist performing as critic.

I

Towards the end of 1871 Howells asked Henry to serve as an occasional art-reviewer for the *Atlantic Monthly*. He probably remembered how entertaining Henry's comments on pictures had been in his letters from abroad to his family and friends. He knew also that Henry possessed what John La Farge called "the painter's eye," a rare and great virtue in a man of letters. For someone with a pronounced verbal gift, Henry had an extraordinary visual sense as well. The two do not always go together. Writers often tend to see less and imagine more: the glimpsed object is but a point of departure for their fancy. In Henry there was a capacity to look with great intentness at the world around him, to see a landscape or a street entire. Through the wedding of his visual sense and his verbal power he dominated and used his other senses. In his novels he shaped his sensory material into striking and evocative imagery, so that sound, smell and touch were made palpable with the greatest of subtlety. The reader has the feeling of having seen James's interiors, for instance, but he has also been made aware of the texture of the furnishings, and of the very smells in the rooms. At every turn James invites us to look: and through sight we are asked to charge our other senses. In his letters to the Nortons he is constantly asking for picture-postcards of what they have seen: his need is always to re-imagine their experience in his mind's eye, to repaint it, as it were, in some concrete mental picture. To look was to feel. He had so far assimilated whole areas of experience that to gaze upon a house, a street, a meadow, was to have lived in that house, and to have strolled in that street or meadow. It is by some such process that the artist learns to deduce the known from the unknown, and it is no accident that in Henry James's late novel, *The Ambassadors*, the little painter Bilham substitutes the word "see" for the word "live." The two had almost equal value in Henry James's personal lexicon.

In accepting a regular task for the *Atlantic*, Henry was not harnessing himself to a "job." He had fought shy of any such commitment from the first. He was merely putting his pen to work on a form of reporting and critical writing he had not hitherto attempted, and he found it congenial alike to his temperament and his mood. He predicted that his work would soon collapse for want of material. There was little to write about. His articles appeared with agreeable consistency for three months —January to March 1872. They were unsigned. After a lapse of two months one further article appeared, this time dealing with an exhibition in New York. Thereafter he had all the Continental galleries to roam in, and he dispatched from London, not long afterwards, a detailed account of the showing of the Wallace Collection in Bethnal Green. He wrote a few more pieces of art-criticism for the *Atlantic* when he returned to Boston two years later, but he never made of this part of his critical endeavour a very prolonged or consistent effort. The miscellaneous art-papers of this time, together with certain later papers, have been collected by John L. Sweeney in a volume appropriately titled *The Painter's Eye*. Mr Sweeney, in his appraisal of their content, reached the conclusion that the novelist was "an amateur, rather than a strict connoisseur" of the pictorial arts, and this is undoubtedly true. He had had what John Ruskin considered a prerequisite to any art-criticism, the experience of holding a paint-brush in his hand. He had also carried a sketch-book with him during his European journeyings. He had, moreover, closely studied the paintings of the masters and learned to write vividly about his experiences as a spectator. He was to value the "picture" and above all else the portrait as a form of expression in art, and to make of it the supreme goal of the writer of fiction. In a late essay on the novel-form he wrote of "man's general appetite for the picture," and of the novel as "of all pictures the most comprehensive and the most elastic." The "given picture of life," "the figures in any picture"—such phrases are to be found at every turn in his essays on fiction, until we discover a final image, in his late lecture on Balzac, in which he contrasts the constructed and integrated novel with the over-documented novel, crammed with excessive data, as "the art of the brush as opposed to the art of the slate-pencil," and "to the art of the brush," he held, "the novel must return."

II

The twenty-eight-year-old critic who reported on an exhibition of French paintings in Boston in 1871, or who evaluated in New York the Metropolitan Museum's acquisition of a group of Dutch and Flemish works, sought above all to illustrate the art of seeing. His language is precise and his art-criticism—like his theatrical criticism later—reflects his enormous grasp of visual detail as well as his possession of standards of aesthetic judgment and appreciation. Any one of the notices he wrote at that time enables us to see him at his gallery task.

If we had been standing at his side in the rooms of Messrs Doll and Richards at 145 Tremont Street, we would have found him for instance scrutinizing a canvas by Decamps and reflecting on the fanciful qualities indulged in by "one of the finest of the modern realists." Decamps belonged to the gifted class of artists —to be found in literature, music, and the drama as well—"whose mission is the pursuit of effect, without direct reference to truth." This painter, Henry said, was superbly endowed for this purpose and seldom missed his effect. His little picture then exhibited in Boston, "The Centurion," had skill, science, experience, all of them substitutes for "the simplicity of genuine inspiration."

He would not confine himself only to generalities. His task as art-reporter was to make his point by describing the painting, and then comparing it to a Delacroix hanging nearby. It was strange, he observed, to discover Decamps selecting a Scriptural subject; he had shown good taste "by touching the theme as lightly as possible." The face of Christ was not even painted—faces were evidently Decamps's weak point. And the reviewer then went on to describe the little group of figures on the canvas, occupying the middle of the scene, "dipped, as it were, in a wash of cool purple shadows; out of this rise mighty, into a glow of afternoon light, the walls and towers and ramparts and battlements of some visionary city of the antique world."

The great success of the picture is in its hint of this pagan vastness (you see the heavy smoke from a perfumed altar rising in the distance) and in the golden luminosity with which the scene is suffused. It seems to us to bear about the same relation to probable fact as some first-rate descriptive titbit of Edgar Poe or Charles Baudelaire; whereas, if we were to seek for a literary correlative for that sadly imperfect Delacroix near by, we should find it in some fragment of Shelley.

Literature and painting have here been mixed a little; and James's own imagination has added perfume to the painted altar. But what artist would complain at having his painting described in terms such as that "only a supremely vivid fancy could have conceived those dizzy and mellow-toned walls and towers and distilled that narrow strip of morbidly tender sky." There was much subjectivity, perhaps, in the "morbidly tender;" it is, however, the criticism of a reflective observer.

In the same notice he goes on to Delacroix, who, "more than any other painter we know, must be judged by the total impression. It is not that, as a rule, he selects grotesque or exceptional subjects; but that he sees them in a ray of that light that never was on land or sea—which is simply the light of the mind. This conceded, we must add that the light of Delacroix's mind produced some very singular optical effects."

The notice is not without the local touch. He begins it by remarking that the paintings are privately owned in Boston, "and united thus in a charming room they afford a pleasant suggestion and premonition of the artistic taste and wealth scattered, potentially at least, through our supposedly sordid American community." The "supposedly sordid" may have been a sop to the readers of the *Atlantic*. It shows us, however, our reviewer looking at pictures with a glance at least at his environment.

ESCAPE

LATE in the summer of 1871 Henry visited Canada briefly, from Niagara to Quebec, again writing articles on his travels for the *Nation*. His little tour began with a boat-trip—from Toronto across Lake Ontario; in due course he studied Niagara and rhapsodized for his readers in the manner of one of his own untutored Americans in his tales—"it beats Michelangelo." This he later modified into a more aesthetic judgment—"in the matter of line it beats Michelangelo." His observations of Quebec were happier; here at least was evidence of an older culture, instead of nature in the raw.

The city had seemed to snatch a past "from our scanty annals" and he wondered what its future might be. Quebec reminded him somewhat of Boulogne-sur-Mer, where he had spent his fourteenth year. He grasped quickly the nature of the French-Canadian society, "locked up in its small dead capital, isolated on a heedless continent, and gradually consuming its principal, as one may say—its vital stock of memories, traditions, and routine." Evenings in Quebec, he thought, might be as dull as Balzac's scenes of provincial life. Did they play *loto* and arrange marriages between their sons and daughters, whose education was confided to abbés and abbesses? He encountered in the streets little old Frenchmen who looked indeed as if they had stepped out of Balzac. Quebec, he mused, must be a city of gossip, for he saw no sign that it was a city of culture. He scanned the windows of the booksellers: a few Catholic statuettes and prints, two or three Catholic publications, "a festoon or so of rosaries, a volume of Lamartine, a supply of ink and matches." James walked in the marketplace and listened to the *patois* of the farmers and noted their "evident good terms with the tin-spired parish church, standing there as bright and clean with ungrudged paint and varnish as a Nürnberg toy." One of them spoke to him "with righteous contempt of the French of France. 'They are worth nothing; they are bad Catholics.' " In these words, and with his searching scrutiny, Henry James caught the unchanged, unchanging note of French Canada.

I

Early in 1872 Henry began to hint in his letters that he had some hope of getting to Europe: it was still "absurdly vague," he told Elizabeth Boott, but he was determined to cross the ocean "by hook or by crook in the late summer or early autumn." If he did so, he said, he could hardly stop short of Florence or Rome. The plan was so "pitifully embryonic" that it was "really cruel to expose it to the rude blasts of the World." A month later he was still speaking of "vague moonshiny dreams" of escape "with what speed I may." What is clear now is that sometime between the beginning of that year and May, when he sailed, he was able to convince the *Nation* that he could write a usable series of European travel-articles for the journal; and he obtained from his father an advance of money for the trip, which he hoped to pay back by literary earnings.

What aided him was the feeling in the James family that it was time for Alice to be given the advantage of foreign travel already enjoyed by William and Henry. This must have been debated for some time, because of Alice's precarious health. The devoted Aunt Kate offered to go as Alice's companion; and it was accordingly settled that Henry would act as escort to the womenfolk, looking after their travel-arrangements as well as being *cicerone* and protector. The plans were broad and the itinerary would depend upon Alice's ability to support fatigue. Alice felt it would be wise not to plunge at once into London, but to reach it by easy stages. Henry acquiesced in this, since it would give him a chance to do a series of pieces on rural England. Switzerland seemed indicated as a place for a vacation in the midst of travel; and Henry hoped that if all went well they might, at the end of the summer, dip into Italy for a month. As far as Henry was concerned the experiment would show whether he could keep his pen profitably busy. He felt strongly that his material lay in Europe; moreover he had solemnly vowed he would return to Rome. Since Alice's travel-plans had to be flexible, he made none himself. Time would take care of them.

II

One day that spring Henry walked to Shady Hill, the home of Charles Eliot Norton, where he had spent many happy hours in the past, to attend the funeral of Susan Norton, Charles's wife. She had died in February, in Dresden, and Norton, in Europe with his young children, had not been able to accompany the body home. Henry had been fond of Susan: he had many memories of their meetings abroad to which the circumstance that clustered about them gave a kind of improvised and providential charm. It was with her that he had gone, one day in England, into Kent to lunch with the Darwins, and afterwards they had taken a memorable stroll through Holwood Park and felt the first breath of the English spring.

Now Susan was dead, after giving birth to her sixth child. The funeral at Shady Hill was sad, simple, touching—"you would have been satisfied," he wrote to Norton. Then he described the scene at Mount Auburn. The day was sombre and there was a momentary relapse into winter after weeks of a dry, monotonous blue sky. On this day there were rolling grey clouds, a "superior seriousness of cloud-scenery." As the mourners stood beside the new grave, a heavy snow began to fall.

On 6 May 1872 Henry, writing to Norton and describing the burial, sought to comfort his correspondent. His thoughtful words showed the long road he had himself travelled during his Cambridge months. He urged Norton to allow himself to experience to the fullest his loss and pain. One had to stand face to face with "the hard reality of things." Henry added that he presumed to speak to his friend in this fashion "out of my own unshaken security." The human soul was "mighty, and it seems to me we hardly know what it may achieve (as well as suffer) until it has been plunged deep into trouble." But Henry recognized that such words might be small comfort to one who had lost a wife and the mother of his children. At the end of the letter he mentioned casually that his departure for Europe was but five days off, and that he counted on meeting Norton somewhere abroad.

Henry had had his season in Cambridge. His own spirit again and again had tested "the hard reality of things." Now his trunk was packed, and if he announced no plans beyond the summer's touring, his own design was clear. He would stay on as long as he could, to show whether his pen could accomplish in Europe what it had failed to do in America—give him freedom and independence, the sense of being footloose and unattached, and above all self-possessed. This, he was now well aware in his "unshaken security," was impossible in Quincy Street.

Book Two

Transatlantic Sketches 1872

*

BROTHER AND NEPHEW

THE SENTIMENTAL TOURIST

A PARISIAN AUTUMN

BROTHER AND NEPHEW

It was as brother and nephew, rather than as writer for the *Nation*, that Henry James sailed for Europe in May 1872; the escorting of Alice and his Aunt Kate seemed a modest price to pay for going abroad. If it meant, for the time being, that he travelled with Quincy Street for company, he knew that at the summer's end his companions would sail for home and he would then possess himself—and Europe. They crossed on the *Algeria*, a sturdy Cunarder which brought them to Liverpool in a little over eight days. The ladies experienced some seasickness; Henry did not miss a meal. On arrival in England Henry promptly booked an October return-sailing for his companions on the same ship.

I

They went first to Chester and its Roman ruins, favourite starting-place for many an American tour. Years later Henry would launch his "ambassador," Lambert Strether, at the little hotel in Chester. Their itinerary took them to Lichfield and Warwick, North Devon and Salisbury; they passed through the rich farmland of the Shakespeare country—"too ovine, too bovine, it is almost asinine," quipped the *Nation* correspondent—and then, reaching Oxford, they wandered from college to college and garden to garden. In London they spent a week, on the theory that cities would be exhausting for Alice; in Paris they lingered only long enough to spend a day with Norton and his children at St Germain-en-Laye and to see a play at the Théâtre Français. While the ladies rested, Henry visited the burnt-out ruins and barricades of the Commune. They took an overnight train to Geneva and presently were settled at Villeneuve, on Lake Leman, in the Hôtel Byron, near the Castle of Chillon. A few years later Daisy Miller, in her flirtatious finery, would make her appearance at nearby Vevey on her road to Rome. During this phase of their travels Alice withstood fatigue remarkably well; indeed she seemed to enjoy the constant activity and the sight-seeing. Henry and his aunt were determined, however, not to force their luck. The stay in Switzerland was designed as a breathing-spell from train and coach, a gain of coolness and quiet.

At the Hôtel Byron they met, by pre-arrangement, their loyal friends, the Italianate-American Bootts, Francis and his daughter Elizabeth, who was Alice's age. Assured of sociable companionship, Henry looked forward to several weeks of Swiss tranquillity.

However a period of torrid weather set in; and after a week at Villeneuve the Jameses and the Bootts moved by way of Berne and Interlaken to Grindelwald, at 3400 feet, partly in the belief that Alice needed a more bracing climate. Here towards the end of July they seemed to have found the answer to their problem; but the heat continued to pursue them. The "two white pyramids of the Fischerhorner" glittered hotly and the snow-crowned granite of the Wetterhorn gave them no sense of coolness. The tremendous Alpine sun drove them higher and higher. This time the Bootts did not join them. Francis was not fond of mountains, and Lizzie liked the sociability of urban hotels. In a letter from Grindelwald, the brother and nephew confessed that "the romance of travel—of *tables d'hôtes*, strange figures and faces, and even of Alps—soon rubs off and the throb of admiration and surprise soon subsides into a tolerably jogtrot sort of pulsation." Nevertheless Henry had been able to distil the romance of travel into four pieces for the *Nation*, the record of their sight-seeing in England. He had also distracted himself by climbing the Faulhorn, an eight-hours' trudge, and was pleased to discover that "my old Swiss legs, such as they are, haven't lost their cunning."

From Grindelwald the Jameses went by slow carriage to Meyringen, and finally to the Grisons, with Alice and Aunt Kate following on horseback. Here they put up at a hotel at Thusis, on the Splügen road. Now the air was too bracing for Alice, and Henry's letters spoke of her being made nervous by it. What this

Queen Hotel Chester. May 23d

Dearest Mother.

The above is a feeble sketch of the position & circumstances of your exiled daughter. She sits before a great bow-window, looking out into an elegant & verdurous garden. The ivy crawls and clambers in along the edges of the casement; the birds make

HENRY JAMES'S SKETCH OF ALICE

From a letter

meant in reality was that she had taken to her bed in one of her habitual collapses. As soon as she could move, they went on to Chur, but Henry was ready to conclude that "Alice has tested stiff mountain air to its condemnation." She had need of the "human picturesque." They were "glutted with mountain grandeur and gloom." A month of Switzerland had been a rather over-solemn entertainment for her.

What was clear to Henry now was that so long as Alice was kept busy in towns and cities she would manage her problems decently well; but left alone to idleness and repose, in high mountain resorts, she sooner or later succumbed to her neurasthenia. Quite naturally he did not tell this to Quincy Street, and it is only in later letters to his sister that we find the record of what really happened during this part of their travels. There seem to have been three occasions on which Alice became ill and had to be nursed and comforted, for Henry was to speak of her "performances at Thusis, Andermatt and Batzen," and during a later illness wrote to her, "I am sorry I am not near you to heal you and comfort you as I then did—as you will vividly remember." He performed his rôle as brother, guide and morale-builder with affectionate loyalty. But Switzerland proved a trial alike to him and his aunt. Long before their journeyings were over, he was eager to be free.

II

After Alice's brief breakdown at Thusis, Henry lost no time in moving his companions to Berne, where they found the Bootts in an old-fashioned hotel amid "a large entourage" of Bostonians. The writer, on his side, was glad enough to be in a city again. He confessed in one of his *Nation* articles that he relished "a human flavour in his pleasures" and felt that there was a more equal intercourse between man and man than between man and mountains. He said he had found himself grumbling on occasion that the snow-peaks of the Oberland were not the marble pinnacles of a cathedral, and that the "liquid sapphire and emerald of Leman and Lucerne are not firm palace-floors of lapis and verdantique." The Jameses enjoyed their visit to Berne and while they feared they might be rushing matters to go to Italy in late summer they set out cheerfully on 26 August, limiting their tour to northern Lombardy and Venetia, with the promise of a return to coolness in the Austrian Tyrol.

Henry's letters to Quincy Street, placed beside his travel-sketches, give us a lively picture of his enjoyment of the changing scene. On a warm August evening they are at Chambéry in lately-occupied Savoy; Alice and Aunt Kate are leaning out of their hotel windows watching a French military band in red leggings, serenading an inspector-general who is banqueting within. That afternoon, while the women rested, the indefatigable Henry had gone sightseeing: at Chambéry he could not resist visiting Les Charmettes, where Jean-Jacques Rousseau had lived with Madame de Warens. The cracked yellow spinet still stood there and on the table lay Rousseau's turnip-shaped timepiece which had once ticked the hours in the great man's waistcoat pocket. After the opulence of Ferney and Coppet, the haunts of Voltaire and Madame de Staël, this seemed poverty-stricken indeed; and the hero and heroine of the place, Henry reflected, had been, after all, first-rate subjects for psychology rather than poetry. Henry was pleased with his little visit: he felt as if he had obtained an illustration which he could mentally insert into a reading of the *Confessions*.

Twenty-four hours later they had negotiated the Mont Cenis tunnel. Old sensations suddenly came to life and made him aware how intense had been his 1869 experience of Italy—the balcony, the Venetian blind, the cool floor, the speckled concrete; the Castello in Turin's square with its shabby rear and its pompous front; the brick campaniles in the mild, yellow light; the bright colours, the soft sounds—it was the eternal Italy and also his personal Italy. Under the arcades the human scene was unchanged: handsome officers, buxom females, civil dandies with religious faith in their moustachios; ladies in lace mantillas, with a little too much display "in the region of the bodice." In Milan they inspected the cathedral; they paused at Lake Como and devoted four dreamy days to Venice. The mosquitoes kept them awake at night, but in the daytime they lived in gondolas and found coolness on the lagoons and in the churches. They ate figs, went every night to Florian's for ices and ransacked the place for photographs of works of art. An afternoon at Torcello was memorable. Two strong-armed gondoliers helped them cut "the wandering breezes of the lagoon, like a cargo of deities descending from Olympus. Such a bath of light and air—colour and general luxury, physical and intellectual."

Austria-bound, they paused at Verona and broke the trip to Innsbruck at Batzen, where Alice had a brief collapse. Henry found Germany "uglier than ever" by contrast with Italy. But, he confided to William, it was a relief to be turning toward Paris again. Their ten days in Austria and Germany seemed long. "What colossal tastelessness!" Henry exclaimed after visiting the *Hofkirche* at Innsbruck. It was a shame to go into a *Hofkirche* to laugh—"but I distinctly smiled." Munich was "a nightmare of pretentious vacuity: a city of chalky stucco—a Florence and Athens in canvas and planks." Nuremberg was only a little better, and Henry was prepared to trade a thousand Nurembergs for "one ray of Verona." Toward the end of the German trip he was convinced—so he wrote from Heidelberg—that he should "listen to the voice of the spirit—to cease hair-splitting and treat oneself to a good square antipathy." He could never hope, he said, "to become an unworthiest adoptive grandchild of the fatherland." So much for William's continuing insistence that he should devote some part of his European sojourn to a period of study and residence in Germany.

Strasburg was gloomy and battered; utterly conquered and fast being Germanized. They crossed the frontier and after a day's hard travel were in Paris again, at the Hôtel Rastadt, in the Rue Neuve St Augustin, where they found the old family friends, the Tweedys, Edmund and "Aunt" Mary, so called because she had been foster-mother to the James's Temple cousins. Henry wrote that they dined with them almost daily and helped relieve "the mutual monotony of our by this time extremely familiar selves." The Nortons were in Paris, and Henry, Alice and Grace Norton had an evening together at the theatre. The sister and aunt were occupied in a round of shopping, visits to dress-makers and milliners, dispatching parcels and trunk-packing, leaving Henry free to roam during long afternoon hours. "Alice has just shewn me a ravishing bonnet," the brother tells Quincy Street, "which will certainly, next winter, be the wonder and envy of all Cambridge." Aunt Kate is weary and eager to go home; "she has had no heart evidently in our journey on her account, and yet her devotion to Alice has been immeasurable." In retro-spect Henry felt that the tour had been of great value. "We seem to have seen a vast deal and to have had innumerable delightful days and hours and sensations." It all appeared to have been "absurdly easy" once it was over. What he does not say is that both for him and Aunt Kate a constant anxiety had undermined many of the days and hours of which he now spoke with pleasure —a pleasure perhaps, in part, that they were of the past.

The brother and nephew was loyal to the end. He crossed the Channel with his charges, paused briefly in London, escorted them to Liverpool and saw them aboard the *Algeria*. With a certain relief he turned from the ship's side. He could now begin his career abroad in earnest.

THE SENTIMENTAL TOURIST

QUINCY STREET had been carefully prepared for the news that Henry was remaining in Europe. Five of his travel-sketches had appeared in the *Nation*; "Guest's Confession," which he had written before leaving, was published that autumn in the *Atlantic*—his father read proofs for him—and during his brief stay in London he had taken Alice to see the Wallace Collection at the Bethnal Green Museum, to write another of his art-pieces for Howells. "A decent little sum" was thus due to him from the magazines. "You have learned, by my recent letters," he informs William, "that I mean to try my luck by remaining abroad. I have little doubt that I shall be able to pull through." He wanted to spend a quiet winter, he said; he would read a good deal. "I shall be able to write enough and well enough, I think: my only question is how to dispose of my wares. But in this, too, I shall not fail." A few days later he told his parents: "I suppose you are resigned to not seeing me this autumn. I can't say that I am to my prospects of exile, but I try to steel myself. Seriously speaking, I expect this coming year or two, over here, to do a great deal for me. It will not be my own fault if it don't."

The verbally fastidious Henry tended to indulge in the colloquial when he addressed his parents; but in this instance his "if it don't" probably was intended as a casual cushion to the quiet announcement that he would remain abroad for longer than a few months. His allusion to the "coming year or two, over here" envisaged a greater expanse of time than he had hitherto mentioned. There remained the practical side. It would be economical, he said, to remain in Paris for a while; he had never lived there, had used it always as a way-station, and would try now to stay out the autumn. His destination, however, was Italy. One reason for going there was that the *Nation* had a Paris correspondent, but none in Rome. Having explained this, he asked permission to draw on his father's letter of credit intended for his and Alice's tour, "to help me on my way to Italy; for the clothes and the journey together would rather diminish my private fund." Fifty pounds, he felt, would "start me in life and carry me ahead for a long time, as regards clothes."

The elder Henry agreed. He proposed that the magazines send their payment for his son's articles directly to him. He would thus be Henry's banker as well as his literary agent. "It is the best plan," Henry replied, little realizing that he was thereby still tethered to Quincy Street. "I shall do very well without ruining you."

I

Henry James's travel-sketches in the *Nation*—his English notes, embodied in four long papers, his Swiss notes and later his record of his journey with Alice into Italy and Germany—readily won a public, for Howells presently was asking him for similar articles for the *Atlantic*; and the *Galaxy* in New York, which had printed some of Henry's tales, was quite prepared to publish his essays. He thus broadened his market at this crucial moment, and by this tolerably easy kind of journalism—easy at any rate for him—gave himself the material foundation for a continuing sojourn abroad. From Quincy Street his brother William kept up a running fire of praise and criticism. He complained of Henry's "over-refinement and elaboration." He offered advice: "Recollect that for Newspaporial purposes, a broader treatment hits a broader mark; and keep bearing that way as much as you can with comfort. I suppose traits of human nature and character would also agreeably speckle the columns." The elder brother's opinions were valued by Henry but viewed with objectivity and aloofness. Was William, after all, qualified to tell Henry how to be "Newspaporial?" His younger brother had the guidance of Howells and the other editors for whom he was writing, but William tended to speak out of his long-assumed authority as first-born: and, one supposes, as Henry's most interested reader. He returned again and again to the charge: Henry had to cultivate directness of style. "Delicacy, subtlety and ingenuity, will take care of themselves." He confessed, however, that he had been surprised at the number of persons who were reading his brother and liking what he wrote. He himself thought "the style ran a little more to *curliness* than suited the average mind."

To such a running commentary Henry finally gave response. Doubtless with practice, he said, he would be able to be a little less refined: yet beyond a certain point he did not feel that this was desirable, "for me at least, who must give up the ambition of ever being a free-going and light-paced enough writer to please the multitude." The multitude, he said, had no taste "that a thinking man is bound to defer to." To write for the few who have taste was perhaps to lose money, but he was not afraid of starving. He preferred to work his material close, to try to cultivate a style. This was the only way, as an artist, that he would not feel himself risking "intellectual bankruptcy." And he had "a mortal horror of seeming to write thin."

It was clear thus from the first that there was a fundamental difference between the two brothers. William, in reality, was pleading for that lucidity which he himself, in so rare a fashion, possessed. He failed to appreciate, nevertheless, the artist side of his younger brother. William was all for communication; Henry was all for artistic statement—and for style. William, to be sure, was to achieve a style of his own, apparently without taking sufficient stock of the artist within himself which made this possible.

II

In writing his travel-sketches Henry, as always, proceeded from a very clear conception of what he wanted to do. The observations of an intelligent traveller were worth recording, he believed, even when the experience was confined to the beaten track. He praised Taine's Italian and English travel-writings because there was in them a constant effort "to resolve his impression into a positive and definite statement." He insisted that the prose of travel had to be a "tissue of images and pictures," such as he found in Théophile Gautier. He was aware also that the travel-writer must keep the reader within a certain angle of vision. Although he designates himself in the *Nation* as "our old friend the sentimental tourist," he is above all "an observant American." His vision may be cosmopolitan, but he tries to use his eyes on behalf of his domestic readers. It takes, he remarks in England, "a poor disinherited Yankee to appreciate the 'points' of this admirable country." During his walks he seeks the "fine differences in national manners" as well as the "foreign tone of things." He remarks: "The tone of things is, somehow, heavier than with us; manners and modes are more absolute and positive; they seem to swarm and thicken the atmosphere about you. Morally and physically it is a denser air than ours. We seem loosely hung together at home, compared with the English, every man of whom is a tight fit in his place."

There is considerable method in James the traveller. His attention is divided between the works of nature and the works of man: his concern is with the works of man—the flow of life into art, the flow of art into life. Descriptive prose by now comes easy to him: he can evoke Devon's flora and fauna with a few brush-strokes—the embankments of moss and turf, the lace-work of trailing ground-ivy, the solid walls of flowering thorn and glistening holly. "They are over-strewn with lovely little flowers with names as delicate as their petals of gold and silver and azure —bird's-eye and king's-finger and wandering-sailor—and their soil, a superb dark red, turns in spots so nearly to crimson that you almost fancy it some fantastic compound purchased at the chemist's and scattered there for ornament." He tosses this off with a spontaneity that carries us with him: but he also likes to get the reader out of the fields and into the towns and cities. He is in Berne and has "the vision of a long main street, looking dark, somehow, in spite of its breadth, and bordered with houses supported on deep arcades, whereof the short, thick pillars resemble queerly a succession of bandy legs, and overshaded by high-piled pagoda roofs." And so to the shops, and the houses, and the windows of the houses, and the human being framed by the window, "a Bernese fair enough, at least, to complete the not especially delicate harmony of the turkey-red cushion and the vividly blooming plants." His eye is always for the architecture, for the buildings by which man has asserted his creative power. In Milan the cathedral may have its shortcomings but "it is grandly curious, superbly rich." Henry hopes he will never grow too fastidious to enjoy it. He likes its "impressive, immeasurable achievement," so that he reflects that perhaps "beauty in great architecture is almost a secondary merit" beside the effect of mass—such mass as makes a building "a supreme embodiment of sustained effort." From this point of view a great building is "the greatest conceivable work of art. More than any other it represents difficulties annulled, resources combined, labour, courage and patience."

Within Milan's cathedral he has other reflections. He sees the altar-lamps twinkling through the incense-thickened air and thinks of fog-lights at sea; and the great columns rise to the roof with the girth and altitude of oaks; but they have little refinement of design, "few of those felicities of proportion which the eye caresses, when it finds them." The Jamesian eye is indeed a caressing eye. Life is not immobile; it is all a human scene. Thus in Turin he pauses before paintings but sees the people in them. In part of Van Dyck's portrait of the children of Charles I he thinks of the young ones not as images on canvas but as living babies; "you might kiss their hands, but you certainly would think twice before pinching their cheeks." He finds "all the purity of childhood" in the picture and also "all its soft solidity of structure, rounded tenderly beneath the spangled satin, and contrasted charmingly with its pompous rigidity." In Venice, at Torcello, he meets a group of children not on canvas, "the handsomest little brats in the world," clamouring for coppers; they are almost as naked as savages, with their little bellies protruding, and they show their handsome hungry teeth; yet they scamper and sprawl in the thick grass; they grin like cherubs and suggest "that the best assurance of happiness in this world is to be found in the maximum of innocence and the minimum of wealth." For an instant he combines art and life: one of the urchins has a smile "to make Correggio sigh in his grave."

His scenes are not always those of the lonely observer looking at children in pictures or children in life. He seems to have found it easy to spend time in "starlight gossip at Florian's." There are always compatriots. In Venice he meets a young American painter in the piazza on the evening of his arrival. The encounter foreshadows the opening scene of "The Madonna of the Future," and he constructs with his eyes what should have been that painter's world, envying him his innocence—the fact that he is "unperplexed by the mocking, elusive soul of things"—and his ability to be satisfied by surfaces, light-bathed, old things and old textures; his mornings in "the clustered shadows of the Basilica;" afternoons in church, or campo, on canal or lagoon; evenings in the piazza feeling the languid sea-breeze throbbing "between the two great pillars of the Piazzetta and over the low, black domes of the church." Thus Henry would have liked to spend his days in the decaying city. "The mere use of one's eyes, in Venice, is happiness enough."

A PARISIAN AUTUMN

HENRY JAMES returned to London after bidding farewell to his sister and aunt and remained just long enough to replenish his wardrobe as he had planned. "Oh, the grimness of London! And, oh! the cookery of London!" He recrossed the Channel with relief. "Even after all its tragedies, Paris has a certain natural wholesome gaiety which is a blessing of heaven." At the Hôtel Rastadt he regained his room and settled contentedly into it for the remainder of the autumn. Little larger than a ship's cabin, it was all the warmer for its smallness, and its window framed a pleasant view of rooftops. He wrote in the mornings, walked in the afternoons, and in the evenings dined out, usually in the Boulevard des Capucines on a *rosbif saignant* washed down by some prime English ale. Then he went to the theatre or simply returned to his room to read quietly by his fire. He was reading *Middlemarch*. Reviewing it later for the *Galaxy* he had qualified praise for it; nevertheless he told Grace Norton that "a marvellous *mind* throbs in every page." He also wrote, during this time, two more travel-sketches and "The Madonna of the Future."

I

He had led a "madder and merrier" life in Cambridge, he remarked to his parents; as yet, the waiters in the restaurants were his chief society. However he found that the daily and hourly spectacle of human life in Paris was "suggestive and remunerative." If he was not meeting the French, he at least had no lack of native society. The Rue de la Paix and the Boulevard des Capucines looked to him like "a perfect reproduction" of Broadway. And there were times when Cambridge seemed to have settled by the Seine. The Nortons had come and gone; the Tweedys had just left for Rome. Chauncey Wright, William's friend, had been at the Grand Hotel, "trundling on tiptoes along the boulevard, as he did at home along Main Street" and as always "serenity purpurine." Samuel Rowse, the Boston artist, drifted in and out. The Lowells were in the Hôtel Lorraine, near the Quai Voltaire, in the company of John Holmes, brother of the autocrat of the breakfast table—"the doctor *minus* versatility and *plus* modesty," said Henry. He felt that Lowell, with all his reputation and advantages, was really indifferent to the world. Instead of moving in Parisian literary circles, "here he is living in the heart of Paris, between his Cambridge wife and his Cambridge friend." They made "a little Cambridge together."

The Seine was in flood. Swollen by heavy rains it looked like a "civilized Mississippi." Henry crossed it regularly to dine with Lowell, with whom he had had only a nodding acquaintance at home. Now they struck up a "furious intimacy." It had begun when Norton asked Henry to take a message to Lowell; the next day Lowell returned Henry's call and "we went out to walk and tramped over half Paris and into some queer places which he had discovered on his own walks." In later years Henry was never to cross the Seine on rainy winter nights "amid the wet flare of the myriad lamps," and note the "varnished rush of the river or the way the Louvre grows superb in the darkness," without recalling his old sociable errands to the Left Bank. He would have preferred to meet French writers and to make French friends; failing this, Cambridge-by-the-Seine mitigated his solitude.

At Lowell's hotel Henry would dine at the *table d'hôte*; the landlord sat with his guests and carved. Lowell's letters to Cambridge, as well as Henry's, give a picture of the dingy room, the food, and the voluble political arguments. "Henry James, Jr, joins us now and then at dinner," Lowell wrote, "and, as luck would have it, the first day he came was a regular field day. A political discussion was got up for his special benefit, and such a row has not been heard since Babel." It was, said Henry reporting the evening to his father, "stupidity expressed in epigrams," by four rather violent conservatives, including the Marquis de Grammont, a French deputy, all with rosettes in their buttonholes, aligned against one republican. The conservatives tried to outdo one another in dreaming up ideas for repressive legislation. "A page of Balzac, full of illustration for the humorist," Henry recalled. "Is this unhappy people booked for eternal chaos—or eternal puerility?" If France would not be a first-class power, Henry was certain that it "can't fail to be a precious second-class one."

II

One evening in mid-November 1872 Henry arrived at the Hôtel Lorraine to join the Lowells and found that Concord had arrived to visit the Parisian Cambridge. Ralph Waldo Emerson and his daughter Ellen were in Lowell's sitting-room; they were pausing briefly on their way to Italy and Egypt. Although Emerson had reached the years of his failing memory, he was still sufficiently alert and interested in the world. He seemed to remember Henry's art-letters, for he proposed that they visit the Louvre together. This they did on the morning of 19 November. Some weeks earlier Henry had paid a similar visit to the museum, accompanying the future professor of art history at Harvard, Charles Eliot Norton; he had written home that "he takes art altogether too hard for me to follow him." Emerson, he now found, did not take it hard enough. "His perception of art is not, I think, naturally keen; and Concord can't have done much to quicken it." Nevertheless he was pleased that he appreciated the splendours of Paris and of the Louvre; even when he had nothing to say, "his presence has a sovereign amenity." He was "peculiarly himself" on the morning during which they walked together through the galleries. To Concord, Ellen Emerson wrote: "Father came home enchanted."

Some years later, in writing his essay on Emerson, Henry recalled this occasion; it had been followed by a similar experience in Italy, and Henry reached the conclusion that there were decidedly "certain chords in Emerson that did not vibrate at all." He wrote: "I well remember my impression of this on walking with him in the autumn of 1872 through the galleries of the Louvre and, later that winter, through those of the Vatican: his perception of the objects contained in these collections was of the most general order. I was struck with the anomaly of a man so refined and intelligent being so little spoken to by works of art. It would be more exact to say that certain chords were wholly absent; the tune was played, the tune of life and literature, altogether on those that remained."

III

Emerson was unworldly; Norton was cold; but Lowell touched Henry deeply—"the oddest mixture," as he was to say, "of the lovable and the annoying, the infinitely clever and the unspeakably simple." The lovable side in the end weighed much more heavily with Henry than the annoying. Lowell was fifty-three and Henry twenty-nine when they met in Paris: and their friendship was to extend and deepen during the remaining twenty years of Lowell's life. On the surface the two seemed hardly compatible: Lowell was a homespun Yankee, a lover of the American vernacular who also much preferred Cambridge to the Champs-Elysées. Henry perhaps remembered this when he spoke of him as having the "simplicity as of childhood or of Brattle Street." His weak point, he wrote to William that autumn, would always be his opinions. His strong point, we may judge, for Henry at least, was that he was the American of his time "most saturated with literature and most directed to criticism." Henry thought his poetry was that of the outraged citizen smiting a lyre, rather than the poetry of the addicted artist; and he smiled gently on Lowell's pugnacious parochialism. "I don't feel as if I should ever get anything very valuable out of him," he remarked on meeting him a year or two after their walks in Paris. Nothing valuable, indeed, for his work, but he got an extraordinary degree of acceptance of himself and the loyalty of a profound friendship.

In Lowell Henry had found, indeed, a kind of rugged yet gentle parent, who could chide him and point out slips of English and typographical errors in his work even while bestowing upon him the fullest measure of affection. "It is because you write so well that I care how you write," Lowell would say. Or he would remark, on finding too many French words in a page of Henry's prose, "You know French well enough to afford writing English." He was proud of Henry's accomplishments, almost as if Henry had been his son.

They took ten-mile walks together that autumn. They browsed endlessly in bookshops and along the quays, Lowell driving great bargains with the antiquarians. If Lowell was bookish, Henry said, he was, in the Parisian streets, "the least pale, the least passionless of scholars." His Puritanism, deeply rooted, had in it "the strong and simple vision, even in aesthetic things, of evil and of good, of wrong and of right." Henry was to remark that there was less of the "peace of art" in Emerson and Hawthorne than in Lowell. This meant that Lowell was less of an artist, and it made him a better companion. It was possible to share his company without experiencing overtones of moral ravage or inner conflict. A broad daylight cheerfulness surrounded the poet. When he couldn't find great pleasures, he was content with small ones. "No situation could be dull for a man in whom all reflection, all reaction, was witty."

Lowell's wit made Paris agreeable for Henry during a November and December otherwise rain-washed and dreary. "*Two whole months* of uninterrupted rain," he wrote to his sister, and yet he lingered while Rome beckoned. Christmas of 1872 was approaching when Henry began to uproot himself from his little room in the Hôtel Rastadt. "I have grown very fond of this massive and glittering capital." He was still walking, play-going, Louvre-going, reading and writing. He had just been to the masked ball at the opera and found it stale and flat—and unventilated. The crowds in the streets, the great pyramids of gaslight, the cabs laden with maskers, all seemed to him like some ancient revel in Babylon. At least this is what he told Quincy Street.

On 18 December Henry took his cab to the railway station. It was evening and the boulevards were filled with holiday-makers. Paris was mild and gay, and Henry wondered whether he wasn't making a mistake in leaving. The journey to Turin took twenty-four hours. He rested for a day, then went on to Florence.

Here he found a letter from his "Aunt" Mary Tweedy. Her husband was ill in Rome with gastric fever. A few hours later, during the evening of 23 December, Henry was once again—after three years' absence—in the Eternal City.

Book Three

Roman Hours 1873

★

A ROMAN WINTER

HE noticed at once signs of marked change since his visit to papal Rome in 1869. The kiosks displayed secular newspapers: in the old sleepy Rome there had been only those of the Vatican. There were also, he remarked, new gas-lamps round the spouting Triton in the Piazza Barberini. He put up at the Hôtel de Rome, in the middle of the Corso, but went out immediately into the narrow, crooked streets that were dark and empty. After the glittering boulevards of Paris, the Eternal City seemed a sleepy *ville de province*. He paused before the Spanish Steps; they had shrunk since his last visit. He climbed them and turned into the Via Gregoriana. All was silent and deserted. At No. 33 he knocked, and a few minutes later was being greeted affectionately by Mary and Edmund Tweedy in a charming little crimson drawing-room. Edmund had been ill but was mending. They wanted him to stay with them, but Henry declined. To accept their hospitality would have made him feel the world was a small place indeed.

Henry awoke next morning to perfect weather. The air glowed and throbbed under a sky of intense blue. Paris had offered him weeks of monotonous rain-washed asphalt. Rome was golden in the winter sun. He called on Lizzie and Francis Boott, his and Alice's midsummer companions, and stayed with them for dinner on Christmas Eve. They fed him turkey and apple-sauce. On Christmas Day he dined with the Tweedys, and drove with Aunt Mary to St Peter's in her open carriage. Henry took great delight in the open-lipped caressing Roman speech of the coachman, Giuseppe, whom he had no difficulty in understanding. During the succeeding days, while Tweedy was convalescent, Henry became Mary's escort; when she wasn't driving to the butcher's and the baker's, they visited churches or drove out over the old and the new Appian ways. At the end of their sightseeing Aunt Mary made him comfortable in the crimson drawing-room, served him excellent dinners and launched him in Roman—that is expatriate American—"society."

The new Rome seemed to Henry hostile to the picturesque. The *monsignori*, who had walked the streets in their purple hose followed by their solemn servants, were gone. There were no more glittering scarlet coaches of the cardinals, that swung with the weight of footmen clinging behind. The Pope was no longer to be encountered, sitting in the shadow of his great coach with uplifted fingers. Instead, as Henry passed the Quirinal, there was King Victor Emmanuel in person, with a single attendant, receiving petitions from a group of men and women. Never, Henry remarked, had royalty been in such hand-to-hand relations with their subjects. The traces of the Risorgimento's triumph were visible. But Italy still had its full measure of beggars; there were still children pleading for coppers with their fine eyes and intense smiles. Was Porta Pia bombarded three years before, Henry wondered, that Peppino should still whine for a copper?

He found it pleasant to sit coatless at the window of his large room in the hotel, while the January sun poured in; flies buzzed round his nose; occasionally he annihilated a mosquito. Or he took his daily walk, often alone, but sometimes with Francis Boott, going down back-streets from the Corso to the Capitol, past the low Capitoline hill and the meagre quadrangle—which made Roman history seem so small—to emerge on the other side at the Forum, where gradually he began to feel a certain sense of the picturesque. Nowhere in Rome was there more colour, more charm, more "sport for the eye"—lounging sun-seekers along the slope, beggars, soldiers, monks, tourists; the legendary wolf accommodated in its artificial grotto; and on high the statue of Marcus Aurelius with its pagan arm extended as in a blessing. Then down to the Forum where the new régime had launched its excavations. As yet only an immense stretch of pavement was laid bare, studded with broken pedestals. Henry liked to lean on the railing with the idlers; he found it an odd feeling "to see the past, the ancient world, as one stands there, bodily turned up with the spade."

I

And so on around to the Colosseum, to gaze on Rome present and past, Pagan and Christian, medieval and modern, and the contrast between bright light and mouldering cruel ruin. He took this particular walk one day when the Roman carnival had filled the Corso with hundreds of masked revellers. As the hubbub died away in the distance, he found himself strolling up a byway on the Palatine hill, from just behind the Arch of Titus. It was steep, but Henry was a stout walker and it led him between high walls and round a bend, past a series of dusty little pictures of stations of the cross. At the end of this path stood the little church of St Bonaventure with a modest façade. Lifting the leather curtain, Henry found himself in a small poor whitewashed interior; the candlesticks were tarnished, the altar was decorated with muslin flowers. Henry would not have remained had he not been struck by the attitude of a solitary priest in the place—a young, pale, kneeling figure, who gave him a sidelong glance as he entered. It was "so charged with the languor of devotion" that Henry remained. He watched the priest visit the altars in turn and kiss the balustrade beneath each one. While the Carnival was creating tumult in the streets, here was one figure kneeling for religion. Henry was struck by his "pious fatigue, his droning prayer, and his isolation."

It gave him, he wrote, a "supreme vision of the religious passion—its privations and resignations and exhaustions, and its terribly small share of amusement." The priest was young and strong, evidently not too refined to have enjoyed the Carnival. Planted there, his face pale with fasting, his knees stiff with praying, he seemed a stern satire on the thousands in the streets. Henry half-expected to see "some heavenly portent out of a monastic legend come down and confirm his choice."

Henry regarded religious passion as "the strongest of man's heart." He accepted "some application of the supernatural idea" as an essential part of life. But like his father, he turned his back on religious controversy and the earthly religious forms. Among the "churchiest churches" in Europe—those of Rome—he was interested above all in the social rôle of religion, the fact that the man-made houses of God had been "prayed in for several centuries by a singularly complicated and feudal society," forming the constant background of a human drama. Abroad, in the streets of Rome, Henry felt himself a part of this continuing drama.

II

His first fears were that he was falling into a Cambridge-by-the-Tiber, analogous to that which he had witnessed in Lowell's hotel by the Seine. On his third evening in Rome he went to a party given by a friend of the Nortons, Mrs Henry Russell Cleveland, and told his mother that its being in Rome made it no different from a party in Cambridge. Here he met Sarah Butler Wister, of Philadelphia, daughter of Fanny Kemble, the actress. Mrs Wister promptly invited him to her "at home," two nights later, and he was introduced to "the terrific Kemble herself, whose splendid handsomeness of eye, nostril and mouth were the best things in the room." Sarah Wister, in Rome with her husband and son, took an immediate fancy to Henry. She was strikingly handsome and possessed a magnificent head of hair to which he made allusion in many letters. She was "literary," interested in ideas, and had much of her mother's energy and force. With a promptness that took Henry by surprise, she invited him to accompany her the next day to visit the French Academy in the Villa Medici.

They went instead to the Colonna gardens, "where we wandered for nearly a couple of hours among mossy sarcophagi, mouldering along heaven-high vistas of ilex and orange and laurel, and lingered at the base of damp green statues." Henry was a little surprised at Mrs Wister's informality; but he was also distinctly charmed. "A beautiful woman who takes you to such a place and talks to you uninterruptedly, learnedly, and even cleverly for two whole hours is not to be disposed of in three lines," he observes in a letter to his mother. But he hasn't time to tell her more. He must be off to the "Cambridge Greenoughs, confound 'em. I have not come to Rome for Cambridge tea fights." "The chapter of 'society' here—that is American society—opens up before me," he writes.

It did, and more largely than he had imagined. The presence in Rome of an eligible and charming literary bachelor, addicted to good manners and good conversation, became known almost immediately in that small, enclosed society. The Terry household in the Odescalchi Palace had two marriageable daughters; the Storys, also with a marriageable daughter, were no less hospitable in their great apartment in the Barberini. Presently Henry is attending musical and theatrical evenings in "the rival houses of Terry and Story." At Mrs Wister's he meets a great beauty of Boston and Washington, Mrs Charles Sumner, separated from her political husband and awaiting a divorce. He encounters the lively and Amazonian Alice Bartlett and the haunting Elena Lowe; and there are the Bootts, with their circle of friends. He complains, but he surrenders himself wholly to this society and to the "sovereign spirit" of the city—the Rome, as it was to become, of *Roderick Hudson* and *The Portrait of a Lady*. He passes long hours in the villas and their gardens, nearly always in the company of some young and attractive woman. Mrs Wister tends indeed to monopolize him. He joins the ladies in gallops across the Campagna, where the lonely arches stand crowned with weeds and softened by time, and the footfall of his horse is muffled in a flower-carpeted terrain: wild roses, honeysuckle, half-buried violets and pale anemones, the white narcissus and the cyclamen. High overhead he suddenly hears the disembodied song of the lark. He meets American artists in palaces and studios; he makes excursions to the Alban and Sabine hills; he visits scenes of antiquity and takes part in picnics, with hampers packed at Spillmann's; the food and wine are laid out on the warm stones of ruined temples. He spends days at Frascati and "ineffable hours" at the Villas Mondragone and Aldobrandini, lying on the grass at the foot of ilexes. Returning from his rambles, he finds friendly doors opening wide to him on all sides.

III

Henry knew that certain of these great doors, in villas and palaces, had opened wide fifteen years before to a distinguished American predecessor, and there were moments when he distinctly felt as if he were following in the footsteps of Nathaniel Hawthorne. The writer from Salem had been "the last of the old-fashioned Americans" in Rome, Henry was to write. An American "of equal value with Hawthorne, an American of equal genius, imagination and, as our forefathers said, sensibility," he observed, would now accommodate himself more easily to the ways of foreign lands. "An American as cultivated as Hawthorne," he added, "is now almost inevitably more cultivated, and, as a matter of course, more Europeanized in advance, more cosmopolitan." A reader could hardly be in doubt who this American might be. And the Roman Americans, whether they were the counterparts of Kenyon, of Hilda or of Miriam, presented to the newcomer an interest all the deeper for having been a part of an earlier novelist's experience. The tight little group of artists and amateurs of Hawthorne's day had grown, to be sure, in the intervening years. American painters and sculptors continued to come abroad, and for good reason. There were no art-schools to speak of in the United States, no great masters with whom to study, nor an "atmosphere" in which they could create. In Rome young American sculptors found the Italian marble and qualified technicians and stone-cutters to handle it: there was alabaster and malachite, lapis and porphyry and the centuries-old work in mosaic. The men who used the brush or the chisel had in the Holy City example and precedent. And in Rome, too, as Hawthorne had shown, there were subjects for the novelist as well. The romancer from Salem had for good reason complained that an expanding America offered no mystery, no ancient wrong, no ruins—only a happy daylight prosperity which was hardly sufficient for a novelist of high imagination.

With these artists came also the dabblers and the dilettantes; this was inevitable and served only to leaven the dedicated population and to provide a greater variety of types. There always were amateurs beside the hard workers; always dilettantes to read poems, admire pictures—and to imitate them. And then in the American colony there were men and women who simply journeyed abroad to enjoy the soft climate of Rome, in preference to the harsher one they had abandoned, and who gave themselves over to the simple pleasures available in the ancient city.

Henry, from the first, was prepared to enjoy these pleasures. Like his character Rowland, he "took to evening parties as a duck to water." He enjoyed society; he was always happy in a Roman drawing-room. He liked nothing better than to find an agreeable corner, next to an agreeable and attractive woman, and such women were not lacking in the Roman drawing-rooms. He accepted invitations and paid calls punctually; in an era when one could not travel in taxis or use a telephone, Henry always came at appointed hours and left his card. He might, like Rowland, do this with "exaggerated gravity," but gravity did not diminish his enjoyment. He thrived more on people than on scenery. He tended, however, to emphasize the emptier side of this society to Quincy Street. Cambridge, after all, was expecting him to be industrious. And he always felt he was not working enough. He feared that his relaxation in society might seem, if not sinful, at least wasteful to his mother and father. "Every week I hope 'society' is over—but it spurts up again," he writes home. He confesses, however, that "I have deliberately taken all that has come of it and been the gainer." The words "Forgive me!" intrude in his letters at odd moments—whenever he describes some particular pleasure he has had, as if that pleasure were a crime committed against William, or Alice, or the generosity of his parents. "I mingle enough in society to give a flavour of magnificence to my life," he says. But he also tells his mother that the American colony in Rome is "a very poor affair indeed." It is limited and isolated, "without relations with the place, or much serious appreciation of it," and so tends to tumble back "upon itself and finds itself of meagre substance." Then he tells his family he has cut down his social life to the very limits of courtesy. Yet these limits seem to be sufficiently wide and absorbing. And was this society as meagre as he claimed? Later he was to speak of the "incomparable *entertainment*" of Rome in "manners, customs, practices, processes, states of feeling," and all this over and above the museum side—objects and treasures and relics. He was speaking in a marked degree of his compatriots, for he had little access to the Italians. "Entertainment" of this kind was the very stuff of life for a novelist, and Henry was seeing how these little figures moved against a grandiose background. Were they not all dancing to good music—and in the noblest ballroom in the world?

THE TWO PALACES

HENRY'S playful allusion to "the rival houses of Terry and Story," as if they were Montague and Capulet, singled out in the American colony two artists who lived in old princely palaces and vied with one another in offering hospitality and entertainment to visiting Americans. The Storys were housed in a splendour almost royal, in an apartment of more than forty rooms, in the Palazzo Barberini, on the slope of the Quirinal. The Terrys were in a lesser palace, in rooms on the second floor of the Odescalchi in the Piazza dei Santi Apostoli, opposite the Colonna Palace. With neither household can James be said to have become intimate. He enjoyed, however, their respective soirées; he found it "a kind of pretty spectacle to go to their houses." There is a particular interest in James's view of William Wetmore Story, whose biography he was destined to write—the sole memoir of this kind which he was to write. In death, as in life, Story was fortunate in the circumstances of his fame, for James's two stout volumes have kept his name alive longer than most of his outmoded creations in stone. The account of this work belongs to a later time: it is unusual in the annals of biography, for it deals with a man Henry did not particularly like, and is told with a sympathy that masks but does not altogether conceal his feelings.

I

One might laugh at Italian palaces, Henry wrote in a travel-sketch—at their peeling paint, their general nudity, their dreariness—but they had the great quality of their design: an elevation and extent. Their doorways and arches seemed meant for cathedrals; their wide windows opened upon panoramas; they spoke of a proud indifference to the cost of materials or of labour.

Both the Barberini and the Odescalchi had been built from designs by Bernini; and while the effect of grandeur went with an effect of gloom, the Barberini could rejoice in brightness of façade and an almost modern gaiety. It had embodied the grandiose dream of Urban VIII, who built it in the late Renaissance out of the "quarry" of the Colosseum. It was "greatness unadorned"—"great lines, great spaces, great emphasis, great reserve."

As Henry climbed the stairs leading to the small door of the right wing, he could hear the splash of the Barberini fountain, "the most Roman note of all," as if by an incessant play of water the Romans would wash away the bloodstains of history. The Barberini had its bloody legends; Lady Coventry had been found murdered on its threshold; and in its gallery hung Guido Reni's turbaned portrait of Beatrice Cenci, in the painted eyes of which Hawthorne had sought with such intensity to fathom dark mysteries. As Henry approached the entrance he passed on one of the landings the bas-relief of a Thorwaldsen lion. The modest doorway, with the name "W. W. Story" inscribed on it, swung open into grandiose reception-rooms. Henry was led by servants in livery into the red drawing-room, or the theatre-room, tapestried and chandeliered, where since the middle of the century this American from Salem and Cambridge had been host to former American presidents, writers, painters, and Roman nobility, secular and ecclesiastical. Story's windows looked out upon "iridescent horizons, accidental pictures . . . terraces, treasures of space." On the morning after one of his receptions Henry wrote to his mother: "An apartment in a Roman palace is a very fine affair, and it certainly adds a picturesqueness to life to be led through a chain of dimly-lighted chambers, besprinkled with waiting servants, before you emerge, sonorously announced, into the light and elegance of a reception-room with a *roof*, not a ceiling."

The picture which Henry was to draw of the lawyer turned sculptor was accurate enough—so far as it went. Story was a genial host; "talk was his joy and pleasantry his habit." He was animated and gay, with a faculty for humour and mimicry: he was interested in ideas, in people—in everything. He asked questions, sought answers, could be demonstrative, and disputatious—an individual incisive and over-assertive, a kind of milder Gilbert Osmond, or even perhaps, in certain aspects, the Gloriani of *Roderick Hudson*, who was a clever man but lacked artistic integrity. To spend an evening in the high-roofed theatre-room, with the play of taper on tapestry, listening to chamber music (say some of the amateur quartets of Francis Boott), or to watch the performance of some of Story's theatricals, meet celebrities, indulge in small talk, offered Henry a strange and fascinating picture of expatriate life. Story was never deficient in anecdote and his Roman memory was long. Severn, Landor, the Brownings, Thackeray, Tennyson, Hawthorne, General Grant, a row of Cardinals and British prime ministers, had paid homage to him in his palace. Pope Pius IX had been his greatest patron. It was he who, on seeing Story's statue of Cleopatra—the statue admired by Hawthorne and described in *The Marble Faun*—paid the cost of transporting it to the London Exhibition of 1862, where it captured the Victorian imagination and made Story famous. But if, in his biography, James offers this image of the sculptor, and creates a memorable Rome of words, it is in his letters of the actual time that we can discover his immediate impressions. On visiting Story's studio in the Via San Nicolo di Tolentino—that studio which is Kenyon's in Hawthorne's novel—Henry told Grace Norton he found the sculptor "in the midst of an army of marble heroines, which were not altogether unsuggestive of Mrs Jarley's waxworks." To Charles Eliot Norton he wrote: "So you're acquainted with Story's muse—that brazen hussy—to put it plainly. I have rarely seen such a case of *prosperous* pretension as Story. His cleverness is great, the world's good nature to him is greater." Story's "endless effigies" were "almost fatally unsimple." Mrs Henry Adams who visited the same studio at this time exclaimed: "Oh! how he does spoil nice blocks of white marble. Nothing but Sibyls on all sides, sitting, standing, legs crossed, legs uncrossed, and all with the same expression as if they smelt something wrong." Her husband's impression, years later, boiled down to the rather general statement in the *Education*: "William Story could not touch the secret of Michael Angelo."

There were, indeed, many secrets Story could not touch, and Henry James, in his biography, offered the ultimate verdict: Story's career, he said, was "a sort of beautiful sacrifice to a noble mistake."

II

In the more modest Odescalchi Palace life was pitched in a minor key, but still with pretensions to style. Luther Terry lived there with his wife, sister of Julia Ward Howe and widow of the sculptor Thomas Crawford. There were three Crawford children, the two marriageable daughters, Annie and Mimoli, and the son Marion, then at school, and destined to popular fame as a writer of romances. Terry had left his native Connecticut at twenty, and spent the rest of his life in Italy. A rough-bearded, lonely man, he was a comfortable expatriate whose work James scrutinized in his studio at 23 Via Margutta with an eye more critical than his host suspected. His studio pleased James: it was situated in a squalid house, in a squalid street, promising gloom within. On ascending the long stone staircase, however, Henry found himself in a pleasant first-floor court, a sort of hanging garden, open to the sky: straight out of this opened the large still studio. Terry showed Henry his work: a painting called *The Artist's Dream*, another *The Vision of St John*—"the queerest old survivals of the American art of thirty years ago. It is an agreeable curiosity to see their author sit and look at them seriously and expound his intentions and yet be on the whole a sensible man of the world." Another writer, perhaps with unintended irony, has described how Americans visiting Rome purchased pictures from Luther Terry as "a grateful memorial" of pleasant sociabilities. This suggests that a certain charm of "salesmanship," genial and without Story's flamboyance, animated his host. The charm was also one of background. The Odescalchi Palace is built of stone and brick round a colonnaded court, and Henry, entering the Terry apartment, found himself in high rooms with coffered ceilings. In the ante-room sat liveried messengers. In the library the books were ensconced in elaborate carved bookcases; and the notable Magenta Room, which is described in the various memoirs of the Crawfords and the Terrys, had panels of pink brocade with oleander and silver-grey flowers in their design; the ceiling was vaulted, and painted with a heavy grapevine trellis on a background of burnished gold. In the centre Bellerophon on Pegasus killed the Chimaera in blue-and-white pastel shades. The presiding genius of the Terry household was Annie Crawford, who, Henry wrote home, "has every gift (including a face so mobile and expressive that it amounts almost to beauty), but she is as hard as flint and I am pretty sure she will never have an adorer. He will have to be a real lion-tamer." The judgment was shrewder than he knew. Not long after, Annie married Erich von Rabe, a Junker baron with a dominating will, an estate in Prussia and violent anti-English prejudices.

III

In addition to Story's pretentious statues and Terry's mediocre paintings, Henry saw the imitative art of other Americans who had come to Rome in the earlier years. He met Harriet Hosmer at dinner at the Storys', and looked at her with much interest, for she was the young woman who, fifteen years before, had escorted Hawthorne to her studio and shown him her statue of Zenobia. Hawthorne had described Miss Hosmer as "bird-like" and wondered how so brisk a creature—she had made a popular statue of Puck—could create work "so quietly impressive." In middle-age she struck Henry as "a remarkably ugly little grey-haired boy, adorned with a diamond necklace, but she seems both 'vivacious' and discreet and is better, I imagine, than her statues." He called at the studio of Eugene Benson, a few doors from Terry's in the Via Margutta; the "irrepressible" Benson, a friend of the elder Henry James, was then a striving painter of landscapes, who never lost his devotion to the classical mode. Henry was to know him later in Venice. He pronounced his work "careful, and conscientious, but very uninspired." Edward Darley Boit and his teacher, Frederic Crowninshield, he met, but left no comment on their work. He called also on an elderly lady artist, Sarah Freeman Clarke, a friend of his father's and of Emerson's, who had long mingled with the transcendentalists, and who had once studied with Washington Allston. Since she was known to Quincy Street he described in detail the black staircase leading to her apartment and the series of drawings she had done after piously visiting all the spots in Italy "reputed to have known the tread of Dante's wandering foot." He found her drawings "mild"; she had invented a delightful pastime for herself.

He was most at home in the studio of Lizzie Boott. She was not a professional, but an aspirant, a conscientious amateur; and Quincy Street was interested in her progress. "Lizzie is as sweet and good as ever. She has a little studio, where she paints little tatterdemalion Checcos and Ninas—with decidedly increasing ability." To Alice: "I had an errand this morning at the Piazza Barberini—(the Boott's)—and found Lizzie in her studio, *en tête-à-tête* with one of the very swell models—a wondrous youth in a sheepskin jacket and bandaged legs and flowing curls and the most pictorial complexion. Lizzie is very busy, happy and good." Again: "Going up early the other morning to make a riding appointment with her, I found her in her studio with a certain little Peppina—the most enchanting little nut-brown child model you can imagine: in structure, colour, costume, everything, the handsomest little miniature woman. There sat Lizzie happily painting this delicious object. Where will she get a Peppina in Cambridge?" And he goes on to say that he had been present one evening in her studio when she showed some of her sepia and watercolour sketches to Boit and Crowninshield. "They, like myself, were much surprised at her fertility, inventiveness and general skill."

There was one other artist of whom James obtained a good view and on whose fate he meditated in later years. Indeed at one time he is said to have sat to him for his portrait, but the painting does not seem to have survived. This was J. Rollin Tilton of New Hampshire, who had come to Rome in the middle of the century. Like Story he lived in the Barberini, but in a more modest corner of the palace. The apartment itself James remembered as "a minor masterpiece of early eighteenth-century tarabiscotage, of contorted stucchi, mouldings, medallions, reliefs of every form, a small riot of old-world elements." The "atrocious Tilton," James called him, not so much for his paintings as his personality. He described him as "a very queer genius. He is great on sunsets and does them (and all sorts of aerial luminosities etc.) very well." But he was "the most blatant humbug in his talk you ever heard—assuring you, every twenty minutes, that Emerson is the 'lens of the Almighty.'" Henry scrutinized his paintings of Italian and Egyptian landscapes, in the manner of Claude, "the stone-pine, the ruin, the sunset," and wondered at Tilton's, one moment of fame in London, when his work was recognized by the Academy. Then he fell from sight, his "reputation sadly, publicly, permanently unfinished." He was still another type of the American artist-failure in Europe.

IV

Although Henry's letters from Rome mention only these artists, it is clear that he encountered others and that he studied closely a series of artistic "cases" which he incorporated into *Roderick Hudson*, the novel he wrote during the following year. He was himself, after all, one of these artists, even if his medium was not marble or paint. What kind of artist could an American be in a foreign environment, Henry seems to have asked himself—an environment as congenial and as soft as Rome, which conspired to make him lazy or imitative; or pretentious, like Story; or mediocre, like Terry; or plodding, like Benson; or inspired but unprofessional, like Tilton. Charles Eliot Norton had written to him during his lonely months in Cambridge: "Born and bred in New England as we were, where the air we breathe is full of the northern chill, and no other philosophy but that of utilitarianism is possible—it is not easy to learn to be content with the usefulness of doing nothing. Italy is a good place, however, for deadening the overactive conscience, and for killing rank ambition." There were examples on all sides, even to the dabblers and amateurs like Sarah Clarke or Lizzie Boott. They came from an as yet half-formed America; they seemed content with so little. What if an artist arrived in this environment with a vaulting ambition, such as Henry's, and felt within himself the stirring of greatness? What might happen to him?

The time was to come when Henry would seek to answer these questions. In *Roderick* there is a memorable scene, not unlike the evening James spent with Lizzie, Crowninshield, and Boit, looking at work and discussing it: it is the scene in which Roderick's friends gather to admire his Roman statues, first fruits of his labour abroad. Roderick is there, all impulse and fire. Gloriani, the clever but cynical opportunist, seems to be an Italian version of Story; Singleton is probably a combination of Benson and Tilton, and the amateur Augusta Blanchard, who lives alone and paints people with their backs turned (because she is "a little weak in faces"), could be both Lizzie and Sarah Clarke. Henry places before us the inspired, the clever, the persistent and the plodding creators. Roderick's candle will burn out in one night. Singleton's goals are too modest: quiet industry satisfies him. Augusta is sincere, but unprofessional. Only Gloriani, the European, will outlive his flashiness and achieve greatness. And it is only when, in the fulness of time, he gains large awareness and insight into life, above "the mere base maximum of cleverness," that he will be saluted as Master. In *The Ambassadors* Gloriani has become what Story never achieved: he is endowed with true greatness. The very lines of his face seem to have been placed there by art—and "then the deep human expertness in Gloriani's smile—oh, the terrible life behind it!" In Rome, in 1873, that vision was not yet possible to Henry. He looked, however, with a critical eye upon his fellow-American creators. But where they worked and abandoned themselves to their momentary experiences by the Tiber, the novelist sought to read the larger lesson of their stunted careers. It would serve as both example and warning to himself.

ROMAN RIDES

ONE day toward the end of January 1873, when he had been in Rome a month, Henry James hired a horse and rode out of the Porta del Popolo to the Ponte Molle (Ponte Milvio), where the Tiber flowed between its four ecclesiastical statues. He rode over the crest of the hill and along the old post-road leading to Florence. He had never been much of a horseman, but he knew how to stay in the saddle. The day was mild, the air filled with a mellow purple glow. As he rode, the beauty of the landscape, the sense of movement, the feeling of power—and of control—took possession of him. After an hour he pulled up and stood for some time at the edge of a meadow. On all sides extended great Roman distances: the country rolled away in slopes and dells, purple, blue, brown. In the Sabine mountains he watched a play of sapphire and amber. In the foreground a peasant jogged along on an ass; far off a grey tower added a painter's touch to the landscape. It was bright, yet sad; alive, yet charged, "to the supersensuous ear, with the murmur of an extinguished life." The experience was altogether strange—deliciously strange. To ride once was to ride again; from that moment he gave to the Campagna a generous share of his Roman days. "I can stick on a horse better than I supposed," he wrote to Quincy Street.

I

Presently he was galloping in the grassy shadows of aqueducts and tombs and taking ditches as if he were a huntsman. Riding doubled his horizon; he could pass with ease from one Roman picture to another. He duly hired a horse by the month and justified the expense to his mother by explaining how good it was for his health. In March he engaged another "nice little horse for a month. He has a charming little character and yet is sufficiently lively to assist me somewhat to learn to ride." By the time this period was up he was boasting that he had taken "four ditches with great serenity and was complimented." Later, looking fondly back on this time, he could only half-believe it had all been true.

In Cambridge he had been a leisurely walker. It was a measure of his new-found freedom that he could now proceed at a gallop over the Roman countryside. "The Campagna," he was to remember thirty years later, "was an education of the taste, a revelation of new sources of solitary and of social joy." His solitary rides yielded him a fund of aesthetic adventure and ideas for stories. The "social joy" is reflected in his letters to his parents. "I am now in the position of a creature with *five* women *offering* to ride with me," he boasted. There was a touch of exultation in these words. His letters convey a sense of well-being. Not a word about his old backache, the "obscure hurt" which had immobilized him during the Civil War and which might have kept him from the saddle.

Not all the days in the Campagna were perfect. The rides were a constant feast of the unexpected. The Campagna was at its best on mild winter days, "when the brilliant air alone suffices to make the whole landscape smile." When the sirocco blew, it was as if he rode in a world without hope. Detail and ornament varied from week to week. In Italy man lived more with nature than in New England: "it does more work for him and gives him more holidays than in our short-summered clime." He could sit in an arbour of twisted vines with his feet in the dirt and think that in February, on the other side of the Atlantic, his feet would be seeking the allurement of the parlour hearth-rug. Henry liked to gaze at sun-cracked plaster and indoor shadows. He liked to stare into the gateways of farms, with their moss-coated stairways climbing outside a wall. It was a comfort not to be in snow-blown Cambridge.

On the homeward stretch, in waning light, he would rein up by an old tavern and buy a bottle of their best; their worst and their best, with shifting price, was always ordinary *vino bianco* or *vino rosso.* There was a ragged bush over the door and within sat half a dozen peasants in indigo jackets and goatskin breeches, their feet planted on the crooked cobbles and their elbows on the table. These were primitive hostelries, with Garibaldi's portrait painted on the wall, or a picture of a lady in a low-necked dress opening a lattice. The taverns often had a yard, with a pine-wreathed arbour casting shadows on the benches, and tables covered with white highway dust. But more often than not, Henry did not follow the highway; he liked to ride along the newly-disinterred walls of Rome. In Boston, a year before, he had looked at raw plank-fences advertising patent-medicines. Now he glanced with contemplative eyes on ancient stones "in which a more learned sense may read portentous dates and signs—Servius, Aurelius, Honorius," the wall-builders, the architects of empire.

II

Servius, Aurelius, Honorius—Henry James on horseback caught from the ancient stones, from the great arches and the towering aqueducts, that emanation of grandeur and that echo of *imperium* which he had known from the first. His earliest memory was of the Place Vendôme. He had lived as a youth under an Empire, a late and diminished one it is true—the Second Empire of France—but filled with the sound of trumpets and of marching feet, and showing bravely the eagles and banners of recent glories. Now, in his adult years, he was reading the signatures of history written across Rome and its Campagna; the very names he plucked from the chiselled stones were those of the great, the imperial time. In Italy the *gloire* experienced as a boy in the Louvre existed on all sides for Henry James. He could identify himself with Servius the wall-builder; or Aurelius the stoic conqueror; or Honorius seeking to shore up Rome against decline; and reflect, with the irony of a poet and a dramatist, upon the incongruous in these ancient stones in which pagan and Christian elements were now mixed timelessly with those of a benevolent bourgeois monarchy. Unlike the romantic poets, he did not gaze upon the past with melancholy or sadness; his pose might be Byronic, but he was a cheerful Puritanical Byron. Nor did the great symbols of stone speak to him as Ozymandias spoke to Shelley. For him ancient stones meant grandeur rather than decay. As he wandered through the Forum, gazing upon the new excavations, the marvel that filled him was not how much of the past had crumbled, but how much still endured. Before the tomb of the Valerii, to which he rode one day, he could muse that it was "strange enough to think of these things—so many of them as there are—surviving their immemorial eclipse in this perfect shape and coming up like long-lost divers from the sea of time." This had been his experience during his earlier visit as well. He found a "peculiar fascination" in things recently excavated: an Augustus dug up some five years before or a "ravishing" little bust of the same Emperor when he was a boy, "as clear and fresh in quality as if it had dated from yesterday." All these relics—the dying gladiator, the Lydian Apollo, the Amazon at the Capitol—spoke to Henry "of the breadth of human genius." And there were times when riding through ecclesiastical gateways, or along the broad arches of the Claudian aqueduct, or skirting the disinterred wall, Henry felt that he might have been "a wandering Tartar touching on the confines of the Celestial Empire." A strange image for a New World man in the presence of an illimitable imperial past. It established a kind of primitive distance from imperial power.

III

If Henry relished the Roman relics as symbols of the endurance of art and of the nature of "glory," he also experienced a profound uneasiness in their presence. Power was acceptable to him only in some attenuated or disguised form; seen in its nakedness, as we know from his dream of the Louvre,[1] it had its nightmare side. Perhaps this was because he had always known it in disguise, behind the quiet mask of resignation of his mother; and by the disguises he himself had assumed when he gave himself a motionless observer's rôle, and kept himself at a discreet distance

[1] Described in *Henry James: The Untried Years*, pp. 73–75.

from objects and people, while his eyes and mind took possession of them. "I keep up a devil of an observing," he wrote to his mother; it was the observing of one who could play omniscient author in the lives of his characters while finding many ingenious technical devices to conceal his omniscience. He was to become, as a consequence of this, one of the masters of the devious in the modes of narration, and was to invent many new ways of concealing the storyteller from his readers. Unadulterated power had all the frightening qualities of open assault. Perhaps this is why we find so many allusions to the equestrian statue of Marcus Aurelius at the Capitol. The statue had been, when he looked at it in 1869, "one of the things I have most enjoyed in Rome. It is totally admirable." It was large and monumental and yet so full of "sweet human dignity—stretching out a long thin arm in the act of mild persuasive command—that affects you like an audible personal voice out of that stony Roman past." This was power masked with kindness; the statue had the countenance of the generous conqueror. Henry contrasted it with his glimpse of the Pope borne through the streets. "As you revert to that poor sexless Pope enthroned upon his cushions—and then glance at those imperial legs swinging in their immortal bronze, you cry out that here at least was a *man*." Henry, in these remarks, paraphrases Hawthorne, who saw in the carved gesture "a command which is in itself a benediction." And he may have remembered that Matthew Arnold had seen in the pagan statue a "portrait most suggestive of a Christian conscience"—in the very heart of Christendom. This softening of pagan imperial authority by something resembling Christian benignity, this mildness in an Emperor who had indeed shrunk from violence—while being committed to it—gave Henry great pause.

His travel-essays and his letters to Cambridge show at every turn Henry's sense of power in his new-found freedom, allied with his relish for the strength and dominion reflected in his Roman surroundings. But his deepest anxieties created by this may be discerned in two tales written during these months. They sprang directly from his Roman rides and his exploration of ancient things: a visit to the tomb of the Valerii contributed to "The Last of the Valerii"; a glimpse of a shepherd asleep in the Campagna, "with his naked legs stretched out on the turf and his soft peaked hat over his long hair," led to the writing of "Adina." The tales were told in Henry's early manner. The speeches are often ranting monologues; in them, however, we see the writer using his new materials and the new world of feeling into which he has entered.

IV

In "The Last of the Valerii" a Roman Count, a kind of sleepy, dreamy, well-fed Donatello, marries a young American girl. In the grounds of the Valerio villa a statue is disinterred, much in the manner in which Hawthorne describes the digging up of a Venus, or as Merimée recounts a similar occurrence in the tale which James translated in his youth at Newport, "*La Vénus d'Ille*." In Merimée's story the statue comes marching into the bridal chamber to claim the young hero for herself. The statue in James's story is a Juno, instead of a Venus, and James brings in a distinct variant on his French predecessor: for the sleepy-eyed Conte Valerio falls in love with the Juno, broods for hours before it, neglects his wife, ultimately abandoning himself to worship and pagan blood-sacrifice. If the tale is thus an amalgam of Hawthorne and Merimée, its dénouement is pure James. "When a beautiful woman is in stone, all he can do is to look at her," the little Roman excavator remarks to the distraught American girl. She takes the hint. The past must not deprive her of the present. The Juno is quietly and secretly buried again. In this way the Contessa restores her warm body to her husband's arms—those arms which had been supplicating and sacrificing to stone. The young daughter of the Puritans has exorcised pagan evil—and triumphed.

The second tale, "Adina," describes the shepherd, Angelo Beati, asleep in the Campagna; he is discovered by two Americans, an irritable and unpleasant classical scholar named Scrope and his friend, a proper Bostonian. Scrope notices that the shepherd clutches in his hand a discoloured object: he drags it from him, and when Angelo awakens, throws a few coins at him. The discoloured object appears to be some ancient jewel. Scrope spends days learning how to clean it. He works in solitude. One midnight, in high elation, he brings to his companion a beautiful golden topaz, carved with a laurel-crowned imperial figure and a frieze of warriors and chariots, bearing the words *Divus Tiberius Caesar Totius Orbis Imperator*.

Emperor of the whole world. The topaz thus belonged to Tiberius, the campaigner in Gaul, Armenia and Germany, the conqueror of the Illyrians: also the Tiberius of the Gospel of St Luke and the murderer of his friend Sejanus. In a long oratorical speech Scrope boasts of his own conquest of the centuries in recovering the symbol of a *totius orbis imperator*. He gives the stone to his fiancée, a young American woman named Adina Waddington. She, however, regards the stone as evil and refuses to wear it. "I should feel most uncomfortable in carrying the Emperor Tiberius so near my heart," she says. Moreover Adina has been attracted to the young shepherd who, with his locks combed and in a suit purchased with Scrope's money, trails the American about Rome claiming he has been cheated. "He has more than his share of good luck," he says when he sees Adina. "A topaz—and a pearl! both at once." One evening Adina breaks off her engagement to Scrope; the next morning she climbs out of her window and runs off with Angelo. "She's better than the topaz," he says. The heavy-hearted Scrope, in due course, pauses on the bridge of St Angelo and commits the stone to the muddy Tiber. As with the Juno, the past is restored to the past —but in this instance Scrope's love is not restored to him.

Henry seems to be saying in these tales that the past contains a fund of evil dangerous to love and to life. Things buried for a millennium lose none of their baleful force when restored to the light of day. Much that lay uncovered in Rome fascinated James; he could speak of the "breadth of genius" it revealed; yet clearly, by the testimony of his tales, he felt that the living—in order to go on living—consorted with it at their peril. The beautiful Juno-mother, the glistening topaz, contained within them a witchery of beauty—and a terrible destructive power. There was something morbid in disinterring them; they conveyed a feeling of mouldering, ancient decay: it was like an uncovering of the dead.

Thus Henry James had arrived at his first clear statement of one of his major themes: the corruption to be found in Europe by an America still innocent. The American Contessa cannot compete with pagan evil. To live and love, she must obliterate her stone rival. Adina will have nothing to do with the topaz: it is "pollution." In both, their innocence resists and defies the evil. If Henry states his case in these clear-cut and even extreme terms, it is because his feeling for evil had in it all the mysterious awe and horror of his father's religious revolt and "vastation." These tales, like the casual turn of an excavating spade, show the buried fear of evil in Henry. The tales of the Juno and the topaz contain, beneath their surface narration, a sense of shock which Henry experienced in discovering the endless beauty of the pagan and the endless threat to his heritage of civilization. On another level they suggest also his intuitive understanding that he would have to bury his personal past, the past of Quincy Street, and make his way in a disengaged present. The solution for him would become clearer as he mastered the lesson of his Roman days. The happy meeting-ground of puritan and pagan could be precisely the ground of art. An artist could be pagan in spirit and remain a puritan in fact. He could thus permissibly enjoy the pleasures of his senses—the very throb of Rome—and aspire to greatness without fear of strange punishment. Henry was engaged in a systematic and searching appraisal of old and new, Europe and America, corruption and innocence. And in this search he aspired to, and dreaded, the fierce power of the artist. The mask of courtesy and the euphemism became his outward defence against any dangerous surge of ambition. In Quincy Street he had to be reticent. Abroad, on horseback, he could be resolute. "It is time I should rend the veil from the ferocious ambition which has always *couvé* beneath a tranquil exterior; which enabled me to support unrecorded physical misery in my younger years; and which is perfectly confident of accomplishing serious things." Thus to his mother at a later time, when it was possible for him to speak out. And to his brother, also during a later phase: "If I keep along here patiently I rather think I shall become a (sufficiently) great man."

He would do more than achieve greatness. He would create a kind of *imperium* of letters, annexe Europe to his native American domain, achieve a transatlantic empire larger than that of other novelists. And like Marcus Aurelius he would offer the world the countenance of a conqueror who was, as Arnold said, tender and blameless—*tendentemque manus ripae ulterioris amore.*

SIX WOMEN

"I AM now in the position of a creature with *five* women *offering* to ride with me." There is a distinct swagger here, a suggestion to Quincy Street that its young writing son is a social success in Rome. The swagger was on the whole justified. There were indeed five ladies—two married, one about to be divorced, and two eligible for marriage—who sought the pleasant company of Henry James Jr, of Cambridge, Mass. He bestowed it generously, yet with his customary caution. Let us look at these ladies, in the order in which Henry named them to his mother, look at them as they sit, well-mounted on their steeds, admirably dressed for the Campagna, smiling and responsive—riding with him sometimes alone, sometimes in a group.

I

First there was Mrs Sumner. Before her brief marriage to Senator Charles Sumner, she had been the widow of William Sturgis Hooper of Boston, who had left her with one daughter. She was thirty-five—five years older than Henry—possessed of a slender, stately form, and what has been described as a "high-bred manner and aristocratic reserve." In Rome she was awaiting her divorce from Sumner. They had parted after a few months; both were ambitious, strong, not easily capable of the compromises of life. "I have seen a good deal of late of Mrs Sumner and adore her," Henry wrote to his father; and to Grace Norton, "With her great beauty (which on horse-back is enormous), she has great honesty, frankness and naturalness." When Henry announced that he "adored" a woman, it was sufficient sign that he was in no danger of "involvement." He had long been a worshipper, at a distance, of idealized beauty. And he enjoyed being seen in the company of a woman who

ALICE MASON (Mrs Charles Sumner)
From a photograph taken in Venice

carried herself with queenly dignity. Some of Sumner's biographers have attributed to his wife a highly "variable" temper and a certain moodiness; she was said to have married him in the belief that he would carry her to the White House. Mrs Sumner knew her mind; she also did not easily tolerate fools. If this gave her the air of being brusque at times, she could never be accused of downright rudeness. She had a high social style, force and presence, and for years after her divorce, when she resumed her maiden name and was known as Mrs Alice Mason, she moved through the expatriate society of London, Paris and Rome in complete possession of her world. She entertained Emerson when he came to Rome; Henry Adams speaks of her with affection and respect in his letters; Sargent painted her; she remained a close friend of Henry James. During that winter Henry rode often with her and with her friend Alice Bartlett. Mrs Sumner and Miss Bartlett shared an apartment in the Via della Croce, and Henry came regularly to see them. "I had one day a famous ride with Mrs Sumner and Miss Bartlett: both admirable horsewomen, especially Miss B., and both very handsome in the saddle. We went far away into the rolling meadows, where the shaggy-vested shepherds feed their flocks, and had a series of magnificent gallops, of which I acquitted myself *à mon honneur*. But for me and my infirmities, they ride at a rather tiring rate." Thus the record for Quincy Street.

Second on Henry's list was Mrs Edward Boit, wife of the artist, and mother of the four little girls who figure in Sargent's large canvas in the Boston Museum. If she "offered" to ride, it seems certain that the young man did not accept the offer. "I shall fight shy of Mrs Boit who, I believe, is an equestrian terror." As we gaze upon Sargent's portrait of Mrs Boit, seated floridly in her later and more matronly years, we may wonder that she could ever have been such a "terror" on horseback, for she became heavy, with the fullness of middle age and of repeated motherhood. But the backward toss of the head, and the effect from a certain angle as if she were winking, suggests a personality with whom Henry may have feared involvement on other than equestrian grounds. He was extremely fond of her from the first

—"a decidedly likeable little woman—bating her giggling." Later he remembered her as "always social, always irresponsible, always expansive, always amused and amusing." She became the affectionate "Iza" of his later letters (her name was Louisa, and she was a Cushing, of Boston, who had married Boit in 1864). Henry spoke then of her as "brilliantly friendly" and also as "eternally juvenile." He liked her merry laugh and her lightheartedness: but this was fifteen years after that Roman spring, and Henry himself had advanced in life to the point where a woman who had the air of winking at him no longer disturbed him. The younger Henry liked to be in Mrs Boit's company at a picnic in the Roman countryside, or in a drawing-room, but she was somehow a threat to his security on horseback.

The third lady in Henry's list was Mrs Wister, and with her Henry rode often, sometimes alone and sometimes in the company of her husband. She inspired no "terror," but also she was not "easy." "I went out the other day with Mrs Wister and her husband. They led me rather a dance, but I took four ditches with great serenity and was complimented for my close seat. But the merit was less mine than that of my delightful little horse." There is ample evidence that Mrs Wister and Henry James were often seen together; not sufficiently often, perhaps, to set tongues wagging, for they were both discreet, but more often than one might have expected in a young writer not accustomed to the unescorted company of a married woman and carefully determined to keep a proper distance from all women. Mrs Wister was eight years older than Henry. Her father had been Pierce Butler, the Southern gallant and slave-holder, who had married the proud and fiery daughter of the Kembles, and taken her from the theatre to tame her to domesticity and a life amid slaves on a Georgia plantation. He might as well have sought to tame a tempest. Sarah Butler had grown up separated from her mother, for Mrs Kemble abandoned her husband and the South and was in England during the Civil War. Sarah married Dr Owen Jones Wister of Philadelphia and they lived in Germantown. This winter, reunited with her mother (Pierce Butler was by now dead), they both had their brief salon in Rome before returning to America,

SARAH BUTLER WISTER
From a snapshot

where Mrs Wister led an active life devoted to her family, society and the arts. Henry had been in Rome but three or four days, as we have seen, when he had a rendezvous with her. It was the first of an unforgettable series.

Then there was Alice Bartlett, "that mighty maiden." She posed no romantic problems. Striking, prominent in American society in Rome, she was distinctly the athletic type of woman. "I feel," Henry wrote after a gallop in her company, "very much as if she were a boy—an excellent fellow." The fine thing about her was her spirit—her "pluck, independence, energy." During the spring Henry came every three or four days to the Via della Croce to improve his Italian by reading Tasso with her. Alice Bartlett was as much a friend of Lizzie Boott as of Mrs Sumner, and Henry was to see her often during the next five years in Europe as well as in Boston, and to salute her marriage with a Texan in these words written to Lizzie: "I think her Texan horizon much more natural to her than her Roman one. She was a European only by accident—not by natural sympathy, and she will become an ornament to the young civilization and the energetic society amid which she is to dwell. Yes, she will break in mustangs, and wear a lasso over her shoulder, and be the Diana of the Far West."

Last on his list was Lizzie Boott. She was the most European of his riding-companions and the one he knew best. Henry had met the Bootts in 1865, the year in which Francis brought his nineteen-year-old daughter back to her home-city of Boston from which he had fled when she was eighteen months old. This had been in 1847, after the death of his wife, Elizabeth Lyman, member of an old Boston family; and two years after the death of their infant son. Frank Boott seemed to clutch the baby girl to him in the fear that if they remained in America death might claim her as well. With her nurse, who was to be with the Bootts for the next forty years, they took boat for Genoa. On this same voyage was William Wetmore Story, also bound for Italy, to make his career as a sculptor, after renouncing the law in Boston. In Italy Lizzie was reared by her father as if she were a hothouse flower, and indeed when Henry transposed her into *The*

Portrait of a Lady he bestowed upon her the name of Pansy. She was given the upbringing of a European *jeune fille*. She had a sweet voice and took singing lessons; she learned to paint at an early age. Her father taught her to swim. Unlike her friend Alice James, Lizzie gave her energies, which were modestly creative, free play, and indulged them to the full. In the end she threw herself into her painting with an intensity that far exceeded her talents.

Henry had spoken of her on occasion as "homely," but the photographs and paintings of her show that she possessed a certain chiselled and refined charm, a rather bland beauty, when she was young. She was warmly American in spite of her markedly European manners. She had spent her adolescence in a large ten-room apartment—an entire wing of the Villa Castellani on the hill of Bellosguardo—one of those large Italian rural residences which afforded space and coolness and a superb view of the Arno valley and the domes and spires of Florence. Here she had met the Anglo-Florentines, the Germans and the Americans, drawn to the city of art: the Brownings and Robert Browning's friend, Isa Blagden; the Trollopes; as well as the visiting Americans—including Hawthorne, who had lived in the adjoining Villa Montauto.

Francis Boott, on his side, whiled away the eighteen years of his daughter's growing-up in Italy by a devotion to music. He took lessons in harmony, singing and piano, but felt rightly he had begun his training too late. His first string quartet was performed at Story's palace in Rome in the 1850's; and certain of his songs obtained a vogue in drawing-rooms on both sides of the Atlantic. There was something strange in this little man, with his prosaic and reasonable temperament, fixed in his habits, simple in his tastes, yet deeply involved in the arts. Henry might be bored with him on occasion, but had an inescapable fondness for him and for his vigorous laughter. It was Lizzie however who became a cherished image in the life of the novelist, the "Cara Lisa" of his letters, a link with Italy, an exquisite Italian memory, and the centre of a drama of which he was to be a fascinated as well as a pained spectator. She was one of the few women younger than himself for whom he acknowledged a "great affection." It was perhaps greater than he knew.

"As Lizzie depends upon me," he wrote to his father, "I shall be chiefly her companion." And so they rode together often, joined sometimes by Miss Bartlett.

II

There was a sixth woman. She did not offer to ride with Henry; indeed she does not seem to have been particularly interested in him. This may have contributed to his interest in her. She attracted him by her beauty, her remoteness, her air of quiet intelligence—her mystery.

His allusions to her are brief and fragmentary. Pieced together they suggest that Elena Lowe, daughter of a Bostonian named Francis Lowe, was a woman of exceptional appearance: rather quiet, she seemed to float in an air of melancholy, yet she carried herself with pride and distinction. Henry spoke of her as an "intensely interesting personage." But whether she really was, he could not make up his mind. She reminded him, he said, of the English Judge of whom it was said that "no man was ever as wise as Lord so-and-so looked!" There are only five allusions to her in Henry's letters, and they are not very illuminating. In March 1873 he writes to his father that he calls occasionally "in the dusky half-hour before dinner" on a girl who is "sweet and very clever," named Miss Lowe. "She is very handsome, very lovely, very reserved and very mysterious, not to have many adorers. But I am not yet regularly enlisted as one of them." He adds: "I've seen no one else in society here who has caused a pulse of curiosity in the least to beat."

In April he tells his brother that Henry Adams and his wife have passed through Rome and that he dined with them. Present on this occasion was Miss Lowe, "beautiful and sad." A few weeks later he writes to Mrs Wister that he has been seeing few people in Rome; however he has seen Miss Lowe once or twice, "though I have tried oftener." In August Henry records that Miss Lowe is the subject of wagging tongues. He tells Mrs

Wister that he met the sad beauty at Assisi, "attended by the painter Bellay." He adds that he heard afterwards that "it was a case for a more suggestive word" than *attended*. From which he implied, we presume, that Miss Lowe was rumoured to be the mistress of the French painter.

A year later, on 29 July 1874, he writes to Mrs Wister that he has read of Miss Lowe's marriage at Venice to a "reputable British gentleman," a consul. "Happy man," and Henry adds, "So much for Bellay." Then Henry goes on to wonder whether the bridegroom is really "so ideally happy." True, Miss Lowe was "beautiful, mysterious, melancholy, inscrutable." Was this simply her "way of seeming, or had she unfathomable depths within?"

Henry went on to say to Mrs Wister that he thought Miss Lowe's marrying a British consul "a little of a prosy performance." He qualified this by adding that she was "certainly handsome enough to have a right to be as prosy as she wished." The performance, however, was not as "prosy" as Henry imagined. He had misread the announcement. The paragraph, which appeared in the 9 July 1874 issue of *Galignani's Messenger*, announced the marriage of Elena Lowe, daughter of the late Francis Lowe of Boston, to Mr Gerald Perry, son of Sir William Perry, retired British consul, and of the late Geraldine de Courcy, sister of Lord Kingsale. Miss Lowe seems to have placed herself in good society. In Elena Lowe and her "mysterious" qualities Henry had found an image for the heroine of his first important novel. When he came to create her he gave her a name which seems to echo the original: Christina Light. Again and again in the novel she is portrayed as an enigma and a "riddle." There are references to her "unfathomable" coquetry and to her nature as "large and mysterious." Elena Lowe seems to have haunted Henry, for he was to love Christina as he loved few of his heroines, and to find her sufficiently attractive and mysterious to want to revive her in a second novel. This he did, and Christina, Princess Casamassima, gave her name to a considerable work of his middle period.

A STUDY IN MAUVE

HENRY'S recurrent complaint to his family was that in Rome he seemed fated to enjoy largely female society. There were men whose company he found agreeable, yet they offered him little of the mental nourishment to which he was accustomed. Neither Story nor Terry nor the younger artists could provide the stimulating literary talk which he had had with Lowell in Paris; or with Howells in Cambridge; or indeed with his brother William in his own home. "You feel altogether out of the current of modern civilization," he wrote to his brother in April. "I often hanker for the high culture and high finish of Paris—the theatres and newspapers and booksellers and restaurants and boulevards." And yet Rome had its compensations: there was something that "forever stirs and feeds and fills the mind and makes a sentient being feel that on the whole he can lead as complete a life here as elsewhere." Groping for words to render this more clearly, Henry ended by telling William that he was held by the "unanalysable *loveableness* of Italy. This fills my spirit mightily."

I

In these circumstances he looked to his women-friends for the intellectual companionship he craved. Mrs Boit certainly did not provide this, nor Lizzie Boott; Alice Bartlett and Mrs Sumner were "both superior and very natural women, and Mrs Sumner a very charming one, but they are limited by a kind of characteristic American want of culture." And he added: "Mrs Wister has much more of this—a good deal in fact, and a very literary mind, if not a powerful one." It is not surprising therefore that we find Henry confiding to Jane Norton that he has seen "almost more of her than of anyone; and yet her beautiful hair is the thing most to be praised about her. It's on the whole the handsomest I've ever seen." To William, later, he also wrote that Mrs Wister was "the one I saw most of." From the first however he seems to have been of two minds about her, unless his criticisms of her were designed to make certain that no one should suspect him of being *too* interested in a handsome bluestocking from Philadelphia. Thus he tells his father that she has "fierce energy in a slender frame," rides, walks, entertains, has musical rehearsals, and "is very handsome into the bargain"—but "she isn't easy." He reiterates that she has beautiful hair, but "on the whole I don't at all regret that I'm not Dr Wister." To William he writes that in a certain light, and at certain moments, with her hat on, she bears "a startling likeness to Minny Temple"—but the likeness, he adds, is all in the face. From Henry's mother comes the comment, "Mrs Wister is too conscious of her own charms to be very dangerous I am told—but beware!"

Henry had no need of such advice where handsome women were concerned. He replied to his mother in a manner designed to reassure her. "Mrs Wister I see from time to time; she is a 'superior' woman (but a beautiful bore. Tell it not in Philadelphia—where I don't believe they know it)". Henry's father considered this remark unkind. Henry agreed it was rather "brutal" and retracted it, expressing the hope that he had not been quoted. He added: "She is a fine person—not 'easy,' but perfectly natural."

It is possible to read too much between the lines of such casual remarks, made for the entertainment of Quincy Street. Nevertheless it is quite clear that Henry saw much of Mrs Wister and that she was not a bore, since he was usually adroit in avoiding banal companionship. His use of the word "adored" in describing Mrs Sumner suggests no ambiguity; she was a woman frankly admired. No such feelings were expressed for Mrs Wister. She was charming, clever, lively—but always not "easy." In reality it was Henry who felt uneasy. He saw himself somehow as "involved" with a married woman; and yet if the thought of a love affair crossed his mind it is not likely to have gone beyond that. Sarah Wister seemed "safe"—married, respectable, a mother, older than Henry. This had its pleasant side. It also created a certain vague anxiety. Mrs Wister brought to the surface unknowingly that conflict which Henry was always to experience and never quite resolve: his struggle between his need to be passive with women and to be boundlessly active as an artist. The artist in him told him to live dangerously, to invite passion, to love. The reasonable self, the well-conditioned conscience, echoed his mother's "beware."

II

Henry James kept a note-book while he was in Rome. All that survives of it are certain pages which he edited and published in the form of an article entitled "From a Roman Note-book." These appeared in the *Galaxy* and were reprinted in *Transatlantic Sketches*. In describing some of his Roman excursions he listed his companions by various initials, including the impersonal "X." But when he revised the book for Tauchnitz, as *Foreign Parts* in 1883, he substituted certain identifying letters. A.M. is Aunt Mary Tweedy; L.B. is Lizzie Boott; Mr E. is Emerson, and X becomes W., Mrs W. or S.W.[1] At the time Henry wrote to Mrs Wister saying that she would "recognize an allusion or so" in his Roman pieces. "Enjoy them and forgive them according to need. You will see—I had to make up for small riding by big writing."

This public record of his Roman adventures shows how frequently and in what circumstances Mrs Wister was his companion:

December 30, [1872]. I went yesterday with Mrs W. to the Colonna Gardens—an adventure which would have reconverted me to Rome if the thing were not already done . . . It's a very pleasant thing . . . to stroll and talk there in the afternoon sunshine.

---

[1] Many years later, revising the article again, for inclusion in *Italian Hours*, James forgot he had already substituted initials in *Foreign Parts* and introduced certain new ones. Most of the later initials tally with the earlier ones; the few differences may be attributed to lapses of memory. The Tauchnitz volume (the text of which I have used here) appeared a decade after his stay in Rome, when Henry was forty; his revisions of 1909 were made when he was sixty-six.

January 26th, [1873] With Mrs W. to the Villa Medici . . . What mornings and afternoons one might spend there, brush in hand, unpreoccupied, untormented, pensioned, satisfied, resolving the picturesque into pictures.

January 30th.—A drive the other day with Mrs W. to the Villa Madama, on the side of Monte Mario; a place like a page out of Browning, wonderful in its haunting melancholy.

February 12th.—Yesterday with Mrs W. to the Villa Albani. Over-formal and (as my companion says) too much like a tea-garden; but with beautiful stairs and splendid geometrical lines of immense box-hedge . . . The Alban mountains of an intenser broken purple than I have ever seen them . . . Mrs W. suggested again the Roman villas as a "subject." Excellent, if one could find plenty of facts, à la Stendhal. A lot of vague picturesque talk would not at all pay.

Middle of March.—A ride with Mrs W. out of the Porta Pia to the meadows beyond the Ponte Nomentana—close to the site of Phaon's villa where Nero, in hiding, had himself stabbed. It was deeply delightful—more so than *now* one can really know or say. For these are predestined memories and the stuff that regrets are made of; the mild divine efflorescence of spring, the wonderful landscape, the talk suspended for another gallop.

We wonder how often talk was suspended for another gallop, and then resumed; the very word "suspended" is an intimation of subjects begun, dropped, begun again in a continuum of conversation. On this occasion:

Returning, we dismounted at the gate of the Villa Medici and walked through the twilight of the vaguely perfumed, bird-haunted alleys to H[ébert]'s studio, hidden in the wood like a cottage in a fairy tale. I spent there a charming half-hour in the fading light, looking at the pictures while my companion discoursed of her errand.

The visits to the Villa Medici were more frequent than the note-book records. Mrs Wister had many friends there including the young artist-director, Ernest Hébert, whose studio they had visited. They took occasional walks in the gardens. One day Henry spied Edmond About and looked at him with soft memories of his youthful reading of About's romantic-pathetic tale of *Tolla*. Henry dined at the Storys' with the Wisters and Hébert, "the Marchese Somebody, a mellifluous Italian master of ceremonies to the King," and Hattie Hosmer. Miss Story sings for them afterwards in her strange but pleasant tremolo. "After the dinner—at 11 o'clock, while you were all virtuously snoozing," he writes his sister, "I repaired with Mrs Wister to the Villa Medici. Here, in a great saloon, hung all round with antique Gobelins—a most delicious apartment—were congregated the twenty students of the Academy, a knot of effete young *attachés*, and three or four formidably fine French ladies. A great deal of solemnity. A little music, and no introductions." They leave at one a.m. "through a tremendous tapestried library and wondrous portico, walking out on the gardens of the Villa, flooded with magical moonlight."

Mrs Wister clearly challenged Henry. She asked questions and he had to give answers; she invited him to join her in appreciating art, experience, history; to have ideas on a hundred subjects while being gallant, attentive, devoted, in a word "involved" in her fancies and moods. The problem for Henry, however, was how to be involved—and yet remain, in the strictest sense, "uninvolved;" how to admire yet not be too admiring. This may explain why praise of Mrs Wister in his letters is usually cancelled out by misgiving. The reticences expressed to Quincy Street are genuine; and in a sense they are invitations to his mother to back him up. But the Roman note-book itself, if we read between its purple-splashed lines, suggests that the friendship had deepening roots and underlying intensities, heightened by the sense of the place and the "divine efflorescence" of the spring. When the moment of parting came toward the end of March, and Dr and Mrs Wister and their son Owen (the future novelist) turned their faces toward Philadelphia, Henry recorded the final ride in a letter to his father. "I took her last ride with her away and away under the shadow of the aqueducts. She is most broken-hearted to exchange Rome for Germantown." Henry may not have been as broken-hearted, yet a distinctly romantic moment in his life had come to an end.

III

Some months later, when he had left Italy and was living in an inn near the Taunus Mountains, at Bad Homburg, he wrote a story which embodied his experiences as a young unmarried man enjoying the friendship of a married woman. Perhaps it was his memory of the purple Campagna, the scarlets and lavenders and violets of Rome, the perpetual lavender satins and purple velvets worn by Mrs Kemble, Sally Wister's mother, or even the name Wister itself, with its evocation of lilac wistaria—at any rate he named the story "Madame de Mauves." The tale embodies the earlier theme of old and new, corruption and innocence, but in more subtle and less morbid form. At the same time it is the first of a long series of stories written by James about idealistic Americans observing, in their rich innocence, complex international marriages.

Euphemia Cleve, a convent-bred American girl, has nourished from her early years those love-romances which stirred the blood of Emma Bovary. The difference between Euphemia and Emma is that Emma acts upon her dreams of an unattainable love by taking a series of lovers. Euphemia is doomed in quite another way: she clings to her illusions and to a dream of the past—of a chivalry unrelated to life and transformed into self-righteous suffering. She has married the young, dissipated Baron de Mauves and when Longmore, the American hero, discovers her she is already an unhappy, rejected woman, deeply hurt by her husband's infidelities and aggressively determined to endure them. Longmore thinks he loves her. They walk along garden paths and shady woods at St Germain-en-Laye (like those of the Villa Medici). For a moment Longmore dreams of taking Euphemia away. What she needs, he tells her, is a husband "of your own faith and race and spiritual substance." Euphemia is unmoved. "I have nothing on earth but a conscience, nothing but a dogged, clinging, inexpugnable conscience." The conscience will keep her from "doing anything very base," she says; it will also "effectually prevent me from doing anything very fine." We might add that it prevents her from doing anything.

Longmore wavers. He is distinctly in conflict. "To renounce—to renounce again—to renounce forever—was this all that youth and longing and resolve were meant for?" And again: "Was a man to sit and deliberately condemn his future to be the blank memory of a regret, rather than the long reverberation of a joy?" Longmore is unable to translate these thoughts into action; he does not put his arms round Euphemia, as a young hero might, and bid her to flee from her wicked husband. To be sure Euphemia's defences are rather formidable; nevertheless they are not put to the test. In a dream which James contrives for Longmore, he is separated from Madame de Mauves by a stream in the forest. He thinks of plunging into it to cross over to her; but he does not act. It is someone else who turns up in a rowboat and conveys him to the other side. When he gets there, Madame de Mauves is by now on the opposite bank—thus eternally unreachable—and the oarsman turns out to have the visage of the Baron.

For the Baron de Mauves, throughout the story, has been more than an indulgent husband. He has urged Longmore to make love to his wife; he sees no reason why she should not accept his own relaxed view of the marriage-tie; it would remove her from her high moral throne and her ascendancy over him. Of this Euphemia is aware. Her conscience stands firm. In the end her fidelity becomes her instrument of revenge. The Baron is overwhelmed by so much virtue and high-mindedness. When his wife closes her door to him, he cannot tolerate the frustration, and Henry James asks his readers to believe that in his despair he blows out his brains. Longmore, who is back in America, is moved at first to rush to her; but he has a second thought. Something holds him back. In the midst "of all the ardent tenderness of his memory of Madame de Mauves, he has become conscious of a singular feeling,—a feeling for which awe would be hardly too strong a name." These are the last words of the tale.

IV

The two preceding tales—those of the recovered statue and the restored topaz—had treated evil and corruption as inexorable historical forces, in an atmosphere bordering on the supernatural and the morbid. In "Madame de Mauves" evil is embodied in the Baron de Mauves, the representative of "Europe," but now as part of everyday life. And while Longmore faces corruption as a Puritan, he does not see it as a force emanating from the devil himself. Evil is quite simply a part of life; a part of the bad that must be taken with the good. Experience hurts; it does not necessarily kill. The tension of "Madame de Mauves" is less the result of extremes and of shock than of human ambiguities. At the end of the story one feels that the Baron, whatever his moral laxities, had a decidedly rigid wife. On the other hand Longmore invokes our attention in much the same way: he too is "difficult." For what James seems to have converted into this tale, is not the person of Sarah Wister, who bore little resemblance to Euphemia Cleve, but his relationship with her in Rome: the young lover is of two minds; yet he is never convinced that he should make love to Madame de Mauves. He merely seems to feel that in this situation he perhaps should try. "Women were indeed a measureless mystery," Longmore ponders, even as his author had pondered, in looking upon Elena Lowe, or in praising and cancelling out his praise of Mrs Wister. In "Madame de Mauves" Henry expressed his ambivalent attitude toward the opposite sex: Longmore wonders at one point whether "it was better to cultivate an art than to cultivate a passion." For Henry the answer was clear. He ended not only by cultivating an art, but by channelling his passion into it.

Sarah Wister saved Henry James's letters: they are propriety itself. She remains in them to the end "Dear Mrs Wister." The letters are warm and gossipy, charged with friendship and memory. "Never, never have I forgotten," he wrote to her, "how some of the most ineffaceable impressions of my life were gathered . . . fifteen years ago in your society." He was to write in much the same way to Alice Mason after the turn of the century: "May *your* way [to Rome] be blessed to you, again, this year—the golden air will bring back something at least of the gilt of the old feeling. I can't think of them (air, feeling, everything) without pangs, yearnings, memories, despairs, almost tears."

We seem to catch the image of Mrs Wister in a tale written almost twenty years after their springtime in Rome, an elegant trifle called "The Solution," in James's high comic manner, dealing with a young man whose teasing friends tell him he has compromised a young lady. When the young man actually proposes to her, the friends realize they have carried a joke too far and must "disengage" him. To this end the narrator seeks the aid of the charming Mrs Rushbrook. She accomplishes her task, and marries the young man herself. In the description of Mrs Rushbrook James seems to be setting down a sketch of Mrs Wister as he had known her:

> She was extravagant, careless, even slightly capricious. If the "Bohemian" had been invented in those days she might possibly have been one—a very small, fresh, dainty one . . . She had a lovely head, and her chestnut hair was of a shade I have never seen since . . . She was natural and clever and kind, and though she was five years older than I she always struck me as an embodiment of youth—of the golden morning of life. We made such happy discoveries together when I first knew her: we liked the same things, we disliked the same people, we had the same favourite statues in the Vatican, the same secret preferences in regard to views on the Campagna. We loved Italy in the same way and in the same degree . . . She painted, she studied Italian, she collected and noted the songs of the people, and she had the wit to pick up certain *bibelots* and curiosities—lucky woman—before other people had thought of them.

For Henry, Rome, Mrs Wister, the rides in the Campagna—the whole mauve-tinted experience—had been indeed "the golden morning of life."

THE MONOCLE

ONE day toward the end of February 1873 Henry James entered the Caffè Spillmann on the Via Condotti, one of his Roman haunts, and observed an English family at lunch—a mother, a father, and a little girl. The father had characteristic Victorian side-whiskers, a large sensitive mouth, a broad lined brow. It was a face serious and captivating. He recognized it at once. Here was the idol of his youth. A decade earlier he had walked through the New Hampshire woods with his young cousins declaiming the verses of Matthew Arnold. Among the earliest of Henry's published reviews had been his notice of *Essays in Criticism*, read with intense emotion in the ink-besmirched proof supplied by J. T. Fields. Some of that emotion can be recovered in the anonymous review when we read it today. In Matthew Arnold the young Henry James had found an intellectual kinsman, an Englishman with a continentalized intelligence like his own, and an individual of "natural sensibilities." "Hundreds of other critics have stronger heads," he had written, "few, in England at least, have more delicate perceptions."

What Henry could not have known was that Matthew Arnold had discovered the unsigned review in 1865 and had written to his sister: "The *North American Review* for July had an article on me which I like as well as anything I have seen." He had proceeded to generalize on the "intellectual liveliness and ardour" he had found among Americans in Europe. One wonders what he would have thought had he known, on his side, that his transatlantic reviewer at that time had been a young man of twenty-two who had just begun his literary career.

On the evening after Henry's glimpse of Arnold at Spillmann's, he found himself face to face with the author of *Essays in Criticism* in one of Story's tapestried rooms. There was no doubt about it: Arnold had a powerful face, but Henry, looking into it, found that it was not "delicately beautiful," as he might have hoped of an individual of "delicate perceptions." Arnold's manner, moreover, was rather easy, mundane, even at moments "somewhat gushing." What seems to have set Henry off particularly in this casual encounter was the "little glass he screwed into one eye."

The author of the Obermann verses with a monocle! Henry had never pictured this. He was prepared to avow to Mrs Wister however that it was "simply *my* want of imagination." Nevertheless he did have to reconcile the empathic verses, in which Arnold eulogized Étienne Pivert de Senancour, Obermann's creator, with this somewhat dapper worldly figure:

> Ah! Two desires toss about
> The poet's feverish blood.
> One drives him to the world without,
> And one to solitude.

Decidedly this chattering Englishman with a monocle was not the Arnold of solitude: this was a rather superficial individual exchanging lightweight talk with the lightweight Story. Arnold was now fifty-one; Henry was thirty—but the Henry who waited that evening for precious words to fall from the lips of Matthew Arnold, his intellectual mentor of a decade earlier, was the Henry of twenty-two, the brooding Henry of the Civil War. And so he wrote that he had "first and last a little small talk with him." The note was almost rueful. "He did nothing to make it *big*, as my youthful dreams would have promised me. He's a good fellow, I should say, but he is decidedly a disappointment, in a superficial sense." To William he wrote that Arnold "said nothing momentous"—as if there were anything momentous to say during a casual social evening at the Barberini. To Norton he wrote: "He is not as handsome as his photographs—or as his poetry. But no one looks handsome in Rome—beside the Romans."

They met again shortly afterwards, at a dinner in the Villa Mattei, home of Baron Richard von Hoffmann and his American wife, Lydia Gray Ward. The villa stood on a hill above the wall of Servius; the place had an ilex-walk lined with ancient sculptures, and the Baron, like the Conte Valerio, was constantly digging up fragments of ancient statues in the soil of his garden. The Hoffmanns served a "vast and ponderous" repast, "all flowers and footmen and dreariness." The Baron seemed ill-fitted to preside over his grandiose establishment. The Baroness chatted at Arnold throughout the dinner. Matthew sat, amid this Romano-American extravagance, his glass screwed into his eye. Once more the talk could only be trivial.

In Rome in 1873 Arnold had no way of knowing how much he and the young American had in common: their admiration for George Sand and for Sainte-Beuve, their strong ties with the Gallic mind. Matthew Arnold was as vocal in denouncing the English Philistine as Henry was in condemning American "vulgarity." Later, when Henry was famous, and Arnold had lectured in America, Henry wrote an article about him for the *English Illustrated Magazine*, defending him alike for his literary views and his entry into theological controversy. What he cherished was Arnold's cosmopolitanism. "I like him—love him rather—as I do my old portfolio, my old shoe-horn," Henry wrote to T. S. Perry, "with an affection that is proof against anything he may say or do today, and proof also against taking him too seriously." Proof too, doubtless, against Matthew Arnold's little wall of glass.

Long after, Henry recorded for posterity his memory of the Roman meeting. It is in his book on Story. He had so admired Matthew Arnold, he wrote, that "nothing could have seemed in advance less doubtful than that to encounter him face to face, and under an influence so noble, would have made one fairly stagger with a sense of privilege." But the sense of privilege had to be postponed. In the Barberini, he wrote, it was "as if, for all the world, we were *equally* great and happy, or still more, perhaps, equally nothing and nobody; we were related only to the enclosing fact of Rome, before which every one, it was easy to feel, bore himself with the same good manners." The "enclosing fact of Rome" concealed in it the memory of a monocle.

A ROMAN SPRING

SPRING came and Henry felt as if the picturesqueness of the Eternal City had increased tenfold. "The days follow each other in gentle variety, each one leaving me a little more *Roman* than before." He abandoned himself wholly to the enjoyment of the new season; he rambled in the Borghese gardens, admired the white roses tumbling over the walls, plucked violets from the roots of high-stemmed pines, and rode with Mrs Sumner and Miss Bartlett who had three horses and placed one at his disposal. The Corso was emptying itself; the Pincio seemed deserted; he had the galleries to himself. One day he escorted Emerson—homeward bound from his Mediterranean journeyings—to see the Vatican sculptures, much as he had escorted him a few months earlier through the Louvre. He found him "as lovely as ever, serene and urbane and rejuvenated by his adventures." In early April the Henry Adamses turned up. Henry dined twice with them, once in the company of Miss Lowe and once at Mrs Sumner's. He had known the historian during his Cambridge months. He found him "improved," and Mrs Adams—the former Marian (Clover) Hooper, whose grace of mind he had once admired—seemed to have had her "wit clipped a little"—but, he added, "I suppose [she] has expanded in the affections."

The warm weather made his hotel-room stuffy, and Henry moved into a little fourth-floor apartment in the Corso—No. 101—where he had a *loggia* with a view of rooftops and two comfortable rooms, vividly upholstered in cobalt and yellow, with magenta *portières*. His landlord sold Catholic images in a shop in the basement and lived with a large family in a curtained alcove down the hall from his tenant. Henry was closely neighboured and surrounded by good-natured Italian volubility. The little Italian maidservant was only too eager to please ("She would even satisfy mother," Henry wrote) and rushed to nail his card to the door downstairs—upside down.

In the waning sociabilities Henry still dined with the Tweedys, paid calls on the ladies in the Via della Croce, was punctually ceremonious at the two palaces. One evening, before the Wisters' departure, he found William Wetmore Story in their drawing-room, seated with a large manuscript, a five-act play on the life of Nero, which he was about to read to Fanny Kemble. He got through three of the acts, and years later Henry remembered that "though my ears . . . were all for Story, my eyes were for our distinguished companion in whom the whole matter was mirrored, commented, silently represented." At the time he saw this performance as a display of Storyesque vanity and "restless ambition." Henry was "unavoidably" absent when the remaining two acts were read on a later evening.

By early April the Wisters were in London, *en route* to America; the Bootts were in the Villa Castellani in Florence, before sailing for a summer in Massachusetts, and Henry's social life was much less of a drain on his time. He had hoped to settle down now to less desultory writing; however he complained that the air was heavy and he experienced a kind of torpor, as if he were living in some lotus-land. "Lingering on here in these lovely languid days of deepening spring," he wrote to Mrs Wister, "I felt as if I were standing on some enchanted shore, sacred to idleness and irresponsibility of all kinds." But not too irresponsible: for he wrote to Quincy Street: "The other day, I became THIRTY—solemn fact! —which I have been taking to heart."

I

Henry was thirty, and he could show, thus far, rather modest beginnings for one who had such grandiose dreams. He had been writing for ten years and he had not yet published a book: he had published only scattered tales, reviews, sketches, and travel-impressions. His months in Rome however had shown him that he stood firmly planted in his career. There is a kind of serene confidence in his letters when he speaks of what he is doing and what he will do. He is a little unhappy that he has not written more; but when the time comes he knows that he will be able to write at will. "Mine is a slow progression, but a progression I believe it is." Rather are there indications that his search is elsewhere: what he is really "taking to heart" is the question of what *kind* of artist he is to be, and its corollary, *how* he is to arrange his artist's life. The short things for the magazines come to him with tolerable ease; yet he feels that he is writing too slowly, because of his "still unformed and childish habits of application." For the rest, if Quincy Street is still tugging at the silver cord, he is learning how to resist the pull. Most important, he has been discovering the meaning of freedom: he is learning belatedly to feel comfortable in the world. Moreover he is finding out that the world appreciates him. His father may offer unprofessional advice; his mother may talk in purely material terms, as she counts his literary dollars; his brother may carp at his prose, but only the other day Norton had written from London that Ruskin was delighted with Henry's comments on Tintoretto in the *Nation*. "You may be pleased from your heart," wrote Norton, "to have given not merely pleasure, but stimulus, to a man of genius very solitary and with very few friends who care for what he cares for." Ruskin had told Norton he wished Henry James Jr had been appointed Slade Professor of Fine Arts at Cambridge rather than Sidney Colvin. "Nothing could have given me more substantial pleasure than your note about Ruskin," Henry replied, "the invidious comparison as to Mr Colvin included." It was clear to him what his resources were and how he would come to use them.

He has misgivings of his own as to the value of art-criticism—indeed of all criticism. He tells Grace Norton that he seriously believes that a moratorium on reviewing for half a century would represent a great stride for civilization. He speaks also at this time of writing *A History of Prose Fiction Since Cervantes*. But what he really wants to do is to write prose fiction, and not its history. "To produce some little exemplary works of art is my narrow and lowly dream," he tells Miss Norton. "They are to have less 'brain' than *Middlemarch*; but (I boldly proclaim it) they are to have more *form*."

The sense of a personal schedule which he will follow,

regardless of the schedules of Quincy Street, is strong in his letters. Both his father and William have easy advice for the son and brother: he thanks them—and follows his own counsel. His father had sounded out a Boston publisher and offered to pay for the printing of a volume of Henry's tales; Henry replied that he was not ready for this. He had little use for most of his published work. "There is the impossibility of the things being printed as they stand, uncorrected. They are full of thin spots in the writing which I should deplore to have stereotyped, besides absolute errors to which I was always very subject." He is prepared to wait until he has written some new stories. His answer shows, moreover, that at last he has his vision of a large theme. "What I desire is this," he tells his mother, "to make a volume, a short time hence, of tales on the theme of American adventurers in Europe, leading off with the 'Passionate Pilgrim.' I have three or four more to write." This was indeed to be his first book. In the same way, Henry indicates to William what his second book will be. William had written expressing appreciation of Henry's articles on French writers and urged him to prepare articles on others, and make a book of them. "I may come to it, some day, but there are various things I want to do first. Just at present I shall write a few more notes of travel: for two reasons: 1° that a few more joined with those already published and written will make a decent little volume; and 2° that now or never (I think) is my time. The *keen* love and observation of the picturesque is ebbing away from me as I grow older, and I doubt whether, a year or two hence, I shall have it in me to describe houses and mountains, or even cathedrals and pictures."

These replies demonstrate the extent to which Henry James had taken the measure of himself, his capacities, his opportunities. When his début as a writer of books was made it would be on the best footing possible. He was never one to rush into print heedlessly. He might be thirty, and his apprenticeship might be long, but genius always has its own time-table. Henry would not be led astray by the well-meaning, if sometimes over-urgent, counsels of Quincy Street.

II

The question of money was quite another matter—a rather ticklish matter—for Henry, perhaps because his father on the whole abandoned finances to his mother, and left it to her to discuss them in detail with her son. She showed, in her letters, certain anxieties. The accounts of Quincy Street, to be sure, had to be closely watched; there was a heavy drain on them. William and Alice lived at home; the younger sons had poorly-paid jobs in the West and often required help; and Henry drew regularly on his letter of credit. It was no less true, however, that Henry was now publishing more and being adequately paid, according to the standards of the time. If, on the one hand, Quincy Street vigorously protected the interests of its writing son, it exercised on the other a certain kind of pressure. This arose from Henry's arrangements to have the magazines pay his father rather than himself. Practical as this measure was in avoiding transmission of money to and fro, across the Atlantic, its consequences were far from healthy. Quincy Street became Henry's personal cashier, and Henry was held accountable to his family for his expenditure—and, as it seemed, for his life—abroad.

There was an understandable maternal interest in the welfare of her son when Mary James wrote as she did after he had been in Rome three weeks: "What are you living on, dear Harry? It seems to me you are living as the lilies, and feed like the sparrows. But I know too that you toil and spin and must conclude that you receive in some mysterious way the fruits of your labour. We have been all along under the impression that your publishers were to send your money to us, and as nothing has come, and nothing has been drawn by the Bankers since Nov. 1st, it is quite a mystery to me."

Henry reassures her. He isn't starving. He had drawn on his letter of credit before leaving Paris. There were inevitable delays in publication and payment by magazines. Life in Rome was moderately expensive: at the hotel he had paid seventy Italian francs ($14) a week for service, breakfast, beefsteak, potatoes, fires and light. His standard was luxurious, perhaps, yet he could not get the same for the price at a poor Boston boarding house. His only "serious expense" had been his riding. He pays $50 a month for a horse, or a little more than $2 for a single long ride. "But this," he explains, "is so substantial a pleasure and profit that I can manage it." It is true, he says, that he is not writing much. This is because it is still a "slow and laborious" process. He is not reading or studying either; he has simply surrendered himself to "seeing 'life' here insofar as it offers itself." He believes that "with practice I shall learn to write more briskly and naturally."

His mother's next letter announces that $250 had been received in Quincy Street for five pieces in the *Nation*, but two articles had been published since, and "I presume they send directly to you."

"We must keep things regular," Henry said early in May in a letter to his parents when he could look back to a certain amount of published work, and knew what money was due. And he set down in two columns the balance sheet of his Roman sojourn:

Drawn by me since Dec. 18th		Paid and to be paid father on my account.	
Paris	£30	From *Nation*	$250
Rome	20	,, *Nation*	75
,,	20	,, *Atlantic*	60
,,	40	,, *Galaxy*	30
,,	20	,, *N.A.R.*	75 (?)
	130	,, *Galaxy* (for story I think I asked $150)	150
= $650 *in gold* (I suppose not more than) $575 at most in paper.		,, *Atlantic* (for story forthcoming)	100 *at least*
$575			$640

He hoped, he said, to reach the stage where payments from the magazines would come in "like revenue." Then as if to make certain, he checks his figures and discovers that his total should have been $740. Maternal pressure, perhaps, was not conducive to good arithmetic. At any rate the final balance was sufficiently reassuring. Henry may not have written as much as he had hoped in Rome, but he had done enough work to clear his expenses. He had at last paid his way by his pen—and all according to his own plan.

III

The time had come to leave. June was approaching. The heat was not yet intense; nevertheless there was a "peculiar quality" in the air. Henry felt he needed something more bracing. In the "loving mood of one's last days in Rome" he went to St John Lateran forty-eight hours before setting forth on his travels. A sirocco was blowing. He experienced a great lassitude. Rome for the moment had become the mouth of a fiery furnace. Gone was the lovely winter aspect of the region: where there had been soft yellow sun and purple shadows there was now green and blue everywhere. The Campagna rolled away in great grassy billows; they seemed to break high above the aqueducts. The Alban hills had lost their azure; they were almost monotonously green. Henry paced the twelfth-century cloister; the shrubs were blooming, the old well was surrounded by dazzling light. He contemplated the façade with its robed and mitred apostles, bleached and rain-washed by the ages, rising in the air like strange snow-figures in the hot wind. He had the museum of the Lateran to himself. He crossed the square to the Scala Santa—the marble steps brought to Rome from the praeterium in Jerusalem—and studied them through a couple of gilded lattices. Impious thoughts crossed his mind: the steps seemed oriental or Mohammedan, and on them, where they were to be ascended only on bended knee, his imagination seemed to place sultanas in silver veils, in silken trousers, sitting cross-legged on crimson carpets.

Henry said his farewells at the rival palaces. He dined with the Terrys *en famille* and his last evening in Rome he spent with Story, who, in his large cool Barberini rooms, usually remained until July. They parted almost affectionately, although he wrote home "I don't care an inordinate number of straws [for him]. Story is too much occupied with himself." As he packed his bags, he seemed to experience a reluctance not unlike that which he had felt half a year before when he was on the point of quitting

Paris. "One would like, after five months in Rome, to be able to make some general statement of one's experience, one's gains," he wrote in the final paragraph of that portion of his Roman note-book which he published. "It is not easy. One has the sense of a kind of passion for the place, and of a large number of gathered impressions." Many of these, he said, were "intense, momentous," but they had come in such profusion that he did not have the time to sort them out. "They store themselves noiselessly away, I suppose, in the dim but safe places of memory, and we live in an insistent faith that they will emerge into vivid relief if life or art should demand them. As for the *passion*, we needn't trouble ourselves about that. Sooner or later it will be sure to bring us back!"

Everything that had happened that winter now took on for Henry "the most iridescent hues." Rome had given him more impressions and more life—the kind of life he needed—than he might have gathered elsewhere in years. He was ready now to write more tales, ready to begin a novel. Years later he was to wonder whether Rome hadn't been "a rare state of the imagination," a Rome of words made by himself, "which was no Rome of reality." Enchanting things could doubtless also happen by the Thames, the Seine, the Hudson—even the Charles—but somehow he did not "thrill at their touch." Only the Roman touch had the ultimate fineness. "No one who has ever loved Rome as Rome could be loved in youth wants to stop loving her," he wrote—almost fifty years later.

Book Four

The Choice 1873–1875

★

WILLIAM

ANGEL AND BROTHER

THE FORK IN THE PATH

THE PALPABLE PRESENT

RODERICK HUDSON

A NEW YORK WINTER

BENVOLIO

WILLIAM

IN Cambridge William James was settling into his career, slowly, and with great difficulty. He was often ill and despondent. And he still lived at home. He had had his period abroad, earlier, before taking his medical degree. Unlike his younger brother, he had found little in Europe to please him save German psychology and German *Gemütlichkeit*. On his return to Cambridge he had relapsed into its quiet life, with a sense of dreary inertia. If there was a pronounced difference in temperament between the two gifted brothers, it stemmed, in part at least, from the marked difference in their relation to the family group. William, first upon the scene, had learned to take the world in his own large stride: he was quick, active, impulsive, nimble of mind, warming to experience. His brother, who had to include William among his elders, had learned in childhood to assert himself from behind a mask of deceptive serenity. Submerged and silent, Henry could find his freedom from family pressures and rivalries only by devious means; and there was always, later, escape to his writing-desk. William was much more vulnerable. He possessed no defensive weapons, save the brilliant counter-attack of wit. Between the son who was active and rebellious, and the son who was peaceful and submissive, Mary James did not remain neutral. She showed a decided preference for the quiet one—he caused her so much less trouble. She also, unfortunately, showed a certain cold disapproval—crushing in its effect—toward her firstborn.

The record of William's early years is a series of sallies into achievement—and a series of retreats from each sally. The more daring he was, the more crushing seemed each subsequent "defeat." Every positive accomplishment gave him a feeling of increasing powerlessness. Success could not alter the sense of inadequacy engendered by maternal coldness and a paternal softness that seemed almost indifference. William himself was—perhaps on this account—to describe brilliantly how the human personality can be split by such conflicting emotions into the "me" and the "not-me." And on one occasion he was to write that "with no attempt there can be no failure; with no failure, no humiliation." This expresses perfectly his personal problem. The trouble was that he could not resist making attempts, though to do so meant having his wings clipped.

His refuge, when pressures became too great, lay in symptoms—strange backaches, headaches, eye-trouble, loss of appetite. These increased his melancholy. He found occasional relief from submerged anger over his lot in a lively verbal play and baiting of his fellow-members in the family. This he accomplished adroitly, so that his teasing invariably provoked good-humour and laughter, but it contained within it certain animosities and deeper barbs. The family, for instance, might call Henry "angel"—as Mary James invariably did. William scoffed back—"angel, hero, martyr." It was he, however, who felt himself the martyr.

The differences between the ultimate work of Henry and William James reflect the personalities thus formed. Behind the intensities and passions of his imaginative life, Henry could be patient, persistent, calculating, secretive. He had in him a touch of Mary James's fixedness of purpose in dealing with practical matters, as well as his father's poetry. William's nature remained openly assertive. For all his years of morbid introspection, he was capable of reaching always the warm sunlight of human intercourse. William was to find himself in teaching and in daily communication with young minds, in his relations with his fellow philosophers and psychologists in many countries. Henry was always to remain rather solitary and subterranean, in spite of an outwardly strenuous social life. He was a recluse of the writing-desk and he harboured and built up his creative resources; the drive to power from his inner fortress was, from the first, compelling. William prodigally expended his in immediate action and wide friendship. He married and had children. Henry remained celibate. William's style was direct and easy, bubbling spontaneously into lucidity. Henry's had in it more art, much greater literary power—and also more indirection. William was all idea and intellect warmed by feeling; Henry was all feeling—intellectualized.

Thus each achieved his originality and his genius. Henry forged an inimitable style and created an *imperium* of letters; William became one of the rare philosophers of this world who could meditate on the conduct of life in the words of the human spirit. Each in his way ultimately broke the silver cords of Quincy Street. The process nevertheless was long. And it was hard.

I

While Henry was in Rome tasting for the first time the happiness of self-possession and freedom, William remained in Quincy Street exposed to an imprisoning emotional climate. He had stayed beyond his youth in an obsolete environment. He enjoyed his father's talk up to a point; his mother was attentive and solicitous, but in a rather uncomfortable way. She tended to be impatient with William's self-absorption. The family surroundings only renewed the conditions which had from far back troubled him. Mary James reported to Henry that his brother complained too much. He had a "morbid sympathy" with physical ailments. He was hypochondriacal; he worried and lost his temper; he had to express every fluctuation of feeling. For thirteen years—from his twenty-third year to his thirty-sixth, when he finally left home—the life of William James was marked by recurrent lapses in health and spirit. He was like a mountain-climber who triumphantly scales a peak, only to be terrified by the height he has dared to ascend. He had tried first to be a painter, and had revealed a striking talent. He thereupon abruptly dropped his brushes and turned to scientific study at Harvard. Young and adventurous, he had gone with Agassiz to the Amazon. He returned in gloom and despair. His sojourn in Europe, the months of his studentship in Germany, seemed reasonably cheerful and profitable; he came back to further depression. He then threw himself into medical study and received his doctor's degree at the time of Henry's "passionate pilgrimage" in 1869. This culmination of his studies ministered in no way to self-esteem. He seems to have had no thought of setting up in practice. It was at this time that William "touched bottom." He wondered whether he would ever bring himself into any harmonious relation "with the total process" of the universe. What he needed was something less cosmic. He had to learn to achieve a harmonious relationship with himself.

There seems to have been a profound involvement with his father as well as his mother: and his later preoccupation with the emotions and memories of amputated persons (including those of his father) may have been prompted not only by an intellectual interest in this psychological problem, but by his own sense that during these years he had been emotionally crippled, as his father had been physically. Such a speculation arises from the record he set down in *The Varieties of Religious Experience* of his "hallucination," which seemed almost a repetition of the "vastation" recorded by the elder Henry James in one of his books. The son not only duplicated the father's experience, but felt a need to duplicate the manner of making it known to the world, that is of putting it into a book. The father had, in a moment of well-being, experienced a presence, an ugly horrible shape, in the same room as himself, and with this had come an intense anxiety and mental disequilibrium that lasted for weeks. William's account also included a horrible shape; it was summoned however from an actual memory, and was therefore not hallucinatory. What he remembered was the image of an idiot youth seen in asylum during his medical studies.

> I went one evening into a dressing-room in the twilight to procure some article that was there; when suddenly there fell upon me without any warning, just as if it came out of darkness, a horrible fear of my own existence. Simultaneously there arose in my mind the image of an epileptic patient whom I had seen in the asylum, a black-haired youth with greenish skin, entirely idiotic, who used to sit all day on one of the benches, or rather shelves against the wall, with his knees drawn up against his chin, and the coarse grey undershirt, which was his only garment, drawn over them, inclosing his entire figure . . . The image and my fear entered into a species of combination with each other. *That shape am I*, I felt, potentially. Noth-

ing that I possess can defend me against that fate, if the hour for it should strike for me as it struck for him.

And William, recalling this late in life, went on to describe how the anxiety endured; how every morning he awoke with a "horrible dread at the pit of my stomach, and with a sense of the insecurity of life that I never knew before, and that I have never felt since."

An anxiety as prolonged and recurrent and as overpowering could stem only from a personal predicament with which he could contend less easily than with the difficulties of the outer world. The outer world, indeed, had presented William with no real difficulties: he had always encountered it with decisive power. It was the inner self that was plagued by phantoms. Possessing a philosophical cast of mind, he translated his anxieties into metaphysical and rationalistic terms: however his preoccupation with freedom of the will during that early period seemed to stem, in part at least, from his own lack of inner freedom. His father, at the time of his vastation, had been able to find solace and security in the writings of Swedenborg. William, living in the age of Darwin, Huxley, Spencer, could not seek answers from visionaries. What he looked for, in reality, was a cure for his soul-sickness (and his bodily ailments) for which his fellow medical doctors—as he well knew—had no remedy. William James "required a philosophy to save him," his biographer tells us, but what he does not say is that William needed to be saved above all from Quincy Street. Ralph Barton Perry has described William James's moral dilemma:

To his essentially interested and ardent nature the counsel of resignation could never be more than a temporary anaesthetic, and he was too profoundly human to find consolation in heaven. He was too sensitive to ignore evil, too moral to tolerate it, and too ardent to accept it as inevitable. Optimism was as impossible for him as pessimism. No philosophy could possibly suit him that did not candidly recognize the dubious fortunes of mankind, and encourage him as a moral individual to buckle on his armour and go forth to battle. In other words, to cure him from his weakness he needed a strong man's medicine. He *was* a strong man, overtaken by weakness—a man of action cut off from action by bodily incapacity, a man to whom no teaching of acquiescence or evasion could be either palatable or nutritive.

Like his father he seems to have found a partial answer in a book. Reading the essays of the French philosopher Charles Renouvier, William was struck by his definition of free will—"the sustaining of a thought *because I choose to* when I might have other thoughts." This was not unlike the senior Henry's discovery of the meaning of Selfhood in Swedenborg. It was not unlike Alice's recognition that she did have a choice over the fate of her body. From this William was to write in his diary words, since much quoted: "My first act of free will shall be to believe in free will."

II

William might believe in free will, but the ghosts that haunted him were not prepared to depart at the summoning of a belief. He found no solution for almost another decade; marriage and the creation of his own home proved in the end his salvation. He had begun his teaching at Harvard in 1872, and although he was appointed instructor in physiology, his mind was already at work upon the problems he was later to deal with in his *Principles of Psychology*. In the spring of 1873 the elder Henry James could report to his son in Rome that William was getting on "swimmingly with his teaching." This letter contains a passage which shows how far his eldest son's observations had taken him and how he was groping towards those studies in psychology and medicine which have captured the imagination of our century. What William had done at this stage, as the father put it, was to give up "the notion that all mental disorder required to have a physical basis." He added: "This had become perfectly untrue to him. He saw that the mind did act irrespectively of material coercion, and could be dealt with therefore at first hand, and this was health to his bones." This was the ground upon which Charcot in France, and William James and Freud—who both listened to Charcot's lectures—were to build certain of the basic tenets of modern psychology.

If William was doing "swimmingly" in March at Harvard, this could only mean that he would probably have a sense of drowning shortly thereafter. His feelings at the end of the semester are well described in a letter to Henry from his mother:

> Will's vacation is fast approaching, only one week's work more. He was late to dinner just now, and came in with his hands full of primroses and cowslips from Grace Ashburner's garden—he had been sauntering in the Norton woods with Sara. He will be glad to get through; he has done his part well, I am sure, although, with his usual self-depreciation, he insists on pronouncing it a very superficial thing. He hears that the class next winter will be three times as large and feels much discouraged with the prospect.

President Eliot offered William a renewal of his appointment and asked him to teach anatomy, with the prospect of a permanent post. William's first impulse was to decline. "I told him I had resolved to fight it out in the line of mental science," he wrote to Henry. He finally changed his mind and accepted. Then he changed his mind again, for he resisted the teaching of anatomy and all that it involved. By the end of May he began to toy with the idea that he might take the year off, and escape to Europe. In a letter to his brother he broached the subject of joining him, and remarked: "I don't know whether you still consider my ailments to be imagination and humbug or not, but I know myself that they are as real as any one's ailments ever were." He wondered whether in Europe he might not suffer from loneliness and *ennui*:

> Here at home there are various modes of killing time, the ride to Boston and back destroys one hour, there are constantly visitors in the house to me or to the others who cheer one up, and one can lounge over meals and in the parlour or look in upon the Gurneys and Ashburners etc., in short escape being shut up face to face with one's impotence to do anything, that I should think a lonely invalid might find rather desperate in Europe.

Henry was in Switzerland when he replied. He suggested that William might find Rome interesting; the place, he said, offered more resources for recreation than elsewhere in Europe. He himself had found that it stole much of his time from his writing. There were many persons to call on and places to visit. Henry's letter answers all William's questions, but it is interesting to note that it contains no attempt to influence William in one direction or another. Henry merely added that he planned to spend the autumn and spring in Florence and the mid-winter in Naples; but if William decided to go to Rome he would be glad to join him there.

William did not reach an immediate decision. For two months he debated, amid fits of despondency and languor, whether to keep his $600-a-year job at Harvard or take leave in pursuit of health. "Poor fellow," wrote his mother to Henry on 1 July 1873, "I wish it was possible for him to learn to live by the day, and not have to bear today the burden of coming months and years." She continued:

> He says the question of being able to do the work that lies before him next winter, and indeed his whole future career, weighs so heavily upon him that it keeps him from rallying. After a very serious talk with him yesterday, Father's advice to him was to give up the idea of working next winter . . . I fear unless his resignation is given in at once, and the whole subject dismissed from his mind, that his recreation will yield him neither pleasure nor profit. He is very desponding about himself, but says that Alice's recovery and yours, especially Alice's (for he considers her weak, nervous condition very like his own present one) give him hope . . . He has such a morbid sympathy with every form of trouble or privation, that he is not strengthening where he most wishes to be. For instance, he broke out last evening on the piazza into a most pathetic lamentation over the servants who had only one armchair in the kitchen. I promised him at once that I would supply the want, and that there should be three.

There is little doubt that if Mary James contributed to William's anxiety, he was far from being an easy son to have under the family roof. In July he was still saying that to go abroad would be a "desperate act." He was particularly troubled by the fact that he would have to ask his father for money, when the younger brothers were already a drain. "Every hundred dollars I take or don't earn is so much less that Father can give them." By August Henry had decided what William's decision would be, for he asked him to bring to Europe certain of his books and some American toothpaste and candy. William finally solved his financial problem by borrowing $1000 from the loyal Aunt Kate and agreeing to pay her $75 a year interest on this capital out of his future earnings. On 2 September he could announce to Henry that "the die is cast! The six hundred dollars' salary falls into the pocket of another! And for a year I am adrift again and free. I feel the solemnity of the moment, and that I *must* get well now or give up." If his experiment failed it would be, he had written to Henry earlier, "that I am a failure and between one or another mode of failing there is little choice." His mother writing a few days later told Henry: "You will find him very much improved in appearance, looking as well as he ever did I think, but still very morbid, and much more given than he used to be to talk about himself. If, dear Harry, you could only have imparted to him a few grains of your own blessed hopefulness he would have been well long ago."

William sailed for Europe on the S.S. *Spain* on 11 October 1873. He paused briefly in London, devoted two days to Paris, and then travelled for twenty-two hours from Paris to Turin, and eleven hours to Florence, the appointed meeting-place of the brothers. He arrived towards midnight and went to Henry's hotel—the Hôtel de la Ville. Henry was asleep and William did not awaken him. Instead he went to his room and before retiring wrote a brief letter to his sister: "The Angel sleeps in number 39 hard by, all unwitting that I, the Demon (or perhaps you have already begun in your talks to distinguish me from him as Archangel), am here at last. I wouldn't for worlds disturb this his last independent slumber." He was going to bed with a light heart—and "the certainty of breakfasting tomorrow with the Angel."

ANGEL AND BROTHER

HENRY JAMES had left Rome as he had planned, late in May; he kept an old vow to himself by visiting the hilltop towns from Perugia to Florence; and then fled the Italian summer to Switzerland. After a stay in Berne, he crossed into Germany and made his way to Bad Homburg, where he settled down in a quiet inn and later in lodgings. Here he spent ten weeks. Homburg was "German pretty," cool, shady, comfortable; the Kursaal, from which gambling had been banished, looked like a tomb. There was, however, a reading-room and a café. Henry strolled in the evenings and listened to fussy band-concerts. Forty years later he could recall "a dampish, dusky, unsunned room, cool, however, to the relief of the fevered muse, during some very hot weather." The place was so dark that he could see his way to and from his inkstand only by keeping the door open. In this retreat he was "visited by the gentle Euphemia, artfully editing the confidences with which she honoured me." In other words, it was here that he wrote his tale of "Madame de Mauves," blending into older memories of St Germain-en-Laye, its setting, the emotions of Rome. He wrote travel-pieces as well and read Turgenev in a new German translation, preparatory to writing an article on him. To his mother he wrote: "I drink, I read and scribble, I stroll in the woods and gardens, I listen to the music at the Kursaal; I think of the tremendously fine things I shall certainly do when I am better." He *was* feeling better. "I have for two years been so well," he told William, "and have now in spite of everything such a standing fund of vigour, that I am sure time will see me through."

He returned to Italy early in October; the record of his trip through Switzerland and by coach over the St Gothard was set down in a series of travel-papers, later reprinted in *Transatlantic Sketches*. By this time he knew that William was on his way to

Europe. Arriving in Florence, he found the place oppressively hot and delivered over to mosquitoes. He accordingly spent some days in Siena; this yielded him an article for the *Atlantic* in which we find him indulging in what was to become a characteristic mannerism in his travel-writings—that of imparting a voice to houses, palaces and monuments, and letting them speak to him and to the reader. "We are very old and a trifle weary," the houses in Siena say to him, "but we were built strong and piled high, and we shall last for many a year. The present is cold and heedless, but we keep ourselves in heart by brooding over our treasure of memories and traditions. We are haunted houses, in every creaking timber and crumbling stone."

Into the midst of these colloquies between Henry and the Old World came his elder brother, bringing the power of his unsentimental wit to bear upon the ruminations of the sentimental traveller. This would have been challenge enough, and of the healthiest kind. However he brought with him also old obscure childhood memories. William, the fresh observer, the quick analyst, the lively eye of Cambridge, was a welcome guest. William, the unconscious bearer of old family wounds, the idealized elder brother—but also the ancient rival of the nursery—was an intruder in Henry's Italian paradise.

I

From Henry James Jr in Florence to Henry James Sr in Cambridge, 2 November 1873:

I wrote to you a week ago, telling you of Willy's being on his way to me—and I had hardly sent my letter when he arrived. He had travelled very fast, stopping only one day in Paris, in his impatience to reach me. A compliment to me! I have delayed writing, as I wished to be able to tell you how he seemed, after a few days' observation. He looks indeed in exuberant health, and I am immensely struck with his change in this respect since I last saw him. He is very much charmed with Florence and spends a great deal of time in going about the streets and to the galleries. He takes it all as easily as possible, of course, but he already manages to do a good deal and has made a beginning which augurs well for the future. He has fallen upon indifferent weather, but the air is happily still very mild. I find great pleasure in seeing him and have plied him with all imaginable questions about you all. I feel almost as if I had been spending a week in Quincy Street. Would to heaven I could!

From William James in Florence to Mr and Mrs Henry James in Cambridge, 9 November 1873:

First—of the angel. He is wholly unchanged. No balder than when he quit; his teeth of a yellowish tinge (from the waters of Homburg, he says); his beard very rich and glossy in consequence he says of the use of a substance called Brilliantine of which he always keeps a large bottle on the table among his papers. His clothes good; shoes ditto he having just cabbaged from me the best pair of garters Conol. & Pwr. ever had in their shop as Mr Power informed me. He seems wholly devoted to his literary work and very industrious. I doubt if I get him home in the spring. The "little affectations" of which Mother spoke I have not noticed. He probably fears me and keeps them concealed, letting them out when foreigners are present. He speaks Italian with wonderful fluency and skill as it seems to me; accompanying his words with many stampings of the foot, shakings of the head and rollings of the eye sideways, terribly upon the awestruck native whom he addresses. His manner with the natives generally is very severe, whereas I feel like smiling upon them and fattening the foot to them all round.

II

It was William James's first journey to Italy and the first time the two brothers had been united on European soil since a far-away German summer of nearly fifteen years before, when their father had deposited them at separate *pensions* in Bonn. For both this reunion was bitter-sweet: a mingling of intellectual delight and of hidden ache. Henry felt at times as if Quincy Street had intruded into his private world. William on his side fretted constantly. He felt the weight of his thirty-one years. He wanted to be "settled and concentrated;" he experienced the need to cultivate a patch of ground which might be humble, but still his own. And so he looked upon the beauties of Florence and the past of Rome with a jaundiced eye, feeling "like one still obliged to eat more and more grapes and pears and pineapples, when the state of the system imperiously demands a fat Irish stew, or something of that sort."

And then Florence invited on the part of the physiology

to Harry's room where I sit
by the pungent wood fire writing this letter
which I did not expect to begin
till the afternoon, while he just
at this moment rising from
the table where his quill has
been busily scratching away at the
last pages of his Turguenieff article, comes to warm his legs and
puts on another log, thus do I
catch his outline.
He says I
don't do
justice
to his
beard,
which I
regret to
say since the
brilliantine regime has become

WILLIAM JAMES'S SKETCH OF HENRY

From a letter of William James to his sister

teacher from Harvard speculations that were artistic and historical rather than anatomical. Once one was in these old Italian cities, historical problems seemed most urgent to the mind. "Even art comes before one here much more as a problem," he wrote to his sister, "how to account for its development and decline—than as a refreshment and an edification." William apparently could not accept Italy as it was, and enjoy it with his senses. He told Henry he feared the "fatal fascination" of the place. It seemed to be taking "little stitches" in his soul. He was too impatient and restless to be completely refreshed. He had been eager to go abroad. He was just as eager, shortly after his arrival, to go home.

He had before him, moreover, the constant spectacle of his younger brother's industry. This was salt on the wounds of his own idleness. Henry spent his mornings at his writing-table, and William's presence in Florence was not allowed to alter this daily schedule. Only when the work was done was Henry ready to lunch with his brother and to explore the artistic and human resources of the city. There are repeated allusions in William's letters to Henry's work-habits. Thus he describes how he goes for a stroll and then, tired of sightseeing, returns to sit by a pungent wood-fire in Henry's room. While he is waiting, he starts a letter to his sister, and Henry, "just this moment rising from the table where his quill has been busily scratching away at the last pages of his Turgenev article, comes to warm his legs and puts on another log."

The record of their Florentine rambles was written by Henry in the eight papers which he published in the *Independent* (the former journal of the Rev. Henry Ward Beecher, to which Henry sent these articles and some book-reviews, in his continuing search for a wider market). The articles were later combined to form "Florentine Notes" in *Transatlantic Sketches*. They show the thoroughness with which Henry viewed Florence in the light of its history and of its artistic meaning to his own time. Occasionally we capture in these notes glimpses of his companion, as he carries out his inspection of Fiesole, or visits the castle of Vincigliata, or ponders the pictures in the Pitti as they "jostle each other in their splendour" and "rather fatigue our admiration."

William is "the inveterate companion" or "my irrepressible companion" or, in one instance, "W——," who names a Baptism of Christ, by Paul Veronese, as the picture he most enjoyed in Florence; or remarks on looking at Santa Croce: "A trifle naked if you like but that's what I call architecture, just as I don't call bronze or marble clothes statuary." Henry picks up these occasional comments where they will serve him best, and commemorates in this way the fraternal explorations. For the rest, he observes the city and its treasures in his characteristic way—an evocation of the sense of the past and of history, a thoughtful survey of its architecture, a view of its paintings, and, with light touches, his sense of the character of its people. The earlier Roman pieces are charged with intense emotion and colour, and the sense of Rome as a sovereign city; the Florentine sketches are more intellectual, more pondered, more "homely." Yet Henry is constantly aware of "the deep stain of experience" in the city, and he has a knack of discovering interesting paintings lurking in obscure corners in the shadows of the Academy or behind the church altars. One gains the impression that perhaps the happiest hours spent by the two brothers were during these rambles; they could commune on the common level of art—that art in which William had first thought he had a vocation; and they could be again, briefly, the two young boys who had wandered, in their teens, along the quays of Paris and in the great salons of the Louvre. It is difficult to say how many words Henry puts into William's mouth, in some of the passages, or how much he lifts from him that corresponds to his own feelings.

It was not especially for the pictures that I went to the Corsini Palace, however; and certainly not for the pictures that I stayed. I was under the same spell as the inveterate companion with whom I walked the other day through the beautiful apartments of the Pitti Palace and who said: "I suppose I care for nature, and I know there have been times when I have thought it the greatest pleasure in life to lie under a tree and gaze away at blue hills. But just now I had rather lie on that faded sea-green satin sofa and gaze down through the open door at that retreating vista of gilded, deserted, haunted chambers. In other words I prefer a good 'interior' to a good landscape. The impression has a greater intensity—the thing itself a more complex animation. I like fine old rooms that have been occupied in a fine old way. I like the musty upholstery, the antiquated knick-knacks, the view of the tall deep-embrasured windows at garden cypresses rocking against a grey sky. If you don't know why I'm afraid I can't tell you."

Henry is probably ringing in personal variations on a theme by his brother; the passage, however, suggests to us the observant, earnest, thoughtful, discussing American sightseers—future novelist and future pragmatist.

III

The Apennine winter descended in full force. William complained of the cold and wanted to move to Rome. Henry was at this moment quite happy with his writing by his Tuscan fireside; nevertheless he felt he should accompany his brother and guide him in the city he had made his own earlier that year. They made the day-long journey by a leisurely train; and, as they passed the Umbrian hillsides which Henry had lovingly admired, William looked upon them and upon the Italian scene with quite other eyes. The ancient walls, the spires, the huddled houses, seemed to the elder brother from Cambridge "wicked and venomous," and in the winter landscape they seemed to him to be "showing their teeth as it were to the world, without a ray of anything externally but the search for shelter and security."

They arrived in Rome during an evening in early December. The air was mild; there was a moon. When they were settled in their hotel, Henry led William to the Colosseum and the Forum. The old stones cast strange shadows; the brothers seemed to be in an endless world of ruin. In the Colosseum they looked upon the clear, silent arena, half in shadow, half in moonlit dusk, with its great cross half-way round, where Henry would place Daisy Miller at precisely such a moment several years later. Henry seems to have been, as usual, delighted with the sad beauty of the ruins. Writing to his father he reported that William "appreciated it fully." William, however, had not wanted to dampen Henry's romantic ardour. His version to Quincy Street expressed the deep revulsion which seized him as he stood on the site where the Christians had shed their blood. It was like a nightmare, and—he said—if Henry had not been with him, he would have fled "howling" from the place.

The decay, the paganism, the traditionalism of Rome, the surfeited atmosphere of "churchiness" appalled the elder brother. He could not find anything to like in St Peter's, writing to his father that "it so reeks as it stands now with the negation of that gospel which it pretends to serve." Nevertheless, after this first acute sense of the mouldering musty aspect of Rome had subsided, the artist in William began to respond to the city's splendour. "Willy, who at first hung fire over Rome, has now quite ignited, and confesses to its sovereign influence," Henry reported towards the end of the year. He admitted however that his brother "enjoys all the melancholy of antiquity under a constant protest." Henry believed this to be a sign of William's elasticity and growing optimism. He greatly valued his impressions, however, finding them "lively and original and sagacious." To which he added his old-time note of younger brotherhood, "my own more sluggish perceptions can hardly keep pace with it."

The brothers had taken rooms at the Hôtel de Russie, a quiet, fashionable hostelry near the Piazza del Popolo. Henry, however, discovered that the little apartment in the Corso of his Roman springtime was vacant, and moved in, leaving William alone at the hotel, with access to Henry's sitting-room, fireside and balcony. As in Florence, while Henry worked, William spent his mornings in solitary sightseeing. At lunch-time he went to a café in the Corso, and there awaited Henry who "comes in with the flush of successful literary effort fading off his cheek." Continuing in his characteristic vein of caricature, William assures his sister that he is dining frugally, and saving his dollars, even to total abstinence from liquor, "to which Harry, I regret to say, has become an utter slave, spending a large part of his earnings in Bass's Ale and wine, and trembling with anger if there is any delay in their being brought to him." He went on: "After feeding, the Angel in his old and rather shabby striped overcoat, and I in my usual neat attire, proceed to walk together either to the big Pincian terrace which overhangs the city, and where on certain days everyone resorts, or to different churches and spots of note. I always dine at the *table d'hôte* here; Harry sometimes, his indisposition lately (better the past two days) having made him prefer a solitary gorge at the restaurant."

From Cambridge Mary James wrote to Henry on 8 December 1873: "Mrs Norton said to Alice, the other day, with quite a sympathetic but serious look, 'I hope your brothers are getting on harmoniously in Italy.' Alice, of course, quite astonished, replied, 'What do you mean, Mrs Norton?' 'Oh! you know your brother William does not like Europe, and especially Italy, and Henry is so captivated with everything abroad.'—You may imagine Alice's consternation and the warmth of her assurance that her brothers never quarrelled and that no mere difference of taste, even if they had any, which she disclaimed, could possibly produce a want of harmony between them." That there was no want of harmony between the brothers is quite true; but it is interesting to discover that at least one neighbour in Cambridge recognized what the mother did not want to avow—the distinctly different temperaments and natures of her sons.

IV

Rome had never seemed more delightful. The weather was brilliant—as brilliant and as clear as the finest Cambridge Octobers, milder than New England's mildest autumn, winter with "all the edge melted off." After the freezing temperatures of Florence, Henry basked in the sunshine on the Pincio; he had fraternal company—in comfortable doses—and he took afternoon walks and drives, dined with William at the von Hoffmanns' in the Villa Mattei, introduced him to the sociable drawing-rooms in the two palaces (the Storys, he reported, "are to be 'quiet' on account of Mrs Story's health: i.e., receive not on fixed days twice a week, but *every evening*, regular"). For Henry—so he told his father—there was the "especial charm of seeing Willy thriving under it all as if he were being secretly plied with the elixir of life." William seemed "greatly contented," and felt constant improvement. "He does in fact a great deal, and walks, climbs Roman staircases and sees sights in a way most satisfactory to behold."

This idyllic life—this Rome recaptured in such an auspicious fashion—did not last for Henry as it might have, into the soft spring. At Christmas William was seized with chills and fever. Fearing malaria, he promptly took train back to Florence. Henry reluctantly followed him there, a day or so later, with their luggage. He found his brother in good medical hands, dosing himself heavily with quinine, and already distinctly improved; he was no longer confined to his bed and was able to get about. Henry felt frustrated. The last thing he had wanted to do was to leave Rome; and while he agreed that William had done well to flee it, he nevertheless gave voice repeatedly in his letters to his deep disappointment.

"I was very willing to abide quietly in Florence in the autumn and attempt no higher flight," he wrote to Alice. "But to go to Rome and take root there, and have all the old satisfactions come crowding back on one and call oneself a drivelling fool to have pretended to exist without them—and then to brush away the magic vision and wake up and see the dirty ice floating down the prosy Arno and find life resolved into a sullen struggle to catch half an hour's sunshine a day on a little modern quay, half a mile long—this is a trial to test the most angelic philosophy. Willy, happily, has no regrets to speak of."

To Grace Norton he wrote in a similar vein. He had been "jerked away from Rome, where I had been expecting to spend the winter, just as I was warming to the feast, and Florence, though very well in itself, doesn't go so far as it might as a substitute for Rome. It's like having a great plum-pudding set down on the table before you, and then seeing it whisked away and finding yourself served with wholesome tapioca. My brother, after a month of great enjoyment and prosperity at Rome, had a stroke of malaria (happily quite light) which made it necessary for him to depart, and I am here charitably to keep him company." Two days after writing this letter Henry suddenly fell ill. He had a splitting headache and a bronchial cough and fever. William brought in a nurse to attend him. The fever abated after three nights and only the headache remained. William could discern no special cause for the illness; he described it to Quincy Street as "an abnormal brain fever." It was not malaria; the headache seemed to be the most uncomfortable feature. Henry too spoke of it as "a strange and mysterious visitation, it would be hard to say just what it was." William dispatched regular communiqués to Cambridge, and at the end of the second week he reported: "He advances steadily and went out driving yesterday. He has just taken a breakfast of poached eggs, chocolate and toast and is sitting now (11 a.m.) by the fire reading the Roman paper. The sun is just beginning to slant into our window, and the sky is as blue outside as it has been almost every day since the middle of November."

V

It seemed once again, as in the time of their youth, that the Angel and his brother could not long remain in each other's company without experiencing a certain amount of physical discomfort. Henry's headache, we may speculate, had an emotional origin; it could have spoken for the vexation and frustration expressed in the letter to Grace Norton, that unvoiced helplessness of rage of his early childhood, when he had to accommodate himself to his elder brother's active schedule of life. There was even a touch of the nursery in the formulation of his chagrin; the plum-pudding snatched from the table, the tapioca substituted for the more substantial dish. The meeting of the brothers in Italy had been that of two gifted adults, each delayed in his search for his rôle in life, and each in the process of finding, in his own way and through the dictates of his own temperament, a solution to his dilemma. But each had brought to this meeting his old boyhood self. Thus while they experienced their new relationship as grown men in the Italian setting, they were in some degree re-experiencing an older relationship as well. Put into the crudest terms, William in Italy could be quite simply a headache for Henry.

Fortunately the elder brother did not linger. He was impatient to be home and he cut short his stay as soon as Henry was on the way to recovery. He proceeded to Venice and then to Dresden to pay a visit to the Tweedys, who were wintering there. Early in March he sailed from Bremen. Quincy Street had nourished a hope that William would bring the lingering literary son back with him, but Henry had no desire to quit Europe abruptly. His illness, he wrote, seemed to have "cleared him up;" he felt better than ever and he wanted to take "a more contemplative and ceremonious leave" of the Old World. To William, in Dresden, he wrote that he wished to "hang on" for three or four months longer. "I don't know when I may come again; and when I do it will be in an older and colder mood, when I shan't relish it as I do now nor get what I can now out of it." He urged William to "drop me from your mind and decide your own course freely." Henry had quite decided on *his*: spring was coming, and he would now remain in Florence. He was writing his series of Florentine sketches, and another tale. "I confess," he informed Quincy Street, "I shall leave Europe without alacrity."

THE FORK IN THE PATH

WILLIAM returned to Quincy Street towards the end of March 1874. Cambridge seemed shruken and small, and he now understood better what Henry meant when he spoke of the "provinciality" of Boston. When he encountered Howells he told him that he had a "newly-quickened sense of the aridity of American life." Howells retorted that American life teemed with suggestions to his imagination. William went to a party at the Bootts'—they had wintered in Cambridge—and found it "dreariness and countrifaction." Henry wrote home amusedly: "I tremble for future days when I learn from Willy that even he finds Cambridge mean and flimsy—he who used to hanker so for it here."

Willy's mood was temporary. Moreover it was necessary for him to make peace with Cambridge, since it was here he wished to build his future. In due course he wrote a letter—a curious letter—reflecting certain of his own misgivings, but designed to warn Henry of the dangers of repatriation. "It is evident," he wrote, "that you will have to eat your bread in sorrow for a time here. It is equally evident that time (but it may take years) will prove a remedy for a great deal of trouble." Henry would have to attune his senses to "snatch a fearful joy" from little things—such as Cambridge's wooden fences—"a joy the more thrilling for being so subtly extracted. Are you ready to make the heroic effort?" William asked. He added: "It is a fork in the path of your life, and upon your decision hangs your whole future."

This is your dilemma. The congeniality of Europe on the one hand plus the difficulty of making an entire living out of original writing and its abnormality as a matter of mental hygiene—the dreariness of American conditions of life plus a mechanical routine occupation possible to be obtained, which from day to day is *done* when 'tis done, mixed up with the writing into which you distil your essence.

I

There was a double edge to this statement which William may not have recognized when he wrote it, so close was he to his own problems, so blind, at this time, to Henry's. Its meaning, however, could not be lost upon his brother. William was saying that Henry could not support himself by his writing and would be wise to take a job when he came home—something Henry had long ago determined not to do. If, in this, there was a degree of William's elder-brotherliness, there was also the general fact, recognized by Henry, that in America, more than elsewhere at the time, to be a writer was to accept the way of loneliness and isolation; and William implied that writing wasn't quite an active, manly, healthy way of existence. The three massive novels of James's middle period were to carry within them this burden of an artist's relation to his society. "The pencil—the brush? They are not the weapons of a gentleman," says the old politician in *The Tragic Muse*. He was in effect echoing, in another form, what William had said to Henry: that the pen wasn't a normal instrument for an American. Summing up, William told Henry that if he were not prepared to face a three-year "slough of despond" he would do well to remain abroad.

It is perhaps difficult for parents and brothers to be aware that there is a genius in their midst; and William's advice to Henry was a rather ungraceful urging that he modify his dream of a literary career and conform to Cambridge. Since William was trying to do this, he expected Henry to be capable of it as well. There seems to have been in William—it remained throughout his life—a certain blindness to the laws of art that dictated his brother's life. He had seen Henry joyously engaged in the act of writing and doing this religiously every day, without understanding the meaning of such dedication. Far from "abnormal," this seemed to Henry the most "normal" thing he could do. He never felt better or stronger than when he had completed a morning's work. A good day's writing gave him a sense of strength, of control over chaos, a victory of order and clarity over the confused battle for existence. William never seems to have sufficiently appreciated that the writing son and brother nourished visions of fame, fortune, literary power—the dream of an artist which was wholly unrelated to everyday logic—and which possessed a logic of its own. Henry was always to refuse to be bound by the expediencies advocated by his elder brother. And he felt none of the urgency William expressed about his future.

II

The writing brother chose not to reply directly to William. "Tell Willy," he wrote to his mother, "I thank him greatly for setting before me so vividly the question of my going home or staying. I feel equally with him the importance of the decision." He listened carefully to his brother's adjurations; they had a certain logic, yet he found them needlessly pressing. He was aware that he was reaching a crossroads in his life, but the alternatives did not seem to him quite as bare and as merciless as William pictured them. He shrank, he said, from William's apparent assumption that a return to America at this time was "to pledge myself to stay forever." He had now had, in all, three years in Europe—a year of wandering during 1869 and 1870, and the two years since 1872 spent largely in Italy. Henry considered this a "very moderate allowance for one who gets so much out of it as I do." He was quite prepared to find life at home not *simpatico* and he knew that "as regards literary work" his life at home would be "obstructively the reverse." Nevertheless he was ready to return "on stern practical grounds." He could find "more abundant literary occupation by being on the premises," and in this way he would relieve his parents of their "burdensome financial interposition." He did not intend to bother too much about that future of which William spoke, but would arrange life as best he could with the present. "The present bids me go home and try to get more things published." He underlined, however, the fact that even if he should make more money at home, the American cost of living would use it up twice as fast as in Europe.

The "burdensome financial interposition" of which he spoke was hardly of his making. He himself was only in a limited way a burden to his father. He had earned $1800 since he had gone abroad, and certain other sums were outstanding. The effect of the parental financial advances, nevertheless, was that Henry seemed chronically in debt to Quincy Street. This was conducive neither to a sense of security nor to a complete feeling of freedom.

III

There was a "fork in the path" before Henry, but it was not the one envisaged by William. At the very moment when Quincy Street was offering its counsels and Henry was preparing reluctantly to go home, the magazines began to compete for his works. His travel-pieces in the *Nation* had created a demand for them in the *Atlantic* and the *Galaxy*. And his efforts to find more outlets for his stories now began to bear unexpected fruit. The first intimation of this was contained in a letter from Howells asking Henry not to send any of his short stories to *Scribner's Monthly*. They were trying to lure away the *Atlantic* contributors, Howells said, "and my professional pride is touched." He admitted that the *Atlantic* could hardly lay special claims on Henry, but it had up to the present published all the fiction he had offered it. He promised it would continue to do so.

Henry, however, had just sold a story for the first time to *Scribner's*. His answer to Howells invoked his personal professional problems. He told Howells that the *Atlantic* would simply be unable to print all the stories he was capable of writing. "I need more strings to my bow and more irons always on the fire." He promised Howells, however, that he would always give the *Atlantic* his best things; and as token of this he sent the first part of his tale "Eugene Pickering" which he had been about to mail to *Scribner's*.

Meanwhile the editor of *Scribner's*, Dr Josiah Holland, had written to the elder James in Quincy Street, proposing that Henry do a serial for his magazine. The father's reply to Holland, composed without consulting his son, reveals at what a pitch of paternal garrulity and amateurishness Henry's literary affairs were being conducted at home. Polonius-like, the elder Henry gave Holland a full account of Henry's illness in Florence, went on to say that he was delighted that *Scribner's* so highly esteemed his work, added that Henry had "no power to push himself into notice, but must await the spontaneous recognition of the world around him," and promised that he would do his best to persuade his son to write the novel Holland requested. He also mentioned that it was his opinion that his son's gifts did not lie in the realm of fiction; "his critical faculty is the dominant feature of his intellectual organization." He hastened to add, however, that Henry did not agree with this estimate. He was certain that Henry would ponder "your flattering proposition very seriously." Of course his son alone must provide the final answer, yet the elder James seemed to know what it would be. He assured Holland, "I incline to think he will answer you favourably."

In the face of William's belief that Henry's writing life was "abnormal" and his father's depreciation of him as a writer of fiction, Henry's reply showed how firmly his feet were planted in the marketplace of letters. For an individual with "no power to push himself into notice" he seemed singularly hard-headed and business-like. He saw at once, what his father had failed to recognize, that there was a singular value in having two magazines competing for his work. He told his father his first allegiance was to Howells, and the first question to be settled was whether the *Atlantic* was prepared to match Holland's offer. "I am pretty sure the *Atlantic* would like equally well with *Scribner* to have my story, and I should prefer to appear there. It must depend upon the money question, however, entirely, and whichever will pay best shall have the story, and if the *Atlantic* will pay as much as the other, I ought, properly, to take up with *it*." Holland had proposed $1000 for the serial. Henry decided he would ask $1200 from the *Atlantic*, that is, twelve instalments yielding $100 a month. He added that if the *Atlantic* declined, he was ready to take the $1000 from *Scribner's*. "The writing and publishing of a novel is almost as desirable a thing for me as the getting a large sum for it. The money-making can come afterwards." And he took the precaution of reminding his father that this new undertaking might involve some further delays in paying his debts to Quincy Street.

To Howells, Henry wrote briefly and candidly. "Sentimentally I should prefer the *Atlantic*, but as things stand with me, I have no right to let it be anything but a pure money question." Howells fairly promptly accepted Henry's proposal and sent him a contract, giving him the option of terminating his serial before it had run to twelve numbers. Henry approved of this, for he desired above all "to write close, and avoid padding and prolixity." It was the first time that the *Atlantic* had taken a work of his unseen, and as yet unwritten.

"My story is to be on a theme I have had in my head a long time and once attempted to write something about," he told Howells. "The theme is interesting, and if I do as I intend and hope, I think the tale must please. It shall, at any rate, have all my pains. The opening chapters take place in America and the people are of our glorious race; but they are soon transplanted to Rome, where things are to go on famously. *Ecco*. Particulars, including name (which, however, I'm inclined to have simply that of the hero), on a future occasion. Suffice it that I promise you some tall writing. I only fear that it may turn out taller than broad."

"I shall immortalize myself: *vous allez voir*," he told his family. He also announced that he would delay his return to Cambridge. A summer in Europe would speed the writing of his novel. "I perfectly perceive the propriety of getting home promptly to heat my literary irons and get myself financially and reputationally on my legs. I have long tacitly felt it; but the moment for action has come."

THE PALPABLE PRESENT

HENRY'S course was now clear. He would remain in Florence until summer, then travel northward. He planned to sail for home late in August. This would give him margin for a few more travel-sketches as well as a running start on his serial. "By the time this reaches you," his mother wrote in April 1874, "you will be mentally launched upon the largest enterprise you have ever undertaken." Everyone in Cambridge, she told him, was delighted with "Madame de Mauves," "so you must be sure not to fall below that." Henry replied to Quincy Street: "I am determined that it shall be a very good piece of work."

During early April, while he was waiting for final word from Howells, he broke his Florentine stay for an excursion to Leghorn; then he went to Pisa, Lucca and Pistoia, incorporating his impressions in an article for the *Nation* entitled "Tuscan Cities." By mid-April, when he was back in Florence, he had received his contract. He could not face the idea, however, of doing a large piece of work in a small hotel-room, and accordingly moved into an apartment at 10 Piazza Santa Maria Novella, on the corner of the Via della Scala. It consisted of a sitting-room and balcony, two bedrooms, a scullery and a china-cupboard. He did not need so large a place, but it cost only $25 a month. "Blessed Florence!" he exclaimed to Alice. "My literary labours will certainly show the good effect of my having space to pace about and do a little fine frenzy. Tell William I find the French restaurant in Via Rondinelli, with the lobsters and the truffles in the window, an excellent place to dine, so that I am altogether most comfortable."

Years later he was to remember the setting in which the first chapters of *Roderick* were written—the shabby, charming, high sitting-room with the glare of May and June piercing the shutters. Re-reading the opening part of the book, which he set in

Northampton, Massachusetts, Henry recalled not New England but the Florentine house, and the view his rooms gave on to the piazza; the sleepy cabstand next to the obelisk, the clatter of horse-pails, the voices of the coachmen, the siesta stillness—all seemed mixed with his prose.

When he was not writing, he took long walks, and paid calls. "Nothing particular happens to me and my time is passed between sleeping and scribbling (both of which I do very well), lunching and dining, walking and conversing with my small circle of acquaintance," he wrote to his mother. The circle consisted of Mrs Lombard and her daughter Fanny, of Cambridge, and Greenoughs, Perkinses and Huntingtons. He described himself as reduced to accepting the Lombard parlour gratefully for half an hour on occasions as the nearest approach to a domestic foyer. Mrs Lombard was a chronic invalid who was always admirably coiffed, a detail which Henry introduced into his tales in describing certain itinerant American ladies abroad. From Quincy Street came the usual warning voice of his mother: "They are both, I imagine, great invalids, so avoid committing yourself farther than you can help with them." Other acquaintances included Dr Gryzanowski ("manners formed in diplomacy, brain formed in Koenigsberg") and his English wife, in their Borgo Pinto apartment with its ballroom-living-room as spacious, said Henry, as a Russian steppe. Florence decidedly was not Rome. Henry missed the full sense of the Italian spring he had so richly experienced the previous year: there were fewer places to catch it —no Campagna, no Villa Borghese, no Colosseum, no long walls overtumbled with cataracts of roses. Against the rugged walls of the Strozzi Palace, however, flowers stood in sheaves, and he had pleasant strolls in the Cascine. James Russell Lowell turned up for a few days and they renewed their friendship of two years before. Henry found great pleasure in listening to him reading some of his poems. "I feel as if I know Lowell now very well," he wrote home.

One afternoon he went to a party in the Villa Castellani on Bellosguardo, one wing of which contained the Boott apartment, and he commemorated the occasion by writing a letter to Lizzie.

"It was an enchanting day, the views from the windows were lovely, the rooms were perfumed with a wealth of spring flowers —and the whole thing gave me a sense that it might yet be strangely pleasant to live in that grave, picturesque old house." He added prophetic words: "I have a vague foreboding that I shall, some day."

I

The writer of thirty-one, who sat in his large shabby room in the Piazza Santa Maria Novella during the Florentine spring of 1874, working on his first important novel, was quite different from the troubled Henry James of four years before who had hurriedly written *Watch and Ward* and hoped it would make his name in American literature. He had passed through a long period of self-searching among his kinsfolk and his fellow-Americans; he had returned to Europe to recover the emotions of his original *Wanderjahr*, and he had sharpened his pen by constant exercise and publication not only of tales but of articles based upon personal experience and observation. He had always had a sense of his destiny; and now he worked with confidence, drawing his material out of the past decade of his life—the days he had spent in Northampton, just after the end of the Civil War, and the days he had spent in Rome a year before—and out of his inner vision as artist. *Watch and Ward* had been a small story set in a vague frame. In *Roderick Hudson* he drew upon a view of life and art which seemed to have greatly enlarged itself in recent months, so that he felt he had in his grasp not merely certain precious moments of existence but a sense of living and feeling—and doing—that would carry him forward in all his future creations.

There had been suggestions of this in his travel-sketches and literary reviews, certain remarks which revealed that in his slow process of growth he had taken possession of a personal philosophy that would forever guide him; it was not a particular philosophy, to be found in works of the old thinkers, nor in his father's religious optimism; it stemmed rather from a saturation with certain aspects of life and of literature, and a happy synthesis of the two—and from his constituted personality: the way in which he had learned to look steadily at—and accept—whatever life might bring into his orbit. In one of his travel-sketches he spoke of "that perfectly honourable and legitimate instinct, the love of the *status quo*—the preference of contemplative and slow-moving minds for the visible, the palpable, measurable present—touched here and there with the warm lights and shadows of the past." Hawthorne's experience had been exactly the opposite. "The Present, the Immediate, the Actual has proved too potent for me," he wrote, and spent his life in conflict over his essential isolation from the society of his time, which he sought to overcome. "I don't pretend in the least to understand our national destinies—or those of any portion of the world," James had written a year earlier to Charles Eliot Norton. "My philosophy is no match for them, and I regard the march of history very much as a man placed astride of a locomotive, without knowledge or help, would regard the progress of that vehicle. To stick on, somehow, and even enjoy the scenery as we pass, is the sum of my aspiration."

The vision of James on his locomotive of history is a vision of a comparatively happy observer and artist; and in his seemingly passive acceptance of life there spoke a writer who shunned movements, or theories (save those involving his art), or prophecies, or advocacy, or didacticism: who preferred the active contemplation of a world in which he had been placed by fate, and which fascinated him to such a degree that the task of observing and recording it (and drawing conclusions from his observations)—from various points of appreciation and ironic judgment—proved sufficient for a lifetime.

The image of the train was to have its variations; Henry was to use it effectively in Lambert Strether's outburst in *The Ambassadors*, in which he recognizes that if man is a creature determined and moulded and carried through life, he still possesses the *illusion* of freedom, and should live by that illusion. Such formulations, it might be said, would tend to arise in the consciousness of an individual with a nurtured aristocratic temperament, one who has known a comfortable and even spacious childhood and faces his environment with a sense of profound security. Experience, for such an individual, is something he takes hold of and feels free to mould in any shape he wishes—as distinct from another type of artist who has to conquer his environment through trial and error and struggle; who, so to speak, creates with one hand while holding on with the other to the very train on whose locomotive Henry, highly perched, is riding. The view of a "palpable, measurable present" could be taken only by one firmly anchored; for Henry's less fortunate colleagues the view was inevitably less measurable and was coloured by friction with the environment, if not by outright war upon it.

In this light we can understand the models to whom James turned, writers like himself who had been able to attain a large view—Balzac, in his "palpable, provable world," teeming with life as if it were a five-ring circus; Thackeray, most certainly, when he pictured his *Vanity Fair*, and showed his characters acting themselves out in it; George Eliot, with her strong intellectual grasp of experience. And to these predecessors Henry could now add the name of a contemporary, Ivan Sergeyevich Turgenev, a novelist with whom he had the greatest affinity, both in his psychological turn of mind and in the aristocracy of his temperament. He had been available to Henry in German and French translations. In the article he had just written about him, while William was in Florence, he saluted Turgenev as "the first novelist of the day."

What strikes us as we read that article is the extent to which Henry, in describing Turgenev, seems to be describing himself. Turgenev was "a story-teller who has taken notes;" his figures were all portraits; "if his manner is that of a searching realist, his temper is that of an earnestly attentive observer;" he had "a deeply intellectual impulse toward universal appreciation." No matter how he shifted his point of view, his object was constantly "that of finding an incident, a person, a situation, *morally* interesting." James speaks also of his "minutely psychological attitude." But it is when he characterizes him as a cosmopolitan and speaks of his relation to Russia, that Henry voices certain of his deepest feelings. "M. Turgenev gives us a peculiar sense of being out of harmony with his native land—of his having what one may call a poet's quarrel with it." Americans could appreciate Turgenev's state of mind, he said, and if they "had a native novelist of a large pattern, it would probably be, in a degree, his own." Also "we gather from his writings that our author is much of a cosmopolitan, a dweller in many cities and a frequenter of many societies." Henry spoke as well of there being in Turgenev the "impalpable union of an aristocratic temperament with a democratic intellect," a remark he withdrew in a later essay describing it as "inane." He said instead that Turgenev understood "the opposite sides of life."

These observations show the extent to which Henry had responded to the Russian. There is in this essay, however, a passage perhaps more important still, revelatory of the view James had reached in his personal philosophy at the moment he began *Roderick Hudson*. In it James used the rather worn image of life as a battle: but the picture he gives us is rather that of a moral and spiritual struggle and a kind of Olympian acceptance of life as something not to be defied, or argued with, but to be coped with and mastered. Revolt, he implies, is futile; and his strongest reproach to Turgenev is that he is a pessimist, and that his work is tinged with two kinds of melancholy, the "spontaneous" and the "wanton." "Life *is*, in fact, a battle," he wrote. "Evil is insolent and strong; beauty enchanting but rare; goodness very apt to be weak; folly very apt to be defiant; wickedness to carry the day; imbeciles to be in great places, people of sense in small, and mankind generally, unhappy." He continued:

> But the world as it stands is no illusion, no phantasm, no evil dream of a night; we wake up to it again for ever and ever; we can neither forget it nor deny it nor dispense with it. We can welcome experience as it comes, and give it what it demands, in exchange for something which it is idle to pause to call much or little so long as it contributes to swell the volume of consciousness. In this there is mingled pain and delight, but over the mysterious mixture there hovers a visible rule, that bids us learn to will and seek to understand.

In literary terms this could be taken as the manifesto of a novelist who was to consider himself, and to be considered, one of the new realists of American fiction. It implies also the moralist, the explorer of spiritual values in human conduct. The battle he chose to observe was the struggle within society for values and standards, for devotion to greatness of mind in art and in the imagination, "the things that, as a race, we like best—the fascination of faith, the acceptance of life, the respect for its mysteries, the endurance of its charges, the vitality of the will, the validity of character, the beauty of action, the sensuousness, above all, of the great human passion." By his embrace and acceptance of all this Henry lifted his work into the realm of psychological truth. For he was a solipsist; and he believed, as Proust did after him, that each human consciousness carries its own "reality," and that this is what is captured and preserved in art. For the rest, he would try to compensate—by technical ingenuity, skill of form, grandeur of style—for elements which he lacked in his own experience. This was at times to make him the historian of the rarefied and the particular, but it would also enable him to render the delicate and the exquisite in the human mind.

II

The pen that now was tracing the history of the passionate and erratic Roderick among the artists of Rome was driven by the nerves and the temperament of an individual impervious on the whole to the great scientific strains of his century. He had not only read but had met Darwin in 1869; the new science, however, the challenge of evolution and the debates about determinism, was to take on particular meaning for Henry only later in its literary manifestations, in the *naturalisme* of Zola. He had met Ruskin, but it was Ruskin's aesthetic observations rather than his social ideas which interested him. So too with William Morris, who yielded him not early socialistic thought but rather a sense of a quaint absorption in personal craftsmanship. The word "measurable" in Henry's view of his immediate world was to acquire in his creative life certain distinct accretions of meaning: he was to place that which was "visible" and "palpable" within the window of a given point of view—that is his characters' angles of vision by which they saw and measured the world around them. For Henry metaphysics could have meaning only when translated into art. He had been freed by his father from orthodox theology and had been spared the religious conflict many New Englanders felt between their will to reason and freedom and the over-powering demands of Calvinism. It was possible for him to abstract his world into a secular drama of good and evil as it affected the life of the mind and the conduct of individuals. He shared with his brother an interest in the "varieties" of religious experience, but he was not religious in the sense that some critics have made him out to be. When he used religious symbols it was to see them as part of the fabric of man's emotional experience. In the James household religious and philosophical discussion belonged to his father and his brother; this was perhaps reason enough for Henry to go in search of other—of aesthetic—ground. Intellectual though he was, he gave a primary place to feeling: "Where there's anything to feel I try to be there," Gabriel Nash remarks in *The Tragic Muse*, and he also says: "Merely to be is such a *métier*; to live is such an art; to feel is such a career." Gabriel, to be sure, is a rather shallow individual. But Henry is drawing upon Arnold, Ruskin and Pater, upon the men who in one form or another, in the Victorian world, urged that life and "awareness" were linked. If he indulged in the discussions of neither the hedonists, the positivists nor the utilitarians, he cultivated a personal doctrine of a ripe and mature civilization in which man faced reality by recognizing and not suppressing feeling and insisted that he, as artist, could not involve himself in larger issues and causes and at the same time cultivate his own modest garden.

He wrote his novel with great care and he recognized, as he wrote, that he was concerning himself more with the life of the intellect and of the emotions than with the life of action. In a letter that summer to Mrs Wister he told her that he was reliving some of his Roman experiences; at the same time he prophesied with complete accuracy what would be criticized in his book—in the precise terms, as a matter of fact, which critics would continue to apply to his later productions: "The fault of the story, I am pretty sure," he said, "will be in its being too analytical and psychological, and not sufficiently dramatic and eventful; but I trust it will have some illusion for you, for all that. Vedremo."

III

"I am still lingering on here in Florence—one of the few survivors of the winter colony," Henry wrote to his mother in June 1874. The hot weather had come; the piazza glared white in the noonday sun and seemed to scorch the eye as he looked out upon the huddled cabmen asleep in their boxes while loungers took their siesta half-naked, flat on their faces, on the paving-stones. Henry darkened his rooms and stayed on; he had no desire to travel and to live in hotels. In the morning he took walks and sought the coolness of the churches; he lunched early in a beer-garden, in the shade of a trellis, and spent the long hot hours of the afternoon in his room, working when possible, or simply taking a siesta along with the rest of the city. His plan was to make for Homburg, as he had done the year before, as soon as the heat became unbearable. His novel was proceeding to his satisfaction, "not very rapidly, but very regularly, which is the best way."

Four days after describing to his mother his way of coping with the Florentine climate, Henry packed and fled. A great heat-wave had descended upon the city. He went to Ravenna for a day, long enough to spend some time studying the tomb of Dante and visiting the two-storeyed dwelling in which Byron had lived. Henry wondered how Byron—even granting the particular attraction of the Guiccioli—could have stood the place for two years; it must have been possible, he decided, "only by the help of taking a great deal of disinterested pleasure in his own genius." Pushing on to Milan he found that even the cavern-like cathedral offered inadequate coolness and he sought the higher altitude of Monte Generoso near Como, which he ascended in a thunderstorm. "In spite of the temperature," Henry wrote to William, "I have been lacerated at leaving Italy." A week here, in a room hardly larger than a cupboard, sufficed for Henry. He made for Switzerland, via the Splügen. The journey is recorded in *Transatlantic Sketches*; he spent a night at Chur and a night at Basel, where he devoted some hours to studying the Holbeins. The thought of renewing acquaintance with Homburg, as he approached it, made him "deadly sick." He had had his fill of it the previous summer. He stopped therefore in Baden-Baden, settling in the Hôtel Royal, an establishment near the Trinkhall and the Kurhaus. The place was "coquettish" and "embosomed in a labyrinth of beautiful hills and forest walks." Besides, he wrote to his father, "Turgenev lives here, and I mean to call on him. Many of his tales were probably written here—which proves that the place is favourable to literary labour."

He did knock on Turgenev's door, only to discover that the Russian was at Carlsbad in Bohemia recovering from a bad attack of the gout. Henry had sent him his article some weeks earlier; and in June Henry's father had written a rather fulsome letter to the Russian informing him that "my son's high appreciation of your genius is shared by multitudes of very intelligent people here. Should you ever cross the ocean, you must not fail to come to Cambridge, and sit with us on the piazza in the evening, while you tell us between the fumes of your pipe what the most exercised and penetrating genius of the old world discerns, either of promise or menace for humanity in the civilization of the new." Turgenev replied cordially and modestly; he said he considered himself in a second or even third place, when compared with Dickens, George Eliot or George Sand. As for smoking a pipe "under your verandah," he was not a smoker, but he would enjoy "a quiet and pleasant conversation with the intelligent men and women of your society." He doubted, however, whether at his age he would ever cross the Atlantic.

Turgenev's letter to Henry, written from Carlsbad, expressed pleasure in his article as being "inspired by a fine sense of what is just and true; there is manliness in it and psychological sagacity and a clear literary taste." Turgenev himself gave proof of his own psychological sagacity by telling Henry that he found it difficult to judge someone else's critical appraisal: that he felt the praise too great or the blame too weak, and this not through "diffidence or modesty," but perhaps because this was "one of the many disguises which self-love enjoys."

"It would please me very much indeed to make your acquaintance as well as that of some of your compatriots," Turgenev concluded, and he gave Henry his permanent address in Paris in the Rue de Douai.

IV

Henry's days in Europe were now numbered. He spent five weeks or more in Baden-Baden and by the end of that time could announce to Quincy Street that he had booked his passage. "Be sure about Sept. 4th to have on hand," he wrote to his mother, "a goodly store of tomatoes, ice-cream, corn, melons, cranberries and other indigenous victuals." Baden was a bore—he had spent there "the dullest weeks of my life," he told Mrs Wister. With gambling forbidden, the resort was given over to band-concerts and tourists, and Henry's greatest solace, when he was not working, was in the walks he took in the Black Forest. "I converse with the waiter and the chambermaid, the trees and the streams, a Russian or two, and a compatriot or two, but with no one who has suggested any ideas worthy of your attention," he said in his letter to the companion of his Roman rambles. He seemed to have made up his mind what he would do once he was repatriated. He would spend the autumn in Cambridge, completing *Roderick*. Then he would try his fortunes in New York. "I have no plans of liking or disliking, of being happy or the reverse; I shall take what comes, make the best of it and dream inveterately, I foresee, of going back for a term of years, as the lawyers say, to Italy."

Henry left Baden-Baden in early August, and then by a Rhine journey entered Holland, where he spent some days paying tribute to the "undiluted accuracy of Dutch painters," and relishing that country's "harmonies of the minor key." He contrasted Amsterdam with Venice—"the way in which the thrifty city imparts the prosaic turn to things which in Venice seem the perfect essence of poetry." He admired the cleanliness and ceremonious thrift of the Dutch, but expressed surprise that the canals of Amsterdam and Leyden, in spite of their waterside trees, offered not "a single bench for a lounge and a half-hour's aesthetic relish of the situation." In Belgium he gave much attention to Rubens—a painter who, he said, painted by improvisation rather than by reflection. "He never approaches something really fine but to miss it; he never attempts a really interesting effect but to vulgarize it." The trouble with him was that "he throws away his oranges when he has given them but a single squeeze."

He had paid what was to be his only visit to the Low Countries, and with his articles on them his European journey—his book of transatlantic sketches—could be ended. Of the fortnight in England before sailing we have no record. He appears to have visited the Tweedys, who had taken an English country house. He sailed on a slow Boston Cunarder, the *Atlas*, encountering on board his old friend Wendell Holmes who was newly married. Our next glimpse of him is in a letter written by Mary James to her youngest son Robertson, at Prairie du Chien:

"Harry has come home to us very much improved in health and looks. When he came in upon us from his voyage in a loose rough English suit, very much burnt and browned by the sea, he looked like a robust young Briton. He seemed well pleased to be home at least as yet, and I trust he will feel more and more for himself, what I daily feel for him, that it is much better to live near his family and with his own countrymen, than to lead the recluse life he so strongly tended to live abroad."

To the same brother Henry gave testimony of his feelings a month later: "My arrival is now a month old, first impressions are losing their edge and Europe is fading away into a pleasant dream. But I confess I have become very much Europeanized in feeling, and I mean to keep a firm hold of the old world in some way or other. But home seems very pleasant after the lonely shiftless migratory life that I have been leading these two years. Cambridge has never looked so pretty as during the last month and I have seen nothing in Europe in the way of weather equal to the glory of an American autumn."

Gradually, he felt, he would get accustomed to the American

scale of things. The only other letters of this time seem to be two undated little notes to Longfellow, testifying to an evening or two spent with him and to Henry's lending the poet some of Turgenev's tales, "the best short stories ever written—to my knowledge."

RODERICK HUDSON

RODERICK HUDSON was the longest and, as James later said, most "complicated" subject he had yet undertaken: that of a promising young sculptor from Northampton, Massachusetts, who is befriended by an amateur of the arts and taken to Rome to study. He shows ready proof of his genius. Pledged from the first to marry his American cousin, he nevertheless falls in love with a great and ultimately unattainable beauty in Rome, a woman of a high and capricious temperament, and is consumed by his passion. He ceases to create and his disintegration is rapid. The moral of the story seems to be that a great physical passion can be fatal to art.

Stated thus barely, the complexity of the story-fabric is not apparent. In reality James began by weaving the familiar situations of his earlier tales into a larger drama and against a richer background. The opening sequence in Northampton is a skilful variation on the familiar Quincy Street problems. Roderick is a second son, unsure of himself in the world, but unlike his creator bereft of a father and elder brother. He is given a new father-brother in the art-patron, Rowland Mallet. Adopted by him, as Nora was adopted in *Watch and Ward*, he is taken abroad not only to fulfil himself but also to fulfil Rowland's hopes for him. Before sailing, Roderick becomes engaged to Mary Garland. Rowland also is attracted to her, although he is, as yet, but half-aware of this. The patron in this fashion is made also a rival of the hero. What saves the Northampton part of the story from the clumsiness of the earlier tales is the clarity with which James pictures the artist's dilemma in the small American town. In a few scenes he makes us feel its limitations and the dull future before the gifted young man, who works in a lawyer's office. For the first time in any fiction James has allowed himself the clearest expression of the American artist's need for Europe.

In Rome, Rowland and Roderick wander about very much as Henry and William had recently wandered. If Rowland is more appreciative of ancient things than William, he is nevertheless present as Roderick's puritan conscience and *alter ego*. Roderick's constant riot of emotion is tempered by Rowland's stuffy sobriety. The young sculptor embraces Europe with all the intensity of his being. He places a Venetian watch-chain round his neck and a magnificent Roman intaglio on the third finger of his right hand. He tries, both in garb and manner, to shake off his parochialism, and project himself into other and more dramatic centuries. But at best Rowland sees him as a "nervous nineteenth-century Apollo."

I

Roderick's first statues are paternal and maternal—Adam and Eve. He also wants to do a Cain and nourishes the ambition of embodying Beauty, Wisdom, Power, Genius, even Daring in marble—and a magnificent statue of America to boot. However, his fear of failure is intense, his feeling of helplessness at times overpowering. "What if the watch should run down and you should lose the key?" says Roderick in one of his monologues. "What if you should wake up some morning and find it stopped—inexorably, appallingly stopped? Such things have been, and the poor devils to whom they happened have had to grin and bear it. The whole matter of genius is a mystery." Roderick, in the Villa Mondragone, talks not a little like James's earlier artist, Theobald, in front of the botched and blackened canvas of his unrealized "Madonna of the Future."

Before we have ventured far into the book we meet a group of artists, and through them James pictures for us the various types he encountered in Rome. They are embodied, as we have seen, in Gloriani, the professional opportunist, the modest and single-minded Singleton and the lady-amateur Augusta. Among them Roderick is distinctly the inspired genius. Next to him it is Gloriani who fascinates James; he has the "impudence of his opinions" mixed with "the mere base maximum of cleverness."

If he possesses some of Story's humbug he has much candour, intellectual liveliness and the courage of his convictions. In his statues, as in Story's, the hideous "grimaces out of the very bosom of loveliness."

We do not know Gloriani's future, however, and during that evening in Rome we would say that the future lies with Roderick. He is the romantic artist of tradition, the artist who "lives dangerously;" and the difference between him and Gloriani is, in part, his new-world freshness, his openness to experience. We have seen him in his Northampton surroundings, a frustrated dreamer; we watch him gradually substituting a life of excess for the placid horizons he has abandoned.

Rowland's observation of Roderick is that "the poor fellow is incomplete." This is true; and it is Rowland who, in a sense, completes him. He possesses the cool measuring mind, the dispassionate heart, which Roderick needs—but also rejects. There is something chilly in Rowland; and in contemplating the two men, so romantically named and so involved in a kind of emotional duel—Rowland the rational, with no real sense of what it means to be an artist, and Roderick the impulsive, with no sense of how to curb his artist's ego—it seems as if James has abstracted the incandescence of his genius and placed beside it his decorous, cautious, restrained self. The one is rendered ineffectual by the other: it is as if James were saying to himself that to be free, impulsive and wilful is to court disaster. Rowland Mallet is thus the watchdog of his own spirit. "You are watching me," says Roderick to Rowland. "I don't want to be watched! I want to go my own way; to work when I choose and to loaf when I choose." Rowland cannot go away. He is literally a watcher, for we see the greater part of the story through his eyes. But he is also Roderick's other self. In the novel Henry seems to be asking himself an unanswerable question: how can the artist, the painter of life, the recorder, the observer, stand on the outside of things and write about them, and throw himself at the same time into the act of living. To fall in love with a beautiful woman—say Elena Lowe—would this not be a disaster for any artist? How become involved in life—and remain uninvolved? James is writing out, in this novel, the brief hint of the young American in "Madame de Mauves"—his puzzled interrogation of himself, whether "it is better to cultivate an art than to cultivate a passion." Any suggestion that the two might be cultivated simultaneously seems to have been excluded from Henry's reasoning. He treats them as irreconcilable. And he was to debate, in his later work, both humorously and tragically, this law of his being. It was as if a wall of glass stood between Henry James and his desires. The glass at least permitted him to look at life. This explains why contemporary critics of *Roderick* complained that there were sections of the book which seemed cold and even "inhuman."

James was sufficiently a Rowland to realize that he could never be a Roderick. Instead of acting out his passions he could invest his characters with them. In this novel the *feeling* self had to die. It was too great a threat to the rational self.

II

Into the life of Roderick Hudson, during his early days in Rome, there walks Christina Light, with her poodle, her grand manner, her shifting moods. (She also is endowed with magnificent tresses like Mrs Wister's.) She has the "step and carriage of a tired princess." She is as much at the centre of the novel as Roderick; and she grows upon the reader as an *achieved* woman of a corrupt society. The daughter of an American adventuress with large social pretensions and an Italian Cavaliere, she has been brought up without awareness of her illegitimacy and prepared for the great marriage she will some day make—prepared for it as some royal princess is prepared for the duties she must assume ultimately in her palace. In Christina, James seems to have set down the deep fascination he had felt in the mysterious and unreachable young Boston woman he glimpsed so briefly in Rome. "Beautiful, mysterious, melancholy, inscrutable," were the words he had used to describe Elena Lowe; for no other woman of his acquaintance had he used such language.

Christina is a strong woman capable of evil, yet redeemed by certain moments of honesty with herself, and her awareness that she is the plaything of forces she cannot change. Her final act—her marriage to Prince Casamassima—is carried out under her mother's coercion. She is never wholly a free agent. In one of her moments of self-abasement she exclaims: "I am fond of luxury, I am fond of a great society, I am fond of being looked at. I am corrupt, corrupting, corruption." Corrupt she doubtless is, in the sense that she is a creature of her world. She carries with her the sadness of her grandeur and all its futility. Miss Blanchard sees this when she speaks of her as "half like a Madonna and half like a ballerina." She is a struggling, questioning *fated* female; in later transformations she will become Madame Merle and Kate Croy.

She was the great success of *Roderick Hudson*. Created as a foil for Mary Garland, representing corrupt Europe as Mary represents innocent New England, she testified in her success to the traditional fascination which evil exercises on the Puritan soul. It was inevitable that she should be all colour and vividness, while Mary is as prosaic as she is dull. If Henry thought Europe when he thought Christina, and New England when he thought Mary Garland, he could not do otherwise.

Years later he was to recognize this and other defects in the book. He had needed his contrast. Mary Garland had to be plain and Christina had to be highly coloured. But what remained in the work, even after he revised it, were certain chilly passages which its contemporary critics shrewdly discussed. One critic in particular gave as an example of this the extent to which Henry's aesthetic feelings were allowed to affect the death-scene, so that Roderick's body is found at the foot of a cliff, washed by the rain and altogether "arranged" as a pleasing statue rather than as the mangled corpse of a young man who had died a violent death.

Henry's friend Mrs Wister wrote an anonymous notice of the novel in the pages of the *North American Review*. It was a calculated affair which gave full recognition to the maturity of the prose and the auspicious character of Henry's emergence as a full-fledged novelist. Mrs Wister liked his observation and recognized his verbal power, and compared his use of language to "the facility of a great pianist." The personages were real and living, but "we do not identify ourselves with them." She added: "We are intellectually interested, but as unmoved as one may suppose the medical class of a modern school of vivisection to be." Her final words must have given Henry pause: "All it lacks is to have been told with more human feeling."

A NEW YORK WINTER

RODERICK HUDSON began its course in the *Atlantic Monthly* in January 1875, and *A Passionate Pilgrim*, Henry James's first volume of tales—the book he had described as being "on the theme of American adventurers in Europe"—came out on 31 January. J. R. Osgood published it and paid Henry a royalty: it was not subsidized by his father, as the elder James had originally proposed. During this month of his début as a novelist and man of letters, Henry chose to "try New York" and discover whether it might serve as a place in which to work. He was acutely aware of his "irresistible longing" to be in Europe; and he left Cambridge for Manhattan with frank scepticism, but also, as he said, "with very loyal intentions." He felt it his "duty to attempt to live at home before I should grow older, and not take for granted too much that Europe alone was possible." Europe for him then meant Italy, and Italy had in some measure been a lotus-land: it did not "lead to anything." He wanted something more active, "and I came back and sought it in New York."

I

The history of his six busy months in the city of his birth clearly confirms the loyalty of his intentions. He seems almost literally to have sat at his work-table day and night and "scribbled," as he put it, in a kind of rage of endeavour to see how much he could earn. He was receiving $100 a month from *Roderick*. He managed to earn another $100 each month from miscellaneous writing, largely for the *Nation*. He contributed one or more book-reviews to almost every issue of the weekly during his stay in Manhattan, and sometimes theatrical and art reviews as well. He was later to say that "it was these two tasks that kept me alive"—his novel and his journalism. At the same time he saw his second book, *Transatlantic Sketches*, through the press, and made arrangements to publish *Roderick Hudson* in book-form at the end of the year. Henry allowed his father to cover the cost of the plates, since Osgood apparently considered it more of a risk than the tales; but it paid for itself rapidly. For the time being, however, once he had completed *Roderick*, he ceased wholly to write fiction. New York, in other words, turned him into a literary hack. What he seems to have proved was that by incessant drudgery he could earn an adequate livelihood for himself in America. He published only one tale during 1875, and it was doubtful whether, with this constant need to feed articles into the weeklies and monthlies, he would find time, or energy, to start another novel. The *Nation* paid him anywhere from $10 to $35 for a review, depending upon its length. He had to read three or four books and write about them to earn as much as he could gain from a single travel-article. What he got from his New York stay was the confirmation that it was better economy for him to live in Europe. New York, he wrote to Lizzie Boott, was "a rattling big luxurious place, but I prefer F——. Excuse me I can't trust myself on that chapter." And in the next sentence he was telling her that if he had been with her he might have "fancied I was again in R——? It will out, you see."

He invoked Florence and Rome; yet they were not in reality the alternatives he was seeking to New York. One of his problems in Italy had been his loneliness: his loneliness, that is, as a writer who would have liked to know colleagues and who wanted the company of men instead of the perpetual female society to which he had been exposed. He had lacked, he told his mother, "a *régal* of intelligent and suggestive society, especially male." Such society existed, he supposed, in Paris and London, but he was not sure how to find it. "I chiefly desire it," he said, "because it would, I am sure, increase my powers of work."

He did not find such society in New York. Manhattan seemed to confine him in the world "uptown" while all its activities went on "downtown" in the world of business. Henry was to remember his isolation during this time. He had discovered not only that "the major key was 'downtown' but that downtown was, all itself, the major key." This reduced "uptown" to being the minor, so that "the field was meagre and the inspiration thin for any unfortunate practically banished from the true pasture." Seated for several months "at the very moderate altitude of Twenty-Fifth Street" Henry felt himself alone with the music-masters and the French pastry-cooks, the ladies and the children. There was "an extraordinary absence of a serious male interest."

II

On arriving from Cambridge early in January, he found two rooms at 111 East 25th Street between Lexington and Fourth Avenues, the Rose Hill section of the city. In its up-island progress since Henry's Washington Square childhood, New York had now fixed the centre of its life in the Madison Square neighbourhood at 23rd Street and Fifth Avenue. This was within easy walking distance of Henry's domicile. His sitting-room was small, but sufficiently comfortable, with a fireplace, and he apparently had next to it a hall-bedroom—if we assume that the rooms in which he placed Basil Ransom, in *The Bostonians*, were like his own. Ransom lived further along the street, in the semi-slum near Second Avenue, which Henry came to know during his sojourn. His picture of the area which James said in the novel he included "for old acquaintance sake"—its unpaved rutted streets, its down-at-heel tenements—shows his familiarity with it: the Dutch grocery, with its fragrance of molasses, its odour of smoked fish and its panniers of vegetables on the sidewalk, the delivery-horse drawn up at the curb, giving the place a pastoral air in the midst of the city; the yawning cellar-doors; the drooping gas-lamps at the corners, the ash-barrels on the sidewalks (he had described these vividly in *Watch and Ward*). It was a sordid, uncivic New York, and on leaving his domicile Henry could see, eastward, the "fantastic skeleton" of the elevated railway, which smothered the avenue "with the immeasurable spinal column and myriad clutching paws of an antediluvian monster."

Few letters of this period have survived. Henry had no time for them. But there is abundant evidence of his industry, for the articles he carried to the *Nation* office at 5 Beekman Street show the range and variety of his book-reviewing. The journal's editor was Edwin Lawrence Godkin, whom Henry had known for the past decade—from the first issue of the journal, to which he had contributed. The book-review department was in the hands of Wendell Phillips Garrison, son of William Lloyd Garrison, the abolitionist. The younger Garrison had been a printer and he was methodical in all things. Thanks to his careful record of payments made to Henry, it has been possible to reclaim his reviews from their anonymity in the *Nation's* pages. Godkin, a Scotch-Irish immigrant, trained in the school of Mill and Macaulay, was now a power in American journalism and was to be a warm friend of Henry's. His flourishing weekly, with its 10,000 circulation—substantial for that era—was prepared to publish Henry alike on books, art exhibitions, theatres. Godkin's assistant was an old friend, Arthur G. Sedgwick, of the Cambridge family into which Norton had married. The novelist occasionally dined with him "at theatrical chop houses," and boasted to Howells of being "a naughty bohemian." "I feel vastly at home here and really like it," he wrote to the *Atlantic* editor shortly after settling in Manhattan. He added, however, "*pourvu que ça dure.*" Later he spoke of this winter as "bright, cold, unremunerative, uninteresting." And to Lizzie Boott he confessed that his life was humdrum; that he was seeing few people, and those "very stupid." Of the seventy notices and articles James wrote during 1875, thirty-nine appeared in the *Nation* during his six-months' residence in New York, two in the *Atlantic* and one in the *Galaxy*. Garrison seems to have given him free choice of the books that came into the office, but Henry's selection was still circumscribed by what was available. He preferred travel, literary essays, biographies of New England worthies, anything relating to America and Europe; he eagerly took all French subjects. But he reviewed also such works as Nordhoff's *The Communistic Societies of the United States*; or *Ismailia*, a narrative of an expedition to Central Africa for the suppression of the slave trade. Many of the volumes were dull; and he wrote until all hours of the night by his smouldering fire. There is no fatigue evident, however, in the writing. His reviews are light, humorous and possess great charm. They have authority; some could be called scholarly, although the imagination of the literary creator frees them from any suggestion of pedantry. What Henry brought to them was his literary awareness and his taste for the flavour as well as the substance of any work he read. Reviewing a volume of essays by Masson, he could speak of "one of those familiar fine passages from Pope, in which the rhythm is that of the pendulum, and the philosophy so bent on keeping terms with the epigram, that one loses half one's faith in its consistency." Reviewing a biography of Ezra Styles Gannett he sketches him rapidly as "a man, we shall say, of an extreme simplicity of organization. He was a born minister; he stepped straight from his school days into the pulpit, and looked at the world, ever afterwards, from the pulpit alone." Reviewing Greville's journal he is fascinated, as always, not only by the way in which the diarist portrayed his society, but by the portrait he left indirectly of himself. He has occasion to refer to Emerson's "magnificent vagueness," and he had clearly been reading Mark Twain's Mississippi instalments in the *Atlantic*, for he on one occasion observes that "in the day of Mark Twain there is no harm in being reminded that the absence of drollery may, at a stretch, be compensated by the presence of sublimity." Speaking of French attitudes toward Fenimore Cooper he remarks that "if we take his trappers and his Indians in good faith, Europeans could hardly do less, and the prairie and the virgin forest, as he portrayed them, had, when contemplated from the Boulevard, a prodigiously natural air." Of Stopford Brooke's essays on theology in the English poets he remarks that "he rather too readily forgives a poor verse on the plea of a fine thought." And so his pen races along, cheerful, easy, carefree, imparting to the readers of the *Nation* accounts of Dr Livingstone's journals, the life of the Prince Consort, the story of a missionary bishop, the correspondence of William Ellery Channing with Lucy Aitken, Taine on Paris, Augustus Hare on Rome—and all with a spontaneity which did not reflect the sheer pressure of production in 25th Street.

His inspection of the New York theatres, as reflected in his *Nation* articles, was not edifying. "The public evidently likes playgoing, and is willing to pay for it—to pay a good deal and to pay often," he wrote. But with the exception of the Fifth Avenue Playhouse this public saw few American plays; it received rather "an Irish image, a French image, an English image" in the tinkered dramas brought from overseas. This was not to say that the American plays at the Fifth Avenue Playhouse demanded much intellectual effort. A concoction called *Women of the Day* was "as preposterous an attempt to portray as it was a dreary attempt to entertain." If the theatre was a "superficial institution" in America, it shared this peculiarity "with other social phenomena." Seeing this play, which he described as "ghastly, monstrous, a positive nightmare," he regretted that audiences in America did not indulge in the old-fashioned freedom of hissing.

The five art-notices contributed to the *Nation* during this period are in his characteristic vein, but one of them, "On Some Pictures Lately Exhibited," in which he discussed the spring show at the New York Academy of Design, takes on special interest since it contains a spirited defence of art-criticism. "We frankly confess it to be our own belief," Henry told the *Nation* readers, "that even an indifferent picture is generally worth more than a good criticism; but we approve of criticism nevertheless. It may be very superficial, very incompetent, very brutal, very pretentious, very preposterous; it may cause an infinite amount of needless chagrin and gratuitous error; it may even blast careers and break hearts; but we are inclined to think that if it were suppressed at a stroke, the painters of our day would sadly miss it, decide that on the whole it had its merits, and at last draw up a petition to have it resuscitated." Although he himself was to abandon this branch of criticism, and was later to feel that he had little sympathy with it, he nevertheless proceeded—as he invariably did—to give a good example to the *Nation* readers of what a perceptive and schooled eye, supported by aesthetic feeling and strong verbal skill, could do in the observation of pictures. Notable particularly during this year was his praise for the work of Frank Duveneck, a painter who had trained himself in Munich and who, on a visit to America, was attracting attention in Boston and New York. Henry discovered certain Velasquez qualities in his portraits: their great merit was their "extreme naturalness, their unmixed, unredeemed reality." They were brutal, hard, indelicate, but "they contain the material of an excellent foundation." Henry added he would "take it hard" if Duveneck failed to do something of the first importance. He was, as it happened, to be a close spectator of Duveneck's evolution during the next decade.

III

The New York winter was cold but there was much brilliant sunshine; and the spring was a mixture of rain and snow. Henry would take the elevated train uptown and walk over to the long narrow tract of Central Park, hugged close by its periphery of mansions. There was a "raw delicacy" in the April air; and in spite of the Park's rockwork grottoes and tunnels, its pavilions and statues, its "too numerous" paths and pavements, "lakes too big for the landscape and bridges too big for the lakes," he at least got some feeling of the vernal season. But spring brought back also memories of Rome. He had written the last part of his Roman novel in 25th Street. And his letters to Lizzie Boott repeatedly lapsed into Italian. "*Mille grazie, cara Lisa, di vostra graziosa lettera, scritta nella vera lingua di Dante—Dio la benedica! Sapete che la vita di N.Y. é nemica di tutta occupazione seria e simpatica e potrete dunque perdonar al mio silenzio fin'ora.*" And he went on to remind Lizzie of her visit to Manhattan a month earlier (he was writing in March) and how they had lunched at Delmonico's. He had never had so much pleasure at such a low price. "*E per provari che non mi ha rovinato vi diro che vi prendo ancora la colazione ogni domenica nello stesso posto!*" His Italian might be a collection of traveller's clichés, but it was impregnated with memories of his transatlantic life. These had been revived a few weeks earlier by a visit to Butler Place in Philadelphia, the home of Mrs Wister, where the recollections of their Roman days two years earlier had seemed vivid amid American winter snows. Mrs Kemble was living at York Place, near her daughter, and Henry remembered calling on her one morning (probably with Sarah Wister), and how the ageing actress was induced to read certain passages from Edward FitzGerald's translation of a Calderón play. Henry was to recall the sunny drawing-room, the morning fire, the "Berlin wools" she was wearing, the way her spectacles were placed on her nose, and her rich English quality. She reminded him of a picture he had once seen of Mrs Kemble's aunt, Mrs Siddons, reading Milton in her mob-cap and spectacles. "Mrs Kemble read, then, as she only could read, and, the poetry of the passage being of the noblest, with such rising and visible, such extreme and increasing emotion, that I presently became aware of her having suddenly sought refuge from a disaster in a cry of resentment at the pass she had been brought to and in letting the book fly from her hand and hurtle across the room. All her 'art' was in the incident."

Mrs Wister introduced Henry to her New York friend, Florence Lockwood, descendant of an old Delaware family, the Bayards. Her Manhattan home provided him with excellent conversation: "a remarkable woman," he wrote to Mrs Wister, "and a very exquisite creature," perhaps too tense, and too *in*tense, but "so singularly lovely that a *tête-à-tête* with her is a great bliss." Years later he was to speak of her as "packed almost hard with thought" and "thoroughly in the grand style." He apotheosized her as "one of the big figures of one's experience."

Henry may have been bored, but New York was hospitable. Thus he speaks of spending an evening at the home of Mrs Botta—Anne Charlotte Lynch—who had married an Italian scholar, Vicenzo Botta, and in West 37th Street maintained a popular literary and artistic salon. Mrs Botta was herself a painter and an amateur poet, one of the rare painters in American art-history whose works are known only through literary allusion, for all her canvases have disappeared. At her parties Henry got a certain sense of transplanted Italian things. And, coming in one day to his rooms, he found a bouquet of flowers sent by his friend Anna Hazard Ward: "They reminded me indeed of the Roman springtime and I howled, fairly, in spirit when I looked at that enchanting cyclamen and thought of the sheets of it one sees at this time in the villas and on the Campagna—and then saw from my window the hideous driving sleet."

Apart from a brief break in his Manhattan stay in April, when he revisited Quincy Street, he continued his hard and narrow course. *Transatlantic Sketches* was published on April 29; in proof-reading it he relived all the stages of his European journeyings, from the time of his going abroad with Alice to his final departure from Belgium and Holland the previous autumn. By June, when the hot weather came and Henry began to think of returning to Cambridge, he felt that his experiment had given him the answers he needed. He might have tried to write fiction instead of book-reviews, and eventually earned an adequate living by doing so. But the New York scene offered him few themes compared with those which he seemed to find abroad; and to write fiction would mean placing himself once again on the Quincy Street budget until such time as his tales would yield revenue. We have no way of determining all Henry's reasoning, how he tried, in his inner debate, to reconcile the alternatives between New York and the capitals abroad, and the choice of a scene for his work as a writer. But his choice had been really made from the first. A few words set down many years later by Logan Pearsall Smith, after first meeting Henry James, suggest the extent to which his decision was a foregone conclusion. The meeting was in Oxford and Smith wrote on 14 May 1888, the day after, to his sister: "In speaking of New York he said that it was impossible to have a picturesque address there, and he told me that he had gone back to New York to live and be a good American citizen, but at the end of a year he had quietly packed up his few belongings and come away."

BENVOLIO

THE one piece of fiction (aside from chapters of his novel) written by Henry James during his winter in Manhattan was an allegory entitled "Benvolio." It was to be his sole venture into this form, since he considered allegorical writing unworthy of the realist in fiction. Allegory, he remarked later, is "apt to spoil two good things—a story and a moral, a meaning and a form." "Benvolio" however had neither story nor moral; it was a *jeu d'esprit*, a fairy-tale Henry set down one day in 25th Street, and its meaning is not difficult to discover, for its author underlines it several times. The tale was frankly like one of Hawthorne's allegories, and the old Philosopher and his daughter in it might have been Rappaccini and Beatrice; only there was no evil in the Jamesian garden and there is none in the tale. Perhaps Henry James, finding himself plying his trade on American soil, felt that he had to fire some salute to his predecessor. "Benvolio" was a modest salute indeed, and its allegory has in it less of the universal than of the autobiographical.

Thus Benvolio, a young-man-about-town, is "more than twenty-five" but not yet "thirty-five" and in the revised version he is actually just turning thirty—in other words he is of Henry James's age. He lives in two chambers in a city; one of them offers him a view of the great square and its teeming life; the other, his bedroom, resembles a monk's cell, and looks out on a quiet garden. He is a man of fashion; like Roderick Hudson, he sports an intaglio, or "an antique Syracusan coin, by way of a pin, in his cravat." He is equally capable, however, of putting on a "rusty scholar's coat" and braving the daylight shorn of all ornament. He is a man of peace, like Romeo's friend who had tried hard to keep the Montagues and Capulets from brawling with one another. What this Benvolio tries to do is to keep the two sides of his nature from brawling: not that they are really at war with each other. On the contrary: Benvolio is very well satisfied, although he thinks he should make up his mind between the life offered him by a certain Countess, a life of great extravagance and much amusement, and the life he enjoys with a young woman named Scholastica, daughter of a Philosopher into whose garden he looks from his bedroom window. The Philosopher, like Henry James's father, thinks the young man altogether best fitted for philosophy, and spends his time discussing the Absolute and the Relative with him. But Benvolio, when he is with the Countess, is inclined to write brilliant comedies rather than philosophical disquisitions.

He enjoys extreme liberty, even though he has a large family. "He tired of people whom he had seen very often, and he had seen, of course, a great deal of his family." His curiosity about all things is great—life, love, art, truth; but he is never able quite to satisfy it, and he is certainly a diffident lover, as the Countess discovers. Benvolio often says he was born "to imagine great things—not to do them."

We do not have to look far to see what the Countess represents in this tale. Benvolio says to her: "You represent the world and everything that the world can give, and you represent them at their best." The Countess is the world, and the world is Europe—when indeed did America have Countesses? And Scholastica is the daughter and granddaughter of Hawthorne's New England—the good studious life seen in the modest unimaginative terms of Quincy Street. Or she might well be also that side of Henry which could function as critic and drudge, as he was doing in New York, when his inner being craved the sensations of Italy, the freedom of Europe, the liberty to write as he pleased. In describing Benvolio Henry wrote that "it was as if the souls of two very different men had been placed together to make the voyage of life in the same boat, and had agreed for convenience's sake to take the helm in alternation." Here he was leading his divided life, the author of *Roderick Hudson* and at the same time of endless anonymous reviews of such books as someone's journey up the Nile, or travels in Tibet, or the book on communistic societies in America. America or Europe? The life of the teeming square, or the life of the monastic cell? The writing of plays for the Countess or the meditative life with Scholastica among musty books which doubtless would require editing or reviewing?—this is the general substance of Henry's little allegory.

There is no resolution. When Benvolio is away from the Countess, and when Scholastica, feeling rejected, flees to the Antipodes, Benvolio misses them both and leads "an extremely fretful and unproductive life." When he resumes his life with Scholastica, he is productive again, but his poems are "dismally dull." If the story arrives at no solution, it seems to imply one: for Benvolio seems to be both critic and creator. They occupy the same boat, and Benvolio is quite content to alternate between the two. Scholastica knows that when Benvolio leads "the great world's life" sooner or later "the pendulum would swing back and he would reappear and bury himself in their books and papers and talks." He would then give her all his confidences: he would read to her "everything he had written since his return from Italy."

And so "Benvolio," published at the summer's end in the pages of the *Galaxy*, evaporated as a tale into thin air, and contained only an ambiguous answer. America or Europe? How reconcile them? How reconcile even more those two natures within himself—the inner America and the inner Europe—the Roderick and the Rowland, that duality which every issue of the *Atlantic* was revealing?

Benvolio's ultimate outburst to the Countess does contain a suggestion. When she has chided him for his infidelity, he tells her that she is destroying the very sense of "contrast" by which he lives: "Don't you see, can't you imagine, that I cared for you only by contrast? You took the trouble to kill the contrast, and with it you killed everything else. For a constancy I prefer *this*." And Benvolio taps his "poetic brow."

It was precisely by contrast, by the vision of the old and the new, the two great worlds between which he shuttled, the Americans in Europe, the Europeans in America, the polarities of the parochial and the cosmopolitan, that Henry was to live. Contrast and comparison were to be the law of his life; and in the performance of this an act of critical judgment was necessary as well as an artistic function. He reconciled both; and he paid his price. He became at once the most intellectual of artists, and the most sentient of critics. And he led always that double life of Benvolio: he courted Europe, and he never forgot America.

I

What strikes the reader in this fantasy is the fact that the two personages dwelling within Benvolio, although quite different, nevertheless manage to enjoy peaceful co-existence: the monastic cerebrating side does not find the artistic worldly self unfriendly: indeed the one seems to admire the other, and the worldly self is never happier than when it is borrowing a page from the monastic self to cast a clinical eye on people and on existence. The spectacle of life is pleasing to both. Benvolio is happy when he looks out on the square and lives with the Countess; he is no less happy when he contemplates the garden and Scholastica. In his philosophy he can be faithful to two women at the same time. There is a frank egotism in the way Benvolio takes up with the Countess, for weeks on end, experiencing only the thinnest kind of guilt at leaving Scholastica; and then, on an impulse, a shadowy memory, a moment's longing, he returns to Scholastica, quite certain that he will find her patiently waiting for him. And now he is oblivious of the feelings of the Countess. The two selves might be different, but they were different parts of an harmonious self. This suggests that in certain fundamental areas Henry was an individual without conflict. He was thus able to see the world as it was and to pursue his aims without hesitation. He could be single-minded in his dedication to literature; and he never doubted his literary destiny.

At the end of his stay in New York, therefore, he did not find himself in any particular dilemma. If there was a fork in his path, he simply had to decide which way to go. He had known from the first that he wanted to live in Europe: the issue he had to decide was just how to do so and to be quite practical about it. It was, as he had said of his *Atlantic* serial, purely a question of money.

He returned to Cambridge in mid-July, knowing that his first two books were receiving good reviews and having an honourable sale. Howells had launched *A Passionate Pilgrim* with superlatives, causing Charles Dudley Warner to remark that if what he said was true "all the rest of you might as well go to bed." "In richness of expression and splendour of literary performance," wrote Howells, "we may compare him with the greatest, and find none greater than he." Henry possessed "a style distinctly his own," and few had the "abundance of felicity of his vocabulary." Other critics did not go to such extremes; they recognized the qualities of the style, but found flaws in Henry's characters. The reviews of *Transatlantic Sketches* were more complimentary; here the critics did not have to contend with fictional method and their varying opinions of James's cosmopolitan bias. The *Nation* did remark however that Henry, as a traveller, imposed certain difficulties on his readers; he not only discussed the objective scenery but also put into his writing the "scenery of his own mind." The critics were unanimous that Henry James Jr was a sensitive, intelligent and cultivated writer and they were aware of the singular maturity of his technique.

Particularly encouraging was the news that in three months Henry's travel-book had sold almost a thousand copies and seemed launched on a long career in the bookshops. Henry had thus finally taken hold, systematically, of a literary place in America: and he had the assurance that his third book would be published by the end of the year. The question to be resolved was how, and in what circumstances, he could now take his leave of Cambridge and re-cross the Atlantic. The best thing he could imagine was to go abroad and "try Paris" as he had tried New York. This time he envisaged a thorough "siege," not a mere visit as in 1872. In the French capital he would probably meet Turgenev. Moreover he had already discussed with the *Galaxy* an idea broached some time before by William, that he should write a series of essays on the important French novelists. Paris would be the best place to do this. The essays might ultimately make up a volume, a substantial counterpart in literary criticism to his travel-book.

At this moment, appropriately enough, when he was poised between his winter's grind in New York and the thought of Paris, Henry James wrote the first of these essays—his first major literary essay. The definitive edition of Balzac's works had recently appeared in twenty-three volumes; and re-reading the novels and tales Henry recaptured his fascination for the professional power and literary dedication of "the first of the realists." "What is most interesting in Balzac," Henry wrote, "is not the achievement but the attempt"—the attempt to recreate the whole of France through the power of language. Even more Henry was fascinated by the sheer persistence and labour of the French novelist, his productivity, his methods of revision, his financial embroilments and the range of his imagination; "the things he invented were as real to him as the things he knew." Through his entire career Henry was to feel strong affinities between himself and the writer he chose as his model. He called him "the father of us all." He was to say later that he had "learned from him more of the lesson of the engaging mystery of fiction than from any one else." There was a marked congruity between James's selection of Balzac as the first of the French novelists about whom he was to write for the *Galaxy* and this moment in Henry's life. Having just published his first novel in his thirty-second year, he alludes to the fact that Balzac had spent a decade trying to write novels before he had learned the world.

> The wings of great poets generally sprout very early; the wings of great artists in prose, great explorers of the sources of prose, begin to spread themselves only after the man is tolerably formed. Good observers, I think, will confess to a general mistrust of novels written before thirty. Byron, Shelley, Keats, Lamartine, Victor Hugo, Alfred de Musset, were hardly in their twenties before they struck their fully resonant notes. Walter Scott, Thackeray, George Eliot, Mme Sand, waited till they were at least turned thirty, and then without prelude, or with brief prelude, produced a novel which was a masterpiece. If it was well for them to wait, it would have been infinitely better for Balzac.

Thus the American writer who had also waited. The autobiographical overtones of this passage, and of the passages in which James describes Balzac's money-needs, suggest that Henry had thought of himself as a Balzacian scribbler during those weeks in

25th Street in which he had turned himself into a writing-machine: Balzac was always, as a writer, "a man of business in debt." "We cannot say how much Balzac liked being in debt," Henry remarked, "but we are very sure he liked, for itself, the process of manufacture and sale, and that even when all his debts had been paid he would have continued to keep his shop."

There was in Henry James, who had just "manufactured" and sold three books in this single year of his début as a full-fledged novelist, a consistent reference back to Balzac in all that he was to do. Balzac was his touchstone for the novel; and years later he was to express astonishment that a writer schooled in things French, like George Meredith, seldom had Balzac on his lips. Henry was to plan his own definitive edition in twenty-three volumes; he was to write a major series of essays on Balzac; and he was to lecture across the American continent on "The Lesson of Balzac." Now, planning once again a transatlantic leap, what more natural than to test the land and city of Balzac, to be himself like one of Balzac's young men from the provinces—even if from the American provinces—arriving in the great metropolis, a metropolis of conquerors, like Balzac or Napoleon, there to conquer not with a sword but with a tireless pen? But how was he to do this? What he needed above all in Paris was some foothold, some regular means of writing that could furnish him his needed revenue, as the *Nation* had done in New York, but without having to work at it to the exclusion of all other creativity.

II

The answer, as he later recorded it in his journal, "loomed before me one summer's day in Quincy Street." He had met in New York John Hay, who had been an assistant secretary to Lincoln, and was now an editorial writer for Whitelaw Reid, publisher of the *New York Tribune*. To Hay, Henry wrote, on 21 July, that he had "a tolerably definite plan of going in the autumn to Europe" to establish himself for a "considerable period" in Paris. "I should like, if I do so," he said, "to secure a regular correspondence with a newspaper." It would be non-political, wholly concerned with manners, habits, people, books, pictures, the theatre, perhaps travel-sketches in rural France. He had noticed, he said, that the American readers were fond of this sort of thing and that "it is as a general thing rather flimsily and vulgarly supplied." He offered to supply it in a "more intelligent and cultivated fashion." In fact he had "a dazzling vision of doing very good things." He added: "I think I know how to observe, and may claim that I should observe to good purpose and chronicle my observations agreeably."

Henry recognized that the *Tribune* had a correspondent—the Frenchman Arsène Houssaye—who was writing the kind of sketches he envisaged, but he felt he could do better. The *Tribune* moreover would have the advantage of having these from an American point of view. If this correspondent's "relations with the paper are destined within the coming couple of months to terminate—and let me not seem obtrusively to assume that they are—or if you are weighing the question of removing them—my proposition may have a certain timeliness." For all this delicate verbal wrapping, James was rather cold-bloodedly proposing to oust the incumbent. It may be that he had already heard from Hay that the *Tribune* was not altogether satisfied with him. Henry may also have known that he wrote his papers in French and that Hay was their translator. Hay promptly sent a memorandum to the publisher urging that Henry be engaged—"you know his wonderful style and keen observation of life and character." Hay added something that Henry had not suggested, that "he has no hesitation in saying that he can beat Houssaye on his own ground, gossip and chronicle, and I agree with him." Henry had not proposed to furnish "gossip," and this was later to be an issue between him and the publisher. Hay proposed that Houssaye be dismissed at the time of Henry's going abroad with the explanation that the labour of translation created extra difficulties for the paper. "In short, this is the statement. You pay Houssaye $30 for a not very good letter, and me Heaven knows how much for translating it. For, say, $20 or $25 James will write you a much better letter and sign his name to it."

Whitelaw Reid saw the force of this argument. He was inclined however to offer $20 a letter in view of the rate he was paying his American correspondents. "It is a smaller sum than I should myself have proposed," Henry told Hay, but if it was "good newspaper payment, I summon philosophy to my aid." Thus it was that on 11 August 1875 Whitelaw Reid recorded this memorandum in the records of the *Tribune*: "Henry James Jr is engaged to do Paris letters in place of Houssaye at $20 gold, per letter, to begin about 25th October 1875." Henry had found the answer to his problem. With $60 or $80 monthly from the *Tribune* he could live comfortably in Paris, augmenting his income by writing fiction. There would now also be royalties from the sales of his books. It seemed to him that he could go abroad on a sounder financial footing than ever before. Even if he were only half as industrious as he had been in New York, he would get along quite comfortably.

He began at once to gather together all available funds. He asked the *Atlantic* to advance the $400 due on the four remaining instalments of *Roderick Hudson*. He postponed his sailing till late October in order to see his novel through the press. He wrote a number of reviews for the *Nation*; he completed his Balzac essay. His father agreed once more to back his needs with a letter of credit. Thus armed, he once more bade farewell to his family, had a final breakfast with Howells, embraced the Quincy Street dog Dido, and set sail on 20 October for Liverpool on the *Bothnia*.

"Harry James is gone abroad again not to return, I fancy, even for visits," Howells wrote to John Hay. The autumnal crossing was stormy. There were gale-winds and the Cunarder tumbled and tossed during its ten-day voyage. Henry discovered that Anthony Trollope was on board and had some talk with him. He was struck by his "plain persistence" in writing every day, no matter how much the ship rocked. "The season was unpropitious, the vessel overcrowded, the voyage detestable," he wrote; "but Trollope shut himself up in his cabin every morning." He had had the ship's carpenter rig up a rough writing-desk and "he drove his pen as steadily on the tumbling ocean as in Montagu Square." Trollope had "a gross and repulsive face and manner, but appears *bon enfant* when you talk with him. But he is the dullest Briton of them all." In the evenings the British novelist played cards with Mrs Arthur Bronson of Boston. Henry on this occasion only just met her; he could little guess how devoted a friend she would ultimately become.

The crossing came to an end at last, and on 31 October, a Sunday, Henry stepped off the boat-train in London and went to Story's Hotel in Dover Street, off Piccadilly, and sat down to a meal of cold roast beef, bread, cheese and ale. It had all happened before. On Monday morning, to get his land-legs, he walked up Piccadilly and into Hyde Park. He would once more patronize the London tailors and take a wardrobe with him for his Paris winter. In the afternoon he sat down and wrote to Quincy Street, the entire family, to "Dear People All"—to his father and mother, William and Alice, and to Aunt Kate to whom the letter would be forwarded, and among whose papers it was found years later. The exclamatory opening sentence would do for all the ensuing decades: "I take possession of the old world—I inhale it—I appropriate it!" He had made his choice: he had consummated his adventure. No conquistador, planting a flag of annexation, could have sounded a note more genuinely triumphant.

Book Five

The Siege of Paris 1875–1876

★

IVAN SERGEYEVICH

IN New York one could not have a picturesque address. Henry's now was 29 Rue de Luxembourg. The street has since been renamed Rue Cambon and has been overrun by commerce. Located in the very heart of Paris, it extends its narrow length from the Rue de Rivoli to the Boulevard des Capucines. In 1875 it was still composed of large residences, with old high garden-walls. Henry had a second-floor apartment consisting of a parlour, two bedrooms, an antechamber which could serve as a dining-room, and a kitchen filled with shining casseroles. The furniture was "clean and pretty." There were mirrors, clocks, curtains, lamps, picturesque candlesticks; there was a woodpile in the kitchen.

From his windows he had a good view, and he was to remember long afterwards the particular light click of the passing cab-horses on the clear asphalt, "with its sharpness of detonation between the high houses." Re-reading some of his writings thirty years later, he recovered between the lines the sounds of Paris of this time. Each morning a troop of cuirassiers charged down the street and filed through a portal into barracks leading to one of the ministries which fronted on the Place Vendôme. Henry had to force himself to remain at his work-table when he heard the hard music of the horses' hoofs. He lingered at the window's cross-bar enjoying the uniforms, the plumes, the splendid animals.

The porter at No. 29 took care of his needs for $6 a month, and his rent was about $65 a month. "When I reflect upon my last winter's disbursements in New York, it is remarkably cheap," he wrote home. His woodpile cost him $5 and his linens less than $2 a month. He confessed to Quincy Street however that he had been rather extravagant in England. His new wardrobe had made inroads on the paternal letter of credit. He was certain that he would rapidly work off this debt. London had been cold, damp, foggy; he had sloshed through the mud and rain, yet had found the place "enchanting" and he would probably have remained there had he not been committed to Paris. Leslie Stephen had been "good and friendly as before;" and he had gone to see the acting of Henry Irving—"clever, but by no means a genius." If he belonged to a London club and were in English society, he said, London would make an excellent domicile; but "if one can't be in London, this is next best."

Henry had arrived in Paris on 11 November. He was settled within the week and on 22 November he dispatched his first letter to the *Tribune*. Eight days later he was reminding the editor of the *Galaxy* of his proposal to write a serial for that magazine. "I have got at work upon one sooner than I expected, and particularly desire it to come out without delay. The title of the thing is *The American*." And in the 15 November issue of the *Revue des Deux Mondes*—the salmon-coloured journal that for years had represented to him the summit of French literature—he discovered a translation of his tale "The Last of the Valerii." His permission had not been asked; literary piracy in the pre-copyright era nevertheless could be a charming form of flattery. It was almost as if his arrival were being trumpeted to the French capital.

I

On the day that he mailed to New York an article entitled "Paris Revisited," destined for the *Tribune*, Henry made his way to Montmartre, and climbing its hilly streets found the out-of-the-way Rue de Douai. No. 50 was a three-storey house, with a low wall between it and the pavement. He passed through an iron gate and a small front courtyard, and on entering was ushered into the presence of Ivan Sergeyevich Turgenev. This was to be, henceforth, one of the sacred moments of his life—his meeting with the tall, white-haired Russian. He was to remember the large sofa, in the green room on the second floor, built to accommodate Turgenev's sprawling figure; the walls draped in green and the *portières* of the same colour. He remembered the white light of the Parisian street, which came in through windows more or less blinded in their lower part, like those of a studio. There was a fine painting by Théodore Rousseau on one wall; a Corot was on another, and also a bas-relief of Pauline Viardot, the singer in whose house Turgenev was living—and whom he had followed into the West, from Russia, as a devoted member of her ménage, ever since her famous concerts in Moscow and St Petersburg. Nothing seemed out of place in the sitting-room. There were none of the odds and ends one expected to find in the rooms of a man of letters; no accumulation of papers; few books; everything seemed put away. Henry recalled however that Turgenev wrote little in Paris; that he did most of his work during long periods of withdrawal to his properties in Russia.

James, who was a short man, seemed to feel himself dwarfed by Turgenev. The Russian was exceedingly tall; his frame was so large as to suggest brute strength. One could see in him the sportsman, the partridge-shooter, the man of the out-of-doors. He had a finely shaped head; his features were irregular and yet there was much beauty in the face; it was distinctively Russian, almost everything in it was wide; his expression, James was to write, "had a singular sweetness, with a touch of Slav languor, and his eye, the kindest of eyes, was deep and melancholy." His hair was abundant and straight; and his beard, trimmed and short, was as white as his hair. There was about him an air of neglected strength and of singularly noble modesty.

Turgenev had asked Henry to come between 11 and 1. Henry seems to have arrived promptly at 11, and for the next two hours, speaking largely in English, the two writers discussed "a variety of topics." In a letter to his Aunt Kate, the first of a series to his family describing his encounter, Henry said he remembered nothing in particular that Turgenev said on this occasion. The novelist spoke English well, but rather stiffly; he remarked to Henry that no language was comparable to the Russian. "He seemed very simple and kind. His face and shoulders are hugely broad, his stature very high, and his whole aspect and temperament of a larger and manlier kind than I have ever yet encountered in a scribbler."

With his characteristic generosity, Turgenev offered to introduce Henry to Gustave Flaubert, and if possible to George Sand, who, however, was now rarely in Paris. There was something benign and gentle in the Russian, "a delightful, mild, masculine figure." Henry had come prepared to like him for his novels. Instead he found a human being whom he could love. "I found him adorable," he said in a long reminiscence written several years afterwards. "He was so simple, so natural, so modest, so destitute of personal pretension." Turgenev seemed to Henry a singularly complete human being, interested in everything, and without a particle of vanity.

This was Henry's first vision of the novelist and there was in it a considerable measure of hero-worship. Later Henry was to discern flaws in the hero, particularly his softness and his passivity. However the liking for him remained unchanged. What Turgenev's view of Henry was we can only deduce: but it is distinctly wrong to say that "the young man did not particularly impress" the Russian writer, as one of Turgenev's biographers remarks. At thirty-two he could no longer be called "young;" and Turgenev received him as a mature *confrère* with courtesy and respect. The evidence points to his finding the American, from the first, charming. He liked him well enough to return his visits promptly, to sit with him for long hours in restaurants discussing the art of fiction and to describe to him his working methods. He came later to see him in England. In address his letters passed from "My dear Mr James" to "*Mon cher ami*," and Turgenev's characterization of Henry to his translator in England, W. R. S. Ralston, is significant in that it refers to him not only as "amiable" and as "having much ability," but as possessing also in his work *un certain penchant à la tristesse*. For a melancholy Russian to discern a *penchant* for melancholy in an American suggests a community of feeling, which Turgenev's letters to James clearly convey. A friend of Turgenev's was to tell Henry later that the Russian spoke of him with an appreciation *qui alla jusqu'à l'attendrissment* and "in a way that he had rarely spoken to him of anyone." Even if we discount this as a possible attempt at flattery, the *attendrissement* matches the other evidence. For presently

Henry was accepted as an intimate of the Turgenev-Viardot household and was invited to its "at-homes."

II

The meeting of the American writer with the fifty-seven-year-old Russian was a meeting of two men who seemed at first glance divided by their years, by geography, language and background. And yet they met on the wide common ground of their cosmopolitanism and their craft, their artistic temperament, their sense of the great sprawling land-mass which each had quitted for the alien yet friendly soil of France, of that Paris where neither may have been wholly at home and yet where both found a kinship of spirit and discovered their brothers in art. It was no accident, perhaps, that Henry was drawn toward Turgenev, or that the Russian on his side should welcome the American beyond the limits of formal courtesy to his home and presently make him known to his French friends. Large historical forces had been in motion behind them: they were, in a strange sense, both products of a powerful ferment in the provinces. Turgenev had himself been an influence in the emancipation of the serfs; Henry had lived through the blood and struggle by which America freed the New World's serfs. If Henry had seen some union between aristocracy and temperament in the Russian, he himself spoke for a similar melting together of these elements, with emphasis on the aristocracy. Russian society, like that of America (as Henry observed), was in process of formation, and the Russian character was "in solution" in a sea of change such as existed also in the United States. These were the analogous backgrounds from which they stemmed. As for the deeper similarities, they might be found in their family history. Turgenev had had to contend with a mother who was an overt tyrant; Henry with a mother who concealed an iron grip: both had emerged with a certain inner softness as well as an ability to "tune in" to the feminine consciousness to an extraordinary degree. What they had in common as artists came from their similar view of their fellow-humans, so that while James was influenced in certain respects by the older writer, there are distinct qualities, resembling Turgenev's, which the American had possessed from the first. Both had the power of creating the atmosphere of place; both knew how to see into the essence of human personality; both were "tidy" to the point of finickiness in their portrayal of character; both were "realists," that is their work has a certain historical and documentary as well as psychological value; both dealt with individuals involved in the problems of their inner life, and both—above all—took a certain melancholy pleasure in their belief in renunciation. If we recognize also that both conceded moral supremacy to certain types of women, while harbouring a sense of the feminine sex as a destructive force, and that both wrote from strong poetic impulse, although they were artists in prose, we can discern how much they could find in one another that was attractive and congenial. They were articulate spokesmen for all that was civilized in their two countries—and a civilization both nations had "imported" from western Europe. Small wonder that Henry, in his first essay on Turgenev, had singled out a series of themes in his novels which might have been his own. Henry found in all Turgenev's young girls "a touch of the faintly acrid perfume of the New England temperament—a hint of puritan angularity."

For all this, it would be difficult to make a New Englander out of Turgenev, or a Russian out of Henry James. In Paris they were both "outsiders," possessing a vision wider than that of their French colleagues. In meeting Turgenev, Henry had discovered a man old enough to be his father, yet young enough to be his friend; and a man of singular allure. He had the gentleness of the elder Henry James without his bristling qualities; and he accepted Henry as an artist, which his father never wholly did. A month after their encounter Henry wrote to Quincy Street: "I have seen him [Turgenev] again several times, with unabated regard. He seems rather older and drowsier than I first thought him, but he is the best of men. He has twice called on me." This was the beginning of their friendship in Paris that winter and spring.

THE LESSON OF THE MASTER

In his later memoir of his Russian friend Henry described the elation he used to experience after being with Turgenev. He always left him, he said, in a state of intimate excitement, "with a feeling that all sorts of valuable things had been suggested to me." This condition was like a man swinging a cane, leaping lightly over gutters, stopping for no reason at all, to look, with an air of being struck, into a shop window—where he actually saw nothing.

What was this enchantment of talk which brought Henry such "valuable things"? He recorded one such occasion in three different essays; and the others, after the years, melted together into a kind of supreme sense of artistic feeling and artistic spontaneity, the example of a man of genius who was sentient, aware, capable of warm human relations, enjoying laughter—even at himself—and seeing life with a kind of detached irony tinged with melancholy. Four meetings stood out, across the years, four vivid scenes of memory.

I

The first had its prelude in Henry's going to call on Turgenev towards the end of January and finding that the Russian had the gout. He was stretched out on his sofa and Henry sat with him for an hour. They spoke of many things, and Henry came away feeling that he had listened to extremely gifted talk; everything Turgenev said had a measured *justesse*. Coming back a few days later, he was told that Turgenev was too ill to see him. He had taken to his bed with an attack of bronchitis. On 31 January Turgenev wrote to Henry: "The last time you came I was ill and had gone to bed. I am not budging from home these days." He invited him to come again.

It was raining when Henry arrived at the Rue de Douai. Once more he is in the green room, and Turgenev is sprawling on his sofa. If he has been ill, he shows little sign of it in his conversation. There is something animated in him, responsive yet reflective too. He begins to speak of his writing, how stories come to him. He tells Henry that he never thinks of a plot. The germ of a story comes in the form of some figure he has known, hovering and soliciting him, or grouping itself with other figures. Before writing about this figure, Turgenev wants to know it intimately; he compiles its *dossier*, as if he were a police functionary, writes out its biography. Only when he knows his character intimately does he become aware of what it will do and how it will act. How his people "look and move and speak and behave, always in the setting I have found for them, is my account of them." Critics observed *que cela manque souvent d'architecture.* Turgenev did not care. He would rather have too little architecture than too much.

As Henry put it, Turgenev was trying to suggest the "intensity of suggestion that may reside in the stray figure, the unattached character," the *disponible* personage, and how, starting with such a figure, he invented and selected and pieced together "the situations most useful and favourable to the sense of the creatures themselves." And Henry could say, years later: "I have not lost the sense of the value for me, at the time, of the admirable Russian's testimony."

It was testimony that confirmed Henry in his own way of story-telling. He too began with his personages: it was the vision of Roderick that had started him on his novel; it was the vision of an American in Paris that was keeping him for long hours at his desk at this moment; it would be a vision of an American girl confronting her destiny that would lead him to *The Portrait of a Lady*. But that winter in Paris he still had the feeling that in working in such a fashion he was putting the cart before the horse; that plots, not people, were what he should be looking for. To have the man he regarded as "the first novelist of the day" give him authoritative reassurance meant everything to him. Turgenev's method had the "immense recommendation that in relation to any human occurrence, it begins, as it were, further back. It lies in its power to tell us the most about men and women." Certain readers, to be sure, would say "We don't care a straw about men and women: we want a good story." But for those who did care, here was a way of work, essentially psychological, in which the author sought the truth of personality and of human behaviour.

And so the long rainy afternoon passed—one of the unforgettable afternoons of his life—and Henry wrote to William that Turgenev "gave me a sort of definition of his own mental process, which was admirably intelligent and limpidly honest. This last is the whole man; and it is written in his face." Turgenev was an *amour d'homme*—a "beautiful genius."

II

The second meeting occurred on another damp day: it is raw outside with the rawness of the Paris winter, but the café in the Avenue de l'Opéra is new and bright, with large settees made for comfort and talk. Turgenev has come from Montmartre to join Henry for *déjeuner*. They eat and they talk. The hours pass. The day wanes: the lamps in the café are lit. The habitués take their places at tables over their glass of absinthe, or sit quietly pondering their games of dominoes. Henry and his Russian friend still linger over their noonday meal. Turgenev talks almost exclusively about Russia: he tells of curious visits paid him by emigrés; he talks of the nihilists he has known, and the remarkable figures that have come to light among them; he dwells on the "dark prospects of his native land." He evokes the steppes and the forests, the great inarticulate Russian masses, the anguish of struggle and revolt. When he is in this vein (Henry later observed) no man can speak more to the imagination of his listener. There is something "extraordinarily vivifying and stimulating" in what he says. They part late in the afternoon: Henry again is in an extraordinary state of elation.

The third occasion: Turgenev and the Viardots by now feel Henry to be a familiar of their entourage. He is invited to

Madame Viardot's Thursday musicals, and to the family's Sunday evenings. The Sunday evenings are devoted to simple sociabilities, mainly charades, that remind Henry of Concord and of the "historical games" of his childhood. Madame Viardot, past her prime as a singer but still a great personality in the musical world, fascinates the American. She is "as ugly as eyes in the side of her head and an interminable upper lip can make her, and yet also very handsome." There is something "strange and sweet" in Turgenev—the same Turgenev of the serious talk and the meditative manner—prancing and crawling on the floor, wearing old shawls and masks, "at his age and with his glories" as if he were a child. "Fancy Longfellow, Lowell, or Charles Norton, doing the like, and every Sunday evening!" One is not sure that Henry's Bostonian eye altogether approves. He describes the *soirées* as "dingy," remarks that Turgenev has "not a gram of dramatic talent" and says that "the whole entourage is much beneath him." Nevertheless he recognizes that he is witnessing a certain type of European spontaneity—spontaneity and capacity for enjoying simple pleasures—in a gifted man. As he puts it to Charles Eliot Norton: "I have seen more of Ivan Turgenev than of anyone else and taken a strong fancy to him. But he is twice my age, and much engrossed with relations of his own. It pays, however, to see even only a little of a man of genius."

One other scene. Spring has come. It is April. Paris throbs with the life of the season. Henry has met a young Russian, Paul, the son of the famous poet and translator, Vassili Zhukovsky, who had been a friend of Goethe and tutor of the Tsar. Paul is a dilettante painter, a good conversationalist. He is also a friend of Ivan Sergeyevich. Zhukovsky invites Henry and Turgenev to dine with him, and turns up with a dark-eyed and sympathetic Russian woman, the Princess Ourousov. Turgenev says he has discovered an excellent place, a little restaurant in the square in front of the Opéra Comique. They find themselves in a low entresol; the food is hardly what they hoped, but Ivan Sergeyevich has never been more charming. He is jovial, prattlesome, entertaining at every moment. Henry delights in the mixture of his wit with his almost infantile naïveté. The evening seems scarce begun before Turgenev leaves. He has faithfully promised Pauline Viardot he will be home by 9.30. The party breaks up. But the three remaining diners do not feel their evening is at an end. The Princess invites Zhukovsky and Henry to her home; she too has her little salon—it is frequented by Turgenev, and certain of the French writers; later Maupassant will be of their number; still later André Gide. Here the American writer and the Russian dilettante are joined by Prince Hohenlohe, the German Ambassador to France; and so another memorable evening comes to an end.

III

There were to be later meetings, reunions in London and again in Paris, but these were the most precious of Henry's year in the French capital. He had seen certain aspects of Turgenev that revealed him as a lovable human being, all the more that he came to be aware of certain of his shortcomings. Did not Flaubert call him a *poire molle*, literally a soft pear? Turgenev himself quoted this and was much amused by it. There was something weak in him; perhaps that was why he was so lovable. He had an "expansive softness, a comprehensive indecision," like so many of his characters. Henry retailed to his parents the local gossip: Turgenev was Pauline Viardot's "slave," she guarded him as if he were a piece of property, she was reputed to have had a child by him; the Viardots treated him as a *vache à lait* and made free and easy with his money. And the 9.30 curfew! All this was told not so much in depreciation but in a tone of regret—almost of jealousy. Madame Viardot stood between Henry and more frequent meetings with the beloved Ivan. Henry may have cut the silver cord of Quincy Street but he had for the moment fastened the dangling end to the Rue de Douai.

This perhaps illuminates a strange passage in Henry's memorial essay in which he remarked, with some irrelevance, that Turgenev "to the best of my belief" ignored James's writings, and "was unable to read them." Henry went on to say that the Russian "cared, more than anything else, for the air of reality, and my reality was not to the purpose. I do not think my stories struck him as quite meat for men. The manner was more apparent than the matter; they were too *tarabiscoté*, as I once heard him say of the style of a book—had on the surface too many little flowers and knots of ribbon."

This seems to be an honest avowal and most of James's readers have accepted it as a fact. However on the basis of our testimony it seems to have been an act of self-depreciation in the very act of exalting his hero. Turgenev's letters, at any rate, do not suggest that he thought Henry's tales were not "meat for men." He praises the early part of *Roderick Hudson* as written with "the hand of a master;" he tells him that the first volume of *Confidence* strikes him as "finer and more simple" than Henry's earlier writings; he assures him that he will read *The American* and give an honest opinion "as one must, where a person possessing an ability such as yours is concerned." When we recall that earlier Turgenev had praised the "manliness" and the "psychological sagacity" of Henry's style, we begin to wonder whether Henry was not offering his subjective view of what Turgenev thought of his work. Turgenev, moreover, was not flattering Henry, since we have the independent testimony of his letter to Ralston urging him to meet James and saying "he has much ability." Turgenev may not have showered unqualified praise on Henry's work, but it is clear that there was esteem for it, and that he gave Henry every encouragement as from an older to a younger writer.

One possible reason for Henry's self-abasement suggests itself. William James had often reproached Henry for his "fancy" writing—the "knots of ribbon"—and the gallicisms sprinkled through his prose; his father praised his essays at the expense of his fiction. Henry may have unconsciously transferred to Turgenev the reservations of Quincy Street. Accustomed to some note of criticism in those dearest to him, holding Turgenev dear, and sensing in him paternal and fraternal qualities, he endowed the Russian with the familiar things of his own life. In assimilating the lessons of his master, he assimilated him also into his inner existence: in setting him up as an authoritative figure he may have seen him in the light of those other significant figures of his early experience, the candid critics of Quincy Street.

COUNCILS OF THE GODS

TURGENEV kept his promise. Three weeks after their first meeting he took Henry to one of Flaubert's Sunday afternoons (it was probably on 12 December 1875) and in a letter a few days later to his friend Perry, written in French, Henry spoke triumphantly of being "in the councils of the gods"—"*je suis lancé en plein Olympe.*"

I

After the solitude of Cambridge and the restless impersonality of New York, it seemed indeed as if Henry had suddenly been transported to some Olympus—an Olympus, to be sure, where the gods were uncommonly talkative as well as bawdy, and inclined to paunchiness: disputing the art of fiction, gossiping about the latest scandals of Paris, discussing the censorship, royalties, publishers, sexual adventures, the theatre, politics. No subject was sacrosanct: all Paris seemed to pass in review. Some of the gods were mortals, younger men like himself, making their careers in literature; and the "immortals," for all their allure, could have feet of clay. Then there were the young god-aspirants: for instance Guy de Maupassant, aged twenty-five, a protégé of Flaubert's, who wanted to write and so far had published nothing.

On that memorable Sunday in December, when Henry and Ivan Sergeyevich climbed to the high end of the Faubourg St Honoré and then mounted five flights of stairs to Flaubert's Parisian perch, it seemed to the American that he was listening to genuine conversation for the first time. Flaubert received, when he was in Paris, on Sunday afternoons from one to seven: his servant had the day off, and he always opened the door himself. He used to embrace Turgenev, as if he were receiving a brother. The Frenchman was tall; the Russian was even taller, both towered over Henry. As Flaubert shook hands with his transatlantic visitor, he greeted him in a timid, friendly way and bothered himself over what he could do or say to his guest. Flaubert had a massive physical development. His face was serious and sober, and he had a mottled complexion, long tawny moustaches and light-coloured salient eyes. He made Henry think of a weather-beaten old military man.

The guests were ushered into a high small room that seemed "bare and provisional," save for a gilded and painted Buddha of considerable size on the chimneypiece. Flaubert wore what Henry described as "a long colloquial dressing-gown," with trousers to match, a costume often affected by French men of letters, and "the uniform of freedom of talk." Here before his cheerful fire the author of *Madame Bovary* dispensed his hospitality.[1] "*C'est un naif*," Turgenev said of him, and Henry agreed. He liked the man; he was not at all what his books had led one to suspect; and there were moments when he was to wonder whether he wasn't fonder of Flaubert than of Turgenev, though he greatly preferred Turgenev's work. On this first occasion Henry met Edmond de Goncourt, then fifty-three, a year younger than Flaubert, and the busy survivor of the fraternal writing team: tall, slender, *type du gentilhomme français*, Henry said of him, unaware of the prodigious journal Goncourt had begun with his brother and was still keeping. Henry is not mentioned in the journal; his stay in Paris was to be brief and too aloof to involve him in that mass of literary gossip and petty hostilities which constitutes the journal's fascination. He was also introduced to Émile Zola, then thirty-five, author of *Thérèse Raquin* and the first volumes of his series of the Rougon-Macquart. "A very common fellow," was Henry's first impression, and he was to continue to shrink from the sordid physical life in Zola's work, and to admire his zeal, his professional loyalty and his personal courage. The only others mentioned as being present on the

[1] In his pastiche portrait of James in *It was the Nightingale* (1934) and earlier in *Return to Yesterday* (1931) Ford Madox Ford interpreted this description to mean that James was shocked at being received by Flaubert in his dressing-gown and considered it an affront to Turgenev and himself. Ford said that ever after James hated Flaubert and his work. There is abundant testimony to the contrary.

first occasion were Charpentier, the publisher, and the poet Catulle Mendès.

James met Alphonse Daudet on his second Sunday visit. This was in mid-January of 1876, about a month after the first. Daudet was Zola's age; his hair hung over his eyes; he had a black wispy Bohemian beard and a visage that was—with his later physical sufferings—to be generally considered "Christlike." James's first impression of him was as negative as that of Zola. He described him as "a little fellow (very little), with a refined and picturesque head, of a Jewish type" and a brilliant talker and raconteur, an extreme imitator of Dickens, "but a *froid* without Dickens's real exuberance." Henry had greatly liked *Lettres de Mon Moulin*, and *Fromont Jeune et Risler Ainé*, but *Jack*, which came out at this time, was "dreary and disagreeable, and in spite of cleverness intrinsically weak."

II

They were charming conversationalists. Henry repeated with delight Flaubert's characterization of Turgenev's talk: the Russian always found "*l'expression à la fois étrange et juste.*" Daudet had said this reminded him of Sainte-Beuve. Goncourt's rejoinder was: "*Sainte-Beuve trouvait bien l'expression juste mais—pas étrange.*" And to Howells Henry wrote that "as editor of the austere *Atlantic* it would startle you to hear some of their projected subjects." On one occasion Zola confided in a matter-of-fact way to the group that he was collecting all the *gros mots* of the language, the familiar talk of the working class, a veritable small dictionary of obscenities. Henry reported that Goncourt on his side said he was interested in an episode he was writing in a novel "into which he was going far." When Flaubert asked him to say what it was, he replied "A whore-house *de province.*" The remark may not have been Goncourt's, but that of the future author of *La Maison Tellier*. Flaubert was gathering, with his characteristic compulsiveness, material for his "dictionary of accepted ideas" out of which he wanted to fashion *Bouvard et Pécuchet*. To Howells James described the consequences of

Zola's collection of the working-class *argot*. Zola's new novel, *L'Assommoir*, was starting its run in a magazine; he was being well paid for it; but the journal had received protests from provincial subscribers against the serial's indecencies, and it looked as if publication would be suspended. The *cénacle* was stirred up, and its opinion was that while this was a bore, it could only do the book good in the end. "Among your tribulations as editor," James told Howells, "I take it that this particular one is not in store for you." On his way down from Flaubert's on another occasion he encountered Zola climbing the long staircase, "looking very pale and sombre," and Henry, who had been asked by Howells to run a serial a full year in the *Atlantic* instead of nine months as planned, saluted Zola "with the flourish natural to a contributor who has just been invited to make his novel last longer yet."

One afternoon Maupassant told a long involved story about Swinburne, two Englishmen and a monkey. "Distinct to me," Henry wrote many years later to Edmund Gosse, "the memory of a Sunday afternoon at Flaubert's in the winter of '75–'76, when Maupassant, still *inédit*, but always 'round,' regaled me with a fantastic tale, irreproducible here, of the relations between the two Englishmen, each other, and their monkey! A picture the details of which have faded for me, but not the lurid impression." Swinburne had been rescued from drowning at Etretat by Maupassant and had invited the Frenchman to the cottage where he was staying. Here Maupassant discovered the strange household. Henry recalled that it was a case of a "resentful and impassioned beast" which had seen a young Englishman installed on the scene "after he [the monkey] was more or less lord of it," and in the end somehow destroyed himself in an access of jealousy. "The drama had essentially been," James recalled, "one of the affections, the passions, the last *cocasserie*, with each member of the quartette involved." But what Henry recalled above all was Maupassant's "intellectual, critical, vital experience of the subject-matter."

Henry did not go every Sunday to the Faubourg St Honoré. He preferred to see Turgenev by himself; and he paid several private visits to Flaubert on week-days. He seems to have visited the *cénacle* about once a month during his stay in Paris. Perhaps he held back because so much of the talk was local and rather "parochial;" no group of Boston Brahmins, discussing the gossip of "the hub," could have been more local. It was strange for James to contemplate: that with his real joy in the wit and intellectual power of the Flaubertians, he found them also distinctly insular. They were "*affreusement bornés*," he told T. S. Perry; and he had to recognize the price a cosmopolitan paid among "provincials" who in this case could hardly be called "exquisite."

Thus after his second visit he remarked to his mother: "They are a queer lot, and intellectually very remote from my own sympathies. They are extremely narrow and it makes me rather scorn them that not a mother's son of them can read English. But this hardly matters, for they couldn't really understand it if they did." Henry was perhaps tailoring his impressions to the horizons of Quincy Street. Turgenev at any rate spoke English fluently; and Flaubert had mastered enough to read Shakespeare. Nevertheless Henry's contemporaries, Zola and Daudet, could not meet him on the ground of *his* language and literature, as he could on theirs, and there was no doubt that the French men of letters were inclined to consider Paris as their country, and to find it all-sufficient. This is the burden of Henry's complaint, even while he finds himself rejoicing at being in touch with men engaged in literary action, "in a manner full of interest for one never previously privileged to see artistic conviction so systematic and so articulate."

III

He was astonished how little respect these men had for the *Revue des Deux Mondes* and with what ease they dismissed certain of the minor novelists he had enjoyed and reviewed: the novels of manners of Victor Cherbuliez, the sentimental sketches of Gustave Droz, the romantic-sentimental of Octave Feuillet. Such writers, he was to say years afterwards, "were not even conceivable" in that room. The matter troubled him a little; was this a failure in his literary taste, or simply the *brusqueries* of young dogmatists? He alluded to the matter in one of his *Tribune* letters:

You ask a writer whose productions you admire some questions about any other writer, for whose works you have also a relish. "Oh, he is of the School of This or That: he is of the *queue* of So and So," he answers. "We think nothing of him: you mustn't talk of him here; for us he doesn't exist." And you turn away, meditative, and perhaps with a little private elation at being yourself an unconsolidated American and able to enjoy both Mr A. and Mr X. who enjoy each other so little. Of course subsequently you do them justice in their mutual aversions, and perceive that some of the qualities you admire in their writings are really owing to their being intrenched behind their passwords. A little school that dislikes every other school, but is extremely active and industrious within its own circle, is an excellent engine for the production of limited perfection, and French literature abounds in books in which particular tendencies have been pushed to lengths which only a sort of artistic conspiracy of many minds could have reached, but which seem like mere blind alleys of thought, where explorers perish, suffocated for want of having taken heed of possible issues to right or left. It is simply the old story that, either in politics or in literature, Frenchmen are ignorant of the precious art of compromise.

This was Henry's impression after the first visit to Flaubert. If he was being made welcome at the *cénacle* it was decidedly not on the strength of his tales which were appearing in the *Revue* during that winter (after the first, three more were published, in rather poor translations). On one occasion, when the name of Gustave Droz came up, Zola muttered an obscenity to Henry, who reported it to his friend Perry, in a letter written in French: "*Tu devrais entendre le ton que prennent ces messieurs à l'égard de Cherbuliez et de Gustave Droz.*" They had as much use for these gentlemen, Henry said, as Perry had for Dr Holland of *Scribner's* and his sentimental preachings. Also "they all detest Dumas [*fils*]—very properly, and predict for him a great fiasco before long. But," added Henry, "they generate poor stuff themselves." To his sister he spoke of "the little rabble of Flaubert's satellites," who were not worthy to tie Turgenev's shoelaces. It also made Henry "sick" to hear Turgenev seriously discussing Daudet's *Jack* with Flaubert. He, on his side, had been enjoying George Eliot's new novel, *Daniel Deronda*, "partly for reading it in this beastly Paris, and realizing the superiority of English culture and the English mind to the French."

"I have seen almost nothing of the literary fraternity," he was to write late that spring to Howells, "and there are fifty reasons why I should not become intimate with them. I don't like their wares, and they don't like any others." Turgenev, he said, was worth "the whole heap of them, and yet he swallows them down in a manner that excites my extreme wonder." We must make large allowance for these complaints—to Howells, to his mother, to Alice—complaints in reality to his own puritan side as well as that of Cambridge. The truth was that he greatly enjoyed himself among his young French peers and he saw more of them than he admitted. As for Flaubert and Turgenev, he sought them out as often as was decently possible. He was to acknowledge that the talk of the *cénacle* had "extreme intensity and variety." He had found at last the male company which he had lacked in Cambridge and in Rome. For all the "narrowness" of the French writers, he seems in the long retrospect—and after the turn of the century—to have cherished their memory.

In the magisterial essays which he wrote in 1902 on Flaubert and in 1903 on Zola, his backward glance reflects old pleasures and an old warmth. He speaks of Flaubert's friends as constituting a "rich and eager *cénacle*" made up almost wholly of "the more finely distinguished" of Flaubert's contemporaries—philosophers, men of letters and men of affairs belonging to his generation and the next. And in the memorial essay to Turgenev he stresses the elements in the Rue du Faubourg St Honoré which were important to him. It was at Flaubert's, he said, that Turgenev's "beautiful faculty of talk showed at its best." Everything the Russian said was "touched with the exquisite quality of his imagination."

What was discussed in that little smoke-clouded room was chiefly questions of taste, questions of art and form; and the speakers, for the most part, were, in aesthetic matters, radicals of the deepest dye. It would have been late in the day to propose among them any discussion of the relation of art to morality, any question as to the degree in which a novel might or might not concern itself with the teaching of a lesson. They had settled these preliminaries long ago, and it would have been primitive and incongruous to recur to them.

They refused, in other words, to be drawn into the Victorian debate between art and morality. "The only duty of a novel was to be well written; that merit included every other of which it was capable." This was the common ground on which Henry stood with these "deep-dyed radicals" and he was never to shift to any other. And it was this that made him recognize, long after, that his year in Paris, for all its shortcomings, "was time by no means misspent." In the end it became "all a golden blur of old-time Flaubertism and Goncourtism! How many more strange flowers one *might* have gathered up and preserved."

PASTEL

In the little high room at the Faubourg's end Henry heard always many voices: but one mid-week afternoon towards the end of March he found Gustave Flaubert alone. He sat with him a long time. They talked freely and Henry found himself greatly liking this prematurely old, sad, distinguished man. Their conversation turned to French writers, and Flaubert gave Henry certain reminiscences of Théophile Gautier, who had been his intimate friend, and whom Henry greatly admired. Not long before, Henry, in the pages of the *North American Review*, had spoken of Gautier as "one of the first descriptive poets;" his verses were always "pictorial and plastic," his sonnets pieces of "self-amused imagery." Flaubert said he preferred Gautier to Musset. "*Il était plus français*," more generally French in the quality of his melancholy. Neither Goethe, nor Heine, nor Leopardi, neither Pushkin, nor Tennyson, nor, as he said, Byron, could at all have matched Gautier in *kind*: other nations had the equivalent of Musset; Gautier, in his "extreme perfection," was unique. And reaching for Gautier's volumes he began to read a poem. It dealt with old and yellowing portraits in oval frames, lying along the quays of Paris, portraits of beauties faded and violated by time, by dust and specks of mud, yet clasping forever their withered century-old bouquets, a poem nostalgic and fragile in its artful sadness. *J'aime à vous voir en vos cadres ovales*, Flaubert read, slowly and in measured tones, *Portraits jaunis des belles du vieux temps*—a kind of distant echo of all the French poets who had written of vanished snows of yesteryear:

> J'aime à vous voir en vos cadres ovales,
> Portraits jaunis des belles du vieux temps,
> Tenant en main des roses un peu pâles,
> Comme il convient à des fleurs de cent ans.

Le vent d'hiver, en vous touchant la joue,
A fait mourir vos œillets et vos lis,
Vous n'avez plus que des mouches de boue
Et sur les quais vous gisez tout salis.

Il est passé, le doux règne des belles;
La Parabère avec la Pompadour
Ne trouveraient que des sujets rebelles,
Et sous leur tombe est enterré l'amour.

Vous, cependent, vieux portraits qu'on oublie,
Vous respirez vos bouquets sans parfums,
Et souriez avec mélancolie
Au souvenir de vos galants défunts.[1]

I

Flaubert rather loudly declaimed these lines—he used to speak of his "bellow"—but the moment was filled with deep emotion for Henry. There was something extraordinarily tender in the way Flaubert showed his affection for his friend's beautiful verses. It may have been the deep sincerity of the massive Norman, and his strong literary feeling; it may have been also the quality of the poem itself, with its suggestion—to the author of "The Madonna of the Future"—of the enshrined dead beauty, but it struck a

[1] PASTEL

I love to see you in your oval frames,
Yellowing portraits of an antique day,
Ladies who hold pale roses, such frail flames
As glow in a century-old bouquet.

The winds of winter, passing, touch your cheeks,
Making your lilies and carnations freeze,
And fly-specks, where you're laid, or dirty streaks
Of mire defile your resting place, the quays.

Gone is the sweet dominion of the Fair:
Only rebellious subjects hail the Dove
Or serve la Pompadour and la Parabère,
Within whose tomb we have interrëd love.

Yet you remain, old half-forgotten prints
Of belles who breathe the scentless fragrance shed
By withered nosegays, nymphs whose sad smile laments
The vanished gallantries of lovers dead.

(Translated by A. J. M. Smith)

strong chord of response in Henry. He always vividly remembered this moment, when the author of *Madame Bovary* had read to him—to him alone—in the quiet little room in the old Faubourg. He described the scene to his father a few days afterwards; he wrote it into his journal half a dozen years later; and in his essay on Flaubert he devoted an entire page to it. To the elder James he said that Flaubert deemed Gautier unique in his extreme perfection, "and he recited some of his sonnets in a way to make them seem the most beautiful things in the world. Find in especial (in the volume I left at home,) one called *Les Portraits Ovales*."

In his journal he gave another name to the poem, referring to it as *Les Vieux Portraits*. And in his final essay he somewhat ruefully confessed he couldn't recall the title. The poem had been new to him; and since that time, he said, he had never been able to discover it in Gautier's works, "hunt as I will in every volume of its author." This was perhaps a happy thing, he believed, since it caused "Flaubert's own full tone, which was the note of the occasion, to linger the more unquenched. But for the rhyme in fact I could have believed him to be spouting to me something strange and sonorous of his own. The thing really rare would have been to hear him do that—hear him *gueuler*, as he liked to call it."

Henry could not recover the poem because he looked for a title with the word *portraits* in it, whereas the poem is entitled *Pastel*. What he had remembered were phrases from the first and last stanzas. The inveterate reader of James may be tempted to see in these verses some of the sentiment that invests the inspection of the "faded pastels" in *The Sacred Fount*; to be reminded of Jeanne de Vionnet who seems to Lambert Strether "a faint pastel in an oval frame," and to recall also the feelings of Milly Theale, standing before the portrait of the Bronzino in *The Wings of the Dove*—her sense of the lady in the picture, long dead, "handsome in sadness" and "fading with time" in her brocaded and wasted reds.

II

There were other week-day occasions at Flaubert's when they talked alone, and sometimes on Sunday Henry was the first to arrive and had the elderly writer to himself. He considered him "the most interesting man and strongest artist of his circle." Turgenev was involved in the Viardot household and not always available; Flaubert had, Henry felt, "an accessibility to human relations" as well as a conception of courtesy. As for the other writers he met at the house, they were distinctly "not *accueillants*;" they made no overtures of hospitality. In part this was traditional French reserve; in part it was because the younger men were preoccupied with their careers; and like Henry they were among the "received" rather than the receiving.

Of Flaubert's art Henry had already spoken in an essay written for the *Galaxy* before he met him, and he was never to modify his view of it. *Madame Bovary* was a masterpiece, this he recognized. His other works were failures. *Salammbô* was as hard as stone; *L'Éducation Sentimentale* was as cold as death; the *Tentation de St Antoine* seemed to be a patchwork covered with pieces of metal. As for *Bouvard et Pécuchet*, the posthumous novel, it was "puerile"—there was "extreme juvenility" in its main idea of trying to make a fiction out of a "dictionary of accepted ideas." *Madame Bovary* alone had enough emotion to take off the chill of the other works. There was "something ungenerous" in Flaubert's genius, and Henry was to note that in all Flaubert's letters there was no mention of "any beauty but verbal beauty."

He talked of Flaubert one day with Turgenev. The Russian said that Flaubert's great trouble was that he had never known a decent woman. He had passed his life exclusively "*avec des courtisanes et des riens-du-tout.*" Neither of them apparently knew of Flaubert's affair with Louise Colet; that had been long ago; and indeed if Turgenev had known, from some old gossip, he would probably have considered her also a *rien-du-tout*. There is a genuine tone of surprise in James's later review of Flaubert's letters as he comes upon his correspondence with the energetic and opportunistic bluestocking. But in 1876, telling of his talk with the Russian, he writes to William: "In poor old Flaubert there is something almost tragic; his big intellectual temperament, machinery, etc., and vainly colossal attempts to press out the least little drop of *passion.* So much talent, and so much naïveté and honesty, and yet so much dryness and coldness."

Flaubert might have a "big intellectual temperament," but Henry distinctly felt that he himself could "easily—more than easily—see all round him intellectually." This was hardly a boast. It reflected Henry's conviction that Flaubert's superiority lay in his being a "painter of aspects and sensations." As a painter of ideas and moral states he was "insignificant." There was however something human and even "august in a strong man who has not been able completely to express himself." In a word, Flaubert was "cold—and he would have given everything he had to be able to glow."

Henry's final verdict on him, set down in the intimacy of his journal, was that he was of "a powerful, serious, melancholy, manly, deeply corrupted, yet not corrupting nature. He was head and shoulders above the others, the men I saw at his house on Sunday afternoons." Exception made, of course, for Turgenev.

PARISIAN LIFE

THAT winter Henry James moved in a sort of cosmopolitan enclave within Paris—among Russians and Americans—but having only glimpses of the French. He felt himself distinctly an outsider even though he had access, as artist, to the Flaubertian *cénacle*; indeed this made him feel more of an outsider than ever. "The half-dozen charming houses to which it would be pleasant to go of an evening do not open their doors to one," he told his mother. No one appeared to receive in the evenings. The only time people were visible was during the afternoon. Six months later, when summer had come, he could announce to Howells that he was "turning into an old, and very contented Parisian." He felt he had struck roots into the Parisian soil and that they could even grow "tangled and tenacious" there. But he added: "Of pure Parisianism I see nothing." The real Paris remained a painted background to his comings and goings among the Muscovites and the society of Boston and New York that had grouped itself in lavish apartments round the Arc de Triomphe.

I

He was to say, years later, that the French are "the people in the world one may have to go more of the way to meet than to meet any other." This was partly because they stayed closer to home. Anglo-Americans travelled more. He recognized also that the people of England and America had more expensive accommodations for entertainment, and that hospitality in France was more national than international. Yet Henry did obtain limited entry into certain French houses and had brief glimpses—all the more tantalizing—of what he would have liked to know. He might have fancied himself a sort of Eugène de Rastignac, laying siege to Paris, enviously eyeing the great houses in the Faubourg

St Germain, yet unable to penetrate their mysterious existence. For one as curious as Henry and as interested in manners, and one as saturated with Balzac, this must have been a chronic exasperation. Godkin had given him a letter of introduction to the political correspondent of the *Nation*, Auguste Laugel, who received him cordially. The Laugels tried very hard to launch their American protégé, and did provide a series of amusing evenings for him; nevertheless these led to no continuous relationships, and provided no opportunities for forming the kind of friendships to which Henry was accustomed in America. Laugel was a French mining engineer and writer on scientific subjects who regularly described for *Nation* readers the drama of French Republicanism in its struggle with Orléanists and Bonapartists. He had "a deadly melancholy tone and manner which depress and distance one," but he invited Henry often to his home. He had been secretary to the Duc d'Aumale, and Madame Laugel obtained for Henry an invitation to a ducal reception, where the American met members of the Orléans family, all save the Comte de Paris, pretender to the throne. He was much amused by a corpulent Princess of Saxe-Coburg who was rather deaf and chatty, and who gave him "a realizing sense of what princesses are trained to." The experience was promptly written into *The American* in the scene between Christopher Newman and the fat duchess. The Laugels also arranged dinners at which Henry met Ernest Rénan and Émile Montégut, who had acquired distinction as a French critic of American literature. Henry liked Rénan: his talk was "really exquisite for urbanity, fineness and wit—all quite without show-off." Toward Montégut he developed an acute personal dislike, so strong that he could no longer read him; he was "a Frenchman of the intense, unhumorous type," who was always "spinning out his shallow ingeniosities with a complacency to make the angels howl."

He complains constantly of being caught in concentric social circles, but he makes the most of them. Through an American friend he is invited to the salon of the old Marquise de Blocqueville, daughter of one of Napoleon's marshals. She is "a literary dowager" and patroness of Émile Montégut, "a very gracious and caressing woman," whose red house on the Seine opposite the Louvre he evoked years later. "She is a great invalid, very corpulent, never leaves the house and has her head swathed in long veils and laces *à la sultane*—but with the remains of beauty." The French have a habit of not introducing anyone to anyone else, and Henry complains that he wanders about among "a lot of people." He tells his brother he will go again to her Monday at-homes, and "by keeping it up long enough shall perhaps get something out of it."

The trouble with many of these salons is their addiction to music. Henry claimed he had an unmusical ear: and he finds "music at Madame Viardot's, music at Madame de Blocqueville's, music at the Baronne de Hoffmann's, music a couple of nights since at Miss Reid's," and hears assorted divas, tenors, string quartets. At Madame Viardot's "I stood the other night on my legs for three hours (from 11 to 2) in a suffocating room, listening to an interminable fiddling, with the only consolation that Gustave Doré, standing beside me, seemed as bored as myself." When Pauline Viardot sang, however, as she now rarely did, it seemed to him "superb." Henry heard her do a scene from Gluck's *Alceste*, which was "the finest piece of musical declamation, of a grandly tragic sort, that I can conceive." Late in the year at Paul Zhukovsky's he listens from 9 to 2 a.m. to a young pianist playing selections from Wagner's Bayreuth operas, then in their early French vogue, before a small Russian circle. "I enjoyed the circle, but I had an overdose of Wagner, whom Zhukovsky vastly admires."

Henry manages to meet assorted figures in the Parisian world. He dines with the new Minister of Education, William Waddington, who has an American wife; he meets the Duc de Broglie one day at the Longchamps military review, whither he has been piloted by Madame Laugel. Becoming an intimate of the widow and children of the Russian emigré, Nikolai Turgenev, distant relatives of Ivan Sergeyevich, he again encounters Rénan and they have a long talk after dinner. He is introduced to the grandson of Jérome Bonaparte, of the American branch of the family, a "fine-looking stupid man." He encounters John Lemoinne, "a dwarfish man with a glittering eye," the writer for the *Débats*, just elected to the French Academy, and Louis de Loménée, the politician, who regales him with an analysis of the Biblical style of American anti-slavery orators. During another evening he is in a private house where the Minister of the Interior, Louis Buffet, is guest and decides that his "physiognomy expresses the beau ideal of toughness." It is all a parade, a kind of reception line in which Henry shakes hands with figures as they pass. There is French wit and French incisiveness in the air all about him. He remains nevertheless simply one of the audience.

Most remembered of all these ephemeral encounters will be his few visits to a certain house in the Rue du Bac. He has gone there with a letter from Fanny Kemble, and met the eighty-three-year-old Madame Jules Mohl. Her memories go back to Madame Récamier, and to Chateaubriand who died in the very house in which she lives. Madame Mohl was actually Scottish; her maiden name had been Mary Clarke. She had herself conducted one of the last of the Romantic salons. "Imagine a little old woman, with her grey hair in her eyes, precisely like a Skye terrier, a grotesque cap and a shabby black dress. It is hard to imagine her as the quondam rival of Madame Récamier and the intimate friend of the Queen of Holland and other potentates. She was very kind and friendly with me." Out of the windows of her third and fourth floor apartments at 120 Rue du Bac Henry looked upon the formal garden of a school for missionary priests, and watched the young novitiates walking up and down, breviary in hand. Madame Mohl talked of Chateaubriand's death, and of how the eighty-year-old Madame Récamier (at whose bedside she sat after her lover was dead) had said with adorable grace "I don't want to seem pedantic, but I wish for nothing now but virtue." It is to this anecdote that Henry alludes in his "project" of the novel which became *The Ambassadors.* There are subtle autobiographical overtones in the passage in the novel in which Lambert Strether, sitting in a garden next to what had been Madame Mohl's house, has the sense of "names in the air, of ghosts at the windows, of signs and tokens." One ghost at the window was perhaps Henry James himself, who had discovered the sense of

Paris in 1876, as Strether would at the turn of the century—without ever penetrating to the heart of Paris itself.

II

Henry saw little purpose in cultivating "the American village encamped *en plein Paris*," but it cultivated him. He found Mrs Mason there when he arrived; she was on the point of leaving for Rome—"a most comfortable creature, especially for so handsome a woman." Mrs Wister's friend, Mrs Lockwood, passed through the capital and Henry saw much of her. He also renewed acquaintance with and greatly came to like Mrs Charles Strong, of New York, the former Eleanor Fearing, who was to be an expatriate all her life. He had met her in Rome in 1869. Mrs Strong had "a spark of the *feu sacré*, an ability to interest herself and *s'enthouisasmer* which is sincere and pleasing." She was a Catholic convert and he was ultimately to see her as "agreeable, shallow, elaborately and unsympathetically dressed, at once very exacting (of attention) and very appreciative, restless, nervous, melancholy, frivolous, querulous, attractive, irritable, irritating and in spite of her fanatical and ludicrous (in its applications) little religion, quite unable to occupy herself. So she occupies her friends!" He went with her to the opera; he liked to have idle talk with her. But she was of the slightly older, married, or divorced, or widowed type of woman he cultivated. Among the unmarried, Henry met that spring one woman at whom he looked very carefully. By now he seems to have made up his mind that he would never marry; however it is interesting to capture, in one of his letters, his first vision of Henrietta Reubell, whom he was to claim as one of his most devoted friends in the French capital. To William James he described her in April 1876 as being twenty-seven or twenty-eight, "extremely ugly, but with something very frank, intelligent and agreeable about her." He went on: "If I wanted to desire to marry an ugly Parisian-American, with money and *toutes les élégances*, and a very considerable capacity for development if transported into a favouring medium, Miss Reubell would be a very good objective.

But I don't." The words "wanted to desire" indicate the extent of his caution. He had nevertheless entertained the thought. Etta Reubell's home at 42 Avenue Gabriel was to be a cherished foyer in the coming decades; and he was to write to her some of his most entertaining social letters. She was for him the perfect example of the perpetually expatriated American. She was to find her way into *The Ambassadors*; with her bejewelled fingers and hearty laugh, she figures there as Miss Barrace, one of the American sophisticates in Chad Newsome's entourage.

Henry was most at home in the household of the Edward Lee Childes, friends of the Nortons, who sought him out and often entertained him. Mrs Childe was French, the former Blanche de Sortiges, and Henry found their intimate dinners pleasant and sophisticated. Childe, a nephew of General Robert E. Lee, did not interest him very much, but he liked Mrs Childe's alertness and vivacity. "I call in the afternoon and find Mme Lee Childe in black velvet by her fire (she is a very graceful, elegant and clever Frenchwoman) with old decorated counts and generals leaning against the mantelpiece." Henry would like to have a *tête-à-tête* with her, but her fireside is always pre-empted. On one occasion he dines at the Childes' and meets a Mrs Mansfield, an Englishwoman steeped in diplomacy, "and the most extraordinary, clever and entertaining woman I ever met. I can't describe her, but some day I shall clap her into a novel. Trollope, with a finer genius, might have invented her." The Childes themselves suggest, in a number of ways, and with modifications, the Tristrams in *The American* and the Franco-Americans in *The Reverberator*.

III

Perhaps the strangest of his American friendships that winter was Henry's association with Charles Sanders Peirce, the physicist, astronomer and logician, who ultimately laid the foundations upon which William James built his philosophy of pragmatism. An aggressive, "difficult" individual, Peirce was swinging pendulums at the Observatory. He learned from William that Henry was in Paris, called upon him, took him to dinner; and the two presently fell into the habit of meeting at regular intervals. William was much amused, for their temperamental difference was great. He told Henry he must find Peirce an "uncomfortable bedfellow, thorny and spinous." He advised him to treat him like a nettle—grasp firmly, contradict, push hard, make fun of him. This was William's way of dealing with Peirce. Henry used his own methods. He recognized that Peirce, who was four years older than himself, was, in his particular way, a brilliant man with a large exploratory mind. He confessed he did not find him of "thrilling interest," but said he was more gentle and urbane than he had known him to be in Cambridge. They helped each other through certain hours of loneliness.

Peirce described Henry to William as "a splendid fellow," not as fond "of turning over questions" as he was. This, he said, was a manly trait, "but not a philosophic one." Henry would have agreed. He was not interested in splitting logic with the philosopher; however, as a novelist he was much interested in Peirce's sense of dislocation in Paris; his feeling that French scientists treated him indifferently; his tendency to live luxuriously, wear extravagant clothes, employ a secretary, yet lead a life of "insupportable loneliness and sterility." Peirce saw in Paris "not a soul but myself and his secretary."

The scientist read *Roderick Hudson* and declared himself an "extreme admirer" of the book. Apparently this was all he read of Henry's work, for one day many years later—in 1909—he manifested a belated curiosity and wrote to William that "one winter, about forty years ago or less, I used almost every day to dine with your brother Harry and we used to talk a great deal about the novels he meant to write." Had the books ever got themselves written? Would William send him—one at a time—"a specimen of each kind that he writes?" William was not too helpful. He sent Henry's latest novel, *The Golden Bowl*, and told Peirce "I hope you'll be able to finish it!" Henry's final verdict on Peirce had been recorded years before, when he was summarizing his Paris winter in his journal: "I saw a good deal of Charles Peirce that winter—as to whom his being a man of genius reconciled me to much that was intolerable in him."

IV

The French were inaccessible; and Henry had hardly come abroad to pay calls on Americans. He was happiest, therefore, with the cosmopolitan Russians. In addition to being received in the Rue de Douai he became a familiar in the Faubourg St Germain home of Madame Nikolai Turgenev, widow of "the William Lloyd Garrison of Russia," who had died in 1871. Henry found these Turgenevs, mother and grown children, "an oasis of purity and goodness in the midst of this Parisian Babylon." He alludes in his letters to their "literally more than Bostonian virtue," and "a virtue worthy of Cambridge." Ivan Sergeyevich and these remote relatives of his, and "a young man whose acquaintance I have lately made, give me a high idea of the Russian nature—at least in some of its forms." The young man was, as we have seen, the dilettante Zhukovsky, a bearded soft-eyed Russian of Henry's age. They liked each other from the first.

Zhukovsky had the manners of an aristocrat and the ardour of a romantic. Turgenev called him a "naïve epicurean." Orphaned early—he was the child of his poet-father's old age—he had been brought up at the Russian court, dandled by empresses and princesses. His mother was German and he had memorabilia of his father's friendship with Goethe, including some of the German poet's drawings ("awful," said Henry). In his young manhood Paul had lived in Venetian palaces. His large Parisian studio and apartment were filled with Italian treasures. Henry described Zhukovsky as "a most *attachant* creature," although he recognized that he was also "a lightweight and a perfect failure." An amateur painter, he was exhibiting two large canvases that spring in the Salon. Henry studied them and decided that if Paul Zhukovsky was "one of the flowers of civilization" he would also never be anything "but a rather curious and delicate dilettante." Henry appreciated his delicacy and enjoyed his company. "He is much to my taste and we have sworn eternal friendship," he wrote to his sister. "He asks nothing better than to make me acquainted with all sorts of interesting Russians." It was Zhukovsky who told Henry that Turgenev had spoken of him with an appreciation that went almost to the point of *attendrissement*, and in a way that he rarely spoke to him of anyone. Henry was pleased, and repeated this to Quincy Street "at the risk of seeming fatuous." Zhukovsky gossiped freely about the Russian writer and describing his "want of will" said that he couldn't even choose a pair of trousers for himself. Zhukovsky spoke also, however, of Turgenev's "absolute goodness and tenderness." This he said could not be exaggerated. There was a great want of will in Zhukovsky also; but he was "very sweet and *distingué*." The two cosmopolitans—the American and the Russian—knocked about Paris a great deal together that spring.

Henry found the Princess Ourousov, Zhukovsky's friend, extremely attractive. A miniature in the possession of her descendants testifies to her youthful beauty. She had a pleasant face, dark hair, flashing dark eyes, a rather characteristic broad Russian nose. Gide, who met her a decade later, described her as being "*d'une beauté plantureuse*." She was the daughter of the great Russian industrialist, the pottery czar, Maltzov, who had built himself a small private narrow-gauge railway on his vast estates. Marie Maltzov had always moved among aristocrats and she had ended by marrying a prince. The family fortune dwindled however, and she was living "without princely splendour." In later years, in Russia, she was to know Tolstoy; during summers at Berchtesgaden Brahms would play for her; in Paris Maupassant frequented her salon; the young André Gide brought Oscar Wilde to meet her. The spontaneity Gide found in her was there when Henry James knew her, for he spoke of her being "as easy as an old glove." He felt he had laid "the foundations of an intimacy" with her, by which he probably meant nothing more intimate than quiet *tête-à-têtes*, of the kind he enjoyed with Mrs Wister or Mrs Mason. Her only fault, he told Quincy Street, was that "she smokes too much." Through the smoke-haze, however, Henry found a woman "of such liberal understanding and culture that conversation with her is a real pleasure." Nevertheless when the Princess introduced her sister, the Countess Panin, Henry felt that she had been eclipsed. The Countess was "a ravishing young widow, and one of the sweetest, freest, charmingest women I have ever met." Henry never achieved the "intimacy" he sought with these women: they were too much out of Paris and he went to live in London. In later years, however, during his Paris visits, he used to call on Marie Ourousov. Turgenev remained a strong link between them.

His Russian friends, he told his father, "are quite the most (to me) fascinating people one can see; with their personal ease and *désinvolture* and that atmosphere of general culture and curiosity which they owe to having (through their possession of many languages) windows open all round the horizon." They opened windows for Henry too, so that moving among them, and among his compatriots, and gaining his glimpses of the French, the transatlantic visitor found himself abandoning certain Cambridge rigidities, taking life a little less hard, giving himself over to the simple pleasures of genial living.

SILK PURSE AND SOW'S EAR

HENRY JAMES had told John Hay confidently that he would write entertaining letters from Paris for the *New York Tribune* and Hay had taken him at his word. He went to some pains in his first letter, and, since he was fresh upon the scene, made it broad and general; his tone was easy, and he chatted about the obvious: the aspect of Paris to a revisiting American, the pre-Christmas atmosphere, the subjects in the daily headlines. The *Tribune* launched its new correspondent with a laudatory editorial, "Paris Through Fresh Eyes," probably written by Hay. It promised an extended series of dispatches by Henry and spoke of him as "one of the best-equipped Americans who have crossed the Atlantic." "No essayist of recent years," said the *Tribune*, "has shown such powers of delicate and intelligent observation, such refined and wholesome humour, such insight into national traits and characteristics and such a felicitous command of pure and idiomatic English as Mr Henry James." Readers could rely upon his embracing "a rather wide field of incident, observation and criticism."

When Henry read his first letter in print he recognized that it was too general and too long, pitched "in too vague and diffuse a key." He also confessed, when the time came to write a second letter, that "I can think of nothing in life to put into the *Tribune*. It is quite appalling. But I suppose it will come." He took refuge in an exhibition of animal statuary, the decorations of the new opera, the renovation of the Odéon. He knew, however, that this was hardly the intimate Paris-from-the-inside type of letter he had promised Hay. His letter was distinctly Paris-from-the-outside, and this accurately describes the seventeen Parisian letters he wrote for the *Tribune*. Three others were published, one about George Sand and two describing Chartres, Etretat, Rouen and Le Havre, in Henry's familiar travel-style.

Henry had perhaps all-too-readily decided that it was as easy to write for the *Tribune* as it was for the *Nation*, and he discovered soon enough the difference between everyday journalism and the literary journalism at which he was adept in the weeklies and monthlies. It was one thing to review a book, or describe foreign manners and foreign art; it was quite another to furnish incident, observation and criticism in a regular column and to find lively subjects. To be "chatty" about Paris and the Parisians was more than he could do. And he had in reality a contempt for newspapers, which he was to express repeatedly in his correspondence and his fiction. Writing for the *Tribune* not only went against the grain; he was temperamentally unsuited for it.

"Subjects are woefully scarce," he wrote to his mother in January; and to his father, two or three months later, he spoke of "a painful dearth of topics to write about." We have thus the spectacle of a man of James's large imagination unable to imagine subjects for a newspaper—and in a city teeming with them. He could hardly make capital of his private encounters with Turgenev or the Flaubert group; and these were subjects that would have had little interest for the average *Tribune* reader at that time. There still remained all Paris to write about, and a strong resurgent France recovering from the Franco-Prussian war and the Commune. James could and did exploit the theatres, the art-shows, occasional books of general interest, newspaper controversies and the human interest in the effervescent political scene—all of which was his province. The newspaper was not relying upon him for ordinary coverage: the seasoned William H. Huntington took care of that; for political stories it could call on its correspondent, John Paul. James was quite free to deal with whatever struck his fancy. And yet a certain acute helplessness pervades his letters. They are readable when he performs in his characteristic magazine vein; for the rest they are rather forced, and often on the dull side. "I am glad my *Tribune* letters amuse you," he wrote to Howells. "They are most impudently light-weighted, but that was part of the bargain." To his father he wrote: "The vulgarity and repulsiveness of the *Tribune*, whenever I see it, strikes me so violently that I feel tempted to stop my letter." He could not however yield to this temptation: he needed the money.

I

Try as he might, Henry James could never speak in the journalistic voice. It was as if a man, otherwise fluent, suddenly reduced himself to a stutter. The voice we hear in the *Tribune* letters is still that of the artist and the artist-critic. When all else failed him, and his *Tribune* pen lagged, he could fall back upon his aesthetic faculty. He could also fall back on his faithful eyes:

> The huge towers of Notre Dame, rising with their blue-gray tone from the midst of the great mass round which the river divides, the great Arc de Triomphe answering them with equal majesty in the opposite distance, the splendid continuous line of the Louvre between, and over it all the charming colouring of Paris on certain days—the brightness, the pearly grays, the flicker of light, the good taste, as it were, of the atmosphere—all this is an entertainment which even custom does not stale.

"Entertainment" doubtless for the mind and imagination of Henry James, but what concern, we may wonder, did the average daily newspaper reader have with "the good taste, as it were, of the atmosphere?" This is the painter-observer at work with blue-grey, pearl-grey and flickering light, but it is distinctly not newspaper reportage; nor was the wandering sentence suitable for journalism. When we travel with Henry to Versailles, where the French Assembly is sitting, we find him abridging his attendance

> in that musty little red and gold playhouse in which the Assembly sits, for the sake of wandering about the terraces and avenues of the park. The day had that soft, humid mildness which, in spite of the inveteracy with which you are assured here that every biting blast is "exceptional," and which consequently piles up your accumulated conviction that it is the rule—is really the keynote, the *fonds*, as they say, of the Paris winter weather.

We can indeed imagine the copyreader struggling with these clauses within clauses, the quoted "exceptional," the *fonds* of the matter.

If the *Tribune* reader was willing to accept the literary tone, the unorthodox sentences, the substitution of colour and atmosphere for hard fact, he could find his rewards, over and above the descriptive felicities. He could tour the salon of 1876 with the patience and vigour required in visiting this annual French display of miles of painted canvas; he could encounter works by Taine, Rénan, Zola, Sainte-Beuve, carefully reviewed and analysed; he could catch Henry James Jr at a ball watching Johann Strauss conduct his waltzes; and on another occasion he would be present to hear Giuseppe Verdi lead his Requiem. In these articles we walk through the foyer of the new opera with Henry and examine the decorations and the gilt; we muse over the traceries and carvings at Chartres; or we travel down the Seine to Rouen looking at scenery and finally relax on the beach at Etretat, when summer takes us away from the capital. Had James been more of a journalist and less of a connoisseur, he might have found more to say when he made his pilgrimage to the Durand-Ruel gallery and examined the exhibition of the early Impressionists which was to pass into history. "I have found it decidedly interesting," he tells us.

> But the effect of it was to make me think better than ever of all the good old rules which decree that beauty is beauty and ugliness ugliness, and warn us off from the sophistications of satiety . . . the "Impressionist" doctrines strike me as incompatible, in an artist's mind, with the existence of first-rate talent. To embrace them you must be provided with a plentiful absence of imagination.

And he went on to say that Impressionists "abjure virtue altogether, and declare that a subject which has been crudely chosen shall be loosely treated. They send detail to the dogs and concentrate themselves on general expression. Some of their generalizations of expression are in a high degree curious."

Allowing for the ampler view which we have, and the triumph of Impressionism since that time, we can see in this account Henry's failure as a reporter. He might quarrel aesthetically with Impressionism, as all the committed "representationalists" did; he nevertheless could have brought his power of description to let his American audience see with him exactly what the paintings looked like. The Impressionists may have failed, in this instance, to impress; what James failed to see was that they were "good copy." He could for instance make such copy of extremes of representation, as when he writes of Meissonier's minutely-depicted battle of Eylau:

> The best thing, say, is a certain cuirassier, and in the cuirassier the best thing is his clothes, and in his clothes the best thing is his leather straps, and in his leather straps the best thing is the buckles. This is the kind of work you find yourself performing over the picture; you may go on indefinitely.

A writer who could characterize a painting of this sort had in his pen the gift to say more than that the Impressionists were "curious." William James's comments reflected his awareness of Henry's problem: "Your first letter was a very good beginning, though one sees that you are to a certain extent fishing for the proper tone and level." Again: "Keep watch and ward lest in your style you become too Parisian and lose your hold on the pulse of the great American public, to which after all you must pander for support."

Had Henry ever obtained such a hold? A search of the columns of the *Tribune* shows that his letters were passively received. The correspondence columns of the paper contain letters of praise for most of the *Tribune's* other correspondents, but no praise and little blame for James. A single derogatory letter may be found in the issue of 22 January 1876, complaining that Henry has harshly misjudged Barye's animal sculptures. But when later Houssaye resumed his letters, a group of readers wrote to commend his work, and expressed the hope that he would be heard from often. And Whitelaw Reid was to comment that not only were the *Tribune's* readers silent, but other journals, which often quoted the newspaper, seemed oblivious of Henry's letters.

This explains Henry's formulation of his *Tribune* experience in his journal six years later. "I wrote letters to the New York *Tribune*, of which, though they were poor stuff, I may say that they were too good for the purpose (of course they didn't succeed)." A much truer statement was embodied in a later tale in which the heroine ruefully confesses that she has agreed to write some London letters for a provincial paper; "I can't do them—I don't know how, and don't want to. I do them wrong, and the people want such trash. Of course they'll sack me."

II

The *Tribune* did not "sack" Henry; but ever after he was to speak as if it did. By midsummer, when he had written twenty letters and received the tidy sum of $400—and knew that he had been as well paid for his work as for anything he had done for the *Nation*—he asked Whitelaw Reid for more money. What he suggested was that he receive half as much again, $30 per letter. He apparently felt that his trial-period with the paper was at an end; perhaps also he knew that Houssaye had been paid more. Certainly the effort he was obliged to put into any one of these letters must have been out of proportion to the amount he received. Reid's reply, at any rate, was unexpected. The publisher offered a compromise. He explained that James's subjects were "too remote from popular interests" and that it was possible to overestimate the "literary culture" of the readers. He reminded Henry that newspaper-readers are people in a hurry who want brevity, variety and topics of sustained interest. They were more likely to read a letter filling one column than a letter filling two (as Henry's had invariably done). He therefore proposed that Henry alter the character of his letters: make them shorter and "newsier," and that he space them more widely—particularly since the United States was entering upon an election year. In Reid's economy this did meet Henry's request for a rise; he was offering to pay the same amount of money for less copy. "You must not imagine," Reid wrote, "that any of us have failed to appreciate the admirable work you have done for us." He added, however, the forthright statement: "The difficulty has sometimes been not that it was too good, but that it was magazine rather than newspaper work."

This was wholly reasonable. Reid was telling Henry that however admirable literary and aesthetic journalism might be, it required a certain process of transformation to be acceptable in the columns of a newspaper. He touched, nevertheless, James's professional sensitivity; and his concluding sentence had a peculiar and painful force: freely translated he was telling James that his work might have been good for the magazines but it was decidedly not good for the paper. Henry was left defenceless. He could hardly try to convince Reid that he had chosen topics of wide interest; he knew all too well how few topics he had been able to scrape up. He knew also that he could not lay claim to having written good journalism or argue that the *Tribune* should publish his work even when it was magazine-work. The terms also offered no ground for negotiation. If he was to receive the same amount for less work, this "less" had also to undergo a qualitative change—be more "newsy," informative, gossipy. A literary hack, a professional journalist, a man accustomed to "tailoring" copy to a given medium, might be addressed in this manner and would not think twice about it. But was it fair to ask this of a literary artist who placed at the service of a newspaper his style, his reputation and his name? Reid could take no other view. James's dedication to his art determined his. The pen which answered the publisher was more incisive than it had ever been in the columns of the *Tribune*.

James began mildly enough. He recognized that his letters were considered not "the right sort of thing for a newspaper;" he had been expecting to hear as much from the publisher. He could readily imagine that the general reader would have little time for him during the excitement of an election year. He was prepared to grant the magazine-quality of his writing. He thereupon selected the one point on which he might counter-attack; since it is clear from what followed that he regarded Reid's letter as an attack. This was Reid's request that he incorporate more news. "I know the sort of letter you mean," he wrote; "it is doubtless the proper sort of thing for the *Tribune* to have. But I can't produce it—I don't know how and I couldn't learn how." He added "it would be poor economy for me to try and become 'newsy' and gossipy. I am too finical a writer and I should be constantly becoming more 'literary' than is desirable." Thus far he spoke with genuine honesty and recognition of his limitations. The next sentence revealed his deeper feelings:

If my letters have been "too good" I am honestly afraid that they are the poorest I can do, especially for the money! I had better, therefore, suspend them altogether. I have enjoyed writing them, however, and if the *Tribune* has not been the better for them I hope it hasn't been too much the worse.

To his father he wrote that Reid "had stopped off my letters to the *Tribune*—practically at last—by demanding that they should be of a flimsier sort. I thought in all conscience they had been flimsy enough. I am a little sorry to stop, but much glad." The episode was to haunt him for years. He was ultimately to make a short story of it, "The Next Time"—"the idea of the poor man, the artist, the man of letters, who all his life is trying—if only to get a living—to do something *vulgar*, to take the measure of the huge, flat foot of the public . . . to make, as it were, a sow's ear out of a silk purse."

What Henry forgot, when he came to make an artistic picture of the creator's dilemma, was that his own had not been comparable. He had simply ventured into an alien medium. The magazine world was quite prepared to accept him and he could work for it in comparative freedom. He did say to Quincy Street shortly after resigning his journalistic chore: "You needn't commiserate me for my *Tribune* cessation; I don't miss the *Tribune* at all; I can use my material to better advantage." He was to demonstrate the truth of this again and again.

THE AMERICAN

HENRY JAMES'S financial situation on reaching the French capital had been as follows: he had drawn upon his father's letter of credit in London to pay for new clothes and for his installation in the Rue de Luxembourg; he had certain miscellaneous sums outstanding from the *Nation* and the *Galaxy*, and had arranged to have them paid directly to him, instead of to Quincy Street: royalties from the book-publication of *Roderick* (it was published in Boston on 20 November 1875) were to be sent to his father to reimburse him for the sums owing him. He was committed to start another novel for Howells, but a certain lapse of time was necessary following the serialization of *Roderick*, just ending. He was, therefore, short of funds. His fortnightly letters to the *Tribune* did not even cover his rent; his fugitive reviewing and other writings would barely feed him. He needed about $150 a month; and the only practical course open to him was to start a new serial, as quickly as possible, in some other magazine. He would have to explain to Howells that he could not afford to wait. Having already had tentative talks with the editors of the *Galaxy*, he wrote to them from Paris on 1 December 1875 that he proposed "to take for granted, as soon as I can, that you will be ready to publish, on receipt of them, the opening chapters of a novel." It was then that he announced he had begun *The American* sooner than expected. He planned to complete it in nine months and his price would be $150 an instalment. He would thus earn in three-quarters of a year more than *Roderick* had brought in during a twelvemonth.

He learned presently that *Transatlantic Sketches* had yielded a royalty balance of $200 at the end of the year, and this money had gone directly to Quincy Street. On January 24 he received a letter from his mother accusing him of extravagance, and informing him that his autumn draft on his father had been "excessive and inconvenient." Henry replied at once. Her words had given him "a wretched hour." It was true, he said, that he had drawn more largely, and at shorter intervals "than could be at all agreeable to you." Nevertheless this had been a necessity of his situation. "I have hardly had my expense off my mind an hour since I have been abroad, and I had arranged my life here, in Paris, well within my means." Paris was not cheap; but it was not as dear as New York and "once under way, as I am now, I am in for nothing that I cannot face." He had not known, he said, that his father's resources were curtailed, or he would have been "doubly and triply careful." He said he was certain that by the end of the year he would have a balance in his favour "and I shall be able to refund and compensate inconveniences." He added: "Banish from your mind your visions of my extravagance. I am living simply as well as physical well-being and decent mental cheerfulness seem, in lonely life, to demand."

The effect of his mother's letter was, for the moment, to undermine Henry's sense of security. He could draw no further on his father; and he had to find ways to keep his pen busy. This may explain his suddenly developing a ten-day headache, not as violent or feverish as the one he had had in Florence when William was with him, but sufficiently uncomfortable to keep him at home. He had to cancel his plans to attend a fancy-dress party at the Viardots', and Turgenev came the morning after, to comfort Henry and describe to him the fun he had missed.

The *Galaxy* did not reply, and Henry stopped writing *The American.* Instead he hastily wrote two tales in his old, pre-*Roderick Hudson* vein—"Crawford's Consistency" and "The Ghostly Rental." He deemed them inferior and sold them to *Scribner's* for $300. Meanwhile Howells wrote to say he would take Henry's serial whenever he was ready to let him have it. Henry ruefully replied: "I took for granted that the *Atlantic* would begin nothing till June or July, and it was the money question solely that had to determine me." *The American*, he said, was the only subject "mature enough in my mind to use immediately. It has in fact been used somewhat prematurely; and I hope you find enough faults in it to console you for not having it in the *Atlantic*." He said, however, that if the *Galaxy* continued to ignore him, or if its editors were not satisfied, he would ask them to forward the first instalment to Howells. His price remained $150 a month for nine instalments.

Howells was determined to keep Henry in the *Atlantic*, and he lost no time in offering to take *The American* if the *Galaxy* did not want it. Henry, on his side, laid down an ultimatum: "If you are unable to begin *The American* at the latest in the May *Galaxy*, I must forgo the pleasure of having the story appear in the magazine. I decided it should be plain that this and the price I fixed per number ($150) were the only terms on which I offered it." He repeated: "These then are my terms—$150 a number—to commence in *May*—and failing this to send the copy instantly to Cambridge." The editors of the *Galaxy* obliged. Howells scheduled the serial to begin in the *Atlantic's* June issue.

I

The American was a firm, rapid stride on the part of Henry James into full literary maturity. The endless debate of *Roderick Hudson* gave way now to determination and action. Henry had found it necessary in his first large novel to create two characters to express his full intention; he was able now to make of these one substantial individual who embodied the active-creative part of himself as well as the still-lingering Cambridge cautionary elements. It took Rowland Mallet, playing God, to complete Roderick; Christopher Newman also wants to play God—to the whole world—but in the process he stands aggressively planted on his own two feet. The novelist's divided and conflicting selves had come together: unified, he could launch them in the Old World, in Paris, where he himself was now launched.

He had told Howells he was writing the novel "prematurely." What he meant by this was that he was uncomfortably close to his materials; there was an almost excessive flow of daily incident from life into his book without prior assimilation of it. The consequence was that this novel, of all James's works, is written, as might be said, "off the top of his head." Yet he had long nourished the image of Christopher Newman. He had thought of him, one day, while riding in an American horse-car, as the figure of a robust American confronting an aristocratic society. The point of his story would be that this American "should suffer at the hands of persons pretending to represent the highest possible civilization and to be of an order in every way superior to his own." The old idea could now be brought together with Henry's new environment. He would write a novel about an American businessman and his siege of Paris, of that Faubourg St Germain about which Henry had read in Balzac, and of which he himself was having only a passing glimpse. He speaks in the novel of "those grey and silent streets of the Faubourg whose houses present to the outer world a face as impassive and as suggestive of the concentration of privacy as the blank walls of Eastern seraglios." The streets he had in mind were the Rue de l'Université, where much of the novel's action takes place, the Rue de Lille and the Rue de Bellechasse, where in later years he was often to call on the Daudets. There was also the Rue du Faubourg St Germain, and the short Rues Monsieur and Madame. Other streets a little farther out of the "*old* residential and noble parts of the city" were the Rue St Dominique, the Rue de Grenelle and the Rue de Varenne, where long after he was to join the group of "sarabandists," as he called them, frequenting the home of Edith Wharton. In Henry's time there were a great many fine old *hôtels* in these streets, with their wide gates and coachyards such as may still be seen in some quarters of Paris. Henry had hoped that some of these gates would swing open for him; he would have liked to visit the Balzacian scenes. His American, Christopher Newman, however, has a much higher hope—that of marrying into one of the Faubourg's old aristocratic families. He reflects, in a measure, some of Henry's frustration at not achieving entrance into this world which Eugène de Rastignac had conquered and in which, through his saturated reading of French novels, Henry felt himself, in his imagination, to be initiate. The result is that the Faubourg which Henry creates is in part the Faubourg of literature, rather than that of life; on it he superimposes the few shreds of fact and the glimpses he himself had had during the reception at the Duc d'Aumale's and his meeting with the Orléanist princess. These episodes would be converted into the great party in the house of the Bellegardes.

Newman is thus an image of Henry's Parisian life of action, while at the same time being a mordant portrait of an American—a portrait indeed so rich in national ambiguities that several generations of readers have seen him largely as an expansive generous warm-hearted hero without sufficiently noticing that he embodies also everything that Henry disliked in the United States. Newman's qualities show the American character in all its forthrightness and innocence as well as in its predatory aspects. Books written in recent years about "the quiet American," "the nice American" and "the ugly American" represent facets of James's hero. The Californian was in some respects "quiet," and his author even claimed for him a certain "shyness," which is nowhere present in the book. He was "nice" in many ways. But there was in him a strong and vulgar streak of materialistic self-satisfaction which Henry had understood from the first and to which many American readers preferred to close their eyes. Constance Rourke, in a brilliant essay on the humour in the book, long ago pointed to the way in which James achieved a remarkable synthesis of an American "type:" his naïveté, his boastfulness, his impatience with cant; but there is also his total failure to grasp deeper human values. Americans reading this book are often apt to overlook that side of Newman which Charles Dudley Warner noticed, when it was still appearing in the *Atlantic Monthly*, and about which he wrote to Julian Hawthorne: "It seems to me the cleverest thing James ever did; perhaps it is too clever. He actually makes us believe it possible to marry a Californian boor to a Bellegarde, and then he cruelly breaks the match."

"Boor" may be too strong a word, but the boorishness in Newman resides not in his pretensions—decidedly superficial—to cultivate art or architecture; it is the side of him which is at once pride in being a "self-made" man and in his crass unawareness that there are things in this world which cannot be bought. Little phrases and occasional sentences throughout the book tell us these things: Henry James however has handled his character so adroitly and placed him so distinctly in the position of an individual wronged and thwarted, that they are not sufficiently noticed. The very description of his protagonist reveals this. Newman has "an eye in which innocence and experience were singularly blended." It is "frigid and yet friendly, frank yet cautious, shrewd yet credulous, positive yet sceptical, confident yet shy, extremely intelligent and extremely good-humoured." There is also "something vaguely defiant in its concessions, and something profoundly reassuring in its reserve." Newman would seem to be that future paradox in the civilized world: the American who is hospitable to life's chances, but who is "committed to nothing in particular" save his own incredible self-assurance.

Christopher Newman begins with the belief that "Europe was made for him, and not he for Europe." He has for his standard "the ideal of one's own good-humoured prosperity." His "specialty" has been "to make the largest possible fortune in the shortest possible time." When the Marquise de Bellegarde says that she is a "proud and meddlesome old woman" his only answer can be "Well, I am very rich." He has made his pile of money, and what he dreams of is a wife; "there must be a beautiful woman perched on the pile, like a statue on a monument." She has, indeed, to be "the best article on the market." Newman is not often embarrassed, for "his unconscious *sang-froid* was boundless." He has "not only a dislike, but a sort of moral mistrust, of uncomfortable thoughts." If he avoids mental discomfort, however, he has no real sense of physical comfort. He may have "a relish for luxury and splendour," yet he "scarcely knew a hard chair from a soft." He has as a prime conviction "that a man's life should be easy" and it is the ease of one who has had a continent to conquer, who has lost and made fortunes in leather, washtubs, copper. At the same time he possesses that morbid fear of idleness which had coloured Henry's days in Cambridge. "Elegant leisure comes hard," he says. He confesses also to never having had "time to feel things."

He does not wave the Stars and Stripes belligerently. However with his wealth he carries the solid belief that his homeland is "the greatest country in the world" and that Americans "could put all Europe in their breeches pocket." Americans, Newman remarks (and it is one of Henry's slyest digs at his erstwhile home), who speak ill of their country "ought to be carried home in irons and compelled to live in Boston." And he adds that "this, for Newman, was putting it very vindictively." When he is told that he has "a sort of air" of being thoroughly at home in the world he ascribes this to the privilege of being an American citizen. "That sets a man up." And what lets a man down, he comes to discover, is being thwarted. Even though he is an American, he cannot arrange life entirely on his terms, or according to his values. "He had a burning, tingling sense of personal outrage. He had never in his life received so absolute a check"—this when the aristocratic family changes its mind. It cannot swallow a commercial American as a son-in-law. Newman finds the sensation of defeat intolerable.

He is never more American than in his belief that "energy and ingenuity can arrange everything," and that a willing American can learn anything. When Newman remarks that the Bellegarde house in the Faubourg is "curious," Valentin asks him whether he is interested in architecture. He replies with a typical statistic that he had visited four hundred and seventy churches during his summer's travel. "Perhaps," Valentin responds, "you are interested in theology."

"You are the great Western Barbarian," he is told, "stepping forth in his innocence and might, gazing a while at this poor effete Old World and then swooping down on it." This is one side of Newman, a side thoroughly dissimulated, however, behind the energy, geniality and "drive" with which he moves through the book, impervious to all save his own anchored dollars and the sense they give him that he can do as he pleases. The novel is a story of an American who discovers in the end that he simply can't.

II

This was the thin ice on which James skated—the thin ice of American national sensitivity—and his performance in the novel, in spite of all the fustian and melodrama, is brilliant. Even though he sketches an innocent Western Barbarian, he shows us also the candour of his innocence and the courage of his ignorance. The central irony of the book is that Newman has not been corrupted by his gold; he is still one of "nature's noblemen" and he can, in the end, be as moral and therefore as noble as the old corrupt Europeans. The truth is that in her own way the Marquise de Bellegarde is simply a European Christopher Newman; she sits upon her aristocratic sanctity with the same tough possessiveness and assurance that Newman sits on his pile of dollars. In the struggle between the two, it is Newman who emerges the good Christian. The woman he loves, or rather prizes, and wishes to take possession of as if she were a railroad or a mine, has immured herself in a convent in a street named the Rue d'Enfer. In this street Newman once again stands before a wall that bars his way, a wall "pale, dead, discoloured." He goes to Notre Dame; and sitting there he hears "far-away bells chiming off, at long intervals, to the rest of the world," [1] and decides that revenge isn't "his game." Critics have spoken of this splendid scene as an act of "renunciation." Newman merely recognizes the realities before him. He could take his revenge, but he will not regain Claire de Cintré. And because the Bellegardes have been cruel to him is no reason for him now to be cruel to them. A good American, a shrewd business man, does not indulge in waste effort.

It is a good ending to the story, and it does impart to Newman an aura of nobility. The original readers of the novel did not experience this. They felt as frustrated as Newman; they had hoped for a happy ending; they had read the *Atlantic* instalments from month to month, in the fond belief that their author would give Newman the prize. Howells pleaded with him to do so; Lizzie Boott, on behalf of herself and Alice Bartlett, asked for the happiness of seeing Newman married. On the other hand Fanny Kemble, in the serenity of her old age, and speaking out of her transatlantic experience, expressed a fear that he should put the marriage through. "*Voyons*," Henry wrote to Howells,

[1] Into his revision of this passage many years later Henry infused more poetry, speaking of "far-away bells chiming off into space at long intervals, the big bronze syllables of the Word."

"they would have been an impossible couple." And he went on to argue that they would have had no place to live: Claire de Cintré would have hated New York, and Newman could not dwell in France. Leaving out Asia and Africa, there would be "nothing left but a farm out West." Newman was confronted by an insuperable difficulty from which the only issue, as far as Henry could see, was forfeiture. The image he chose was singularly apropos: it described the barriers of the Faubourg and the Rue d'Enfer: "We are each the product of circumstances and there are tall stone walls which fatally divide us. I have written the story from Newman's side of the wall, and I understand so well how Madame de Cintré couldn't really scramble over from *her* side! If I had represented her as doing so, I should have made a prettier ending, certainly; but I should have felt as if I were throwing a rather vulgar sop to readers who don't really know the world and who don't measure the merit of a novel by its correspondence to the same." In replying to Lizzie Boot the also argued that Claire wasn't really in love with Newman and "that in putting it into Newman's power to forgive and contemptuously 'let off' the haughty Bellegardes, I was doing quite the most dramatic and inspiring thing." He reminded Lizzie: "I am a realist."

This is the fundamental point. In telling Howells that his unhappy ending corresponded to life, and in insisting that he was a realist, Henry James overlooked the essential fact that he had written a romantic novel. His persons were real enough; their backgrounds were real; but the story of what happened to them moved across that borderland of the actual and the imaginary which Hawthorne liked to celebrate—although Hawthorne's "imaginary" often went as far as the supernatural. Henry's resided simply in the melodrama of his plot, that element of the arbitrary in his situation which he endowed with plausibility, but which, on the whole, was quite as impossible as any melodrama can be when it is closely scrutinized. Having aroused the reader's sympathies on Newman's behalf, and having made the reader endure the death of the charming Valentin, Henry continued to turn the bright sunshine of the book into depressing gloom by locking up Claire in a convent and crushing Newman in an unhappy ending no more "real" than would have been a happy one. It was not so much a question of throwing a sop to his readers as making the book true to itself; given the book's initial character, its ending was false. Henry was to recognize this in later years; he did substitute a happy ending when he dramatized the novel; and in his late preface he made the romanticism of the book his greatest plea for the reader's acceptance of its improbabilities. He recognized that the Bellegardes "would positively have jumped at my rich and easy American" and not have minded any drawbacks; moreover there were "few drawbacks to mind."

This being the case, why did Henry insist on breaking off the marriage instead of seeking means to unite his lovers—as lovers usually are united in romantic novels. This was always to be one of his problems; and we may speculate that having ruled out marriage for himself he found it genuinely difficult to offer it to those of his heroes with whom he was in some way identified. The marriage tie, to Henry's vision, was a tie which enslaved: and women represented a threat to man's sovereignty. They were lovely creatures to be admired, to meet in drawing-rooms and have a *tête-à-tête* with in some quiet corner; one could ride with them in the Campagna—all this was possible, and nothing more. To accept them as mates was to court the disaster symbolized by Roderick's fate. Henry's tales of the artist-life invariably contain the admonition that marriage could only be a burden to the creator, a distraction, a form of servitude fatal to art. Identified with Newman as an active and independent individual, Henry shut up Claire de Cintré in the convent as he shut women away from himself. And in endowing Claire with weakness and inconstancy he underlined his sense of women's fickleness as well as his own fear of them. One of the pot-boilers written for *Scribner's* during the period when he was waiting for an answer from the *Galaxy* shows the extent to which Henry was pondering this question. In the tale, "Crawford's Consistency," the genial hero, Crawford, like Newman, falls in love with a young woman, strongly in the clutches of her family, who at first accept him and then turn him down. The action in this instance is perhaps genuinely irrational and inconsistent: the Bellegardes, after all, offered good reasons for their repudiation of the match. Crawford, on the rebound, marries a common woman who ends by ruining his life and ill-treats him to the point of pushing him down some steps and crippling him. This crude story, based on an anecdote told Henry by his father, reflected an old and tried theme in his tales—from the very first one written when he was turning twenty. It embodies his two visions of woman: the young and the unattainable; or the cruel and the destructive who reverses rôles with the husband and in this instance wields her strength to the point of physical violence.

Bernard Shaw was to say to Henry years later that an author can give victory to one side as easily as to another; this was a truth in Shaw's didactic theory of art which hardly fitted the aesthetic world of Henry James. Certainly it did not apply to tragedy, where the inexorable course of events admits of only one solution. In *The American* Henry James decidedly did have the choice: and in his strong feeling that such a choice did not exist, he revealed his commitment to the only solution he could envisage.

III

It is clear that Henry realized only in retrospect that *The American*, for all its attention to the real, was a form of the romantic. Nor, apparently, was he aware that, for all his seriousness, he was writing a high comedy. "I suspect it is the tragedies in life that arrest my attention, more than the other things, and say more to my imagination," he wrote to Howells even while he was writing his monthly instalment of the comic chapters of *The American.* To be sure, anyone reading the earlier tales of James's, in which he dealt with American adventurers in Europe and their impassioned brooding as they proclaimed their disinherited state, would hardly have discerned in them the writer of comedy. For one who felt himself to have this penchant for the tragedies of life, Henry managed to write an amazing number of successful high comedies during the next few years: upon them, indeed, he built his greatest fame. In *The American* Henry for the first time revealed to the full the two genuinely original elements in his work that were to constitute his claim to renown during the first half of his writing life: his grasp of the contrasts in manners between America and Europe, and his subtle vein of humour, as original as any in the nineteenth century. Certain critics recognized this as soon as they read his new novel. "Among American story-writers," said the reviewer of the *Globe*, a newspaper published in the city to which Newman would have confined recalcitrant Americans, "Henry James stands alone—imitating no one, and, as yet, having no imitators." This was completely true. Earlier writers had barely sketched his American-European theme; and none had seen the humour in it. Indeed Henry himself was not yet fully aware of all that he carried of it in his head. What was discernible in *The American* was the sureness and lightness of his touch. To grasp his vividness and humour one must read the unrevised version of the novel, that version which readers of the *Atlantic* had from month to month and which, with very little change, was issued in volume form in 1877. The later version, systematically and exhaustively revised in 1905 for the New York Edition, is almost another book—perhaps a better one, in terms of structure and style, but it lacks the pristine qualities, the visual sharpness and the intensity with which Henry, feeling himself as good as the Europeans, wrote this tale in a Paris that kept him at arm's length.

The touch of comedy is present on almost every page—save those which James gives over to unutterable melodramatic gloom. Even when he is describing the death of Valentin, however, he is unable to resist the comic delineation of the aristocrats round the deathbed: and there is even buried humour, for one of them hands Newman a volume of Faublas, which we may be certain was known to few of the *Atlantic* readers—*Les Amours du Chevalier de Faublas*, an ancient frivolous novel of seductions and *amours* that would have made the strait-laced American shudder. James himself felt the allusion recondite; in his revised version he substituted Choderlos de Laclos' *Les Liaisons Dangereuses*, which served the purpose equally well.

Henry's scenes between Newman and the aristocrats are nearly always on a double plane of comedy: the exchange of wit is constant, and quite often it contains also an element of mockery of which Newman is unaware. Thus when Newman offers a recital of his life to the Bellegardes and tells them of his sisters' early marriages, he mentions that one of them had made a match with the owner of the largest india-rubber house in the west. "Ah," observes the Marquise, "you make houses also of india rubber." And young Madame de Bellegarde takes up the cue: "You can stretch them as your family increases." Newman finds this hilarious, wholly unaware that between the lines they are laughing at him. This is the kind of wit Oscar Wilde was to put successfully on the stage. The fat duchess asks Newman whether it isn't true that he has founded an American city and would be richer still "if you didn't grant lands and houses free of rent to all newcomers who'll pledge themselves never to smoke cigars." This concept of the marriage of feudalism with puritanism is but one of the ironic ways in which James keeps the play of comedy constant. Or simply the casual remark of the Marquise de Bellegarde, when she first meets Newman: "You're an American. I've seen several Americans." To which Newman archly replies, "There are several in Paris." And not least the charming touch of old M. Rochefidèle, who has seen his American long ago, "Almost the first person I ever saw—to notice him—was an American." Newman learns it was "the great Dr. Franklin."

This is the comedy which flows easily from the characters and from the situation in which Henry placed them. The dialogue throughout the book is vivid and lively. If Newman himself proves he can indulge in give and take, it is only to make himself more pleasing to the grand and the mighty of the Faubourg. The Marquis does concede he is polite, the Duchess finds him very amusing. He is guilty of one serious error and it is his undoing—when at his engagement party he asks the Marquise to parade with him among the guests, as if to give him the *cachet* he lacks. She does up to a point, but she reaches a moment when she has to say to him "This is enough, sir." His failure in tact has been complete. Advertising and salesmanship, so to speak, have overcome shrewdness and caution. From this point Newman's good fortune goes into decline.

IV

Roderick Hudson had represented Henry's final dialogue with Quincy Street, a last tug at the silver cord. He had made his choice, and his story of Christopher Newman was symbolic of his own stepping-forth into the world—as a new man. But the vivid personalities of Quincy Street, the conflict of its strong egos, remained. The rivalry with William emerges in *The American*, no longer in the complaining terms of the Cambridge time, but simply as a hard fact of life. The unpleasant Marquis de Bellegarde, who is fifteen years senior to his brother Valentin (as William was fifteen months older than Henry), represents one extreme of old feeling; the other is the portrait of the American clergyman Newman encounters during his travels. And here, at last, William recognized himself. "Your second instalment of *The American* is prime," he wrote. "The morbid little clergyman is worthy of Ivan Sergeyevich. I was not a little amused to find some of my own attributes in him—I think you found my 'moral reaction' excessive when I was abroad."

By the same token, the second son, Valentin, in this version of Henry's familial experience, is charming, ineffectual and doomed. Dominating the book is the matriarchal old Marquise, the archetypal mother-figure of all Henry's work, in whose hands husbands are crushed or robbed of their manhood, or—as in this instance—actually murdered. The melodrama harks back to James's first blood-and-thunder tales.

The book's reception in America was mixed. It was, however, read more attentively, and aroused more discussion, than anything James had done before. The character of Newman was generally liked, although some reviewers felt Henry might have found a nicer American to oppose to the aristocrats; and Henry's friend T. S. Perry was not even sure that Newman had made an honest fortune; he wondered "which side of the market he operated upon." The style, the technique, the narration were universally praised. The strongest fire of the critics was reserved for the plot: the failure to provide a happy ending, they argued, was inconsistent with what the story had prepared them for: and certain critics again significantly saw Henry's detached and "cold-blooded" attitude towards his personages. This might be "realism," yet it revealed a critic, an analyst, "rather than the sharer of strong feeling." The originality of James's international theme was recognized, and nearly all the critics were prepared to consider the novel an important contribution to American literature. They were not yet prepared however—and this they said—to place Henry beside Hawthorne, or Trollope, or Dickens—or for that matter George Eliot.

IN THE PROVINCES

HOWELLS liked *The American* and decided that he would spread it through twelve monthly issues of the *Atlantic* instead of nine. Henry agreed to take the same price for the twelve as he had asked for the nine, since the amount of copy he had to produce was unchanged. This would yield him $1340. Henry's livelihood was assured until the following year.

Spring came, the chestnuts bloomed, and the soft warm days enabled Henry to loiter in the cafés when his writing was done. Even as he worked at his instalments of *The American* he had the feeling of "the life of the splendid city playing up in it like a flashing fountain in a marble basin." Everything in his environment could be grist to his mill. There was a little joke he heard (and repeated in his *Tribune* correspondence), that of the hard-working maidservant who saved up thirty crowns to give herself a dowry, and then was asked why she had married a hunchback. "What sort of husband can one get for thirty crowns?" she replied. The joke emerges in the pages of *The American* when Noémie Nioche asks Newman: "What sort of a husband can you get for 12,000 francs?" His warm friendship with Paul Zhukovsky is reflected in the friendship between Newman and Valentin: it has the same quality of camaraderie. And one day a distraught American girl knocked at Henry's door to inform him that she had read *Roderick Hudson*, and to beseech his help. Would he intercede in a duel about to be fought over her between an American and an Englishman? Whatever vision Henry may have had of his pacific self trying to stop a flourish of pistols and swords was dissipated by the fact that the rivals could not wait on romantic formalities. In traditional Anglo-American fashion, they slugged it out. And so probably the more fatal duel in *The American* had its genesis in life as well as in literature.

I

The time had come to say farewells. It was May. The Princess Ourousov had left. Turgenev was leaving. He was returning to Russia for the summer, hoping to finish *Virgin Soil.* Wishing to see as much of him as possible before his departure, Henry joined the Viardot household for charades once again on a Sunday evening, and again watched the Russian novelist scampering about on hands and knees; and then he called on him one morning shortly after and found him "more charming than I had ever seen him." There was such "an extreme sense of *justesse* in his great Cossack body" that Henry felt like embracing him. A day or two later Turgenev joined Henry and Zhukovsky at dinner and "was again adorable"—but once again he had to return to Madame Viardot at an early hour. Late in May Henry went to Flaubert's last Sunday afternoon in the Rue du Faubourg St Honoré; he had an hour alone with the author of *Madame Bovary*, after which he said his summer goodbyes to the *cénacle*. He could not know then that he would never see Flaubert again; and that eight years would elapse before he would renew his friendship with Goncourt, Zola, Daudet, Maupassant—in the later full tide of "naturalism."

Zhukovsky remained in the city for a while and Henry attended various musical evenings at his studio. A later tale called "Collaboration" describes one such evening. When the Bootts turned up in Paris, Henry arranged a dinner-party for them. Zhukovsky found Boott "*extrêmement sympathique*" and thought he looked like one of Titian's men; and Lizzie, to Henry's surprise, revealed great fluency in French. The Bootts established themselves near Paris, at Villiers-le-Bel, where Lizzie studied painting with the French master, Thomas Couture. Henry thought him "a vulgar little fat and dirty old man." But Lizzie said he was an admirable teacher.

July came, and Henry was still in Paris. It was hot and he frequented the cafés, drinking beer, watching the crowds, dining in the Champs Elysées under the trees, beside ivy-covered walls. Or he would take a penny steamer to Auteuil, eat fried fish at a *guinguette* on the river-bank, and return to Paris on top of a horse-car. For a change he would dine in the Bois de Boulogne and drive back through the woods at night in the cool air. "Your last few letters," William wrote to him, "have breathed a tone of contentment and domestication in Paris which was very agreeable to get. I'm afraid though that your native snobbery will wax wanton on your intimacy with crowned heads and that you'll be more intolerably supercilious than ever if you do return home." From Elmwood, Lowell wrote: "Don't get to be too much of a Mounseer and come home as soon as you can." Henry had no thought of return; but he was forming his opinions of the French. "The longer I live in France," he wrote to William, "the better I like the French personality, but the more convinced I am of their bottomless superficiality."

II

One day in late July Henry packed his bags, reserved his apartment for the autumn, and took a boat down the Seine, to Rouen, to Honfleur, to Le Havre. He inspected the bourgeois streets of Rouen, which Flaubert knew so intimately, and wrote about them in one of his last letters for the *Tribune*; Honfleur had all the charm of an Old World fishing port; and in Le Havre the cool breezes at the hotel by the waterside, the waves, the sky, gave him a ship-board feeling. He finally settled at Etretat, taking lodgings near the beach and his meals at the Hôtel Blanquet. He bought himself a fishing cap and canvas shoes; he wore his old clothes; and for a month he wrote peacefully, giving over his spare time to the exploration of the fishing villages, taking long walks across the dunes, or lying on the beach watching the French bathers. He found the Boston-Roman Edward Boits living in an old house nearby, and went on excursions with them, once to the restaurant of *la belle Ernestine*, where they breakfasted in the orchard in front of the house and found some rather offensive American young men with a party of French actresses. Henry trudged ten miles to see the races at Fécamp, and admired the "plastic" landscape of Normandy. At the Casino one day he studied Jacques

Offenbach, sitting placidly over his drink; and on evenings he went to the light operas.

During one of his strolls he found a shepherd flat on his stomach, resting among his shorn sheep. He had been tending sheep for thirty-five years. When Henry remarked that it was pleasant to do so under such beautiful skies, the shepherd observed rather dryly that in thirty-five summers there were a certain number of rainy days. Henry looked at the closely-knit French families taking their summer holidays, and mused on the differences between French matrons and their American sisters. "I have never seen such richness of contour as among the mature *baigneuses* of Etretat. The lean and desiccated person into whom a dozen years of matrimony so often converts the blooming American girl is not emulated in France. A majestic plumpness flourished all around me—the plumpness of triple chins and deeply dimpled hands." He went on to analyse the difference in manners between America and France and the institution of the *jeune fille*. He did not believe it was a hardship for French girls to be tied to their mother's apron-strings until they were wedded, especially since the girls always knew that the parents were busy planning to marry them off. "Mademoiselle is married certainly, and married early, and she is sufficiently well informed to know, and to be sustained by the knowledge, that the sentimental expansion which may not take place at present will have an open field after her marriage." The subject interested him during all the years to come. Ultimately it yielded him a complex dialogue-novel, *The Awkward Age*. Turned round, it was the very essence of "Daisy Miller."

III

He had promised Edward Lee Childe and his wife that he would visit them in their château near Montargis, at Amilly on the Loiret, and in August when he set out to keep his promise he half-regretted he had given it. He would have gladly stayed on at Etretat. He passed through Paris, paid a fleeting call on the Bootts, and then took the train to Montargis, where Childe met him. In the warm August evening he drove with his host to the *castel* of Varennes. They reached it in a vague twilight; it looked like the setting of an opera; the castle on its island in the heart of ancient France with its wide clear moat and its turret, surrounded by walls at least three feet thick. The lover of the picturesque in Henry responded at once: and presently he found himself in a comfortable Blue Room, with a washroom in the turret, and a valet to attend him. He had not expected to be entertained in such a baronial style. Varennes turned out to be "an exquisite sensation—a memory I shall never lose." It was an initiation into years of country visits. Mrs Childe, being French, promptly took her American visitor on a series of excursions. In another château Henry had a lively meeting with the Baronne de Triguеté, a woman of eighty, "with the strength of an ox," who took a great fancy to him and insisted that he spend a week with her in her château, offering all the inducements of her pastoral existence. Henry begged off. He did accept an invitation to an enormous *déjeuner* with her, at which a large party of guests was assembled, "the most heroic and succulent old *déjeuner de province* that can be imagined. Under her roof I should have died in thirty-six hours of an indigestion of game and melons." He met also the Comte de Bressieux, the Baronne's nephew. Thus if he had not breached the Faubourg St Germain he could at least gather material about the provincial gentry. And indeed one château seen during his visit to Amilly, the Château Renard, served as model for the gloomy Fleurières of the Bellegardes.

Henry was fascinated by the relics of old feudal life. Mrs Childe played Lady Bountiful as she went from cottage to cottage. It was like a George Sand novel. "We made a dozen visits, in a dozen queer little smoke-blackened big-bedded, big-clocked kitchens, and everywhere I was charmed with the nature of the people—their good manners, quaintness and *bonhomie*, and the way they did the honours of their little huts." He spoke of his pleasure in seeing "this strange, thrifty, grasping, saving, prospering France, where alone the commercial disasters of the day are not felt. Some of the 'peasants' we saw yesterday are worth sixty and eighty thousand dollars, made franc by franc."

In the Childe household was a handsome boy of six, with long eyelashes, an orphan nephew. Henry took a great liking to him, and was to know him later as Paul Harvey, diplomat and man of letters (still later the learned compiler of the *Oxford Companion to English Literature*). An attractive boy, a country house, a tower, a valet: there seems to be here an early coming together of elements which were to figure in one of Henry's most famous tales, "The Turn of the Screw."

IV

At the end of August Henry decided to visit south-western France. He went directly to Biarritz but found it crowded and unpleasant. He retreated to Bayonne with the intention of glancing at it, and stayed a week. He would have stayed on, but unseasonal rains proved depressing and Henry decided to return to Paris. Before doing this he crossed to San Sebastian and enjoyed a limited glimpse of Spain: he studied a life-sized Virgin in a church with a flamboyant façade and felt that she was as solid as a character in Cervantes; in fact, he said in his travel-sketch, "I addressed her as Doña Maria of the Holy Office; whereupon she looked round the great dusky, perfumed church, to see whether we were alone, and then she dropped her fringed eyelids and held out her hand to be kissed. She was the sentiment of Spanish catholicism; gloomy, yet bedizened, emotional as a woman and mechanical as a doll. After a moment I grew afraid of her, and went slinking away."

In Bayonne he found his friends the Childes, whom he had visited so recently. They were staying at a castle above the town, the Casa Caradoc, and Henry was invited to dine. "I enjoyed the dinner," he wrote to his father, "in spite of my taking it hard to see a depressed English governess sitting in servitude to French people." And then, with the Childes, their hosts, and a couple of young officers from the local garrison he went once again to San Sebastian to see a bullfight. He liked the spectacle and remarked that the ladies who sat beside him often yawned, but never shuddered. He liked the toreadors as well, "yet I thought the bull, in any case, a finer fellow than any of his tormentors, and I thought his tormentors finer fellows than the spectators." Henry's summer had begun with an abortive duel; and it ended with a bull-fight. "A bull-fight will, to a certain extent, bear looking at, but it will not bear thinking of." He never visited Spain again.

A CHANNEL CROSSING

HENRY returned to Paris on 15 September 1876 and discovered that, despite his precautions, his apartment had been let. He was promised another, on the fourth floor, but would have to wait until it was vacated. He accordingly took a room in the Rue de Beaune, in Lowell's old hotel, and certain final pages of *The American* were written there. A few days later he moved outside the city, to St Germain-en-Laye, where he stayed at the Pavillon Louis XIV. The autumn days, after the rains, were clear and beautiful, and he worked quietly here until he was able to move into his rooms. He saw the Bootts off to Italy, and had a desire to go south himself. He had decided, however, that he would spend a second winter in the French capital; and in the high *salon* of his new quarters, at 29 Rue de Luxembourg, a room in which there was a black-framed Empire portrait-medallion suspended in the centre of each white panel, he worked on his last instalments. The Indian summer was beautiful: his casement windows were always open, and once more the "thin, quick, quite feminine surface-breathing of Paris" provided the final accompaniment to the sad ending of Christopher Newman's romance. In the last pages Henry had Newman, on an impulse, cross the Channel to visit England. The same impulse now came to him.

He had for some months, in his letters home, shown signs of impatience with France. Like Newman, he seems quite simply to have lost interest. A long letter to William, written from Etretat (and much-quoted since), gives the more extreme expression of his feelings: his satiety with the French mind, his belief that all he had got out of France was a great deal of the Boulevard and "third rate Americanism." He had gone so often to the Théâtre Français, he said, that he knew its repertoire by heart. He had done with the French, he told his brother, "and am turning English all over." A more moderate statement was written to his mother that autumn. He felt, he said, that another six months of Paris would suffice. "Charming and supremely easy it is, on its material side, but (as I have found it)—most innutritive on its social. Still, anyone who has ever lived in Paris will always have a corner of affection for it in his heart and will often go back."

By the time he had written the last words of his novel he had made up his mind. His recollection of this period of transition is recorded in a summary in his journal: "I settled myself again in Paris—or attempted to do so; I had no intention of giving it up. But there were difficulties in the Rue de Luxembourg—I couldn't get back my old apartment, which I had given up during the Summer. I don't remember what suddenly brought me to the point of saying—'Go to; I will try London.' I think a letter from William had a good deal to do with it, in which he said, 'Why don't you?—That must be the place.' A single word from outside often moves one (moves *me* at least) more than the same word infinitely multiplied as a simple voice from within. I *did* try it."

Although his mind was made up early in November he remained for almost a month. He renewed his friendship with Zhukovsky, the Princess Ourousov, and the Nikolai Turgenevs. He was delighted to see Mrs Mason again. But for his "flimsy compatriots" of the Paris set he felt a complete indifference: the idea, indeed, of beginning to play at "society" with them once more was intolerable. He no longer had his *Tribune* correspondence, which might have justified a continued sojourn. "There is nothing else, for me personally, on the horizon," he told Quincy Street, "and it is rather ignoble to stay in Paris simply for the restaurants."

He had written a long article on Balzac before taking up residence in the French capital. And now, on the eve of leaving, he wrote another. This time he reviewed Balzac's letters, lately published. They fired his imagination. For the first time the story of Balzac's fierce dedication, his methods of work, his stubborn professionalism, his grandiose sense of *métier*, was told in detail. Certain phrases from the letters were to be echoed again and again by Henry in his correspondence with his family during the coming years. He seems to have been fascinated by Balzac's Napoleonic promises to those nearest him: glory justified everything, glory would pay for everything. Henry saw in this a "magnificent egotism" and an "incomparable power." As Henry prepared to cross the Channel he could say to himself that he had now fully mastered the lesson of Balzac. He too could possess, as artist, a kind of massive egotism; he too was not to be swayed from his course where his craft was concerned; and he too would try to fill Quincy Street with the reflected rays of the glory he was certain he would attain. Ambitious and resolute, Henry left Paris without regrets. It was but one more step in his advancing career. He had "tried" New York. He had by now spent a full year in France, largely in Paris. He was about to try London. In his journal a single sentence offers the best reason for his departure: "I saw that I should be an eternal outsider."

Henry crossed the Channel, Boulogne to Folkestone, on 10 December 1876.[1] The Parisian weather was beautiful to the last. It was hard to leave. He had retraced his steps to the now-familiar Rue de Douai and found Ivan Sergeyevich as he had often found him, stretched out on his green sofa, with his gouty foot. The Russian was as affectionate as ever. He talked in great detail of *Virgin Soil.* Henry asked him to give the English translation rights to his friend T. S. Perry. Turgenev willingly consented. He made Henry promise to write from London; he promised he would answer. "*Adieu, cher ami,*" the Russian said as they parted. The friendly words, the tone, went to Henry's heart. Ivan Sergeyevich had been "adorable" to the end.

[1] In his journal Henry recalled that "I went to London in November 1876." This was however a slip of memory, as his correspondence reveals.

Book Six

The Conquest of London 1876–1878

★

THE OBSERVANT STRANGER

LONDON CLUBS

A BIRD OF PARADOX

A LITTLE JOURNEY

DAISY

THE TWO SECRETARIES

A POSITION IN SOCIETY

THE OBSERVANT STRANGER

"I TOOK a lodging at 3 Bolton Street, Piccadilly," Henry was to write in his journal (some half-dozen years later), "and there I have remained till today. I have *lived* much there, felt much, thought much, learned much, produced much; the little shabby furnished apartment ought to be sacred to me. I came to London as a complete stranger, and today I know much too many people. *J'y suis absolument comme chez moi.*"

He fell into London during the dark and sleety winter of 1876 as if he had lived there all his life. "I took possession of it," he said; and it also took possession of him. Bolton Street was two streets from Half-Moon Street, in the very heart of Mayfair, where he had stayed in 1869. It is a short street. One end looks out upon the Green Park; the other opens into Curzon Street, where Becky Sharp lived. In his comings and goings he thought of it as her street, and Thackeray's, "just as I was to find fifty other London neighbourhoods speak to me only with the voice, the thousand voices, of Dickens."

He moved into his lodging on 12 December, and the next morning awoke to his first domestic breakfast—bacon, eggs, slices from an "exquisite English loaf," cups of tea, served by a dark-faced maid with the voice of a duchess. "You may imagine the voluptuous glow in which such a repast has left me," he wrote to Alice. To his mother he wrote: "I am very glad I wasted no more time in Paris. I shall work here much more and much better, and make an easier subsistence."

Although his windows on the first floor looked on to the street and he had a balcony, it could scarcely be said that he had "a view;" at best he could obtain a sideways glimpse of the Green Park. He used to sit writing with a featureless, sooty, brown brick wall facing him across the way, the wall of a great house, Lord Ashburton's. For Henry, however, it had "a vast convenient neutrality." It was like the curtain of a private theatre. When he went out into London, the curtain rose.

It rose on a city that endlessly delighted him. The season was dark and wet; the fog was "glutinous," as if Thames mud had been spread in solution over the housetops and chimney-pots. And yet Henry experienced a contentment such as he had never known in Paris. "I like the place," he told his mother; "I like feeling in the midst of the English world, however lost in it I may be; I find it interesting, inspiring, even exhilarating." He took long walks in the rain. He brought home armfuls of books from Mudie's Library and read them by his fire. Sometimes it was so dark that he had to light his candles at noon. Whatever mood the dark and the fog induced, he felt that London was "on the whole the most possible form of life"—that is for one who took it as he did. "I take it," he wrote, "as an artist and a bachelor; as one who has the passion of observation and whose business is the study of human life." New York's streets had been "fatal to the imagination," and besides he had had to work too hard. Paris was bright and spacious, but he did not feel at home there. London, in spite of its "agglomerated immensity," became "home." It was "ugly, dusky, dreary, more destitute than any European city of graceful and decorative incident." Brown brick house-walls stretched for miles in perpetual monotony, corroded with soot and fog, pierced with stiff straight slits that figured as windows. The light leaking and filtering from the cloud-ceiling turned harshness into softness, gave subtle tones to objects and buildings, created beautiful pictorial effects. London was certainly "not agreeable, or cheerful, or easy, or exempt from reproach," and yet, James added, "it is only magnificent." It was "the most complete compendium of the world." The human race was better represented in it than anywhere else. It was a veritable kingdom for a novelist. A generation of French writers had had their Paris, and Balzac had made of it his world. Henry would be one of those who possessed London. He would assimilate its streets, its clubs, its society. It was the London of Defoe, of Dr Johnson, of Dickens, of Thackeray: there was no reason why it could not become, by a process of observation and absorption, the city of a transatlantic stranger, an American, born in New York, who as a boy in 14th Street had read *Punch* and the English novelists.

I

When Henry tried later to recall the beginnings of his London life, he noted that "little by little I came to know people, to dine out, etc. I did, I was able to do, nothing at all to bring this state of things about; it came rather of itself." This was true. But that cold December, when all London seemed like a great grey Babylon, he made certain initial overtures to mitigate possible loneliness. Shortly after his arrival he got into touch with a young Englishman named Benson, who had visited the James family in Quincy Street. Benson promptly invited him to lunch at the Oxford and Cambridge Club and introduced him to Andrew Lang who, "though a Scotchman, seemed quite a delightful fellow." Henry called also on G. W. Smalley, the London correspondent of the *New York Tribune* whom he had met in Paris. Smalley "has a very pretty house and wife, and is very civil." There was also a young Englishman whom Henry had met the previous summer at Etretat, Theodore Child, a graduate of Merton who wrote for the *Pall Mall Gazette*. Child invited Henry to lunch with him at the Arts Club on Christmas Eve 1876. He was Jewish, and Henry had hitherto known few Jews: he conceived of them as he had known them in certain plays and novels—outlandish, with beaked Shylockean noses and Fagin-like beards: Child did not fit the stereotype. He was lively, literary, aesthetic. Henry wrote to his mother that he was "a Jew and has a nose," but he added that he was "handsome and looks very much like Daniel Deronda." They distinctly liked each other, and this was the beginning of a rewarding friendship.

If these sociabilities promised well for London, that Christmas was perhaps the loneliest of Henry's life. The holiday fell on a week-end and he spent three solitary days in a tightly-shut city with blank streets and wet vistas of sooty bricks. His Yuletide letter to Quincy Street ended with "your lone literary exile." But as soon as the festivities were over, he found himself the object of traditional English hospitalities. A lady he had met at Smalley's (her name is not mentioned in his letters) invited him to a "heavy London dinner, composed of fearful viands and people I didn't know." Here he was introduced to Frank Hill, editor of the *Daily News*, his wife, who reviewed books, and Lady Hamilton Gordon, daughter of the astronomer Herschel. He was invited also to the home of a Mrs Pollock, who had heard from the Smalleys that he was in London. She had read him in the *Atlantic Monthly*. "Who she is I haven't any idea," he wrote home; but he goes out of pure civility to discover himself in the home of the distinguished jurist and his wife, the future Sir Frederick and Lady Pollock, who would remain his friends during all his London days. At still another dinner he meets Sir Charles Dilke, a rising political figure, and discovers their common interest in French literature. He dines in due course with the Andrew Langs, "a very nice fellow with a pleasant graceful mind and a great facility and understanding." He finds him the most gentlemanly of the London journalists, but Lang publishes too much and writes too easily, using "his beautiful thin facility to write everything down to the lowest level of Philistine twaddle." Dinner leads to dinner. Thus at the home of Sir William Power, K.C.B., "a very polite and pleasant Irishman," son of Tyrone Power, the actor, he encounters the ubiquitous Mrs Cashel Hoey, cousin of the then unknown Bernard Shaw, "a curious and interesting specimen of the wondrous type—the London female literary hack."

"I am getting quite into the current of London life," Henry wrote to Quincy Street. He had been in England barely six weeks.

II

As he began to see London interiors and the comfortable side of the Victorian world, he could not help contrasting them with the raw London through which he often walked late in the evening after dining out. He had had glimpses of it from carriages during his childhood, seen it then as Dickens's London: but now it seemed to him rather the London of Hogarth. There were too many gin-shops, "too many miserable women at their doorsteps; too many, far too many, dirty-faced children, sprawling between one's legs." Also the young ladies of these neighbourhoods were too ardent, "too addicted to violent forms of coquetry." And one dark night, against the dismal background of fog and sleet, Henry came upon "a horrible old woman in a smoky bonnet, lying prone in a puddle of whisky." The vision struck him as symbolic. "She almost frightened me away," he wrote.

In France, in Italy, he had seen poverty and squalor in many forms. But it had there a certain out-of-door picturesqueness. In London it became "the hard prose of misery." Strolling at Easter into a crowded Westminster Abbey, he was driven away by an odour that "was not that of incense." Proceeding early one March morning to Barnes Bridge to watch the Oxford and Cambridge boat race, he stood in the midst of "a dingy British mob, with coal smoke ground into its pores." The landscape was sodden and dank; the view was of taverns, railway-bridges and Thames mud. In this setting the only aesthetic experience was the sudden view of the two crews—"great white water-swimming birds, with eight feathered wings" caught in the morning light. Later, spending a day at Epsom and watching the Derby, Henry was struck by the general intoxication of the crowd. He found the women "too stout, too hot, too red, too thirsty, too boisterous, too strongly accoutred." And he described with great minuteness a youth who had made of himself "a mere bag of liquor," too inert and too limp to be shoved, with any ease, into his carriage.

The crude state of poverty in London gave Henry pause. He was struck by "the rigidly aristocratic constitution of society; the unaesthetic temper of the people; the private character of most kinds of comfort and entertainment." The Victorian world was carefully organized to preserve—to reinforce—respect for traditional institutions. This was one way of maintaining national stability. To a member of America's upper middle class, nourished in a continent in which society was in a state of flux, England's codes and rules, and its stratified class-structure, proved a revelation. They gave Henry a standard by which he could greatly enlarge the process, begun long ago, of comparing peoples and their manners. Church and State, Religion and Science, Progress and Poverty, God, Duty, Immortality and British Domestic Virtue—all seemed to have their firm and hierarchic place in Victorian England:

> In the sight of the English people getting up from its tea and toast of a Sunday morning and brushing its hat, and drawing on its gloves, and taking its wife on its arm, and making its offspring march before, and so, for decency's, respectability's, propriety's sake, taking its way to a place of worship appointed by the State, in which it repeats the formulas of a creed to which it attaches no positive sense, and listens to a sermon over the length of which it explicitly haggles and grumbles—in this exhibition there is something very striking to a stranger, something which he hardly knows whether to regard as a great force or a great infirmity.

Surely, Henry thought, this was a conformity as starched as Prussian militarism. It seemed to him there was little difference.

The thought did occur to him that in a nation in which the explosive force of the British personality was repressed to this extent, there had to be some safety-valve. Where had the Britons placed the "fermenting idiosyncrasies" that had been corked down? He did not find an immediate answer: but he was to see it in due course, in the Piccadilly riots, the Irish agitation, the Dilke scandal, the Parnell case, the trial of Oscar Wilde.

Now he stood in Trafalgar Square and watched the Queen—no longer the slim, small woman of his boyhood, but an ample widowed matron—ride in state to open the Parliament over which Disraeli presided and where in a matter of weeks she would be proclaimed Empress of India. He noted at the same time that, on the other side of the square, men marched with placards and banners expressing various forms of social unrest and focusing them through demands for the release from prison of the Tichborne claimant.

"The upper classes are too refined," Henry was to write, "and the lower classes are too miserable." The judgment may have seemed to him in later years too summary, too unsubtle. His revising pen altered it to read: "The better sort are too 'genteel,' and the inferior sort too base." This might be the measure of the distance he was to travel from Bolton Street into the life of England's leisured class.

III

Henry was to become the historian of "the better sort." But he was not to lose sight altogether of the Hogarthian London of this early time. He was to ask himself, during the ensuing years, what life would be like to one who had not had his own singular good fortune: he had found in England "freedom and ease, knowledge and power, money, opportunity and satiety;" he was to acknowledge in his late memoirs that he had had "an excess of opportunities." For him the doors of London opened "into light and warmth and cheer, into good and charming relations." Yet the place "as a whole lay heavy on one's consciousness." And this heaviness Henry tried to deal with and understand in the brooding novel of his middle years, *The Princess Casamassima*, which he described as having its origin in his habit of walking the streets " during the first year of a long residence in London." He had walked a good deal, "for exercise, for amusement, for acquisition and above all I always walked home at the evening's end, when the evening had been spent elsewhere, as happened more often than not." And he added: "One walked of course with one's eyes greatly open." His observation of poverty and high life in England was that of an intellectual and a humanitarian; it was not that of a reformer. He had called himself in his earlier English articles "the sentimental tourist." He called himself now "the observant stranger."

He insisted upon the "stranger." He had no desire to change his status of outsider, even though he was to become identified with much of English life. As he explained to Charles Eliot Norton, "I am not at all Anglicized, but I am thoroughly Londonized—a very different thing." As an "observant stranger" he could describe without necessarily passing judgment; he could also compare; he could—as he was about to demonstrate—satirize Americans with the same ease as the English. But he had no desire to be a satirist. His forte was irony. Later when Lizzie

Boott praised his English sketches, he said he had sought "the happy medium of irony—to be ironical enough without being too much so." To his friend Perry he wrote that when he would make a book of these essays it would be "very complimentary and urbane," but it would also have "many *sous-entendus* and much reserve." He confessed that he had withheld a great many impressions. "One can't say everything when one is settling down to enjoy the hospitality, as it were, of a country."

One couldn't say everything; nevertheless Henry managed to say a great deal. His remarks contained nothing that had not been said in one form or another by Arnold, or Ruskin, or Morris, or by du Maurier in his caricatures, or by Gilbert in the verses Sullivan set to music. Henry was abroad in the London of Victoria, and he could describe British philistinism as readily as Matthew Arnold could inveigh against it. But what happened now was that Henry began to make certain comparisons; he could on the one hand compare London with Paris; even more, he was taking possession of a social structure of such strength and depth that he was enabled to indulge in comparative study of Anglo-American manners. British responsibility, British leisure, British traditions, the longevity of British institutions, could be compared with American irresponsibility, American failure to enjoy leisure, the as yet comparative absence of tradition, and above all the absence of *standards* generally. On the other hand Henry's patience with the British upper classes often wore thin; and he rejoiced in American forthrightness. When William wrote to him that as an American he should be studying life in Washington rather than London, he replied that he would come to this in good time. "I know what I am about," he wrote, "and I have always my eyes on my native land."

To Grace Norton he was to write on 7 July 1878:

In one sense I feel intimately at home here, and in another sense I feel—as an American may be on the whole very willing, at times, very glad, to feel—like a complete outsider. There are some English institutions and idiosyncrasies that it is certainly a great blessing to be outside of. But I suppose one may claim to feel at home in a place when it ceases to be a land of mystery and vagueness—when one's impressions have become continuous and mutually consistent. I have learned a good deal about British manners and the British mind (thinking on the whole finely of the latter and meanly of the former)—and they no longer have any terrors—or even perplexities—to me. There are times indeed when I seem to myself to carry all England in my breeches pocket.

Again and again he spoke of liking London as "a big city and a regular basis of mundane existence," but he adds that he sometimes gets "woefully tired of its people and their talk. There seems something awfully stale and stupid about the whole business." To his mother he writes at another moment that he finds English society "a collection of mediocrities, mounted upon the pedestal of their wealth, their family, their respectability, their consecrated habits etc." To be sure, he adds, it could be said that "the great stock of society is everywhere a set of mediocrities and that those who have pedestals are better than those who haven't." Even while complaining he continued his London round; it might bore him, but it also fascinated; he found it difficult to stop.

"It was, in fine, dear Charles," he wrote to his friend Norton ultimately, "a very happy inspiration of mine, two years since, to come to London to live; so thoroughly have I attached myself to its mighty variety and immensity, so interesting do I find the spectacle of English life, so well do I get on, on the whole, with people and things, so successfully, on the whole, do I seem to myself to assimilate the total affair." He had a real tenderness for the "personal character of the people. It seems to me many times the strongest and richest race in the world—my dream is to arrive at the ability to be, in some degree, its moral portrait-painter."

IV

And this indeed he became, although he was to paint even more successfully the moral portrait of Anglo-American manners and relations: to paint them once and for all, so that his pictures were as prophetic as they were real. The man who dissected the nature of the international marriage and pictured the young American beauties trailing through Europe to become duchesses and princesses did not explicitly foresee the time when a cinema star might occupy a small European throne; but he in effect predicted it, for it is as implicit in his stories as the ultimate marriage of a British king to a Baltimore woman. "For a Bostonian nymph to reject an English duke is an adventure only less stirring, I should say, than for an English duke to be rejected by a Bostonian nymph," he was to say in his essay on the art of fiction.

The tales Henry wrote during the first year of his residence in England, no less than the essays, testify to the accuracy of "the observant stranger." Only a man who had, as he told Norton, "successfully" assimilated the total affair could write stories which foreshadowed as well as depicted the manners and customs of international society. And it was with the same accuracy that Henry, at the end of his first year in Bolton Street, wrote a prophetic letter to his brother William. The passage begins with Henry's discussion of the continuing fear of England's involvement in the Russo-Turkish war. He had been dining out, and had listened to the army men indulging in "the densest war talk." In the light of his close attention to the talk, he went on to tell William that he wasn't sure he could accept the arguments of the peace-at-any-price school:

> At any rate I believe that England will keep out of war for the reason that up to this stage of her relation to events in the East, her going to war would be simply for the sake of her "prestige," and that the nation as a whole, looking at the matter deliberately, have decided that mere prestige is not sufficient ground for a huge amount of bloodshed. This seems to me to indicate a high pitch of civilization—a pitch which England alone, of all the European nations, has reached. It has been curious to see that all the French republican papers have lately been denouncing her fiercely for not pitching into Russia—the defence of prestige being a perfectly valid *casus belli* to the French mind.

And then came the prophecy:

> It certainly remains to be seen whether in material respects England can afford to abdicate even such a privilege as that. I have a sort of feeling that if we are to see the *déchéance* of England it is inevitable, and will come to pass somewhat in this way. She will push further and further her non-fighting and keeping-out-of-scrapes-policy, until contemptuous Europe,

growing audacious with impunity, shall put upon her some supreme and unendurable affront. Then—too late—she will rise ferociously and plunge clumsily and unpreparedly into war. She will be worsted and laid on her back—and when she is laid on her back will exhibit—in her colossal wealth and pluck—an unprecedented power of resistance. But she will never really recover as a European power.

This, said Henry, was "the vision I sometimes entertain, and which events, doubtless, will consummately bring to naught." By the time 1914 came he had probably forgotten his prediction: and in our own time we can look back at the Battle of Britain and see how Henry James, more than half a century before, had understood and spoken—almost in Churchillian cadences—of the deepest nature of the people in whose midst he had made his home. Where Henry erred was in a further remark in this letter that Britain's "stubbornly aristocratic social arrangements" made compulsory military service in England difficult against a Europe armed to the teeth: gentlemen would not stand in the same ranks with peasants, servants, town boys—cads in short. Perhaps from the moment in the Victorian era in which he was speaking he was right. He could not foresee the levelling that was to occur in the twentieth century, or perhaps he misread here the unifying power an enemy exerts. The passage testifies however to James's uncanny ability to see reality and to read its meaning with unerring logic. This was possible in all matters in which his deepest personal emotions were not touched—where he could be distant, detached, and surgically analytical.

LONDON CLUBS

JOHN LOTHROP MOTLEY, nearing the end of a busy life as historian and diplomat, called on his fellow-countryman in Bolton Street early in February 1877 to tell him that he had put him on the honorary list of the Athenaeum Club. This meant that Henry had temporary access to a club in England which gathered under its substantial roof in Pall Mall the country's eminent men of letters, philosophers and churchmen. Henry had hitherto had little experience of clubs. Elected to the Century in New York two years before, he had never had occasion to take his place in that association of artists and amateurs. On his arrival in London he had briefly used the Savile, thanks to G. W. Smalley of the *New York Tribune*, as he was later to have temporary access to the Travellers' and the St James's. At the Athenaeum he could not only dine sociably at the end of a long day's writing, but he had the use as well of a fine library and occasion to meet certain of his peers. He had complained to T. S. Perry that London was less convenient than Paris for a "lonely celibate." The club admirably extended his sense of home; it was, so to speak, a luxurious annexe to his lodgings. "Such lounges and easy chairs!" he exclaimed to Quincy Street. As he settled down into one of them he pronounced the Athenaeum "the last word of a high civilization."

"I am writing this in the beautiful great library," he told his father in a letter on the club's stationery of 13 February 1877. "On the other side of the room sits Herbert Spencer, asleep in a chair (he always is, whenever I come here) and a little way off is the portly Archbishop of York with his nose in a little book. It is 9.30 p.m. and I have been dining here. An old gentleman put himself at the table next to me and soon began to talk about the 'autumn tints' in America—knowing, heaven knows how, that I came thence. Presently he informed me that he was the son of Sir Richard Westmacott, the sculptor; and that the old gentleman on the other side of him was a nephew of Lord Nelson etc. etc. I give you this for local colour (it is a great blessing, by the way, to be able to dine here, where the dinner is good and cheap. I was seeing arrive the day when London restaurants, whose badness is literally fabulous, would become impossible, and the feeding question a problem so grave as to drive me from the land. I am not sure that some day it won't)."

There were to be other intimate glimpses in his early club life. Remembering his Thackeray, Henry relished describing to his sister the dignitaries sprawling or reading their papers—"all the great chairs and lounges and sofas filled with men having afternoon tea—lolling back with their laps filled with magazines, journals, and fresh Mudie books, while amiable flunkies in knee-breeches present them the divinest salvers of tea and buttered toast." And seeing certain of Alice's favourite authors at the club he proceeded to satirize them: "Lecky the historian, and Green ditto (author of Alice's favourite work—the fat volume which she gave me) have just come and seated themselves in front of me: two such grotesque specimens of the rickety, intellectual Oxford cad that I can't forbear mentioning them. Only du Maurier, in *Punch*, could do them justice; and if Alice could see in the flesh her little wizened, crawling Green, with eyes like ill-made button-holes, she would take to her bed for a month and renounce her 'historic-reveries.' The delights of London are only equalled by its disillusionments."

The London club was to become for Henry James thus a necessity, a means by which he gave himself a more spacious existence than he had in his Bolton Street rooms. Here he could make—and meet—friends; he could entertain fellow-writers and reciprocate certain hospitalities; it was a place as fundamental to his existence as the old coffee-houses had been to an earlier London. Unfortunately his access to the Athenaeum had its term. For some time he went to the Travellers', thanks to Charles Milnes Gaskell and Frederick Locker; and for a good while to the St James's, haunt of young diplomats, where he paid a monthly fee. In all he was guest in seven London clubs before his election to one he could call his own. This happened much more promptly than he anticipated. Before he had been six months in England he was put up for the Reform Club by Frank Hill of the *Daily News* and C. H. Robarts. The Reform was the Athenaeum's neighbour in Pall Mall, the club of the country's liberals in the political and literary walks of life. It could not boast as many celebrities as the Athenaeum, but it was one of the best clubs in London, and materially "the most comfortable corner of the world." He was to be elected in May 1878, apparently with the help of Sir Charles Dilke, "who, poor man, appears to have found time (up to his neck in the House of Commons as he is) to read and be 'struck' by my French essays."

"*J'y suis, j'y reste*—forever and a day," he announced triumphantly to his father and drew £42 on his letter of credit to pay his entrance-fee. He told his sister that his election had "doubled my 'selfhood,' as Father would say," and added, "bookless and houseless as I am, [it] is a great blessing, and since my election I have done nothing but sit there and read Jowett's Plato and Beaumont and Fletcher."

THE BIRD OF PARADOX

Henry Adams had sent James a letter of introduction to Richard Monckton Milnes, Lord Houghton. Characteristically enough the English peer invited him to one of his familiar breakfasts before Henry had a chance to use the letter. Lord Houghton's breakfasts by this time were legendary. The "bird of paradox" was a great collector of celebrities. Henry Adams considered him "the first wit in London, and a maker of men—of a great many men," and he wrote in the *Education*: "A word from him went far. An invitation to his breakfast-table went farther." Monckton Milnes had written verses as a young man and had been Keats's first champion. In Parliament his speeches had been too literary. He had, said Adams, an "almost Falstaffian mask and laugh of Silenus." But Adams had known him during the earlier decades. In 1877 Lord Houghton was sixty-eight, a little rusty but still as eager a collector of celebrities for his breakfasts as he was of rare volumes and erotica. He had cultivated the art of being a man of the world, almost as if this were a profession. Disraeli, disguising him as Mr Vavasour in *Tancred*, had written: "Mr Vavasour's breakfasts were renowned. Whatever your creed, class or country—one might almost add your character—you were a welcome guest at his matutinal meal, provided you were celebrated. That qualification was rigidly enforced."

We may judge then that by Lord Houghton's standard Henry could consider himself a celebrity—or certainly on his way to becoming one. The breakfast-groups could hardly be said to resemble Flaubert's *cénacle*; fame rather than dedication to art seemed the fundamental criterion. However they were occasions for pleasant talk, high gossip and a kind of extended fellowship among "personalities." Henry never compared it with the Saturday Club to which his father belonged in Boston; and yet one might have seen an analogy—with the distinction that in Boston the faces were nearly always the same, while at Lord Houghton's there was endless rotation and variety. We have no record of the men Henry met at the first breakfast he attended. He seems by that time—a bare twelve weeks after settling in London—to have become sufficiently blasé about such occasions. He had been discovering that most of the Englishmen he met were, as he told Quincy Street, "of the 'useful-information' prosaic sort." There is a note of world-weariness in his speaking of the first breakfast to William as composed of half a dozen men "all terribly 'useful-informationish,' and whose names and faces I have forgotten." But he is bidden again by Lord Houghton to another gathering, the Cosmopolitan, a kind of "talking club, extremely select," and here he encounters, amid a little knot of parliamentary folk, his fellow-passenger of two years before, Anthony Trollope.

Henry found Lord Houghton to be "very kind and paternal" and "a battered and world-wrinkled old mortal, with a restless and fidgety vanity, but with an immense fund of real kindness and humane feeling. He is not personally fascinating, though as a general thing he talks very well, but I like his sociable, democratic, sympathetic, inquisitive old temperament. Half the human race, certainly everyone that one has ever heard of, appears sooner or later to have stayed at Fryston Hall. This represents an immense expenditure of hospitality and curiosity, trouble and general benevolence."

By the time Henry wrote this he had passed from being a breakfast-guest to a dinner-guest and to visiting Lord Houghton in the country. At one dinner he encountered Tennyson, Gladstone, and the excavator of Troy, Dr Heinrich Schliemann. Henry sat next but one to Tennyson. He described the Bard as swarthy and scraggy and less handsome than he appeared in his photograph. He talked exclusively of port wine and tobacco; "he seems to know much about them, and can drink a whole bottle of port at a sitting with no incommodity." He had a strange simplicity, "and seemed altogether like a creature of some primordial English stock, a thousand miles away from American manufacture." Henry continued:

Behold me after dinner conversing affably with Mr Gladstone—not by my own seeking, but by the almost importunate affection of Lord Houghton. But I was glad of a chance to feel the "personality" of a great political leader —or as G. is now thought here even, I think, by his partisans, an ex-leader. That of Gladstone is very fascinating—his urbanity extreme—his eye that of a man of genius—and his apparent self-surrender to what he is talking of, without a flaw. He made a great impression on me—greater than anyone I have seen here though 'tis perhaps owing to my naïveté, and unfamiliarity with statesmen.

By the end of the winter Henry was considered by Lord Houghton not merely one of the famous men in his collection, but a personal friend. He, the "collector," asked Henry, just before leaving for Paris, for an introduction to Turgenev and Flaubert. Henry gave him a letter and urged him to get the Russian to take him to the *cénacle*. "I am sure," Henry wrote, "the others won't do me the honour to remember me, though I often used to meet them at Flaubert's."

A LITTLE JOURNEY

BETWEEN the time of his first solitary Christmas in 1876 and the Easter of 1877 Henry James firmly established himself in the London world. Since he was unable to place a serial while *The American* was appearing, he continued to support himself by fugitive writing and he sold ten articles during that year to the *Galaxy*, for which he received $1200. Four of them completed his French series begun in 1875 with the essay on Balzac; one dealt with his previous summer in France; five were devoted to his discovery of England. He was also able to place three articles for the first time in *Lippincott's*, and these, with his usual writings for the *Nation* (which yielded him about $400), brought his earnings for 1877 to about $2500. With the prospect of a serial for the *Atlantic* in 1878, Henry felt at ease financially and was able to plan a trip to the Continent.

He remained in London until midsummer and then discovered the pleasures of country visits. Henry Adams had urged him to stay with his friend Charles Milnes Gaskell, and when he received the invitation he gladly went to Wenlock Abbey, a ruin in Shropshire, partly restored and modernized, where he spent several pleasant days. "You feast on the pictorial, you inhale the historic," Henry wrote. "It is not too much to say that after spending 24 hours in a house that is 600 years old, you seem yourself to have lived in it for 600 years." He enjoyed the sensation of stepping from the medieval stone gallery—where the monks used to pace—into a modern drawing-room. Another invitation to visit friends in Warwickshire was gladly accepted, and Henry found himself in a great house, in an immense park, where there were grazing deer and massive ancient oaks. He mingled with some fifteen friendly guests, and "the combination of the spacious, lounging, taking-all-day life, the beautiful place, the dinner-party each night, the walk to church across such ideal meadow paths with such a lovely young Miss Bouverie (the product of similar agréments in Devonshire)—all this was excellent of its kind."

Still in Warwickshire, he stayed with the Carters (Mrs Carter being a sister of Henry's Parisian friend Eleanor Strong) at "The Spring," near Kenilworth. Mr Carter was an ardent Liberal, "extremely intelligent and high-toned, devoted to workingmen's clubs, snubbing the parson, buying out taverns etc." (We catch a glimpse of him later in "Lady Barberina.") The place was small and charming, and across the lawn, from the drawing-room window, he looked straight at the world of Sir Walter Scott, the romantic mass of Kenilworth Castle. Henry began his visit by going to a party at the old rectory and dancing all evening with shy, rosy Warwickshire maidens. "The women dance ill," he told Lizzie Boott, "but they are soft and clinging." Another day the party went to Stratford to visit Mrs Kemble's second daughter, Mrs James Leigh, who lived "in a divine old rambling, wainscotted, brown-chambered manor house" on the Avon. Mrs Leigh, wife of a clergyman, talked much to Henry of Philadelphia and her nostalgia for the Georgia rice-fields.

I

Before crossing to the Continent Henry gathered together his French essays—as William had long ago urged him to do—and sent the manuscript to the firm of Macmillan, which had expressed an interest in publishing him in England. He had not thus far brought out a book or published an article in the country in which he had now established his home, although certain of his volumes had been imported into England and in a few instances reviewed in that temperate and condescending way in which literary journalists often greet a new writer. The reviews had noted his advent upon the American literary scene, praised his accuracy of observation and felicities of style, criticized his characterizations and measured him in general by the standards of Victorian fiction. They found plot and story wanting, and an excess of character-analysis instead of incident. However only about eight notices of any length had appeared in England since the publication of Henry's first volume of tales. He was, in other words, largely unknown. In the United States he had built up a reputation by a long process of periodical publication, and during the past two years by the appearance of two novels, his tales and his travel-book. There existed thus for Henry a serious problem: what sort of début should he make in England, where he would, so to speak, come before the reading public "cold." He had remarked some months earlier to T. S. Perry that if the British "want a novelist, they want also a critic." He could offer them both, but it probably seemed to him that the most cautious thing he could do would be to publish this modest volume of essays. He no longer considered *Roderick Hudson* suitable; he felt he could do much better. He apparently was not sure that *The American*, just out in Boston and New York in book-form, would do; he felt that it had been written too hastily. A volume of essays would be a cautious venture: if it failed it would not injure his reputation as a writer of fiction—and he could prepare a proper and bold entry in that character into English literature. In other words we have the interesting spectacle of Henry James deciding with characteristic deliberation to appear in England not as a novelist but as a critic of novelists, and not as a writer of tales or of travel but as an authority on French literature, especially on French realism. Indeed he seemed to think the book particularly suited for the English, since he never published it in the United States. He accordingly deposited a manuscript titled *French Poets and Novelists* at the offices of the Macmillans, and was ready for his trip to the Continent.

II

First there was Paris. The city glistened in the September sun after the soot of London. The Parisians had cut a wide boulevard from the ornate Opéra to the chastely-columned Théâtre Français—the Avénue de l'Opéra—knocking out many old streets familiar to Henry from his earlier years. He viewed the change with misgivings. The avenue was imperial, yet it substituted for things old and cherished a kind of blank, pompous, featureless sameness—and the smell of asphalt. It achieved, to be sure, a splendid thing; it linked the great temple of French music at one end with the great temple of French comedy at the other.

Henry looked at the French people with new pleasure. They were alert, bright, vivacious. From the moment he saw the porters in their blouses on the quay at Boulogne, he felt himself rediscovering old agreeable sensations. It was a pleasure to have lunch at the railway buffet; to be offered soup without having to ask for it; to find a pint of Bordeaux at his plate, to be given a napkin, to take up a long stick of French bread and break off a crisp, crusty morsel. In Paris he returned to the familiar café on the boulevard for his breakfasts. The *garçon* remarked that *monsieur* had been away a long time, led him to his favourite table and brought him his usual newspaper. Henry noticed the familiar faces of certain habitués, sitting over their drinks or their dominoes. He was prompted to compare them with the gentlemen he saw in the London clubs. In London he could discern a majestic social order massed behind the clubmen. What was behind these Frenchmen was probably not adapted for exhibition. Behind the English—whatever their personalities or even their irregularities—there was reared an immense body of private proprieties and comforts, domestic conventions, theological observances.

Henry was in no hurry to reach Italy. He found a couple of shabby rooms off the Champs Elysées, above the Palais de l'Industrie, in the Avénue d'Antin, with a charming view of tree-tops tinted by early autumn. Here, in spite of his being on holiday, he did his daily writing. The rest of his time was devoted to Paris and to his friends. Almost his first act was to inform Ivan Sergeyevich of his arrival. Turgenev had kept his word; he had corresponded with Henry. His warm and affectionate letters were filled with melancholy over the Russo-Turkish war. "We have missed you here," he wrote when the younger man described his London life, "but I suppose we mustn't complain since you are, after all, satisfied with your stay—and are able to work." It was a question of adaptation, "but we would have all been so happy if you had come back to *adapt* yourself to Paris." *Virgin Soil* had not only been a failure in Russia; one had even heard the word *fiasco* mentioned. Turgenev, who usually wrote to Henry in French, added: "*La fortune n'aime pas les vieillards—même en littérature.*" He had lately read Zola's new novel, *L'Assommoir*. It wasn't immoral—it was simply "devilishly dirty!" If he were a cartoonist for *Punch*, Turgenev wrote, he would amuse himself by drawing a cartoon captioned: "Queen Victoria reading *L'Assommoir*."

Henry had reviewed *Virgin Soil* in the *Nation*, and praised the book while recognizing that it was not the best of Turgenev. The Russian wrote to him: "Something was lacking in this last work which a spirit of such fine perceptions as yours must have discerned: a sense of freedom. I wrote always under a cloud." In August Henry had sent him *The American*, which he had acknowledged from his country house at Bougival, near Paris. Turgenev was despondent; things had not gone well; his affairs were in confusion; the war preyed on his mind. "I am so distant from all literary activity that I ask myself whether I have ever been active—and whether it was really I who wrote books which had a beginning, a middle and an end." And he told Henry: "I count on seeing you." When he learned of his arrival he sent a note in his rather stiff English: "I am very glad that you are in Paris and very desirous to see you. In my present state of mind I rather avoid to see human faces—but you are naturally an exception." He came into the city and they breakfasted at Bignou's, in the Boulevard des Italiens. Turgenev talked incessantly of the war. He expected total collapse on the part of the Russians; the badness of the generals, the viciousness of the system of having ignorant Grand-Dukes as commanders-in-chief, could produce no other result. He doubted whether such failures would produce an uprising of the Russian people. The Tsar could with impunity "do absolutely what he chooses with them." All this gave Ivan Sergeyevich sleepless nights and dreadful visions.

Henry saw Turgenev several times, visiting him in his spacious chalet at Bougival on the Seine, next to the summer home of the Viardots. On one occasion Ivan Sergeyevich and Henry lunched nearby with the Nikolai Turgenevs, who were Bonapartists, and it pleased the American writer to hear the Russian novelist come up "with a larger republican and generally liberal profession of faith than I have heard him utter before. He was magnificent." On the whole, however, Henry wrote home, "Russians, just now, are depressed and depressing company."

Elsewhere in Paris Henry renewed certain friendships. He dined with Theodore Child, who was now Paris correspondent of the *Daily Telegraph*; he saw Mrs Kemble on her way to London from her usual Swiss summer; and during this visit he became a closer friend of Henrietta Reubell, whom he had appraised so carefully in 1876. They began to have the intimate chats and meetings which were to continue across the years. "Not the least poignant" of his Paris memories, he wrote to her when back in London, were those of the hours spent in her "admirable little salon."

And finally he went to the theatre. One evening he saw *Le Demi-Monde* by Dumas *fils*, at the Théâtre Français, and came away with a feeling of "lively irritation." He had seen the play several times before. On this occasion it had been brilliantly acted by Delaunay and Mademoiselle Croizette. Henry found it very difficult to swallow the morality of the piece. It was one of those characteristic nineteenth-century dramas exploring the fate of a "woman with a past" of which *La Dame aux Camélias* was the prototype. The heroine of *Le Demi-Monde* seeks to marry a respectable young man who loves her. The young man's friend, whose mistress she has been, is determined to prevent the match, and is quite prepared to tell a lie so as to make the woman compromise herself. Henry, walking the lamp-lit streets after the theatre, found himself wondering whether an English audience would consider this kind of conduct gentlemanly and fair. "Madame d'Ange has blots in her life, and it is doubtless not at all proper that such ladies should be led to the altar by honourable young men." Nevertheless an English audience, even while not condoning her irregularities, would also dislike the ungentlemanly behaviour of the former lover. He would be judged a "meddlesome" individual, and his victim would certainly not be considered "fair game."

Later Henry found himself wondering whether he might not give another turn to the situation. What if an American lady—say with a long list of divorces—tried to crash her way into British society? What if a British matron sought to uncover the American woman's past? Would an American gentleman tell? He did not know it that September in Paris, but he had found the *donnée* for one of his most amusing "international" comedies, "The Siege of London."

III

Early in October Henry went to Rheims, inspected the great cathedral, and wrote a pleasant article for the *Atlantic* on it and on the champagne country. Then he took the train to Turin, lingered there briefly, and proceeded to Florence. He found Frank Boott looking rather old; Lizzie was her usual busy self. They were "a most friendly, lovable, pure-minded, even touching couple," and Lizzie was the same "noiseless little active and productive force as ever." Boott's devotion to his daughter was "more intense and absorbing than ever and his unremitting attention to every stroke that she draws or paints, half-touching, half-amusing."

He had had an earlier glimpse of the Villa Castellani, had even used it in *Roderick*. But this was the first time that James had had an opportunity to see the quiet life of the Bootts on Bellosguardo, its limited nature, and their constant industry, Lizzie with her painting and Frank with his music. (One is reminded of the old Professor and Scholastica in "Benvolio.") During the week Henry stayed in Florence, he left his hotel by the Arno daily, passed over the Ponte Vecchio, walked to the Roman Gate, then climbed the steep and winding way to the villa along a narrow road bounded by mottled, mossy garden walls. He spent long afternoons on the sunny terrace, or sauntered along it by a moon that threw shadows on the buildings below in the softly-scooped hollow of the hills.

He knew the Bootts well enough to describe what he saw in the columns of the *Atlantic* without seeming to invade their privacy, in an article entitled "Recent Florence." He spoke of the "row of high-waisted cypresses," the grassy courtyard, the long serene horizontal lines of the other villas, flanked by their trees, disposed on the neighbouring hills; beyond the city the changing colours of the mountains, the shifting shadows. "What a tranquil, contented life it seemed, with exquisite beauty as a part of its daily texture!" he wrote. And he went on:

When such a life presents itself in a dull or ugly place, we esteem it, we admire it, but we do not feel it to be the ideal of good fortune. When, however, the people who lead it move as figures in an ancient, noble landscape, and their walks and contemplations are like a turning of the leaves of history, we seem to be witnessing an admirable case of virtue made easy; meaning here by virtue, contentment and concentration, the love of privacy and of study. One need not be exacting if one lives among local conditions that are of themselves constantly suggestive.

It was charming entertainment for a week: to walk about and look at the villas; Montauto with its tower, where Hawthorne had lived; the Brichieri, associated with Mrs Browning; and other ample houses built with thickness of wall and depth of embrasure; to wonder at the height of the cypresses and the depth of the loggias; to walk home in the fading light noting on westward-looking walls the glow of the opposite sunset. In imagination Henry found himself renting each villa at which he looked. And yet there seemed to be something melancholy in the place. The fanciful stranger could only murmur to himself: "Lovely, lovely, but oh, how sad!"

The very terms of this passage, the picture of the elderly man with the daughter he had reared in Italy, in the continental manner, the setting—all this appealed to Henry's mind and imagination. In writing this travel-sketch he little knew that he was recording a setting for Gilbert Osmond and his daughter Pansy. They would not resemble Frank and Lizzie Boott, but the image of the villa, and of the couple in it, was to serve his need in the novel that was slowly taking shape in his consciousness, and that he was presently to start writing near this very place. Perhaps we may discern also in the article the germ of a much later subject: for in the observed relationship of a father and a daughter leading a self-sufficient life, he had the theme of an ultimate novel as well which he would call *The Golden Bowl.*

IV

In Rome he found a little apartment in Via Capo le Case, No. 45, the "rather ragged and besmirched establishment" of a Cavaliere Avvocato Spinetti. His rent was modest and the rooms were flooded with sunlight. On his first evening he made his pilgrimage to the Colosseum. There was no moon; the place seemed shrunken and prosaic. "When even picturesqueness intermits, then fallen Empires are fallen indeed," he observed. The excavations had gone on apace; Rome seemed "very modern." As for the American circle of three years before, Story was in Boston and the Terrys had had financial reverses. Henry spent some hours with Mrs Tilton in the left wing of the Pantaleone apartment in the Barberini, she defending the charms of Rome and Henry lamenting the changes that had come about. "Rome has changed and I have changed," he told Quincy Street. A few days later, however, he was writing to Grace Norton: "The old enchantment of Rome, taking its own good time, steals over you and possesses you, till it becomes really a nuisance and an importunity." He had hoped to get some work done; the sunshine and the atmosphere drew him constantly out of doors. He saw Alice Bartlett and met a Mrs Hawker, who lived in the Palazzo Bonaparte and was her friend. The Bootts arrived from Florence to spend the winter in the Holy City, and before Henry knew it five weeks had slipped by. Macmillan by this time had accepted *French Poets and Novelists* and sent it to the printer; proofs would be forthcoming shortly; in fact he expected to find batches of them in Paris. He reluctantly decided to cut short his enjoyment of Rome's turquoise mornings and topaz afternoons and took train for the French capital.

Before leaving, however, he recaptured the old pleasure of riding in the Campagna—the golden atmosphere, the violet mountains, the flower-strewn grass, the lonely arches crowned with wild weeds and crumbling in the sunshine. All the lost sensations were there: the cool yellow wine handed him at some suburban *osteria* as he sat in his saddle, the peasants lounging in their leather leggings, the shepherds and their flocks. His previous rides had been in the springtime. Riding now in the autumn he found certain differences: there were other kinds of flowers—the faded fields were made rosy, for instance, by "little pink autumnal daisies."

It may have been while they were galloping over the daisies of the Campagna, or one evening while they were together with the Bootts. At some point Alice Bartlett had occasion to mention an episode which had occurred in Rome during the previous winter. The evidence points to its having been Miss Bartlett, for James was to write later that he had the story from a friend then living in the Eternal City, "since settled in a South less weighted with appeals and memories"—and of his Roman friends it was Alice Bartlett who lived ultimately in South Carolina. Her anecdote concerned a simple and uninformed American woman who had been trailing through the hotels of Europe with a young daughter, "a child of nature and freedom." The girl picked up, with the best conscience in the world, a good-looking Roman "of a rather vague identity." The Italian seemed astonished at his luck. He was serenely exhibited, and introduced, in the Victorian-Roman-American society, where "dating" was much less relaxed than it is today. Miss Bartlett seems to have furnished few details. There had been some social setback, some snub administered to the innocent girl. Henry's pencil made a brief record of this seemingly inconsequential anecdote.

V

One of the first things that confronted him on his return to England, on all the railway book-stalls, was a pirated edition of *The American* with a dramatic picture on the cover showing tall Christopher Newman, flanked by Valentin de Bellegarde carrying a candle and Claire de Cintré, rather more blonde and less dignified than she was ever intended to be. These were the days of piratical publishing, and if Henry may have felt pleased at being so widely displayed—prematurely—in England, he also had the chagrin of recognizing that he would receive not a penny from the sale of this popular edition. His feelings moreover were not assuaged when he opened the volume. It was "vilely printed" and carelessly edited; whole paragraphs were omitted. Nor was he happy to receive proof from Germany of his growing fame—a pirated translation of the same novel, with a happy ending substituted for his own. Quite clearly it was time for him to take hold of his affairs as a writer not only in England but on the Continent.

What Henry did not see was the confidential report which John Morley had written for the Macmillans on *French Poets and Novelists*. The document, preserved in the Macmillan archive, reads rather quaintly today and shows Morley's blindness to Henry's essential qualities—a blindness that was to persist to the end. He reported that the essays were sensible and refined, free from narrowness and prejudice, and that they served their turn as fugitive criticism. "Of charm, delicacy, finesse," he said, "they have none. They are prosaic to the last degree, and *as criticism* not at all interesting." He had compared them with Sainte-Beuve and "Mr James, by such a test, must be called mediocre." The book might have some slight sale; nevertheless Morley did not believe it would make a deep literary mark. "The style wants *cachet* and distinction, and the method wants depth and subtlety." He concluded: "It is honest scribble work and no more."

Morley was right perhaps in saying that Henry's essays were not comparable to the work of Sainte-Beuve (who, to some extent, had been Henry's model). But, as a reader, Morley erred in seeking a French parallel to essays written for an English-speaking audience. What was much more important was that there had been no book in English as important as this one, on the new French writers: and the real question was whether these essays, written originally for American magazine audiences unfamiliar with France's mid-century writers, could serve a similar function in England. What Morley failed to recognize, and perhaps could

THE AMERICAN

Illustrated cover of "yellow-back" pirated issue

not have done at the time, was that Henry had singled out with critical accuracy the very writers who were ultimately to be influential in the English-speaking world. The essays on Balzac and on Turgenev (whom Henry here included as if he were French) were for that time remarkably prescient; and a reader today would quarrel with very few of James's subjects. When the book came out early in 1878 certain of the Victorian journals dismissed the essays as dealing with the "indecent" novelists of France. A qualified reviewer such as George Saintsbury, however, welcomed the volume, pronounced the papers on George Sand and Balzac to be "admirable" and astutely pointed to resemblances between Turgenev's work and James's. The only essay in the collection which was a distinct failure in appreciation was the one devoted to Baudelaire. Henry lagged in his understanding of symbolism, as he lagged in his grasp of impressionism. Moreover he was never a good critic of poetry. His method in general was to seek the personality of the writer in his work. This caused Saintsbury to argue that the book was too biographical, and not sufficiently critical. Henry believed, however, with Sainte-Beuve, that a critic could not but read a writer's works as the expression of the man. The critic had to remember that the artist "is present in every page of every book from which he sought so assiduously to eliminate himself"—an idea Proust was to echo in another form in arguing, as it happened, against Sainte-Beuve.

That the Macmillans decided to bring out the book in spite of Morley's adverse report may have had more to do with the firm's shrewd publishing sense than its opinion of the volume. The publishers had recognized that Henry was a productive writer, and they wanted to handle his work in England. If *French Poets and Novelists* would not make money, it would nevertheless place him under their wing. Henry, on arriving in Paris from Rome, found the bundles of proofs awaiting him and spent ten days there reading them—and paying visits. He had an opportunity to see Turgenev several times—"very bad with the gout" —at Bougival. He wrote to his mother that he was "better friends with him than ever."

He recrossed the Channel just before Christmas 1877. Fanny Kemble had asked him to join her at Alverston Manor House, Stratford-on-Avon, at the home of her daughter. He arrived on Christmas Eve, and we catch a glimpse of him, in a letter of Mrs Kemble's, as "our dark-bearded, handsome American friend," helping to trim the tree in the large nursery with its open arch roof, oak rafters and huge chimney. "Our American friend seemed very well pleased with all the ceremonies of the day, including church service in Shakespeare's church." The weather was brilliant. The picturesque house, with its big fires and its hangings of holly and mistletoe, provided a distinctive final setting to a remarkable year in Henry James's life—the happiest and most "lived" year yet. He had found an anchorage in London. *The American* was in its second edition in the United States, and Tauchnitz had just bought it for a Continental edition. He had profited by its success to revise minutely his old novel *Watch and Ward*, of six years before. *French Poets and Novelists* would be out in February and Macmillan was already asking for simultaneous serialization, in *Macmillan's Magazine*, of his next *Atlantic* novel. He faced the coming year with great and confident expectations.

DAISY

"My London life flows evenly along, making, I think in various ways, more and more a Londoner of me," Henry wrote to William at the end of January 1878. "If I keep along here patiently for a certain time I rather think I shall become a (sufficiently) great man. I have got back to work with great zest after my autumnal loafings, and mean to do some this year which will make a mark. I am, as you suppose, weary of writing articles about places, and mere potboilers of all kinds; but shall probably, after the next six months, be able to forswear it altogether, and give myself up seriously to 'creative' writing. Then, and not till then, my real career will begin. After that, *gare à vous*."

The passage reads as if Henry were proceeding according to a deliberate time-table. He must be patient for a "certain time;" he will make his mark "this year;" he will, after the next six months, be ready to begin to write in earnest. There was insight here into the inner calendar of his life. For what came to pass was that Henry wrote "Daisy Miller" during that winter; it was accepted by mid-April for the *Cornhill Magazine*—the journal of Thackeray and Trollope—and was published within six months. After that Henry was to be considered by the world "a (sufficiently) great man."

I

Almost the first thing Henry had done after returning from the Continent to his fireside in Bolton Street was to write the tale suggested by Miss Bartlett's anecdote: that of the American girl snubbed in Roman–American society. The story reads today—has always read—as if it had flowed spontaneously out of the tip of Henry's pen; it has a splendid lucidity and a vividness of form and detail; a kind of ironic laughter echoes between its lines until it reaches its final, gently-sketched scene of pathos. The circumstantial detail of "Daisy" lives with extraordinary authenticity, for it was transposed directly from Henry's half-dozen years of Continental journeyings. The little crimson drawing-room in the Via Gregoriana, where Mrs Walker turns her back on Daisy—we have seen Henry there, in January 1873, visiting the Tweedys; Vevey and the Castle of Chillon—this was where Henry and Alice joined the Bootts during their long-ago summer of Swiss travel; the Colosseum by moonlight, William's touch of the Roman fever, Giovanelli as a *cavaliere avvocato*, the Protestant cemetery—all spill over into fiction from felt backgrounds and Roman springtimes to give the tale its air of freshness and reality; there is no lingering and no explaining; the story moves with quiet, swift incident and an inexorable logic of its own.

That logic resides above all in the image of Daisy Miller. Miss Bartlett had no need to describe the young lady of her anecdote—Henry had seen her in her multitude, stepping confidently ashore from the transatlantic liners, in fine dresses with flounces and ribbons, carrying her head high, talking in her thin, gay voice, possessed of the *tournure* of a princess. Young Daisy is a clear and dancing image—pure nineteenth-century Schenectady or Utica, exposed to the bright Swiss summer-sun on Lake Geneva and the turquoise skies of Rome. For all her brilliant array of dresses and her air of sophistication, she is garbed in the innocence of Eve, in all her nakedness, before the tasting of the apple.

He had first submitted the tale to the editor of *Lippincott's* in Philadelphia, who returned it without comment. Henry was not certain why, and he found the absence of comment grim. He accordingly asked a friend (perhaps Leslie Stephen) to read the story; the opinion he got was that the editor had probably rejected it because he considered it "an outrage on American womanhood." Henry himself was not convinced; he thought that perhaps the story was simply too long. At any rate he submitted it to the laconic Stephen of the *Cornhill*, who accepted it "with effusion." In fact it was sent to the printer at once, and Henry made his bow for the first time in an English magazine in the June and July 1878 issues. His failure to assure himself of American publication lost him the valuable magazine market in the United States; the story was pirated immediately both in New York and Boston, and when Harper's brought it out in their Half-Hour Series as a pamphlet it sold 20,000 copies in a matter of weeks. It was priced at twenty-five cents and this meant that Henry's royalties were negligible. "I have made $200 by the whole American career of Daisy Miller," he told Howells. The tale was destined, however, to be "the most prosperous child" of Henry's invention.

II

Daisy Miller had a sub-title; Henry called it "A Study," perhaps to suggest that he had written the equivalent of a pencil-sketch on an artist's pad, rather than a rounded work. Later he said it was because of "a certain flatness" suggested in the very name of his heroine. And indeed the slightness of the story has made a later generation wonder why it should have proved so attractive. A modern reader, unrehearsed in the history of manners, would wonder, for instance, at the social fuss which occurs merely because an American girl "dates" an Italian. The informality of the twentieth century can little understand the formality of the nineteenth; and the snobberies of Roman–American society seem exaggerated to the point of caricature.

The story of Daisy's short-lived adventure in Europe begins in Vevey at the Trois Couronnes, where the Europeanized American, Winterbourne, meets in the garden of the hotel the little American boy Randolph, who is boastful, unhappy, full of misplaced energy and a quite justifiable sense of being dragged about Europe when he would rather be at home. While the stiff and formal Winterbourne—through whose eyes we see Daisy—chats with the boy, his sister joins them, and presently they are talking quite familiarly to one another, even if they have not been properly introduced. Her name is Annie P. Miller but everyone calls her Daisy. She is a pleasing flirt. "Did you ever hear of a nice girl that was not?" she asks. She expects young men to give her their undivided attention, and she arranges to go, unchaperoned, with her new acquaintance to visit the Castle of Chillon. Winterbourne's aunt, who knows all the proprieties, sniffs her disapproval, between migraine headaches; the best she will allow Daisy is that "she dresses in perfection—no, you don't know how well she dresses." For the rest, Winterbourne admits that the girl is rather "uncultivated." "She is very common," says his aunt.

Daisy is described to us, more often than not, in negatives; she is not insipid, and she is not exactly expressive; there is no mockery in her, and distinctly no irony. She has a bright, sweet, superficial little visage; her features are eminently delicate. "There isn't any society," she claims in describing her experiences of Europe, and she adds "I have always had a great deal of gentlemen's society." Her misfortune is that she does not know the European definition of a gentleman and believes her own conception of one to be universal.

Later that year, in Rome, Winterbourne meets her again: we still see her through his eyes. As in the anecdote, she has acquired a charming Italian; his name is Giovanelli; he has a moustache, is attentive, and if he does not understand her flirtatious nature, he "must wonder at his luck." Winterbourne perceives quite clearly that Daisy is not interested in marrying him and that the Italian does not hope to marry her; but he enjoys her company, and she is pleased to have a "gentleman" dance attendance on her, as her boy-friends did in Schenectady. It never occurs for a moment to Daisy that she is the subject of gossip, and that her behaviour violates the European code; that young girls simply do not go about without a chaperon. When Mrs Walker overtakes her and Giovanelli in the Pincian gardens and points out to her that what she is doing "is not the custom here," Daisy replies ingenuously enough: "Well, it ought to be, then!" The girl has no standards; she sets her own; she has never been given any; she does not even know what "standard" means. And even when she is snubbed in Mrs Walker's drawing-room, she does not comprehend the meaning of the gesture. She cannot accept the notion—it is fundamental to her nature—that conduct anywhere can be different from what she has known in Schenectady.

Winterbourne is unable to decide whether this bright, young, admirably turned-out example of the new American generation is "honest" or frivolous, whether she is innocent or wicked. A true Jamesian male, he never quite makes up his mind. When he encounters Daisy and Giovanelli rambling late in the evening in the Colosseum he thinks his worst suspicions may be right. The story moves swiftly to its dénouement. Daisy catches the Roman fever and dies of it; and "by the raw protuberance among the April daisies" in the Protestant cemetery Winterbourne and Giovanelli exchange the remarks which are, so to speak, her epitaph. "She was the most beautiful young lady I ever saw, and the most amiable," says Giovanelli—whose name expresses youth and irresponsibility—and he adds "she was the most innocent." Winterbourne, whose name expresses the frosty stiffness Daisy had complained of in him, can only stare at the grave and decide that Miss Miller would have "appreciated one's esteem."

III

If the tale of the girl from Schenectady is now a piece of superseded social history, one aspect of it has assumed a new importance: this is the unerring vision which James had of the total abdication, by the mass of American parents, of all authority over their children. The entire discussion of "permissiveness" in our time and the re-evaluation of progressive education make James's picture of the two Miller children singularly relevant. Daisy is allowed to wander about Rome with Giovanelli at all hours of the night; it is she, not her mother, who exercises authority over the travelling group; both in turn abdicate authority to Eugenio, the courier, who is treated as if he were a member of the family. Nine-year-old Randolph does as he pleases.

"Did you get Randolph to go to bed?" asked the young girl.
"No; I couldn't induce him," said Mrs Miller, very gently.
"He wants to talk to the waiter. He likes to talk to that waiter."

Daisy recalls that "it isn't so bad as it was at Dover."

"And what occurred at Dover?" Winterbourne asked.
"He wouldn't go to bed at all. I guess he sat up all night—in the public parlour. He wasn't in bed at twelve o'clock: I know that."
"It was half-past twelve," declared Mrs Miller, with mild emphasis.

The logic of this is that nine-year-olds apparently must be talked into going to bed, instead of being simply put there; and Randolph's rugged individualism is but the pioneer version of a generation of spoiled young allowed to dominate the American scene. Henry had remembered well the glimpses he had had of children asleep in leather chairs in the lobbies of Saratoga hotels at a late hour of the evening. He was to continue, in his tales, to portray the consequences for a civilization of an absence of standards and codes, of a society knowing no rules, and of a "freedom" which consisted in a kind of meaningless pampering of the young—offering the future citizens of his country neither a sense of history nor a charted course in life and civilization.

He was to give forcible utterance shortly after "Daisy" to this picture of the new American generation in a tale of comparative manners, "The Point of View," in which a repatriated American woman at Newport writes:

> The country is made for the rising generation; life is arranged for them; they are the destruction of society. People talk of them, consider them, defer to them, bow down to them. They are always present, and whenever they are present there is an end to everything else. They are often very pretty; and physically they are wonderfully looked after; they are scoured and brushed, they wear hygienic clothes, they go every week to the dentist's. But the little boys kick your shins, and the little girls offer to slap your face! There is an immense literature entirely addressed to them, in which the kicking of shins and the slapping of faces is much recommended. As a woman of fifty, I protest. I insist on being judged by my peers. It's too late, however, for several millions of little feet are actively engaged in stamping out conversation, and I don't see how they can long fail to keep it under. The future is theirs; maturity will evidently be at an increasing discount. Longfellow wrote a charming little poem called "The Children's Hour," but he ought to have called it "The Children's Century."

Seventy-five years after this was written, it is possible to say that the nineteenth—and the twentieth—century had indeed belonged and belongs to the American child.

"Daisy Miller" remains a remarkable story even if the manners it portrays are outmoded; it has a spare economy, a quick painting of background and a chasteness of narrative, in its summary sketching of American ignorance confronted by American rigidity abroad. It remains also the prototype of the "international" story. Henry was to write many more important and more brilliant tales, but "Daisy Miller," like its name, is a fresh and early flower still blooming among his works, "the little tragedy," as Henry explained to a lady who wrote to him, "of a light, thin, natural, unsuspecting creature being sacrificed as it were to a social rumpus that went on quite over her head and to which she stood in no measurable relation." The achieved pathos of this predicament softens Daisy's hardness of surface, and makes her a victim not only of parental and national ignorance, but of her own innocence. Winterbourne, at the end, can only wonder whether he hasn't lingered too long in Europe, whether a civilization—or absence of it—was developing in his native land which he did not know or understand.

IV

The story, as literary history knows, was an extraordinary success, but not the *succès de scandale* which legend has attributed to it. There was nothing in the public reaction to warrant any suggestion of "outrage." On the contrary, Daisy was distinctly liked by many American readers. She was a girl of spirit and from the American point of view, as Edmund Wilson has observed, that spirit went marching on. She resisted the inflexibility of the Europeanized Americans and stood her ground as a "child of nature and of freedom." Only one reviewer seemed to feel that she was unreal; the others, in general, complimented James on his portrayal of certain types of Americans travelling abroad—types, they said, perhaps too often found in Europe. The vogue set off by Daisy continued for a long time afterwards: she became a perennial figure—and "a Daisy Miller" was to be a much-used descriptive phrase whenever some particularly charming, forward young lady from America showed up in Continental surroundings. For a time there were "Daisy Miller" hats in the millinery shops, and presently another book appeared titled "An English Daisy Miller," by a magazine-writer named Virginia W.

Johnson. The little book was "Dedicated to American Women" and its general theme followed Henry's, substituting an English girl for the American. Henry's story was widely translated.

James had discovered nothing less than "the American girl"—as a social phenomenon, a fact, a type. She had figured in novels before, but never had she stood in fiction so pertly and bravely, smoothing her dress and asking the world to pay court to her. Hawthorne's American girl in Rome, Howells's American girl in Venice, had not been contrasted with Europe; and those Europeans who were reading Louisa May Alcott had a picture of the American girl largely in her domestic surroundings. The rustling young ladies on the verandahs at Saratoga, the busy beauties of uptown New York, the graceful, idle females of Newport, suddenly became Henry's great subject; and all by the simple turn of exhibiting them in their finery as in all the stages of their timidity or insolence, their doubt or their triumph—at the moment of their encounter with Europe and their refusal to yield their heritage of American innocence. The magazines now clamoured for his tales and Henry addressed himself to making the most of his advantage; in fast succession there came from his little sitting-room in Bolton Street "An International Episode," "The Pension Beaurepas," the short novel *Confidence*, and in due course such tales as "A Bundle of Letters." Henry James made himself the acknowledged master of the "international situation" and he was to use it on a large stage, with substantial characters, in major novels yet to be written. What he had begun in *Roderick Hudson* and *The American* as stories of American experience in Europe had now, by extension, been discovered by Henry to be social documents and to have the possibility of being rendered with a light touch and with the exploration of all the ironic, pathetic, comic as well as tragic elements in the theme. "The Americano-European legend," Henry was to call it in the end. And it was his creation, his peopled world. He was to deal with the American girl and the American woman—and the American man as well—exhibit them for almost half a century in their march through foreign countries and their exposure to foreign societies. A critic in the *Edinburgh Review* was prompted early to reflect on the strange new types which James had brought upon his horizon: American men who corresponded not at all to the popular notion of travelling Americans, and certainly less Philistine than Englishmen abroad, looking at churches, admiring works of art, indulging in civilized conversation, and contemplating their fellow-Americans—Winterbourne, for instance; Daisy Millers who availed themselves in Europe of the liberality and licence permitted to young unmarried women in the United States. Their unconventional behaviour and their seeming indiscretions might scandalize Europeans, the reviewer felt; but he noticed that even when their passing flirtations were tinged by romance, they usually married for satisfactory settlements. American women in all their variety passed before Henry: the timid, the adventurous, the self-made, the divorcée in search of respectability, the heiress in search of a princedom, the demure maiden in the European *pension* engaged in an earnest quest for "culture" and self-betterment —and always the chase for the husband. And these were all but a series of sketches from which he would paint his larger, full-length portraits. In a late preface he was to define the various states which he depicted, the predicaments of these fresh, positive, beguiling ladies. They were innocent and they were democratic; they were woefully ignorant of any concept of society—any sense of the old hierarchies and standards; they suffered from an acute state of "queenship," being the spoiled darlings of American men who in the "young roaring and money-getting democracy" were busy with their own affairs, possessing none of the leisure the European males of the upper classes enjoyed in courtship. American men wooed strenuously and when they married spent their days creating fortunes for the use of the women-folk. "An American woman who respects herself," says one of James's married ladies, "must buy something every day of her life. If she cannot do it herself, she must send out some member of her family for the purpose." Thus she explains one of her functions: and in a country of absentee husbands, women, in their reinforced egotism, assume supremacy; they take over education; they exercise such control as they can over the young. It is either excessive or excessively relaxed. James's concern for some years was to be with "the practical, positive, passionless young thing as we let her loose on the world."

To be sure, much that James wrote was true of any newly-rich society; and the absentee husband existed in Europe as well—indulging in his adulteries while his wife indulged in hers. What was new for the Europeans was the general freshness and innocence of these products of the new society, their spirit of conquest, their belief in themselves and their ability for self-improvement: above all the strange new egalitarianism, which nourished the legend that an American could do anything. These newcomers to the ancient civilization came from an order of wealth rather than of aristocracy; and James's picture of them contained a large measure of affection even while he satirized and criticized.

If "Daisy" provoked controversy it was precisely in the ranks of society. The drawing-rooms of Boston and New York echoed with it. "There are many ladies in and around New York today," observed the *New York Times* in June 1879, "who feel very indignant with Mr James for his portrait of Daisy Miller, and declare it is shameful to give foreigners so untrue a portrait of an American girl." The foreigners did not need Henry James Jr to give them that portrait; they were to see the American girls in their thousands down to modern times. "Harry James waked up all the women with his Daisy Miller, the intention of which they misconceived," Howells wrote to Lowell. "There has been a vast discussion in which nobody felt very deeply, and everybody talked very very loudly. The thing went so far that society almost divided itself into Daisy Millerites and anti-Daisy Millerites. I was glad of it, for I hoped that in making James so thoroughly known, it would call attention in a wide degree to the beautiful work he had been doing so long for very few readers."

Henry was to tell an anecdote many years later: how in Venice one day a lady-friend observing two young American girls had spoken of them to him as "Daisy Millers." This was to lead to a remonstrance from a second lady who was with them in their gondola. She remarked that *these* crude creatures were the real Daisies, about whom James had not written, and that the one he had created was a distortion, because he endowed her with form and prettiness and pathos and bathed her in the beautiful light of his own imagination. Henry was quite prepared to agree. "My supposedly typical little figure was of course pure poetry, and had never been anything else; since this is what helpful imagination, in however slight a dose, ever directly makes for."

V

By the time "Daisy Miller" appeared in the *Cornhill* during midsummer 1878, Henry James, writing with speed and assurance, had posted to Howells all four instalments of the serial he had promised him a year earlier—a short novel narrated in 100 pages of the *Atlantic Monthly*. In writing it Henry kept two promises he had made to his friend: he remained within the space allotted to him (the novel actually fills 91 pages), and he made up for his unhappy ending of *The American* by giving the reader no less than three marriages at the end of the story. *The Europeans* reversed the "international situation," to which Henry was, for the time at least, committed; instead of taking Americans to the Continent, he transferred two Europeans to America, to the Boston of 1840, even as in his next tale he was to place a British peer and his friend in midsummer Manhattan, and presently take the two to enjoy the breezes and the American girls at Newport.

The Europeans began its four-month run in the *Atlantic* in July 1878, the very month in which "Daisy Miller" was beginning its long vogue, in both legitimate and pirated form. The new work further enhanced James's popularity. Written in the same clear ironic prose, the short novel possessed neither the compact beauty of "Daisy" nor its power; it was simply a light and readable satire. Its characters were without development, almost stock personages; what sustained them was the beauty of the writing. In this novel Henry was saying that the puritans of New England's "silvery prime" possessed no *joie de vivre*. They are described as "of a pensive cast; they take things hard." Mr Wentworth, the head of his clan, looks "as if he were undergoing martyrdom, not by fire but by freezing," and he welcomes his

European relatives not through any human sense of hospitality but solely as an "extension of duty." When the European-American, Felix, wants to paint his portrait, he solemnly replies: "The Lord made it. I don't think it is for us to make it over again."

"What a pleasant house!" observes Felix on entering the New England dwelling. "It's lighter inside than it is out." He expatiates on its features: "It's very clean! No splendours, no gilding, no troops of servants; rather straight-backed chairs. But you might eat off the floors, and you can sit down on the stairs." The inhabitants of this bright establishment are sad; they "take a painful view of life." "Nothing makes them happy. No one is happy here." The Baroness observes, "You Americans have such odd ways. You never ask anything outright; there seem to be so many things you can't talk about." Henry's epigrams have none of the mannered qualities of Oscar Wilde's but they are emphatic in their quiet truths. "Nothing exceeds the license occasionally taken by the imagination of very rigid people." "Curiosity, pushed to a given point, might become romantic passion." "You are all so afraid here of being selfish." "I am told they [Bostonians] are very sincere; they don't tell fibs." James was to repeat this remark in the first paragraph of *The Bostonians*.

The writing contains this kind of sustained wit and brilliancy; and there are fine atmospheric touches; the horse-cars, the sunsets, the Boston streets, the steel-engravings of religious mottoes on the walls—all painted in clear water-colours. If, on the one hand, James gave Howells more marriages than he had asked for, he remained on the other hand true to himself: the important marriage of the story does not take place. Mr Acton, the congenial New Englander who has travelled in the East and is not altogether parochial, cannot bring himself to propose to the interesting and glamorous Eugenia; he is not sure she is an "honest" woman; he is quite sure that she does occasionally tell a fib. Eugenia accordingly returns to her little European duchy and her morganatic marriage, while her younger brother, an easy bohemian, marries the uninspired though romantic Gertrude Wentworth. James did not take this work very seriously, nor did he intend it to be anything more than the comedy he made of it. Nevertheless it has all the quiet tenderness of an old-time novel; and when it came out as a book in the autumn of 1878 it found a wide public both in London and in Boston. To be sure, certain Boston reviewers, among them T. W. Higginson, murmured very much like James's characters in the novel, at his imputation of parochialism in the Boston way of life. But the best notices felt, quite rightly, that the work was inferior to *The American*, that the characters were puppets, and that Henry had not tried very hard.

In Madrid the new American minister to Spain, James Russell Lowell, chuckled over the novel. He had grown up with Mr Wentworth's generation, and he wrote to Henry, "You revived in me the feeling of *cold furniture* which New England life has often *goose-fleshed* me with [so] that I laughed and shivered at once." Before going to Spain, Lowell had asked the State Department to appoint Henry as secretary of legation. He now congratulated himself that it had refused his request. The department had taken the view that one senior inexperienced diplomat in a legation was enough. Lowell had not even consulted Henry, who, on learning of his proposal, had been worried lest he should get the appointment. He felt that it would have been difficult to decline it. He had never taken a position of any kind, and had no desire to assume one at the very moment when he was achieving the greatest measure of personal freedom and success he had yet known.

VI

As 1878 drew to a close Henry wrote one more tale. This was his story of Lord Lambeth on Broadway and in Newport, his offer of marriage to a young American bluestocking and her rejection of him. James placed great store by his idea of having a young girl from Massachusetts reject a British peer. In "An International Episode" Bessie Alden constantly admonishes Lord Lambeth for taking no interest in his responsibilities as one of his nation's aristocrats. The story begins brightly with the two

Englishmen dawdling in a hot New York filled with mosquitoes; but it wanes a little once the Englishmen reach Newport—and becomes even thinner than *The Europeans*. The characters are mere sketches, and the tale is designed to underline the bad manners of certain members of the British aristocracy and the "thoughtfulness" and democratic feeling of the American girl. There had been, perhaps, a little too much laughter at Daisy Miller's expense in England, and Henry did not want to appear in the invidious rôle of a satirist to the English world of Americans abroad. His suspicions were borne out by a review of "An International Episode" (after it had appeared in the *Cornhill*) written by Mrs F. H. Hill, wife of the editor of the *Daily News* whom James had met socially in London. Mrs Hill accused James of caricaturing the British nobility, and of putting language into its mouth which it would never utter. Henry on this occasion replied, since he knew the lady, and the letter is a magisterial defence of his work and his art. It is the only letter extant which he wrote to a reviewer.

In it Henry defends himself against having made his Englishmen repeat "I say" too often. He had studied English colloquialisms, he told Mrs Hill, during his period at the St James's Club, and had heard "more 'I says' than I had ever done before." And then he defended himself against Mrs Hill's charge that in describing the manners of the two rude English noblewomen he was expressing a view of English manners in general. The passage that follows, addressed to this one reviewer, can be applied to a whole generation of critics which subsequently was to read more things into James's stories than he ever put into them:

A man in my position, and writing the sort of things I do, feels the need of protesting against this extension of his idea in which, in many cases, many readers are certain to indulge. One may make figures and figures without intending generalizations—generalizations of which I have a horror. I make a couple of English ladies doing a disagreeable thing—*cela c'est vu*: excuse me!—and forthwith I find myself responsible for a representation of English manners! Nothing is my *last word* about anything—I am interminably supersubtle and analytic—and, with the blessing of heaven, I shall live to make all sorts of representations of all sorts of things. It will take a much cleverer person than myself to discover my last impression—among all these things—of anything. And then, in such a matter, the bother of being an American! Trollope, Thackeray, Dickens, even with their big authoritative talents, were free to draw all sorts of unflattering English pictures, by the thousand. But if I make a single one, I am forthwith in danger of being confronted with a criminal conclusion—and sinister rumours reach me as to what I think of English society. I think more things than I can undertake to tell in 40 pages of the *Cornhill*. Perhaps some day I shall take more pages, and attempt to tell some of these things; in that case, I hope, there will be a little, of every sort, for every one! Meanwhile I shall draw plenty of pictures of disagreeable Americans, as I have done already, and the friendly Briton will see no harm in that!—it will seem to him a part of the natural fitness!

To his mother he wrote of the tale: "It seems to me myself that I have been very delicate; but I shall keep off dangerous ground in future. It is an entirely new sensation for them (the people here) to be (at all delicately) *ironized* or satirized, from the American point of view, and they don't at all relish it. Their conception of the normal in such a relation is that the satire should be all on their side against the Americans; and I suspect that if one were to push this a little further one would find that they are extremely sensitive. But I like them too much and feel too kindly to them to go into the satire-business or even the light-ironical in any case in which it would wound them—even if in such a case I should see my way to it very clearly."

But Henry was soon to discover the expense of subtlety: it was not the last time that he would find his ironies mistaken for cruelties, his humour turned into vast generalizations.

Whatever the sensitiveness of his readers, whether in London or in Boston or New York, Mrs Hill's review was more than a straw in the wind. It showed that Henry was being read, and that even his "light-ironical" was being taken more seriously than he intended. He had the sense at last of his power, of the writer whose image of society becomes the mirror in which society looks at itself. He had come to England two years ago comparatively unknown and had moved with the silence of an observer through the English scene. Now he was a literary lion, an authoritative voice, a recognized artist. It had been a swift and remarkable success—a conquest of an alien society and an alien audience;

and this he had accomplished by his pen alone, the force of his imagination, his genius.

His third Christmas in England was a far cry from the first in Bolton Street, or even the second with Mrs Kemble. This time he went into Yorkshire to be the guest of Charles Milnes Gaskell; and to greet the new year at Lord Houghton's. It was "a hideous part of England—the Yorkshire manufacturing country, which is blighted and darkened by smoke and cinders, and the presence of a dreary population." The population formed "a not very attractive element in that great total of labour and poverty on whose enormous base all the luxury and leisure of English country-houses are built up." Gaskell drove him in a sledge through the deep snow to Bretton to call on Lady Margaret Beaumont, grand-daughter of Mr Canning, "a drawling, lisping fine lady enclosed in her great wintry park and her immense, dusky, pictured, luxurious house—with her tea-table at one elbow and a table-full of novels at the other." Lord Houghton took Henry to visit the old Duchess of Somerset, a one-time "Queen of Beauty," and now "a dropsical, garrulous old woman." The "Bird of Paradox" was as usual charming to Henry. "Lord Houghton has just come into my room [Henry remarks in the midst of writing a letter to his sister Alice] to know why I haven't come to afternoon tea, and plumping himself into my armchair, is apparently lapsing into social slumber. He is a very odd old fellow—extremely fidgety and eccentric; but full of sociable and friendly instinct, and with a strong streak of humanity and democratic feeling. He has begun to snore violently and I must finish my letter as I can."

The letter is not finished. Henry goes down to dinner and listens with delight to endless anecdotes told by Mrs Procter, intimate pictures sketched by her of Carlyle, arriving at Basil Montagu's, her father's, earlier in the century and leaving with a bundle of borrowed books carefully wrapped up in a big blue calico handkerchief "—but I must check my frivolous gossip, dearest sister," Henry writes late in the evening, "in which I have indulged in the hope of affording you a little innocent amusement."

The new year is coming in over the frosty land. "It is just 12 o'clock—1879. My blessing on it for all of you. I hope you are having a reasonable winter—here it is a very different affair from the two last and the Yorkshire climate has given me back the chilblains of infancy. Love to dear parents, from your *devotissimo*. H. James jr."

THE TWO SECRETARIES

THEIR names were Hoppin and Nadal. William Jones Hoppin was First Secretary of the American Legation in London and Ehrman Syme Nadal was Second Secretary. Mr Hoppin was sixty-three, perhaps a little old to be starting a career in diplomacy. A successful lawyer and a man of means, he had been nominated to the post by the new administration of President Hayes and had arrived in the British capital a few weeks before Henry James. The First Secretary had practised at the bar in New York for many years. He was a gregarious individual with an interest in the arts. A bachelor who had written verses, translated plays from the French and was conversant with the latest art criticism, he had felt that he must accept this call to national duty; moreover the idea of descending upon London, in the Indian summer of his life, appealed to him. If his post was not that of a full-fledged Minister, it was the next best thing to it—and indeed for a period between the ministry of Mr Welsh and that of Mr Lowell he did act as *chargé d'affaires*.

Mr Nadal, the Second Secretary, was a Virginian, twenty years younger than Mr Hoppin. He had served in the London Legation at the beginning of the seventies and then returned to New York to be a journalist. He had written his impressions of London social life and sundry articles for the magazines. Now he was resuming his diplomatist's career. The two Secretaries had distinctly different temperaments; they belonged to different generations and different sides of the once-divided nation. Mr Hoppin was a strenuous Yankee, Mr Nadal a relaxed southerner. The only thing they shared in common, over and above their responsibility to their position, was an ambition to succeed socially in the British capital.

I

Mr Hoppin, in all that he did, showed the signs of his Puritan upbringing and his New England sense of duty. Although a man of wealth, he had carefully resigned all his financial involvements before coming abroad; and while he could have afforded a large establishment he took a modest place and engaged only a housekeeper. Having a long legal experience, he performed his duties punctiliously. Feeling also that this was to be the largest experience of his life, he began to keep a *Journal of a Residence in London.* Since he remained in London for a decade, the journal is of some amplitude: it runs to twelve large bound volumes in which Hoppin's regular entries, written in a neat and flowing hand, are embroidered by all the mementoes of his London life: theatre-programmes, newspaper-clippings, restaurant-menus, and other memorabilia. The journal itself, never published and preserved in the Houghton Library at Harvard, provides an interesting record of the comings and goings of Americans in London and the official activities during the ministries of Pierrepont, Welsh and James Russell Lowell. It records also Mr Hoppin's mild pleasures, largely cultural and social, in the capital. In New York Mr Hoppin had moved in the very best circles. He was a member of the Union League Club and a founder of the Century Association. He wanted to discover good society in London, to meet amiable ladies and to frequent celebrities. Henry Adams, writing to Lowell when the latter was named Minister to England, told him that "Hoppin is rather sensitive, and you will perhaps need to be a little careful to humour him." Hoppin was indeed inclined to be fussy and compulsive; but he had great respect for Lowell and served him faithfully and well. Nadal later described his elderly colleague as "a cultivated and very agreeable man, about as good a type of American gentleman as it would be possible to find."

Mr Hoppin would not have been flattered, since he considered Mr Nadal rather a lightweight, and his journal abounds in his irritated sense of his colleague's laxities. It was true that Nadal contented himself with doing as little work as possible, dawdling about London and cultivating the English and whatever literary folk came his way. His *Impressions of London Social Life*, published in 1875, and his later volume of reminiscences, reflect his superficial and amiable view of life. Henry James had reviewed the first book during his winter of work in Manhattan; he described it as a "gentlemanly book," in good taste and free of indiscretions. But Nadal's observations seemed to Henry "vague and ineffectual." Mr Nadal was a little more assertive than Mr Hoppin, but not disagreeably so. Mr Hoppin, on his side, felt that his years, his social and diplomatic position, could always speak for him. He seemed, therefore, a trifle shy. At least twice during his London residence he was the subject of particular comment in the press. The first was when, during a Guildhall dinner, he announced his rank so indistinctly (and insisted on calling himself *chargé d'affaires*, when he was, in effect, American Plenipotentiary for the occasion) that the heralds' voices stumbled over the French and sank to a whisper. Mr Smalley, reporting to the *Tribune* that the German Ambassador was cheered, added that the "American diplomatist would not have been less warmly greeted had his presence been made known with equal distinctness." The other occasion involved questions of dress. Edmund Yates, who had been the subject of an historic quarrel between Dickens and Thackeray, inserted a paragraph in his gossip-column in the *World* which read: "Mr Hoppin, the American *chargé d'affaires*, has taken to attending courts and drawing-rooms in a nondescript uniform, which includes 'breeches.' Will he be censured by his Government?" The *Daily Telegraph* apparently scoffed at this, by referring in an article on the opening of Parliament to "the defiant simplicity of the white tie and swallow coat of the American representative." Mr Hoppin noted apropos of the "breeches" that it was the same dress he had always worn, and which had been worn by all members of the Legation since Reverdy Johnson advanced the matter with Lord Clarendon in February 1879. A journal-entry of a few days later records a dinner at which Henry James, the Henry Adamses, Lady Hamilton Gordon and Mrs Duncan Stewart were present and there was "a great deal of joking about my 'breeches.' "

II

Early in 1877, when Mr Hoppin had been in London but a few months, he met Lord Houghton. So far as we know he was not invited to his breakfasts. But the literary peer had always liked Americans, and he gave Mr Hoppin a card to the discussion club, the Cosmopolitan, to which Henry James had also been invited. On a Sunday evening in March Mr Hoppin directed his footsteps to 30 Charles Street, Berkeley Square, at about eleven—for the discussions were usually held informally and at the evening's end. He surveyed the large gloomy house which seemed deserted save that its skylight, covering the topmost storey, was illuminated. The building had served as a studio for the painter George Frederick Watts. Mr Hoppin entered, found that Lord Houghton was not yet there, and was persuaded by the doorman to take off his coat and hat and mount the stairs. Here he discovered a large barnlike studio with an immense mythological picture on the side-wall. There were tables with tea-cups, three bottles of spirits, and a provision of soda. Six or seven gentlemen were seated round the fire. None rose; no one noticed Mr Hoppin. "This was characteristically English," he wrote in his journal. He marched about, looked at some of the pictures, and when Lord Houghton did not show up re-descended the stairs.

Another gentleman was just arriving. He was rather short and stocky, and wore a dark beard. He spoke to the doorman and then turning to Mr Hoppin introduced himself as Henry James, an American; he said he too was waiting for Lord Houghton, and the two mounted the stairs again. Mr James knew one of the men, Mr Edward Dicey, and introduced Hoppin. Presently Lord Houghton arrived and "everything thenceforth was smooth and easy."

The incident was banal enough, save that Mr Hoppin recorded the circumstances without giving any indication of the talk. This is one of the exasperations of his journal. It retails facts, but it seldom describes; it has the true flavour of a dry diplomatic report. After this evening the name of Mr Henry James begins to appear with a certain frequency in the journal. Thus it records that they met at the St James's Club on 6 January 1878. Mr Hoppin's account of that occasion reads: "I dined there last evening for the first time. Henry James, the author, was there, who had been introduced by Nadal, and I joined table with him. Nothing remarkable in the talk—I think that men [who] live by writing for the magazines on current topics seldom ventilate their choice ideas. They keep them to be fresh in the market. The dinner was not so good as I had expected."

Perhaps Mr James did not care to ventilate his "choice ideas" to Mr Hoppin; for a later account of James's talk, set down by Nadal, says that "James talked incessantly and with the originality and somewhat of the authority of those who read aloud to you their thoughts out of their own mind. His talk was very alert and eager."

Nadal and Henry had met at the American Legation during the 4 July reception of 1877, four months after the novelist's first encounter with Hoppin. Nadal too has left us a record of the occasion: "A rather dark and decidedly handsome young man of medium height, with a full beard, stood in the doorway and bowed rather stiffly, as if he were not to be confused with the rank and file of his compatriots. I was at once struck by his appearance." He is introduced and when he discovers that James lives in Bolton Street mentions that he had had rooms there when he first came to London, at No. 6. Henry invites him to come and see him. "Mine are No. 3, the half of your old number; you can remember it by that." Nadal in due course comes. He remembers that the door was opened by a slender dark young woman. Henry explains she is not a servant but a relative of the landlady. "She's an English character," he explains. "She isn't a lady and she isn't a woman; she's a person." He was always discussing English class-distinctions, and Nadal noted that he made a point constantly of saying he was a foreigner. He resented, he told Nadal, the remark made by a lady of the middle class he had visited when she said: "That is true of the aristocracy, but in one's own class it is different," meaning, said James, "her class and mine." Henry did not wish to be "adjudged a place in English society in accordance with English standards."

Nadal's memories of James are also recorded in a factual manner, but with more perception; they seem circumstantial, and reasonably authentic. Nevertheless Henry James, like Mr Hoppin, would have considered Mr Nadal a superficial reporter. To his sister Alice he wrote that "the little second secretary of legation" was "a most amiable nature but the feeblest and vaguest mind, and socially speaking, a perfect failure here—though he is not aware of it and it doesn't seem at all to have embittered him. He is a wonderful specimen of American innocence." And to Norton he wrote after Lowell became Minister, "I wish he had a pair of secretaries that ministered a little more to the idea of American brilliancy. Lowell has to do *that* quite by himself."

III

If Henry James had been able to read over Mr Hoppin's shoulder as he wrote in his steady straight-line hand the record of his London doings he would have discovered that, unlike Nadal, Hoppin knew that he was a failure in London society, and it made him very bitter. It was in the second year of their acquaintance, after the 1878–79 Season, that Mr Hoppin was prompted to write an essay in his journal to which he appended the bold title, "The Position of a Stranger in London Society." This little essay stemmed from Henry's remarking, on meeting Mr Hoppin, that he had dined out that winter no less than 140 times, a figure somewhat higher than that which he had given Grace Norton two months before, when he had said he had dined out 107 times. In the intervening period he had apparently eaten thirty-three additional dinners. Mr. Hoppin obviously had been crushed.

This great success of James leads me to inquire how it is that some people succeed so well here while others constantly fail. I class myself decidedly among the failures. I make new acquaintances but they never lead to friendships. I meet a woman at a dinner, I talk to her as pleasantly as I can—I hear afterwards that she speaks of me as agreeable. But she never asks me to her receptions or dinners. There was Mrs Douglas Salters, for instance, whom I took in to dinner at Mr Washington Jackson's. She enjoyed my talk, I know—but she never asked me to visit her. I am satisfied that youth and personal appearance have a good deal to do with such matters. An old fellow like myself with an unprepossessing exterior has but a small chance. I don't write this by way of complaint. I merely state the facts. I amuse myself sufficiently without these attentions.

Nevertheless Mr Hoppin was determined to understand the Jamesian success and to explain it to himself. He felt that society in London was so immense that a man could attract attention only by having high rank or personal attractiveness—or the art of enlisting attention and regard. In London one had no time to "*grow* into favour. You must strike for it at once." He returns to the novelist:

Henry James is good looking, has good manners, but more than all, he is a popular author. People read his books and their curiosity is piqued to know him. I don't think he talks remarkably well. I believe he keeps his most piquant ideas for his novels—but he has that dash of cynicism which is in fashion. There is nothing that pleases a woman so much as to hear some spicy ill-natured *Wort* about her best friends. A kind-hearted man who is naturally disposed to like people—to admire beauty—to find out who is becomingly dressed—has no chance at all in companion with an ill-natured growler who growls in an original tone.

Mr Hoppin then speculated on how he might have achieved success. If he had allowed the word to spread that he had an income, and if he had entertained more and had a larger establishment, "this would have brought all the angular old maids and widows with their projecting teeth and big feet to term and I should have been enormously in request." There was one comfort. "Such kindness as I do receive is for myself and not for my money."

From dispassionate analysis Mr Hoppin had moved to a distinct *apologia*; in the process he made no further reference in this entry to Henry James.

IV

In their talk about society and social success in London, Nadal gained the impression that Henry James did not want to be "in smart English society because he really preferred the company of smart people. It was rather that he did not like to feel that he was shut out from that or any other kind of company." He told Nadal that he wanted "to be taken seriously" by the English. This was a phrase he often used. He particularly detested "that excluded feeling." Nadal added: "I dare say also that he wanted to be enough in smart company to know what it was like. He wished to be an international novelist, and desired to know that as well as other parts of English life." Lafcadio Hearn, who had undergone a more difficult expatriation than James's, also remarked on this. "There are very few men strong enough to stand the life of society and to write," he observed. "I can think of but one of importance—that is Henry James—but his special study is society."

One day Nadal spoke critically of certain Americans who had pursued social success in London and had been snubbed. Nadal had disapproved of their attempt: he saw no reason why they should have exposed themselves to rudeness at the hands of London's social leaders. Henry James's reply was perhaps the most significant of all that Nadal set down:

"I don't agree with you. I think a position in society is a legitimate object of ambition."

A POSITION IN SOCIETY

In his late years Henry James was to look back on the old Victorian society in London, which he had known intimately, as some strange other-world. "Nowhere so much as in England was it fortunate to *be* fortunate," he wrote, and that remained the tone of his reminiscence. He had said as much in the early days of his English domicile; he reaffirmed it in the grandeur of his final style. "I confess without scruple," he was to write, "to have found again and again at that time an attaching charm in the general exhibition." He was writing when the guns of the First World War had already opened up across the Channel, obliterating decades of memory and of "progress." That world had been, he could see, "the fool's paradise really rounded and preserved, before one's eyes, for those who were so good as to animate it."

And thus he could speak of "the extinct societies that once were so sure of themselves," of the "thousand dimmed illusions" and "certain complacencies of faith and taste." It had been the day of the "blandly idle and the supposedly accomplished," of "amiabilities and absurdities, harmless serenities and vanities, pretensions and undertakings, unashamed." But this was the after-sight, the backward-vision, the philosophical musing on the elapsed historic moment. In 1878 and 1879—the two great years of Henry James's descent upon and conquest of London—it had all been a swiftly moving adventure, this return of an American to the past of his culture and his race, and his deep plunge into a society comparatively small and comparatively unquestioned. A society, as W. H. Mallock wrote, "mainly founded on the hereditary possession of the land, its nucleus being the heads of more or less ancient families whose rent rolls enabled them to occupy London houses and play an agreeable and ornamental part in the business of entertaining and being entertained for the few months called the Season. It was part of the order of Nature." Hyde Park, at certain hours of the day, had the aspect of a garden-party; Piccadilly "was a vision of open carriages brilliant with flowerlike parasols, high-stepping horses and coachmen, many of whom still wore wigs." For the American from Cambridge this London, which he could observe both as "insider" and "outsider"—and move about in with much greater freedom than if he had been an Englishman—provided an endless opportunity for observation, exploration and discovery. And he was in the fortunate position of being admirably equipped to take it in a large American stride.

I

If in France Henry James had but walked the periphery of society, in London he was presently caught in its full tide. It was, as we have seen, a gradual and almost imperceptible process: one call led to another, one dinner to another, until he was constantly dining out. At first he accepted invitations to luncheon as well; very soon, however, he had to take precautions against being drawn into the morning and afternoon leisure of the upper classes. Only his evenings were dedicated to the pursuit of his "legitimate ambition." It was he who in reality was pursued—pursued to the point that, after a year or two of strenuous social life, he tended to flee London or to frequent it during the "dead season." For the time, however, he gave himself over to the social process with the same systematic care he had exercised in the planning of his professional career. During his first winter he was the observer and explorer; by the time the second came round he had achieved literary fame and was in continual demand. It was during this winter of 1878–79 that—by the count of his engagement-book and Hoppin's record—he dined out 140 times. One may suppose this to represent an almost unparalleled account-keeping of sociability and gregariousness. To have had the stamina to face so many evenings of talk—not all of them good talk, by any means—so many heavily-loaded tables, so much "stuffy" Victorian formality, was some kind of test of endurance. Henry endured; he thrived on it. It completed his "Londonizing process."

His dining-out among celebrities dated from his early weeks in London, when he was as yet known to but a few, and when he had been "launched" by his fellow-countryman, George Washburn Smalley, one of the most respected of American journalists abroad. Smalley had made his name as a war correspondent on the fronts of the Civil War. Since that time he had written dispatches from the Austro-Prussian and the Franco-Prussian wars as well. A New Englander who had grown up among abolitionists, he had known little of "society" in his youth, and now went in for it, Henry observed, tooth and nail. He was received everywhere in London, and was in every way a "man of the world," with the result that the intimate dinners at his home were usually distinguished occasions, an Anglo-American meeting-ground. Henry had sat down during that winter with Mr Froude, the historian and biographer, Mr Kinglake, whose book of eastern travels had enchanted him during his adolescence, his fellow-American Mr Motley, and with Mr Browning. Henry's attention focused first of all on the poet, also one of the heroes of his youth; and on Kinglake, who, sitting beside him, was "a most delicious, sweet, old man, as urbane and deferential as Emerson." Browning, however, was a bit of a shock. He was "no more like to Paracelsus than I to Hercules," he wrote home, and to Howells he said he was "a great chatterer, but no Sordello at all." At sixty-five Robert Browning was a hardened diner-out. The young novelist and the old poet were to find themselves often at the same lamp-lit Victorian tables.

"Robert B. I am sorry to say," he writes to Alice, "does not make on me a purely agreeable impression. His transparent eagerness to hold the *di de la conversation* and a sort of shrill interruptingness which distinguishes him have in them a kind of vulgarity. Beside which, strange to say, his talk doesn't strike me as very good. It is altogether gossip and personality and is not very beautifully worded. But evidently there are two Brownings—an esoteric and an exoteric. The former never peeps out in society, and the latter has not a ray of suggestion of *Men and*

Women." He was to continue to find Browning an idle gossip; but he was to say of him also that he was "the writer of our time of whom, in the face of the rest of the world, the English tongue may be most proud—for he has touched *every*thing, and with a breadth!"

II

And so Henry was launched. At first he was invited to the great houses of London because of his personal charm and wit; as his work began to be published in England, he presently found himself much in demand, not only for dinners but as guest in country houses. The new life is reflected almost step by step in the correspondence with Quincy Street; to his mother and sister he enumerates the various dinners and deftly sketches certain of his dinner-companions; to his father he mentions the personalities which would interest him; with William he is inclined to be a little more cautious and he generalizes more. William after all is critical, and Henry is always flexible in his epistolary skills. "I suppose William will call me a 'fat snob' for mentioning these names," he writes to his mother after enumerating certain diners, "but if they amuse Alice and you, I don't care for William."

(In England three years later William was to write to Quincy Street: "The way he worked at paying visits and going to dinners and parties was surprising to me, especially as he was all the time cursing them for so frustrating his work. It shows the perfect fascination of the whirlpool of a capital when once you are in it." It was more than fascination. It was all part of a writer's daily work.)

During these early London years Henry came to see many walks of English life as represented at these social occasions. He studied the English inevitably with greater attention than he had bestowed upon British scenery and British ruins. There was first of all the fascination of meeting the writers whom he already knew intimately through their works. Browning was but one instance. He meets Walter Pater at the home of the Hertz's, German Jews living in a pleasant house in Harley Street. They "are insatiate lion-hunters and most naif in their pursuit of notabilities." Pater is "far from being as beautiful as his own prose," and though Henry chats with him he does not tell Quincy Street what they chatted about. George Meredith he encounters at a dinner in the home of the Positivist, J. Cotter Morison; he finds the novelist "a singular but decidedly brilliant fellow, full of talk, paradoxes, affectations, etc. but interesting and witty, and of whom, if he didn't live in the country, I should see more. He hates the English, whom he speaks of as 'they.' "

"Their conversation is dreary," said Meredith on this occasion to Henry, "their food is heavy, their women are dull."

At the home of Madame du Quaire (he had met her at Madame de Blocqueville's in Paris) he meets Matthew Arnold for the first time since their long-ago encounters at the Barberini. "I cannot get over a feeling of pleasure that he writes just as he does; even his limitations have a practical excellence." Later at W. E. Forster's he meets Arnold's entire family and sits next to the eldest daughter, "as pretty as an American girl and chattering as freely."

Then there is the Thackeray-Stephen-Ritchie circle. He had met Leslie Stephen in London long before, and the editor of the *Cornhill* had been kind and hospitable. He encounters him now after the death of his wife, the former Miss Thackeray, and finds him "rendered more inarticulate than ever." Later he meets his new wife (whose second daughter, yet unborn, will be Virginia Woolf) and is charmed by her beauty. Henry decides Stephen is too aloof to be a good companion. He finds himself rather fond of the surviving Thackeray daughter, recently married to a man much younger than herself, Richmond Ritchie. He takes her in to dinner on one occasion, "further advanced toward confinement than I have ever seen a lady at a dinner party." She is "lovable and even touching" in her "extreme good nature and erratic spontaneity." He tells Grace Norton that she has "the minimum of common sense, but quite the maximum of good feeling." He is invited to the home of the famous Victorian dilettante, Charles Hamilton Aidé, "an aesthetic bachelor of a certain age and a certain fortune, moving apparently in the best society and living in sumptuous apartments." Here he meets George du Maurier, "a delightful little fellow." They will become close friends. Early in his dining out he re-encounters Trollope, "a very good genial ordinary fellow—much better than he seemed on the steamer when I crossed with him." At Sir Robert Cunliffe's, a friend of Henry Adams, he meets the talkative poetaster and civil servant F. T. Palgrave, who will ultimately be remembered for that substantial symbol of his era, his anthology of poetry, *The Golden Treasury*. Palgrave takes a great liking to Henry, and frequently visits him in Bolton Street in the morning on his way to his office in Whitehall, thus breaking into the novelist's working hours. "Palgrave is the biggest talker in England or the world—it's a current there's no standing against—and he is frightfully abusive of everyone and everything save a very small number of perversely-chosen idols. But his bark is worse than his bite." And again: "He is, I imagine, the most disappointed man in England. He was the great man of his day at college and was expected to set the world on fire. But here he is at middle-age only an inspector of schools and an editor of little books of verse. He feels it much and it has soured him."

He meets the well-known Positivist, Frederick Harrison, "who in spite of his aspect, complexion, hair-brushing etc. as of a provincial second-rate dandy, is very good company. The contrast between Harrison's Comtism, communism etc. and his highly ornate and conventional appearance, is most singular." There is also W. H. Mallock, then the talk of London because his *New Republic* had just been published, "a most disagreeable and unsympathetic youth, with natural bad manners increased by the odious London affectation of none. He strikes me as 'awfully clever;' but I opine that he will produce no other spontaneous or fruitful thing." The judgment was accurate.

III

Not all the dinners are pleasant. "I dined last night," he writes to William, "at the New University Club with Ernest Myers and four or five *çi-devant* Oxford men who are supposed to be choice spirits—Andrew Lang—a leader writer for *The Times* etc. I suppose this strikes you as an attractive occasion and in the stillness of Harvard Street excites your envy and speculation. But it failed to give me a sense of rare privilege—owing, partly, I think, to the ungemütlich *associations* I have, humanly, with Oxford—dreary, ill-favoured men, with local conversation and dirty hands. (All men in London, however, have dirty hands.)" He writes in the same vein of a dinner at the Albert Diceys', "who are good, but decidedly too ugly, useful-informationish, grotesque-Oxfordish, poor-dinnerish etc., too surrounded with emulous types of the same not to make one feel that one can do better."

A dinner at Frederick Locker's—the writer of light verse and celebrated bibliophile—proves deadly dull, Lord and Lady Thurlow, General Hamley etc. Thurlows speechless; Hamley disagreeable; Henry listless with a horrible cold, the Lockers trivial, and the room freezing. But if this can happen on one evening, there can be others when a pleasing incident colours the stuffiness of the diners and the dinners. In one of the great houses he finds himself sitting next to an ugly little wizened old woman who is very entertaining and reminiscent. She is the great dancer Taglioni. She has run through her various fortunes and in the evening of her days gives lessons to the daughters of the aristocracy. She tells Henry that she is well-received *dans le monde*. "*J'ai ma position de femme mariée*," she says, "*et puis j'ai ma position de—Taglioni!*"

He meets the British scientist in the person of T. H. Huxley, "a delightful sympathetic man" to whose home he is invited, a "pleasant, easy, no dress-coat sort of house" in St John's Wood, in Marlborough Place, where Henry had lived as a boy. The Huxleys are like New Englanders and charming. "Huxley is a very genial, comfortable being—yet with none of the noisy and windy geniality of some folks here, whom you find with their backs turned when you are responding to the remarks that they have very offensively made you. But of course my talk with him is mere amiable generalities. These, however, he likes to cultivate, for recreation's sake, of a Sunday evening."

He meets the British soldier, embodied in the personality of

Sir Garnet Wolseley—in a great house in Portman Square, filled with Queen Anne bric-à-brac "to a degree that quite flattens one out." Here he finds "plain women, gentlemanly men etc. Sir Garnet is a very handsome, well-mannered and fascinating little man—with rosy dimples and an eye of steel: an excellent specimen of the *cultivated* British soldier." In the ensuing years they will become good friends.

He meets editors and publishers as a matter of course; and in certain houses, less rigidly Victorian, the stagefolk are beginning to be received. There are cosy dinners at the home of Mrs Rogerson—Christina Stewart Rogerson—one of London's more informal hostesses, who compensates for her homeliness by her dark skirts and white shirts of the finest linen with stiff cuffs and links, and Highland shoes with large silver buckles. He describes her as "a clever liberal woman, who invites me every four or five days." It will be chronicled that he said of her: "If she had been beautiful and sane, she would have been one of the world's great wicked women." At her table the novelist meets his fellow-countryman, James McNeill Whistler, "a queer but entertaining creature," whom he has sharply criticized in certain of his anonymous accounts of the London galleries published in the *Nation*. "They may be good studio-jokes, or even useful studio-experiments," Henry had written of Whistler's nocturnes and arrangements, "but they illustrate only what one may call the self-complacency of technicality." And he had echoed his own remark about the Paris Impressionists: "It may be good to be an impressionist; but I should say on this evidence that it were vastly better to be an expressionist." Whistler invites Henry to one of his Sunday breakfasts in Chelsea. "He is a queer little Londonized Southerner and paints abominably," Henry writes home. "But his breakfasts are easy and pleasant, and he has tomatoes and buckwheat cakes. I found there Sir Coutts and Lady Lindsay (the Grosvenor Gallery people)—who are very sociable (and Sir Coutts the handsomest man in England)."

Elsewhere he meets Frederick Leighton, the Holman Hunts, Thomas Woolner the sculptor, "a good plain conceited fellow," and Samuel Lawrence, "the artist who did your bad portrait in the dining-room," he tells his father, "a very kind, soft little man: who, when I told him he had done my father's portrait, said that was what every American told him."

IV

Henry looks with curiosity at certain Englishmen, fortunate in all the circumstances of their life, and yet limited by their fortune to a kind of passive elegance, and the superior forms of conformity. Thus he has close observation of Henry Adams's friend Charles Milnes Gaskell, "an originally good fellow, depraved by snobbishness, over-many possessions and a position giving him all sorts of opportunities for taking himself and his luxuriant appurtenances with praeternatural seriousness." Or "nice young Sydney Holland," whom he sees in Scotland, the grandson of Sir Henry Holland, "one of those manly, candid, good-looking young Englishmen who only need a touch of genius, or of something they haven't got, to make one think that they are the flower of the human race. As it is, they come near being it."

There are the historical-political figures, for example James Bryce, whom James was to know during all his London years. The author of the famous work on the Holy Roman Empire calls on Henry in Bolton Street and takes him to Oxford as his guest during Commemoration, where Henry watches the conferring of honorary degrees. Bryce always talks well and is "distinctly able." However he possesses three conflicting dispositions—literature, law and politics—"and he has not made a complete thing of any of them." Henry sees him as belonging to the class of "young doctrinaire radicals (they are all growing old in it) who don't take the 'popular heart' and seem booked to remain out of affairs. They are all tainted with priggishness—though Bryce less so than some of the others."

Bryce later takes Henry to Cambridge, to Trinity, to dine with a kind of Oxford and Cambridge co-existence club, composed of half and half, and half in residence and half non-resident, meeting alternately at each university. The dinner is dullish. He has

Henry Sidgwick on his right, and the others include Dicey, Godfrey Lushington, Leslie Stephen, Vernon Harcourt and Dilke. Dilke takes him fraternally by the arm and walks Henry over the place and shows him "all its lovely picturesqueness." Henry decides that "in detail, I think, it beats Oxford; though inferior in *ensemble*."

He studies Dilke closely. "The man who is shooting ahead much faster than anyone else is Charles Dilke. His ability is not at all rare, but he is very skilful and very ambitious, and though he is only thirty-five years old, he would almost certainly, if the Liberals should come into power tomorrow, be a cabinet minister." And again: "Dilke is a very good fellow, and a specimen of a fortunate Englishman: born, without exceptional talents, to a big property, a place in the world, and a political ambition which —resolute industry and the force of social circumstances aiding— he is steadily *en train* to realize. And withal, not a grain of genius or inspiration. But he is only now emerging—much less radical than he began—from his early cloud—his having attacked the Queen and *cremated* his (deceased) wife." Pure political ability such as Dilke's did not appear to Henry to be a "very elevated form of genius." The flaws discerned by Henry in Sir Charles's personality were to lead to his undoing in a celebrated scandal.

This was Henry's vision of London dinner-tables; but it is possible, in the memoirs of the period, to discover how he was seen by others. When Justin McCarthy, the journalist and Member of Parliament, came to write his reminiscences, towards the end of the century, he devoted the following paragraph to the novelist, and it casts an interesting light on James's "position" in the London world:

Henry James is an American who may be said to have thoroughly domesticated himself in London Society, . . . No man is more popular in London dining-rooms and drawing-rooms than Henry James, and a first night at a theatrical performance would seem incomplete if his familiar figure were not to be seen in the stalls or in one of the boxes. Henry James, too, has an interest in political life, and dines with leading public men in the London clubs which represent the one side of politics and the other. He is a delightful talker, and in his talk can develop views and ideas about every passing subject which can clothe even the trivial topics of the day with intellectual grace and meaning. Every now and then some vivid saying or some sparkling epigram comes in, and indeed, there is only, so far as I know, one thing which Henry James never could do in any conversation—he never could be commonplace.

This can be taken as a large verdict in which many other volumes of Victorian reminiscence concur.

V

There came a time when he wrote to his sister Alice (it was in May 1879) that his dinners were falling "into a sort of shimmering muddle" in his memory, and in fact he was rarely tempted to keep them very distinct. There was one he had given himself, at the Reform Club, to a small and select circle, John Cross, Edward Piggott, Andrew Lang and Mowbray Morris: "the thing was pleasant and the dinner was good." He went on:

I am trying to think over my other dinners, but for the life of me I can't remember half of 'em. There was one at the Bishop of Gloucester's; I sat between the Bishopess and one of her daughters—a curious location, and not a lively one; the Bishopess being a regular Mrs Proudie and the daughter very deaf, I was sustained only by watching the fine sincere gallant-looking old face of Sir Henry Rawlinson (the orientalist), who sat opposite to me. Then there was one at the Stansfelds' at which I took in to [dinner] Mrs Jacob Bright, the essence of Birmingham and the flower—a rather faded one—of the middle class. Then there was one at Lady Holland's where I took in a large, plain, buxom Miss Lowther, a young woman of high fashion, and had on the other side of me Lady Carnarvon, who, though "nice" and pretty, has not the genius of conversation.

The passage has in it certain foreshadowings: there is a dinner in *The Wings of the Dove*, in the home of a woman whose name is but a slight variant on the name Lowther, in which a Bishop figures among the guests; and the reader wonders what function this churchman fulfils in the novel, where he is never again mentioned although he has been pointedly described. It is almost as if, in writing the passage, Henry was recalling one or another of his old London dinners, and bringing in all the characters he remembered round the table. The dinners of his fiction were to be in the end composites of old dinners eaten during the Victorian decades. "If you dine out a good deal in London," he wrote to William, "you forget your dinner the next morning—or rather, if you walk home, as I always do, you forget it by the time you have turned the corner of the street. My impressions evaporate with the fumes of the champagne." He was becoming distinctly jaded. "The genius of conversation in the great upper middle class is not a dazzling muse; it is a plain-faced, portly matron, well covered up in warm, woollen garments and fond of an after-dinner nap." And again: "I am tired of the 'common run' of the London world and of the British upper middle class. I can meet them and get on with them; but I can't expatiate upon them." Writing thus to his mother he adds: "Such is the penalty of having a nature so tiresomely framed as that of the 'artistic' H. J. Jr."

If he had written at the beginning of his life in London to Lizzie Boott, "My personal life is much less *thin* than on the Continent," he could now write of his "excess of opportunities" —"I have too much material—in the way of observation I lay it in at the rate of a ton a day, and already am much embarrassed for storage room." Writing to Grace Norton he expresses the wish for some American to talk to, like herself, or her brother, to unburden himself of his many impressions. "Everything is corked up, the feelings, impressions, judgments, emotions, of every kind, that are being perpetually generated, and that I can't utter to a single Briton of them all with the smallest chance of being understood."

He had reached the point where he might still be a foreigner, but he no longer felt he was a stranger. "I am living here too long to be an observer," he writes to Grace Norton on 8 June 1879:

I am losing my sense of peculiarities and differences—I am sinking into dull British acceptance and conformity. The other day I was talking to a very clever foreigner—a German (if you can admit the "clever")—who had lived a long time in England and of whom I had asked some opinion. "Oh, I know nothing of the English," he said, "I have lived here too long—twenty years. The first year I really knew a great deal. But I have lost it!" That is getting to be my state of mind, and I am sometimes really appalled at the matter of course way of looking at the indigenous life and manners into which I am gradually dropping! I am losing my standard—my charming little standard that I used to think so high; my standard of wit, of grace, of good manners, of vivacity, of urbanity, of intelligence, of what makes an easy and natural style of intercourse!

He quickly adds however that his words about his "standard" must be taken with a grain of salt, and he apologizes to Miss Norton for treating her as if she also were "a dull-eyed Briton."

The truth is that I am so fond of London that I can afford to abuse it—and London is on the whole such a fine thing that it can afford to be abused! It has all sorts of superior qualities, but it has also, and English life generally and the English character have, a certain number of great plump flourishing uglinesses and drearinesses which offer themselves irresistibly as *pin-cushions* to criticism and irony. The British mind is so totally un-ironical in relation to itself that this is a perpetual temptation.

He continued to abuse London, to abuse the Season, to complain about the pressures of his life—and went on dining and visiting and observing.

Book Seven

A Reasonable Show of Fame 1878–1879

★

THE OBJECTIVE GENIUS

THE BACHELOR OF BOLTON STREET

THREE OLD WOMEN

VISITS

A DINNER AT THE REFORM

CARTHORSE AND RACER

THE BARD AND MR BROWNING

VOLTAIRE IN PETTICOATS

C'EST MON PLAISIR . . .

THE OBJECTIVE GENIUS

THE year 1878 had been Henry James's *annus mirabilis*. The new year, whose arrival he had welcomed amid the snows of Yorkshire, saw the establishment of his fame on both sides of the Atlantic. Magazines wanted his tales. He had created a vogue. He himself made allusion to it in a story in which a French Academician, writing from America, says: "They have a novelist with pretensions to literature, who writes about the chase for the husband and the adventures of the rich Americans in our corrupt old Europe, where their primaeval candour puts the Europeans to shame. *C'est proprement écrit*: but it's terribly pale." Some of it was pale; and Henry sometimes stretched his material rather thin. But he knew that his style, his charm, his observation, could stand him in good stead even when he had little to relate. He could spin conversations out of thin air, with a deftness pleasing to magazine-readers. And then there were many kinds of magazines: he could afford to write "thin" for some of them; he did not like the illustrated ones, because he considered illustration an affront to the written word. Therefore *Scribner's*, which later became the *Century*, continued to receive what he regarded as his poorer efforts. His best was still reserved for the *Atlantic Monthly*.

He lost no time, now that his name was known in England, in consolidating his reputation by bringing before the transatlantic public those works which had already appeared in America. In the process he edited them carefully. This was to become his established procedure—all that he wrote was revised from magazine to book, from edition to edition. The rapid production of his works in England made him seem a prodigy of letters: a succession of volumes came from the house of Macmillan; in the history of authorship few novelists have seen through the press in a single year so many volumes. "An

International Episode" came out in America, in the Harper Half-Hour pamphlet series, at the end of January 1879. In England in February Henry brought out three tales in two volumes, "Daisy Miller, "An International Episode" and "Four Meetings." In March the English edition of *The American* appeared; in May a completely revised version of *Roderick Hudson*. In August he began a six-part serial in *Scribner's*, entitled *Confidence*, which came out in book-form in December on both sides of the Atlantic. Meanwhile he had assembled some of his earlier stories for the British public, and these appeared as *The Madonna of the Future and Other Tales* in October (he included "Madame de Mauves," "Eugene Pickering," "Longstaff's Marriage," "Benvolio" and "The Diary of a Man of Fifty"—a new tale). Finally, at the end of the year, he was to complete his brilliant little study of *Hawthorne* for the English Men of Letters Series. It was published in December.

This was not all. He managed, in the midst of this activity, to write the tale of "The Pension Beaurepas" for the *Atlantic*, "The Diary of a Man of Fifty" for *Harper's*, and "A Bundle of Letters" —a tale written in a single long sitting, in Paris, which he was persuaded by his friend Theodore Child to print in Child's small English-language newspaper, the *Parisian*. Henry was happy to please him; but he once more forgot the risk he incurred—that of being pirated in America through prior publication abroad. Pirated he was, within a matter of weeks, by a friend of the James family, who produced the tale in a pretty paperback form in Boston. When Henry's parents spoke with pleasure of this publication, they received an angry answer: their son pointed out that the "friend" was, in effect, boldly robbing him. In the absence of copyright he had no legal redress.

He was showing thus in his daily life a Balzacian fertility; and with it something Balzac did not possess; a perfection of style and of form, a neatness of prose that seemed to belie the rapidity of his writing. When Quincy Street became worried lest he be exhausting his physical powers, he replied (to William): "I am as broad as I am long, as fat as a butter-tub and as red as a British *materfamilias*. On the other hand, as a compensation, I am excellently well! I am working along very quietly and steadily, and consider no reasonable show of fame and no decent literary competence out of my reach." He added, for William's benefit, that he was decidedly not bloated morally: "I am philosophic to leanness—to stringiness. Physically it's another affair."

Later, to his mother, who also expressed uneasiness at his perpetual social life and seeming over-work, he wrote: "Perturb yourself not, sweet mother, on the subject of my headaches, of my exhausting life, of my burning the candle at both ends, of being nipped in the prime of my powers—or of any other nefarious tendency or catastrophe. I never was better, more at leisure, more workable, or less likely to trifle in any manner with my vitality, physical or intellectual. I wish you could see me in the flesh. I think a glance would set your mind at rest." In spite of daily long walks, fencing, weight-lifting, he did indeed put on considerable weight during this period. "I am in superb health," he wrote home, "and so fat that my flesh hangs over my waistband in huge bags. My appearance attracts general attention."

It was not his plumpness which attracted attention. On London staircases everyone turned to look at the American with the well-trimmed, silky beard which, Rebecca West was told by one who met him, gave him the appearance of an Elizabethan sea-captain. He was, for the moment, a much-discussed author. What disturbed him was that so far his financial returns were not keeping pace with his reputation. "I have got a good deal of fame and hope some day to get a little money," he wrote to his friend Perry. "I have had, I think, more success with the dull British public in a few months than with that of my native land in all these long years that I have been scribbling to it. This fact, of course, helps me to be comfortable and contented here." To Howells he wrote in the same vein: "My fame indeed seems to do very well everywhere—the proportions it has acquired here are a constant surprise to me; it is only my fortune that leaves to be desired." To his brother he wrote: "My reputation in England seems (considering what it is based on) ludicrously larger than any cash payment that I have yet received for it. The Macmillans are everything that's friendly—caressing—old Macmillan physically *hugs* me; but the delicious ring of the sovereign is conspicuous in our intercourse by its absence. However I am sure of the future—that is the great thing."

His royalties were small; he was nevertheless commanding larger sums from the magazines and certainly "crowding" his market. He had sufficient money to live at ease and to travel; he was no longer tied to the Quincy Street letter of credit. And he possessed a great serenity. When his parents expressed concern lest he be embittered by the British criticism of "An International Episode" his reply was: "I honestly believe that it would be impossible to be less at the mercy of common criticism than I. I know too perfectly well what I intend, desire and attempt, and am capable of following it in absolute absence of perturbation. Never was a genius—if genius there is—more healthy, objective, and (I honestly believe) less susceptible of superficial irritations and reactionary impulses. I know what I want—it stares one in the face, as big and round and bright as the full moon; I *can't* be diverted or deflected by the sense of judgments that are most of the time no judgments at all."

This was to be his attitude towards his critics during all his years of success. Although at first he was interested in what they said, he ultimately became indifferent to them. He went about his business with all the assurance of his craft and all the power of his creativity.

THE BACHELOR OF BOLTON STREET

He had long ago made up his mind he would not marry. It was not so much a matter of making up his mind, as of following his inclination: given his difficulties with younger women, and his comfortable relationship with elderly widows and old ladies, he saw no reason why he should change his pleasant celibate status for one that might prove a threat to his art and his personal sovereignty. In his tales dealing with writers and painters he is always clear about this. The most famous of this group, "The Lesson of the Master," turns the question of matrimony into a joke: the great writer advises the young dedicated novice against marriage—against what he calls the "idols of the marketplace"—among which he includes "placing one's children and dressing one's wife." "One's children interfere with perfection. One's wife interferes. Marriage interferes." The young writer takes his advice and breaks off his engagement, only to learn later that the Master—widowed—has married his former fiancée. The story ends in an irony; nevertheless its lesson is as clear as the Master's, and it is repeated in such tales as "The Next Time," in which the gifted writer is forced to resort to journalism in order to support his family; or it is stated in violent terms, in "The Author of Beltraffio," where the writer's wife considers his books so horrible that she allows their boy to die during an illness rather than have him live to read them. It is one of James's terrible tales—a Medea-story which reveals his deepest fear of woman: that she can rob him of all his creative power and of his progeny. In "The Lesson of the Master" the writer is forced by his marriage into the marketplace. "My wife makes all my bargains with my publishers for me, and she has done so for twenty years. She does it consummately well; that's why I'm really pretty well off." And all this is obtained at the price of shoddy work: "I've led the life of the world, with my wife and my progeny; the clumsy, expensive, materialised, brutalised, Philistine, snobbish, life of London." The Master talks in this vein, even to confessing that his wife had made him burn one of his books. Wives not only harnessed their writing husbands to their pens; they were censors as well.

I

"I am too good a bachelor to spoil," Henry wrote to Grace Norton. "That sounds conceited—but one may be conceited in self-defence, about a position with which the rest of the world associates a certain idea of the ridiculous."

And in a letter to Lizzie Boott, four or five years later, when she returned to the question—as all his lady-friends did periodically—he wrote:

> What strikes me most in the *affaire* is the want of application on the part of society of the useful, beneficent, and civilizing part played in it by the occasional unmarried man of a certain age. He keeps up the tone of humanity—he stands for a thousand agreeable and delightful things. People ought really to be ashamed not to feel better than that *what* one is doing for it. *Dunque, cara Lisa, non mi sposero mai—mai!*

By remaining a bachelor Henry could live modestly; instead of having to find a house, or a large apartment, he could for the present remain in his little rooms in Bolton Street, for which he paid two and a half guineas a week (about $50 a month). This was not altogether cheap, at the time, but it was well within his means—and he was in the heart of London. His routine of life was as simple as his establishment. His hours of writing and reading—he always had some pile of proofs to read when he wasn't reading books—were also the hours during which he seems to have built up rather than depleted his reserves of energy for the other—the strenuous complicated social—side of his existence. He rose usually after a sound sleep, having taken a long walk before going to bed. He began work without breakfast. He would eat a substantial mid-morning *déjeuner*; and he would write sometimes for five or six hours on end after that. Only in the late afternoon was he ready to cultivate his leisure with the same elegance as the members of the British upper classes. The only exception he made for lunching out was on Sundays. At the end of his work-day he paid calls, went to tea, or during free evenings turned to his club to read the newspapers before his solitary meal. He enjoyed dining at the club. It was a pleasure to eat in peace, when there was no need "of swallowing inscrutable entrées and tugging at the relaxed bell-rope of one's brain for a feeble tinkle of conversation." After dinner he would chat with fellow-clubmen, or read in the library, or write letters. He dealt with a voluminous correspondence—there was Quincy Street, and his continental friends, and the usual social "twaddle" in answer to invitations. There was also his business correspondence, for he took care of all his publishing arrangements. Thousands of his rapidly-scrawled letters survive; everyone kept them, even his relatives who were admonished to burn them. There was too much style in them, too much charm. The recipient could not bring himself to destroy so much liveliness, warmth—and life.

II

London was particularly delightful to the bachelor when he could be solitary; after so much social intercourse he enjoyed the "dead season," during which Society moved to its country houses and estates. Henry liked the quiet that descended on the city. At night he could hear the creaking boots of the lonely policeman passing along Bolton Street; and in the morning the sharp double-tap of the postman bringing the usual deluge of mail. He enjoyed the routine irruptions of the domestics into his rooms bringing him his tea and bread-and-butter, or his chop and potatoes. On occasion he would record the talk for Quincy Street:

H. J. (to the maid): Can't you do anything in the world with potatoes but thus drearily boil them?

The Maid: Oh dear yes, sir, certainly, we can *mash* them!

H. J.: That comes to the same thing. No other way?

The Maid: I don't think we have heard of any other way, sir.

H. J.: You can't fry them?

The Maid: I don't think we could do that, sir. Isn't that French cookery, sir?

Whereupon Henry remembered Turgenev's dictum, a reminiscence of the Russian's winter in England during the Franco-Prussian war, "*Que voulez-vous? Un pays où on ne sait tirer parti ni des œufs, ni des pommes de terre!*"

On another occasion Henry described a new domestic, hired to replace the maid "who had grown grimy in my service, and who went away to marry a deformed cobbler, dwelling in a little mews, out of Curzon Street." When the new maid arrived Henry said: "You had better tell me your name, please."

She: Well, sir, it might be Maria.
H. J.: It *might* be?
She: Well, sir, they calls me Maria.
H. J.: Isn't it your name?
She: My name's Annie, sir, but Missus says that's too familiar.

"So I have compromised," Henry told Quincy Street, "and call her Annie-Maria." And he went on to explain that "it is part of the British code that you can call a servant any name you like, and many people have a fixed name for their butler, which all the successive occupants of the place are obliged to assume, so that the family needn't change its habits." He was to make use of this, in "A Bundle of Letters," where the English girl writes: "Lady Battledown makes all her governesses take the same name; she give £5 a year for the purpose. I forget what it is she calls them—I think it's Thompson." The English girl adds: "Governesses shouldn't have too pretty a name—they shouldn't have a nicer name than the family."

III

Life was never dull for an individual absorbed in his work and in his world as Henry was. If he felt lonely he walked in the park; there was always something to look at and to study; and by this time he seems to have had enough friends at whose door he could knock of an evening. We get glimpses of him even knocking, on occasion, at Mr Hoppin's door, and the First Secretary makes a literal record of the talk of two bachelors about their common acquaintances.

Last night while I was dining [wrote Hoppin in his journal in November 1880] *Henry James* called and I asked him to take a part of my soup and braised mutton. He was pleasant in his talk. I don't think he appreciates the *high tone of domestic life* at home while he attaches an undue importance to *society* in Europe. To be sure, as he says, there's no such thing as *society* in America. It is an auxiliary—an accident—an occasional diversion there. Here it is a paramount occupation.—We spoke of the circle of which we see a good deal—Mrs Rogerson, Lady Gordon, Mrs Hughes, etc. These women appear to have no other idea than to divert themselves. Every evening is pre-engaged for theatres or dinners. It is the business of life. At home the business of life is to make the family fireside happy. *Gallantry* takes up a good deal of the time and thoughts of the women here.

Mr Hoppin's observations were rather on the prosy side, and his examples were the reverse of felicitous. Mrs Rogerson's children were full-grown and her husband was a drunkard. There was no fireside to make happy. Lady Hamilton Gordon was a woman of a "certain age." Mr Hoppin and James discussed, to judge from the journal, what it was like to bring "an imaginative sentimental New England wife into such surroundings." The elderly diplomatic bachelor and the thirty-seven-year-old literary bachelor thus made their tour of the London social horizon and dwelt on the dangers of scandal. At the end of the entry Mr Hoppin generalizes: "Scandal spares nobody in this society. A beautiful Countess, one of the professional beauties, is supposed to have had an *amour* with her groom before she was married, and the most dreadful stories of a similar character have been circulated about the noble Duchess——!"

THREE OLD WOMEN

THERE were three old women in London society, ancient, seasoned, full of the world and its ways, who took their special places in Henry James's life: places more important than those of the younger women he constantly met. Their longevity and experience—he once said that their combined ages amounted to about 250 years—made them objects of the deepest interest to him. They were creatures of an older order; they offered him a continuing relation with the past. This alone, however, would not perhaps have sufficed. They were also high-spirited, witty, full of old stories; and they were imperious and demanding. There was something in their nature that made them especially attractive to the novelist. Some hidden appeal brought him into close touch with them and made them important to him in a round of days already crowded with people and action. Writing at the time of George Eliot's marriage to John Cross, a man much younger than herself, Henry told his mother: "Old women are marrying young men, by the way, all over the place. If you hear next that Mrs Kemble, or Mrs Procter, or Mrs Duncan Stewart is to marry *me*, you may know we have simply conformed to the fashion. But I will ask your consent first." When Henry wrote this Mrs Kemble was seventy-one, Mrs Procter eighty-two and Mrs Duncan Stewart eighty-three.

I

For Henry, Fanny Kemble was "the first woman in London." She was also "one of the consolations of my life!" Thirty-two years older than the novelist—and in fact one year older than his mother—Fanny Kemble became one of his great attachments. What had begun as a nodding acquaintance in Rome in 1873, and had been followed by a brief and friendly meeting in Philadelphia in 1875, had blossomed into a valued intimacy by her fireside in Cavendish Square: that of a former great lady of the stage, who had led a tempestuous life on both sides of the water, with an attractive and gifted writer. In the 1870's Fanny Kemble was still sufficiently active to accompany Henry to art-exhibitions and on occasions to the theatre—where she was often unrestrainedly demonstrative, weeping profusely or exclaiming violently, over memories of her own stage career. She possessed great strength of character and of will; and a blazing artistic temperament. The images Henry found for her were nearly always fiery ones—when they were not symbols designed to express the subterranean qualities of her nature. She was a volcano in eruption: or she gave him "a positive sense of having a deep, rich human nature and having cast off all vulgarities." Mrs Kemble, he wrote, "has no organized surface at all; she is like a straight deep cistern without a cover, or even, sometimes, a bucket, into which, as a mode of intercourse, one must tumble with a splash." Sometimes he compared her to the Alps.

Such a temperament made for much amusement in conversation; more often than not it gave rise to the unexpected and the dramatic. There was, too, a rather ugly side to Mrs Kemble, which Henry seems to have been incapable of perceiving: she possessed a kind of hard, even cruel aggressivity. She was capable, for instance, of saying that G. H. Lewes looked as if "he had been gnawed by the rats—and left." Henry, who would have shuddered at such an image on someone else's lips, laughed when Mrs Kemble uttered it—and repeated it in a letter to Quincy Street.

Fanny Kemble was a link with the early part of the century, with the great figures of the London stage and London drawing-rooms. As a rule Henry did not like actresses and the "mountebank" side of their art. Mrs Kemble however was an actress who had a strong aversion to the stage, and who had, in spite of this, mastered it; she brought to it an intelligent competence as well as a remarkable personality. And she remained, until she was a frail old lady, a powerful presence, a great histrionic voice possessed of a beautiful utterance; it made her talk a continual source of delight. She always had anecdotes to tell, and certain of her stories were transformed by Henry into novels and tales; the original story of *Washington Square* stemmed from her. Even her casual remarks furnished ideas for his stories, as his notebooks reveal. Proud of spirit, high of temper, she gave Henry a vision of female grandeur that surpassed all others in his experience. "My sublime Fanny," he said of her. She had a "human largeness" to which he could respond; and she brought out in him all that was most filial and charming, so that in turn she could delight in him. "Oh, friend of many lonely hours," Mrs Kemble wrote in a sonnet which she sent to him; and in turn he could speak of the "grand line and mass of her personality." Long after she was dead, Henry carried, so to speak, the beat of her heart with him: her legacy to him was her travelling clock. "I think of you almost as if you belonged to me," she had written to him. In many ways he did belong to her.

II

Mrs Procter—Anne Benson Procter—had known almost everyone of importance during the nineteenth century. She had anecdotes of Shelley and Keats, stories about Byron, Coleridge, Wordsworth, Southey, Landor. She once made a list of her famous friends and it filled two closely covered sheets of notepaper in double column. Henry considered her "the best talker I have met in England." Fanny Kemble called her "the queen of newsmongers," but Henry wrote to the actress, "What a capacity for *caring*—taking sides, resenting etc.! I don't see why, when one *minds* as much as that, one shouldn't live forever." On the New Year week-end, when Henry was visiting Lord Houghton at Fryston Hall, and found Mrs Procter among his fellow-guests, he wrote that "considering she is eighty years old, she is, at breakfast, lunch and dinner, a marvel. She abounds so in reminiscences and in *esprit* that one of her speeches chases another from one's mind. She has known literally every one." And to his sister Alice he retailed an anecdote told by Mrs Procter about herself which incidentally helps to characterize her:

Mrs Procter (*to Sydney Smith, at the end of a dinner*): Who is that at the end of the table?

Sydney Smith: Macaulay.

Mrs Procter: What? *The* Macaulay? I haven't heard him speak a word all dinner.

Sydney Smith: I gave him several opportunities, but *you* always took advantage of them.

Long after she was dead Henry was to write: "It was her tone that was her value and her identity, and that kept her from being feebly modern." He said also that she testified to a stouter and harder world than that of the Victorian era: her memory went back to the time of Napoleon and to personalities who belonged to the eighteenth century. Henry's final tribute to her was: "She was a kind of window in the past—now it's closed there is so much less air."

But the profile of her which G. W. Smalley sent to the *Tribune* at the same time suggests other aspects of her personality. "She had regal notions of what was due to her, and there was occasionally something imperious in her way of expressing her wishes." He said also her idea of human nature was "perhaps a little cynical." Kinglake had called her "Our Lady of Bitterness." Smalley added that she uttered her bitter sayings in a felicitous manner: nevertheless "her skill in the use of the knife was surgical." He concluded by observing that she had masculine qualities—energy, decision, abruptness, "clear ideas of what she wanted and how to get it." Like Mrs Kemble she possessed an overbearing side to her nature.

She was nearly eighty when Henry met her, and it got to be a little joke between them that he would some day marry her. Thomas Hardy, calling on her in 1879, saw a photograph of Henry James on her table and made this note in his diary: "She says he has made an offer of marriage. Can it be so?" "I expect soon," Henry wrote at this time to his mother, "to hear that I am engaged to Mrs Procter *aetat* 82. I have indeed proposed to her several times, but she seems to think she can do better. As poor old William Hoppin, the American Secretary of Legation here, age 67 or so, was lately reported to be about to espouse Mrs

Duncan Stewart, who is 83 or so, you will see to what an advanced period people here are assumed to keep up their interest in life."

III

The third of these women was Mrs Duncan Stewart, a lady who wore voluminous capotes and capes of old lace and black velvet. She was said to have been the natural daughter of an earl; she had been brought up in a convent in France and was distinctly Gallicized. At twenty-four she had married Duncan Stewart, a merchant, and had lived for years in Liverpool, bringing up several sons and a daughter. The daughter was the Mrs James Rogerson to whose home Henry was frequently invited and where he met Whistler. Mrs Stewart, widowed in 1869, settled in London and became a fixture of its society. She had limited means and lived in small rooms at 101 Sloane Street, where she gave pleasant luncheon parties. She had known Washington Irving and Leigh Hunt and counted Disraeli among her friends. On 29 February 1884 Henry wrote to his sister: "We are having the first cold of the winter and Mrs Duncan Stewart is dead. But the cold is bright and wholesome and Mrs Stewart had become a kind of talking melancholy ghost. She was a charming old being, however, and I shall miss her much. Some day I shall put her into a book." In the same letter he said: "I have seen Mrs Kemble and find her constantly a little more and a little more broken and, as it were, indented. I shall never put *her* into a book."

In his working notebooks, three years after Mrs Stewart's death, in sketching the tale which became "A London Life" he wrote: "There must be an old lady—like Mrs Duncan S.—only of rank—a genial, clever, worldly, old-fashioned, half comforting, half shocking old lady, whom she [the heroine] goes to see and talk with." He describes the forthright Lady Davenant who, in the tale, tries to comfort the hapless American girl, Laura Wing, very much as Mrs Stewart must have appeared to him—"full of life, old as she was, and had been made, finer, sharper and more delicate, by nearly eighty years of it." She expects a great deal of attention; the witty expression of her face shines "like a lamp through the ground glass of her good breeding." In the tale, as in life, Mrs Stewart has firm opinions and is capable of strong quick sympathies.

In other words Mrs Stewart too possessed a certain hardness and sharpness; and this emerges when one reads her letters to Mr Hoppin which he preserved in his scrapbook-journal. They are brief, amusing, flirtatious—at eighty. She chides him for neglecting her; she points out that Mr James does not neglect her. One gains a sense of a lively, demanding woman with a rough fund of witty attack and a sharpness of tongue, when the occasion warranted. Indeed in one letter to Quincy Street Henry characterized Mrs Stewart as "an old reprobate of a woman."

IV

"I constantly hear," Henry wrote to his mother in 1880, "that I have been 'very attentive' to numerous spinsters and widows, and also that many of my well-wishers think that I should be 'so much happier' if I would only marry." He was writing in reply to rumours reaching Quincy Street that he was engaged. His sentence might have been amended to read "elderly widows and spinsters of a certain age." That Henry was attracted to older women because they offered him the polished surface of London wit and cultivation and their long social histories, is understandable in an insatiable student of manners. What is less understandable is his inveterate choice of women who were strong, domineering and had in them also a streak of hardness, sometimes even of cruelty. These women probably appealed to him because such qualities were distinctly familiar: Mary James had been quite as hard, firm, sovereign, but more devious. Indeed during all the years of his childhood he had learned how to make himself agreeable to such a woman.

His various writings suggest that he looked for the same qualities in younger women. A gentle passive feminine creature like Lizzie Boott pleased him, but she was an open book: he would never have thought of marrying her. She had no mystery in her; life with her would have been rather dull. A "beautiful, mysterious melancholy, inscrutable" woman like Elena Lowe intrigued him so much that he sought for years to understand her, as his fiction shows. Mrs Kemble, with a mind like a deep cistern or a well, had unfathomable depths: one never knew what she would bring up from below the surface. And she was also safely old. In the light of this and of Henry's various heroines, it is possible to speculate that if Henry had ever married, he would have sought a young woman who outwardly seemed in full possession of herself and in full conformity with the laws of her sex, but who beneath the surface belonged to the order of the all-demanding and governing matriarchs. Henry could not consciously allow himself to look at this side of his mother; he had been too completely brought up to the idea of her self-effacement and her spirit of sacrifice.

He was able to create in his novels, however, a whole race of formidable and sometimes terrifying female power-figures: the Mrs Gereths, Madame Merles, Kate Croys, or the child-destroyers, Rose Armiger of *The Other House* and the governess of "The Turn of the Screw"—"bad heroines," women seen ambivalently as destructive and yet containing within them qualities distinctly likeable. He could create them without recognizing wholly that they embodied certain deadly accurate aspects of the older women in his life. His experience of the manipulating, manœuvring, meddling woman had been always with the elderly female. When he encountered certain spinsters closer to his own age, spinsters still possibly marriageable, he tended to subject them to all the play of his often-irresistible charm and then was astonished to discover that they were not merely as receptive as the older ladies—they also expected an offer of marriage. It was a form of blind egotism on his part; a psychological failure to recognize that his ways of placating the demanding older woman might be regarded as a wooing by a younger one. Henry was to fall several times into this serious error, and it is reflected clearly in certain of his later works.

Finally, when he came to distinctly younger women, the full contradiction asserted itself: they were charming, they were sometimes beautiful, soft, clinging, intense, and Henry could only ask himself, as he asked of his image of Elena Lowe—could they really be trusted? Even so simple and *insouciante* a creature as Daisy Miller is a puzzle to the frosty American, Winterbourne. Is she a flirt, or is she virtuous? Is she simply heartless in her innocence, or a hard and cynical young woman assuming a mask of gentility? It is interesting to note that a tale he wrote immediately after Daisy had made him famous, "The Diary of a Man of Fifty," was a return to Roderick Hudson's original bafflement. The diary-entries in the tale are dated as of the time of the writing of the first chapters of Roderick, and in the city where he wrote them. It is the story of a middle-aged man, returning to Florence where, a quarter of a century before, he had turned his back on a difficult woman (as difficult as Christina), whom he had decided he could no longer trust. Now he meets a young man in love with this woman's daughter, and thinks his old experience is being re-enacted. He tells the ardent young lover, whom he regards as his youthful self: "You admire her—you adore her, and yet secretly you mistrust her." The young man tries in vain to persuade him that the circumstances are different. "You can't rid yourself of the suspicion that at the bottom of all things she is hard and cruel, and you would be immensely relieved if some one should persuade you that your suspicion is right." Henry could never rid himself of this suspicion: but in this tale the marriage does take place—and the narrator ends by wondering whether he had really been right or whether his old suspicions had been ill-founded. There is in this a long foreshadowing of the ambivalence of *The Sacred Fount*. More important, in terms of Henry's own life, it reveals the uncertainty and anxiety young women created for him, and suggests why he decided that he would never marry.

During this time, when he could easily laugh at the possibility of his marrying the Mrs Kembles and Mrs Procters of the London world, he wrote to Grace Norton (who, in Cambridge, was another version of this sort of woman): "I am unlikely ever to marry." His reason was hardly convincing: "I should pretend to think just a little better of life than I really do." Besides, he said, he had become used to his unmarried state, and "an amiable bachelor here and there doesn't strike me as at all amiss, and I think he too may forward the cause of civilization."

There was to be no doubt that the bachelor of Bolton Street was to forward the cause of civilization: his very experience of the over-riding female had created a permanent damage within himself in his relations with women: and in that marvellous way in which nature insists on compensations and solutions, his constant effort to repair the damage, to understand what had gone wrong, gave him the necessary distance and aloofness—even while creating momentary blindnesses—that enabled him, of all novelists, to undertake the writing of *The Portrait of a Lady*, and to create a whole generation of American girls.

Strangely enough the Second Secretary of Legation, the lightweight Mr Nadal, had a perception of this. Trying on his side to do what Mr Hoppin had done, that is analyse Henry's success in London, he felt that Henry proved attractive to women of all ages because he was genuinely distinguished "in a marked degree, both as a young man and an old one." Secondly he "possessed an inscrutability which piqued their interest and curiosity." But more important still, women liked him, said Nadal, for his sympathetic and delicate discernment of their own qualities. "He seemed to look at women rather as women looked at them. Women look at women as persons; men look at them as women. The quality of sex in women, which is their first and chief attraction to most men, was not their chief attraction to James." This was an accurate observation.

VISITS

THERE was no way of getting to know the English better, Henry felt, than by seeing them "through their great invention of country-house life." The letters of the novelist to his family and friends in Cambridge are filled with his accounts of visits to many great as well as simple homes in England and Scotland: the life led there, the large parties, the hunts, the open-air scenes and the company, interesting or dull. Henry felt that the upper classes in England depended on country visits in order to "get at each other," an indispensable complement to the fugitive contacts of London. "It is certainly a thing they have brought to great perfection," he told Grace Norton, "and if one can stand the occasional dullness and the superabundance of poor unanimated talk, one can get much that is entertaining and interesting out of it."

Periodically Henry embarked on a round of visits; during his first years he enjoyed their novelty and their variety; he welcomed the break they offered in the rhythm of his London days. As the years lengthened he became increasingly discriminating; but this was only after he had been surfeited, and had, in the process, seen many corners of England. His visit to Charles Milnes Gaskell at Wenlock Abbey during his first summer in England had been but a foretaste. After "Daisy Miller" the visits multiplied greatly, and in the autumn of 1878 he made his first trip to Scotland, to stay with Sir John Clark, an "amiable, demonstrative, appreciative" friend and his "rather satirical invalid gentlewoman of a wife." The weather was splendid, the hospitality generous, the company "inoffensive," and Henry wrote with rapture of the breezy moors, the brown and purple hills, the rich mixture of autumn mist and sunshine. There were highland sports, long rambles over the sun-warmed heather: Henry had never before been on the moors and for three days he had a feast of them.

Even though he was not a sportsman, he enjoyed watching the frightened grouse starting up across the blue. He made a trip to a ruined castle on horseback and returned stiff and sore from his hours in the saddle, only to go to a ball and dance polkas half the night. Lily Langtry, the great beauty, was present and Henry watched her in a highland reel (which she had been practising for three days) with young Lord Huntly, a very handsome fellow in a kilt who leaped, hooted, romped and reminded Henry that ancient Caledonian "barbarism" still lurked among the Scots.

There was a visit of a different order, "not a very interesting episode." At Wenlock Abbey he had met Lady Portsmouth and promised to come to her great house, Eggesford Manor, in North Devon.

> The place and country are of course very beautiful and Lady P. "most kind;" but though there are several people in the house (local gentlefolk, of no distinctive qualities) the whole thing is dull. This is a large family, chiefly of infantine sons and daughters (there are 12!) who live in some mysterious part of the house and are never seen. Lord P. is simply a great hunting and racing magnate, who keeps the hounds in this part of the country and is absent all day with them. There is nothing in the house but pictures of horses—and awfully bad ones at that. Yesterday, before lunch, I walked in the grounds with Lady Rosamund, who is not "out" and doesn't dine at table, though she is a very pretty little pink and white creature of 17; and in the p.m. Lady P. showed me her boudoir, which she is "doing up" with old china etc.

Lady Portsmouth takes Henry for a drive in her phaeton through lovely Devonshire lanes. In the evening the nursery *corps de ballet* comes into the gallery with governesses, and dances cachuchas and minuets "with the sweetest docility and modesty" while Henry and the other adults applaud. The next day the weather turns bad, and Henry sits alone "in a big cold library of totally unread books, waiting for Lord Portsmouth, who has offered to take me out and show me his stable and kennels (famous ones)." Henry, writing home, says he will try to get away the next day. "I don't think I could stick out a Sunday here." Though there are innumerable flunkeys about the house, he tries in vain to get the fire refreshed. Two or three come in and look at it, but it doesn't appear to be their business to bring in coal.

The visit to the stables is deferred until after lunch. It finally takes place and Henry goes the rounds with Lord P. and a couple of the other visitors—forty horses, mostly hunters, and a wonderful pack of foxhounds "lodged like superior mechanics."

Then there was Lord Rosebery, his Rothschild wife and their vast estates, Mentmore, the Durdans, Dalmeny House. Rosebery was destined to be one of the last of Victoria's prime ministers. He possessed great conversational gifts; he was an active racing man; and he was vigorous in politics, capable of rousing large audiences by his oratory. His enemies called him an opportunist; his friends recognized him as a hard-working Liberal, possessing strong intellectual qualities and an unyielding nature. Henry met him somewhere in London, probably at the Reform Club, and enjoyed his hospitality on a number of occasions, watching his political career and his rise to power with unabated interest. Late in the autumn of 1880 he was invited by Lady Rosebery to Mentmore, the great house built by Mayer Amschel Rothschild in 1851. His fellow-guests included John Bright, the idol of Birmingham and champion for many years of the middle-class in Parliament, and Lord Northbrook, the last Liberal Viceroy of India. Sir John Everett Millais, the painter, one of the originators of the Pre-Raphaelite movement, was there part of the time, and Henry took a walk with him to the stables where three winners of the Derby were trotted out in succession for them. Lord Rosebery, "with youth, cleverness, a delightful face, a happy character, a Rothschild wife of numberless millions to distinguish and demoralize him, wears them with such tact and bonhomie, that you almost forgive him." Lady Rosebery Henry found "large, fat, ugly, good-natured, sensible and kind." He continues:

I have spent a good part of the time in listening to the conversation of John Bright, whom, though I constantly see him at the Reform Club, I had never met before. He has the repute of being often "grumpy;" but on this occasion he has been in extremely good form and has discoursed uninterruptedly and pleasantly. He gives one an impression of sturdy, honest, vigorous, English middle-class liberalism, accompanied by a certain infusion of genius, which helps one to understand how his name has become the great rallying-point of that sentiment.

He reminded Henry a good deal of "a superior New Englander—with a fatter, damper nature, however."

As Henry wrote this letter, the guests were at tea in a vast hall "where an upper gallery looks down like the colonnade in Paul Veronese's pictures and the chairs are all golden thrones belonging to the ancient Doges of Venice." Henry had withdrawn from the glittering scene "to commune with my mammy," and his letter had in it those thoughts which he knew would be found agreeable in Quincy Street. He is meditating by his fire "on the fleeting character of earthly possessions." The footman arrives and lays out his things. "You may be interested, by the way, to know that Lord Rosebery said this morning at lunch that his ideal of the happy life was that of Cambridge, Mass., 'living like Longfellow.' You may imagine that at this the company looked awfully vague, and I thought of proposing to him to exchange Mentmore for 20 Quincy Street."

He was to have a later view of John Bright, during a week-end at Oxford, as guest of George Brodrick, the Warden of Merton. In addition to Bright, Lady Sarah Spencer and the Charles Roundells were there. He found the stay "tainted with that Oxford priggery, which is not one of the things I enjoy most." The college itself was filled with romance for him: he relished the six-feet-thick window-embrasures, the thirteenth-century rooms, the garden. Bright he now found (it was in 1884) "one of the least interesting types in England." He had fallen into rather boring prattle, mildly senile. Henry had sent him some of Longfellow's poems which Bright now described to him, and he went on to describe "a splendid novel by General Lew Wallace—of which he related the plot at extraordinary length." No doubt *Ben Hur*. "His 'culture,'" wrote Henry to Grace Norton, "is so narrow, his taste so bad, and what remains of his intellect so weak, that I wondered greatly that a 'great statesman' should have coexisted with such limitations. It made me think that great statesmen may sometimes be very measurable creatures.

However John Bright was never, and never pretended to be that: he was simply a great orator, with a special gift of speaking which, having died out, has left him childlike and bland, and rather bare." The word *bare* was apropos. For Bright wrote in his diary, after he had told Henry about Lew Wallace: "Sat up late for two nights with Mr James. Conversation on America interesting."

From Mr Hoppin's unpublished *Journal of a Residence in London*, Sunday, 12 December 1880:

I had a pleasant call from Henry James a few evenings ago. He had been staying with the Henry Hollands and with the Roseberys. He described the luxury and elegance at Mentmore as something fabulous. The Roseberys move from one country residence to another and then to their house in town, always finding each establishment completely mounted and ready for the entertainment of any number of guests without the least trouble and forethought on their own part. Lady R. is large, coarse, Hebrew-looking, with hair of no particular colour and personally unattractive.

James thinks there is a great drawback in making a country visit. Although we hear a great deal to the contrary, a guest must give up much of his personal independence. To be obliged to be agreeable morning, noon and night for several days is a great task upon one's spirits—if not one's intellect. It is better that we should never go into society excepting when we are in a mood for it and when we can show ourselves at the best. . . . Mr Bright does not seem to have made a pleasing impression.

Another Christmas (1880), and this time he is the guest of the commanding officer in the Government House at Devonport, the official residence of General Pakenham, who commands one of the big military districts into which England is divided. General Pakenham is nephew by marriage of the old Duke of Wellington. The house stands on the edge of Plymouth Sound, looking straight across the narrow channel at Mount Edgcumbe, the most beautiful "nobleman's seat" Henry has seen in England. On Christmas Day several of the guests and Henry cross the little body of water and stroll on the Mount. The place seems to him a paradise. Mrs Pakenham, a former American belle, is now intensely Anglicized. There are two sons home from Eton and destined, like their ancestors, to go into the Army. The day after Christmas Henry is taken by a young Captain Brand, son of the Speaker of the House of Commons, aboard his ship, to be present while he reads the service, the Chaplain being absent. Henry breakfasts with the officers in the wardroom, and is conducted over the man-of-war, one of the old-fashioned big line-of-battleships, "rather antiquated, but very prodigious." After that he is taken in a boat about the bay and shown strange gunboats and torpedoes. Captain Brand is "a simple sensible child of the gentry, smelling of Piccadilly more than of the salt sea-navy, who has found his career easy for him by reason of his birth, and yet is probably none the less an excellent officer." Mrs Pakenham urges Henry to stay for the big New Year's ball. Henry begs off. He would be lost, he feels, in a wilderness of redcoats. He goes instead to the Clarks', who have come down from Scotland to Cornwall in the winter, and is driven by Sir John far away to Penzance and then to Land's End. The morning is soft and moist. He stands meditatively watching the winter Atlantic heaving gently round the outermost point of old England. After that he is glad to recover his fireside in Bolton Street.

A DINNER AT THE REFORM

THE occasion was modest enough and yet one of those evenings that Henry was later to remember with deep pleasure. This time it was not he who dined out; it was he who was the host. In June 1879 there arrived from Paris a brief note from Ivan Sergeyevich written in his elegant and quaint English. He was leaving Paris for Oxford; the university "does me the unexpected honour of making me a D.C.L." The "promotion" he said would take place on 18 June: in a week. He would quit Paris on Sunday evening, arrive in London on the Monday, go to Oxford the same day. However on his way back he had "the greatest desire of seeing you, myself." He proposed that they have "a quiet dinner" on Friday the 20th. He added an "*à bientôt*, in every case."

A year and a half—a momentous year and a half—had elapsed since Henry had sat beside Ivan Sergeyevich's gouty bedside. He was overjoyed at the prospect of seeing his valued friend again, and this time it seemed to him that he should forgo the pleasure of the intimate dinner Turgenev offered him. Instead he would share the great Russian with certain of his London friends. He accordingly proposed to him that he give a little dinner in his honour at the Reform Club: it was a way of fêting the honorary degree. It was also a way of greeting the Russian from Henry's now more elevated station in the literary and social world.

The dinner was arranged, and at the last moment Henry was able to add to the list of his guests a familiar from Cambridge. "The other night, John Fiske rose, moon-like, above my horizon, apparently very well and happy," Henry wrote to William, "and I immediately invited him to dine with me to meet Turgenev next week—the latter coming over by invitation to receive the D.C.L. degree at Oxford—a very pretty attention to pay him—(to which

I imagine James Bryce chiefly put them up). He has promised very solemnly (by letter from Paris) to dine with me on the 20th; and it is quite on the cards that he should play me false; but I trust he won't. I wish you were here to adorn the feast. Fiske on his return will tell you about it." Henry probably remembered the diverse occasions on which Turgenev had, at the last minute, cancelled appointments in Paris: the sudden attacks of gout, his complicated involvements with the Viardots, the demands made upon him by his fellow-Russians. His visits to London were always provokingly brief. Henry knew Turgenev liked the English, but he was not at all sure he liked London.

The group that gathered round the table at the Reform Club was a curious one: it seemed more philosophical and political than literary—but then Turgenev had given Henry very little notice, and during London's crowded social calendar at the end of June it must have been a problem to get the right combination of guests. Henry invited W. R. S. Ralston, Turgenev's translator; J. Cotter Morison, the Positivist; John Cross (who was to marry George Eliot a few months later) and Mowbray Morris, of *Macmillan's Magazine*. Bryce and young Hugh Arnold-Forster (ultimately Secretary for War under Balfour), who were not able to dine, joined the party later in the evening.

"Dinner at 8 o'clock at the Reform Club with Henry James," wrote Fiske exuberantly to his wife. "Turgenev was the hero of the occasion, and he is splendid—not unlike Longfellow in appearance. James Bryce, the great historian, was also there, and my ever-delightful Ralston. Magnificent dinner, and brilliant conversation. Ralston walked home with me at midnight."

"It was all extremely pleasant, dear Ivan Sergeyevich being at his best and most charming, which is not saying little," Henry wrote to his mother. "His simplicity and sweetness are as great as his wit and intelligence, and his conversational powers are flavoured (excuse the culinary expression) by the most captivating *bonhomie*."

At Oxford, Bryce, as Regius Professor of Civil Law, had extolled Turgenev's influence in the emancipation of the serfs. The novelist had received his honour in the company of John Ruskin and Sir Frederick Leighton, as well as the British Ambassador to St Petersburg and the Governor of Fiji. Turgenev was delighted. And he was pleased with the gift made to him of the gown he had worn at the ceremony. It would serve admirably for the Sunday charades at Madame Viardot's.

CARTHORSE AND RACER

For Henry, Turgenev was a touchstone with which to measure the English novelists. Thus, writing some months earlier to W. E. Henley, he pointed out that the Russian was the exact opposite of Meredith. Turgenev didn't care a straw for an epigram or a phrase; Meredith cared enormously for them. Turgenev wasn't a whit literary, but simply human and moral. Meredith was a mannerist, a coquette—like "that pitiful prostitute Cherbuliez." (In the fullness of time Henry was thus sharing the *cénacle's* contempt for Cherbuliez, and in language almost as harsh as Zola's.) So too, in thinking of George Eliot, he observed that she was a philosopher, while Turgenev was a poet. One could call Turgenev a "magician"—a word he would never apply to George Eliot. The Russian cared for the aspect of things; she for the reason of things.

Henry nevertheless looked with high regard and affection upon George Eliot and what she had accomplished for the craft of the novel. He hoped that he would meet her again: there had been one brief occasion, in 1869, during his grand tour, when Grace Norton had taken him into the presence of the rather overpowering lady—brief because a son of G. H. Lewes was writhing on the floor in the next room in a fit of pain and Lewes himself had gone to the apothecary for morphine. Now a Londoner, no longer a tourist, Henry embraced the first occasion to pay his respects to her. Early in April 1878 John Cross had invited him to a dinner at the Devonshire Club at which Lewes was present. "Capital talk and stories," Lewes wrote in his diary at the evening's end. Henry's version to Quincy Street was slightly different: "I sat next to Lewes, who is personally repulsive, but most clever and entertaining. He is rather too much of a professional *raconteur*—he told lots of stories; but he recounts very well—chiefly in French. He remembered, as soon as I was introduced to him, my queer visit to George Eliot in 1869, with Grace Norton, and asked me to come back, which I shall do."

He did—probably on 21 April 1878—and reported to William: "The Leweses were very urbane and friendly, and I think that I shall have the right *dorénavant* to consider myself a Sunday *habitué*. The great G. E. herself is both sweet and superior, and has a delightful expression in her large, long, pale, equine face. I had my turn at sitting beside her and being conversed with in a low, but most harmonious tone; and bating a tendency to *aborder* only the highest themes I have no fault to find with her. Lewes told some of his usual stories, chiefly French."

There is no record that Henry went back to this exalted Sunday salon. But he was destined to meet the Leweses once more under strange circumstances. The story of that encounter has become a celebrated anecdote, for Henry James fashioned it himself in the fragmentary pages of what would have been the third volume of his autobiographies: how, being taken by a hostess, Mrs Greville, with whom he was staying in Surrey, to visit the Leweses in their house nearby, he realized on arrival that they were not altogether welcome guests. It was a drenching afternoon; the bland and benign George Eliot stood beside a fire in a chill desert of a room with the master of the house guarding an opposite hearthstone, and both conveying to Henry's keen observation that if they greeted them with a show of warmth they "should more devoutly like it when we departed." In his reminiscence he relates, with a sense of the high comedy of it (and perhaps with self-depreciatory irony), how they left shortly after, and Lewes, seeing them to their waiting carriage, suddenly rushed back into the house and brought out a couple of blue volumes Mrs Greville had lent to the household. "Ah, those books—take them away, please, away, away!" And Henry recognized ruefully that the two blue volumes were *The Europeans*—and that neither George Eliot nor Lewes apparently had in the least "connected book with author."

Lewes was to die shortly afterwards; and not long after that George Eliot married John Cross. She was sixty; he was twenty years younger. When word reached Henry, who was then in

Florence, he wrote to Cross on 14 May 1880: "I have congratulated friends before on their approaching and accomplished nuptials; but I have never had the privilege of doing so in a case in which I felt (as today) all the cordiality of mankind mingling with my individual voice. Don't let this mighty murmur drown my feeble note." It apparently didn't, for the novelist herself, writing to a friend a few days later, said "Johnnie had a graceful letter of congratulation from Mr Henry James, who is still at Florence."

George Eliot lived but a few months longer. To his mother Henry wrote that her death was all the sadder in that "she, poor woman, had begun a new (personal) life: a more healthy, objective one than she had ever known before. I doubt whether she would have written, but she would have lived—and after all, at 60, and with a great desire to live, she was still young."

A few days later he paid his respects to Cross. He was received in the novelist's "beautiful little study they had just made perfect" and sat in the chair George Eliot used to occupy.

> She was surely an extraordinary woman—her intellectual force and activity have, I suspect, never been equalled in any woman. If, with these powers, she had only been able to see and know more of life, she would have done greater things. As for the head itself, it was evidently of the first order—capable of almost *any* responsibilities. She led a wonderfully *large* intellectual life—and Cross said that her memory and her absolute exemption from the sense of fatigue, were more amazing the more he knew her. He, poor fellow, is left very much lamenting; but my private impression is that if she had not died, she would have killed him. He couldn't keep up the intellectual pace—all Dante and Goethe, Cervantes and the Greek tragedians. As he said himself, it was a carthorse yoked to a racer: several hours a day spent in reading aloud the most immortal works.

To Henry's vision there had been two elements in George Eliot—the "spontaneous and the artificial." It was almost as if within her there were also the carthorse and the racer: the carthorse wrote *Romola*, so to speak, and the racer *Middlemarch*. Her spontaneous side enabled her to observe life and to feel it. But she had fallen into a high-minded circle which had compelled her to give an exaggerated attention to lofty generalizations. In the process spontaneity was tethered to the intellect; when she felt life in her works she was at her best; when she tried to feel "views" upon life, she became a burden to her story-telling. To her genius, at its best, he paid and continued to pay homage—and his greatest tribute was to be paid in his writing of *The Portrait of a Lady*, which in a certain sense can be called a "George Eliot novel" written by James in the way he believed she *should* have written.

THE BARD AND MR BROWNING

It was on the day after Henry's visit in the downpour to George Eliot and Lewes, when his two blue volumes had, in a manner, been hurled after him, that the "friend of the super-eminent," the loquacious and eccentric Mrs Greville, took him to still another celebrity living near her Surrey cottage. This time Henry was an invited guest; they were expected at Aldworth and Alfred Tennyson suffered from no lapse of memory about the identity of his visitor. He had met Henry at Lord Houghton's, and had talked to him with much warmth about one of his tales. Henry never revealed which tale it was; but he did feel this was some kind of compensation for the rebuff at the Leweses'. (Tennyson's memory, to be sure, could have its lapses as well. There is a pleasant anecdote, in Henry's autobiographical fragment, of his being some time later with Lowell at Tennyson's table. Luncheon began with an embarrassing silence, broken finally by the Bard's growling at Lowell: "Do you know anything about Lowell?" Mrs Tennyson had to come to the rescue with a "Why, my dear, this *is* Mr Lowell!")

On that autumn day Mrs Greville, whom Henry described as a large, elegant, "extremely near-sighted and extremely demonstrative lady" with a genius for "friendship, admiration, declamation and expenditure," brought Henry to Tennyson's mansion, and when they had lunched the Poet Laureate was urged to read a poem. They went upstairs to his study. One of the great poems of Henry's youth had been "Locksley Hall" and this was the poem he asked for. Tennyson growled it from its noble cadenced beginning through its great length to its finale: it wasn't Flaubert's *gueuler*, but it was a continual monotonous vocalization.

Henry sat at one of the windows that windy watery autumn day; sometimes the glass was sheeted with rain. He asked himself whether this were really he, and whether this was the Laureate;

he wanted to pinch himself when he remembered the emotions this poem had aroused in him in his youth; he wondered why he did not swoon for very ecstasy. It was all the reverse: he felt no emotion. Tennyson did not provoke it. He felt none of the vibrations of those long-ago days at Newport, or the effect upon him of the volume of Tennyson's poems, which his father had given him when he was a boy. "Why in the name of poetic justice had one anciently heaved and flushed with one's own recital of the splendid stuff if one was now only to sigh in secret 'Oh dear, oh dear'?" What had happened was that the author lowered the whole pitch. Henry heard him "take even more out of his verse than he had put in." Tennyson, in a word, wasn't Tennysonian.

On this same occasion there was a certain humour in the way in which Victoria's Poet Laureate pricked up his ears when the chattering Mrs Greville mentioned a French relative whose name was Laure de Sade. Tennyson promptly launched into a discussion of the works of the Marquis de Sade, enumerating titles, and saying many things, with only Henry, among those present, aware that he was speaking of an author one did not mention in polite Victorian society. Tennyson wasn't aware: he was merely reciting "useful information." Mrs Greville listened with "the blankest grace to her friend's enumeration of his [M. de Sade's] titles to infamy, among which that of his most notorious work was pronounced. It was the homeliest, frankest, most domestic passage, as who should say, and most remarkable for leaving none of us save myself, by my impression, in the least embarrassed or bewildered; largely, I think, because of the failure—a failure the most charmingly flat—of all measure on the part of auditors and speaker alike of what might be intended or understood, of what, in fine, the latter was talking about." Henry pondered this phenomenon: the Laureate who had become a mere growling voice; who spoke words—his own—without feeling, and facts without knowledge.

"I went to lunch with Tennyson," Henry wrote to Charles Eliot Norton. "I was staying near him, with an amiable and clever, but fantastic and ridiculous Mrs Greville, and he took me up into his study and read aloud—not very well—'Locksley Hall,' from beginning to end! I don't know whether you saw anything of this author, who personally is less agreeable than his works—having a manner that is rather bad than good. But when I feel disposed to reflect that Tennyson is not personally Tennysonian, I summon up the image of Browning, and this has the effect of making me check my complaints."

Henry held Browning in high esteem; and if at moments he was depreciatory, he was to recognize, when he recalled the contrasting figures of the Laureate and Mr Browning, that there was a distinct difference of temperament—that the scales weighted in favour of the latter. Whatever Tennyson had been, he was, as a "Bard," a growler of his own lines. Browning on the other hand—but we have Henry's exact impression: "One of my latest sensations was going one day to Lady Airlie's to hear Browning read his own poems—with the comfort of finding that, at least, if you don't understand them, he himself apparently understands them even less. He read them as if he hated them and would like to bite them to pieces."

If there was hate, there was at least emotion. Browning might be "loud, sound, normal, hearty," a presence "bustling with prompt responses and expected opinions and usual views." He possessed withal an intellectual eagerness to put himself in the place of other people; and there was in him "a restlessness of psychological research." If in his personal delivery of the fruits of his own genius he tended to harshness, "the result was that what he read showed extraordinary life." During the Tennysonian audition at Aldworth it had seemed as if there were no question of life. The mistake was Henry's. He had made, in his mind, quite another image of Tennyson. He had supposed him to possess all the fine flush of his own youth. That day Henry learned "what a Bard consisted of"—as he learned earlier in Browning something of the truer nature of feeling—in life and in poetry.

VOLTAIRE IN PETTICOATS

HENRY ADAMS and his wife arrived in England during the early summer of 1879, and sought out Henry in Bolton Street. James had seen very little of them since their meetings in Rome six years before. They were fresh from their voyage, rather tired and bedraggled, and his first impression—for he looked at them with the new eyes of distance and time—was that Adams could never "in the nature of things be a very gracious or sympathetic companion." Marian Adams (the Clover Hooper of his youth, Minny Temple's friend) struck him as "toned down and bedimmed from her ancient brilliance." These were first impressions; he revised them in due course. The Adamses settled in furnished rooms, two streets away, in Half-Moon Street, and Henry James got into the habit of dropping in to see them. He took them to a Sunday afternoon at the Grosvenor Gallery and introduced Clover to Mrs Duncan Stewart—"delighted my dear in Americans," the veteran lady told Clover; "they are all so charming." The generalization was rather sweeping, but Henry came to agree as far as it concerned his old-new friends, formerly of Cambridge and now of Washington; they were "both very pleasant." Later that autumn, when they met in Paris and spent many evenings together in restaurants and theatres, he wrote to Quincy Street, "I have become very fond of them—they are very excellent people."

There was, however, a fundamental opposition of temperament between the two Henrys. The historian was interested in large generalizations; the novelist was concerned with the particular. Henry Adams's relationship to the past, to history, was a means by which he attempted to unravel the riddles of man and the personal New England riddle of himself. Henry James's relationship to the past was that it was part of a continuum of man's imagination. He was willing to deal with it only as a vast accumulation of creative awareness applicable to a palpable present. Adams was trussed up in the rigidities of ancestry and up-bringing and was always struggling to be free. James accepted the world as it presented itself, and constantly moved to larger freedom. In his later letters to Adams he gently chides him, holding up the delights of spontaneity and the blessing of occasional obedience to impulse. The two men respected each other while having to recognize how different were their visions of life. For James it was all an act of joyful and imaginative curiosity; for Adams it was a gloomy questioning of personal experience that he could not reconcile to the eternal flux of history. The two Henrys had a patch of common ground. Henry James sought to create laws for novels; Henry Adams was seeking the laws of history. Yet even here there was a marked difference—that between a man who establishes order in his own world, as James could do, and a man who interrogates the entire world to extract a meaning from it. When Henry James read Adams's anonymous novel *Democracy*, he found it clever, although the satire seemed to him "a good deal too coarse." "Who is it by, or attributed to?" he asked his friend Perry. "A man or a woman? It is good enough to make it a pity it isn't better." At the end the novelist was to speak of Adams's "rich and ingenious mind," his "great resources of contemplation, speculation, resignation."

"Henry is very sensible, though a trifle dry," was his comment during this period in London and Paris. He added: "Clover has a touch of genius."

Henry had always liked Clover Adams. Long ago he had spoken of her "moral spontaneity." Now he had occasion to see how sharp, how cutting she could be; how she subjected everything that came under her view to a mordant and often highly humorous aggressivity. She had an abundance of wit: and an intense Americanism. Europeans were people to be judged, appraised and usually condemned. We know her in a great measure from her letters, and they—like Henry's to Quincy Street—were often written as family entertainment. Nevertheless the form they take, in their ever-present astringency, tells us much about this lively and yet self-doomed creature. "Mrs Adams," Henry wrote to Grace Norton, "in comparison with the usual British female, is a perfect Voltaire in petticoats."

The Adamses, after their trip to France and Spain, returned to London for the winter of 1879–80 and we catch glimpses of them in various great houses, often in the company of Henry James. They entertained in their own pretty house, which they took for the season, at 22 Queen Anne's Gate. Mr Hoppin notes in his diary after dining there that Henry James, the Matthew Arnolds, Lady Strangford and Mrs Duncan Stewart were among the guests. "The talk," he tells us, "was very good. Arnold was particularly genial and loquacious." Lady Strangford he describes as a rank Tory "with unreasonable prejudices against Americans."

Henry saw much of the Adamses. We can glimpse him on a Sunday afternoon, 22 February 1880; Adams, writing at this moment to Henry Cabot Lodge, records: "Harry James is standing on the hearthrug, with his hands under his coat-tails, talking with my wife exactly as though we were in Marlborough Street." What the Adamses offered Henry was the American companionship for which he longed in London: they were the kind of Americans he had wished for when he had written to Shady Hill, months earlier, that there were things he could never say to an Englishman. "The Henry Adamses are here," he told Lizzie Boott, "very pleasant, friendly, conversational, critical, ironical." He had sat up with them till one o'clock that morning "abusing the Britons. The dear Britons are invaluable for that." To Quincy Street he observed: "It is agreeable to have in London a couple of good American *confidants*."

The Adamses were "not at all crazy about London." Long before they left they were frankly homesick for Washington. When in the autumn of 1880 the time came for their departure Henry, again to Grace Norton, offered a summing up of what their presence in England had meant to him:

I go in an hour to bid farewell to my friends the Henry Adamses, who after a year of London life are returning to their beloved Washington. One sees so many "cultivated Americans" who prefer living abroad that it is a great refreshment to encounter two specimens of this class who find the charms of their native land so much greater than those of Europe. In England they appear to have suffered more than enjoyed, and their experience is not unedifying, for they have seen and known a good deal of English life. But they are rather too critical and invidious. I shall miss them much, though—we have had such inveterate discussions and comparing of notes. They have been much liked here.

Henry was to observe them in due course in their native surroundings, and the time was to come when "Voltaire in petticoats" would make her appearance in one of his American tales.

Even as these *confidants* were leaving, a turn of the wheel brought to London the charming elderly Yankee who had made bright Henry's autumn in Paris eight years before. Lowell had been shifted from Madrid to the Court of St James's, and it was a little like the changing of the guard—for Mr Hoppin recorded in his journal that when Mr Lowell arrived in London Mr and Mrs Adams were at Victoria Station to greet him. Glad as Henry was that his old friend was assuming these onerous responsibilities in the British capital, he wondered whether he would be very happy—or successful—in his task. For once his doubts proved groundless.

During Lowell's London years his friendship with Henry deepened into an affectionate and enduring intimacy, built upon their common Americanism and their common foundation of literary allusion. Thus was constituted a strange little American corner for the expatriate novelist; Lowell and his two secretaries, Hoppin and Nadal.

C'EST MON PLAISIR . . .

THE joys of the "dead season" in London were short-lived for Henry James. He discovered soon enough that if the importunities of English society ceased at certain times of the year, there arrived at such times on Britain's shore—and on his doorstep—many of his strenuous compatriots. There were days when he gave himself over entirely to entertaining old American friends, acquaintances of his brothers, Albany and New York relatives, and a continuing procession of literary pilgrims. American friends from the Continent would seek him out also, and while he enjoyed seeing some of them, they made great inroads into his working hours. If he had said to William that he always had his eyes on his native land, his native land, more often than not, had its eye on him.

Among the earliest of his visitors after fame had come to him was a Boston lady who thought herself descended from Scottish royalty—from Robert Bruce—and believed Mary Stuart to be an ancestor: and who, accordingly, conducted herself as if she were a Queen. Her motto, on the seal she ultimately designed, was *C'est mon plaisir* . . . and being fortunately endowed, she could suit her life to her motto and her motto to her life. Whether Isabella Stewart Gardner had met Henry James in Boston earlier we do not know; but it is from this time that his letters to her, preserved in Fenway Court, are dated. She came abroad early in 1879 with her husband, and presently Henry James was telling her how to find her way to Burne-Jones's studio and hoping "to see you often—if you will allow me." He was a busy man, however, and probably was not available as often as the regal Mrs Gardner would have liked. The novelist's relationship to Isabella was handled with the same firmness and ingenuity that governed all his dealings with exalted—and self-exalted—personages. He quite fell in with Mrs Gardner's wish to be treated as if she were royalty.

He was prepared always to be the most humble of her courtiers —but his tone was that of *noblesse oblige.* His letters were written as if he were flourishing a plumed hat before her and making formal obeisance. And yet he very carefully maintained a kind of distance designed to show Queen Isabella that it was he who was bestowing favour. For Henry understood her very well, and she greatly amused him. "Look out for my next big novel," Henry wrote in one of his earliest letters to her, in a purring prose. "It will immortalize me. After that, some day, I will immortalize you." If Isabella was Queen, in this game of *politesse*, it was apparently because Henry chose to make her so.

Henry James's letters to Isabella Stewart Gardner—almost a hundred of them preserved in the Venetian palace she ultimately built in Boston's Fenway, shoring up European remnants and ruins in an architectural *salade russe*—are masterpieces of epistolary grace and persiflage. He indulged constantly in the mock-ironic, and Isabella was flattered. If he suggested that she shed tears for the failure of one of his plays, it was to add that her tears were, of course, pearls. He put it, indeed, with much more delicacy than that: "Drop a tear," he wrote when the dramatized *Daisy Miller* was rejected by managers in New York and London, "a diminutive tear (as *your* tears must be—small but beautifully-shaped pearls)." There is more flattery than meets the eye: Mrs Jack was an ardent collector of pearls. Or he could begin with an endearing compliment: "Why are you so perverse?—Why do you come to London when I am away, and [go] away from it just when I come back?" Having made his flourish he could quietly add: "Even your bright presence there does not make me repent having fled this year from the Savage Season." And then the forcible conclusion: "You wouldn't have made it tame—so what good should I have got? I hope you have found it as wild as you like things."

Isabella must have found this exhilarating, and Henry had his fun. Such letters could have been written only by someone who, at bottom, really liked the self-inflated, wilful, and driven Mrs Gardner. Henry could rail at her in the privacy of his notebooks, see her as one of the tide of transatlantic "barbarians" over-running Europe, carrying off shiploads of spoils—while at the same time he penetrated the façade and understood that Isabella's acute state of queenship concealed a certain strange shyness and timidity, a certain unsureness that no real Queen could have: and that she was cultivating her high imitation of the regal to keep firm ground, at times, under shaky feet. Bernard Berenson was to call his patroness "the serpent of the Charles," but Henry saw in her some qualities that belonged to Eve rather than to the serpent. "I think she is too amiable to become *really* fashionable," he wrote to Mrs Daniel S. Curtis, who lived in a real Venetian palace on the Grand Canal and who, if she wasn't treated as a Queen, was saluted as a female Doge. "I see her succeeding better at Grand Hotels than at grand manners. She tries too hard and listens too sympathetically—bless her innocent (after all) heart." We must allow for the fact too that Isabella would have shown her least disagreeable side to a courtier as powerful and as adroit as Henry James. There were times when he was much less patient. "Mrs Jack [Gardner] returns to Paris tomorrow," he wrote to Henrietta Reubell. "She is not a woman, she is a locomotive—with a Pullman car attached."

During the summer and autumn of 1879 Henry went sight-seeing with Mrs Gardner on both sides of the Channel. On one occasion in Paris the Boston Gardners and the Washington Adamses, accompanied by Henry, dined at a *café chantant* in the open air and then went to the *Cirque*, after which they ate ices at a wayside café. The experience could not have been lost on Henry: an imperious-aggressive "Queen" juxtaposed with a "Voltaire in petticoats" in a setting such as Manet painted. "I remember those agreeable days last summer in London and Paris," Henry wrote later, "those talks and walks and drives and dinners." Thus Isabella took her place in the pattern of Henry James's days and years, and fixed her image in his work: for if one of his great themes was the chase of the American girl for the husband, another was the chase of the wealthy American for the artefacts of Europe.

Book Eight

Portrait of a Lady 1879–1881

★

PROVINCIAL STORM

THE FRAIL VESSELS

FATHERS AND DAUGHTERS

A NEAPOLITAN EPISODE

FENIMORE

A BAND OF EGOISTS

VENICE

PROVINCIAL STORM

WILLIAM JAMES was married in July 1878 to Alice Howe Gibbens, a Boston schoolteacher and a woman of considerable charm and refinement. She came from Weymouth, Massachusetts, of an old New England family, and had lived abroad for several years with her mother. The marriage took place in the very month of "Daisy Miller," and William, in the first flush of his honeymoon and of his release from the paternal hearth where he had lingered to his thirty-seventh year, resumed his vigorous criticism of Henry's work. We shall never know exactly what he wrote to his brother, for Henry destroyed William's letters of this period. William, however, kept Henry's and from these we can deduce some of his strictures. The elder brother attacked the slightness of *The Europeans* and objected to the ending of "Daisy," which seemed to him frivolous. He asked for greater "fatness and bigness" in Henry's stories. To the author of these works, flushed with his recent success, William's observations seemed as ill-founded as they were ill-timed. His reply is sufficiently documentary: "I was depressed on reading your letter by your painful reflections on *The Europeans*. But now, an hour having elapsed, I am beginning to hold up my head a little." He felt that William tended to take such works "too rigidly and unimaginatively." William, he said, seemed to think that "an artistic experiment was a piece of conduct, to which one's life were somehow committed." Henry added: "I don't trust your judgment altogether (if you will permit me to say so) about *details*; but I think you are altogether right in returning to the importance of subject. I hold to this very strongly." William's criticism of "Daisy" was simply "queer and narrow," Henry said, and any creative artist would so judge it. (William had felt that Henry's remark about Winterbourne's attachment to a lady in Geneva was out of place immediately after the scene in the cemetery.) Concluding, Henry explained to his brother that being "very artistic" he had a constant impulse to try experiments of form, on which he had no intention of wasting "big" situations. "It is something," he said, "to have learned how to write, and when I look round me and see how few people (doing my sort of work) know how, I don't regret my step by step evolution."

I

There was nothing new in William's criticisms; Henry had long been accustomed to them. What was new between the brothers, however, was the fact of William's marriage. This represented, in Henry's long and close attachment to his brother, a distinct and quite sudden alteration of an old relationship, the oldest and closest of Henry's life. Their fraternal alliance of affection and competition, of joint discovery of the world, had been formed in the nursery and during their childhood companionship abroad. Their rivalry was strong; their love for each other was also strong. The burden of Henry's early tales, in which he and William figure, had been always that however much they were unlike in taste and temperament, they were united by invisible bonds. The combined effect on Henry of William's marriage and his critical outburst seems to have been more powerful than might be imagined. The language in which Henry congratulated William is in itself suggestive. "I have just heard from Mother that you had decided to be married on the 10th ult.; and as I was divorced from you by an untimely fate on this occasion, let me at least repair the injury by giving you, in the most earnest words that my clumsy pen can shape, a tender bridal benediction." Even if we regard this as a slightly awkward attempt at humour, we must recognize that the pen raised in blessing has set down the words "I was divorced from you by an untimely fate on this occasion." In a certain sense there had been—on the grounds of their old attachment for each other—a kind of "divorce." And what is interesting is that in the ensuing weeks Henry wrote his worst novel, or at any rate a piece of fiction that might be considered a regression to the days of *Watch and Ward*. It is incongruously sandwiched between two minor masterpieces, *The Europeans* and *Washington Square*, and it bears the uncommonly ineffectual title of *Confidence*. Its plot is like an old eighteenth-century comedy, or a theme for a strange three-figure ballet, in which two young men (the familiar closely united but strongly differentiated young men of the early tales) become involved with a woman named Angela. *Confidence* is the only work of Henry James's in which this name occurs, and it may be of some significance that the familiar "Angel" is here feminized. First one of the young men loves Angela; she rejects him and he marries someone else. Then the other young man wants to marry her. She accepts him, and in the climax there is much dashing about and a frantic scene of jealousy in which the first young man offers to divorce his wife if Angela will still have him. Angela herself, all insight and perception, sets everything to rights. In some strange way this novel goes through a series of comings-together and fallings-out, and its personal statement appears to contain strong elements of rejection, jealousy, and a need for self-consolation. One would have to go very deeply indeed into Henry's inner life to unravel so intricate a series of fantasies. What we can usefully recall, however, are the fundamental elements in the relationship of the two brothers. In his old age Henry was to speak of the "abasement" of being a younger sister or brother. And he was to remember a striking episode of childhood, when William had rebuffed him by saying that he only played with boys who cursed and swore. This had certainly been one way of calling him "Angela" rather than "Angel." What is involved here may not be so much a relegation of Henry to a feminine rôle as to a kind of second-class citizenship.

II

Henry's sense of having been sharply criticized and pushed aside in his brother's life would probably not have had consequences beyond the feeble little novel, which ran through its six instalments in *Scribner's* and yielded him the tidy sum of $1500, had there not been another occurrence at this time of a much more public nature. Once Henry had finished *Confidence* he began his critical study of Hawthorne, a work he took to Paris with him and completed there in the autumn of 1879. It was written for the English Men of Letters Series, and was published in England and in America soon afterwards. In England it was warmly received; indeed Macmillan's promptly invited Henry to do a study of Dickens for the same series. In America it quite abruptly raised a storm in the press which amazed, disconcerted and finally deeply disturbed Henry.

In writing the book Henry felt that its tone was "gentle and good-natured." He had not tried to find any original material, although he had had some talks with Julian Hawthorne, the novelist's son, who was then living in England. For his biographical facts Henry relied on George Parsons Lathrop's *Study of Hawthorne*, and for the rest he based himself squarely on the works then available and Mrs Hawthorne's edition of the *Notebooks*.

The *Hawthorne* had not been out long before Henry realized that he had in some way profoundly irritated his American reviewers and critics. The first intimation came from Quincy Street. His mother spoke of the book as having taken some courage to do. Henry wondered why. "Mother thinks me very 'bold,'" he wrote to his father, "to have braved the probable wrath of the Boston critics; but I am not conscious of any great audacity." His mother, however, was right. Not only the Boston reviewers but those of New York attacked Henry for adopting a "foreign" attitude toward Hawthorne, and for his emphasis on the parochial quality of New England life in Hawthorne's day. For the first time American critics began to suggest that Henry was losing his native point of view by his continued residence abroad. Certain of the reviewers felt that he had treated Hawthorne with too much condescension. Others were angry at the repeated use of the word "provincial." A careful reading of what Henry said shows nothing truly offensive, but the tone of the book, and certain of his formulations, evoked a sharp, if characteristic, outburst of chauvinism. Henry's argument ran as follows: America had been bare of society and history when Hawthorne came upon the scene; finding no rich social fabric, such as

English novelists could draw upon, the romancer tissued his work out of haunted Puritan memories of New England. In depicting the America of the earlier part of the century, and in describing the elements "absent" from American life, James distinctly touched certain sensitivities in a nation that had tended to be self-adulatory rather than self-critical. "In the United States, in those days," Henry had written, "there were no great things to look out at (save forests and rivers); life was not in the least spectacular; society was not brilliant; the country was given up to a great material prosperity, a homely *bourgeois* activity, a diffusion of primary education and the common luxuries." Such sentences, while accurate enough, seemed to certain of Henry's reviewers depreciatory. A formulation such as "in the light, fresh American air, unthickened and undarkened by customs and institutions" invited challenge. It little mattered that in saying these things Henry had taken his cue from Hawthorne himself. Indeed the most celebrated—and condemned—passage in the book was nothing more than a series of variations on a theme from Hawthorne's preface to *The Marble Fawn*. Hawthorne had written: "No author, without a trial, can conceive of the difficulty of writing a romance about a country where there is no shadow, no antiquity, no mystery, no picturesque and gloomy wrong, nor anything but a commonplace prosperity, in broad and simple daylight, as is happily the case with my dear native land." It was in the light of this passage that James went on to make the famous enumeration of the things "absent" from American life in Hawthorne's time which existed for British novelists. The passage is often quoted, but seldom in context, so that it does make James sound as if he were advocating adoption by the United States of those very British institutions which America had abjured. This was the offending passage:

> The negative side of the spectacle on which Hawthorne looked out, in his contemplative saunterings and reveries, might, indeed, with a little ingenuity, be made almost ludicrous; one might enumerate the items of high civilization, as it exists in other countries, which are absent from the texture of American life, until it should become a wonder to know what was left. No State, in the European sense of the word, and indeed barely a specific national name.

No sovereign, no court, no personal loyalty, no aristocracy, no church, no clergy, no army, no diplomatic service, no country gentlemen, no palaces, no castles, nor manors, nor old country-houses, nor parsonages, nor thatched cottages, nor ivied ruins; no cathedrals, nor abbeys, nor little Norman churches; no great Universities, nor public schools—no Oxford, nor Eton, nor Harrow; no literature, no novels, no museums, no pictures, no political society, no sporting class—no Epsom nor Ascot! Some such list as that might be drawn up of the absent things in American life—especially in the American life of forty years ago, the effect of which, upon an English or a French imagination, would probably as a general thing be appalling.

Henry went on to say that "the American knows that a good deal remains; what it is that remains—that is his secret, his joke, as one may say." In this variation on Hawthorne's theme James was also echoing the very cadences of still another of his predecessors, James Fenimore Cooper, who had written in his "Notions of Americans" that there was "no costume for the peasant (there is scarcely a peasant at all), no wig for the judge, no baton for the general, no diadem for the chief magistrate." Cooper had further said: "In short, it is not possible to conceive a state of society in which more of the attributes of plain good sense, or fewer of the artificial absurdities of life, are to be found than here." For these reasons, and the fact that men found with ease other avenues to wealth and honour than the strenuous avenue of authorship, Cooper considered the outlook for American literature in his time hardly promising.

Even Henry's friend Howells was critical. The effect of the book upon him is reflected in the anonymous review he contributed to the February 1880 issue of the *Atlantic*. "We foresee, without any powerful prophetic lens, that Mr James will be in some quarters promptly attainted of high treason," Howells said. He felt that Henry had over-insisted on American provincialism. "If it is not provincial for an Englishman to be English, or a Frenchman French, then it is not so for an American to be American; and if Hawthorne was 'exquisitely provincial,' one had better take one's chance of universality with him than with almost any Londoner or Parisian of his time."

Howells expressed delight in certain of the chapters, but as for Henry's enumeration of the things absent from American life,

Howells said, "we have the whole of human life remaining, and a social structure presenting the only fresh and novel opportunities left to fiction, opportunities manifold and inexhaustible."

III

Henry judged Howells's review "handsome and friendly;" and in a long letter to his editor told him that the *Hawthorne* had been "a tolerably deliberate and meditated performance." He admitted that he had used the word provincial too many times; he also pleaded guilty to over-working the word "dusky." But on the main point of provincialism and nationalism Henry insisted that "I think it extremely provincial for a Russian to be very Russian, a Portuguese to be very Portuguese; for the simple reason that certain national types are essentially and intrinsically provincial." As for his enumeration of "absent" things, and his argument that the novel of manners required an old civilization, this seemed to Henry to be a truism in any discussion of fiction. "It is on manners, customs, usages, habits, forms, upon all these things matured and established, that a novelist lives—they are the very stuff his work is made of." In saying "we have the whole of human life remaining" Howells had begged the question. There was that much less of life when there were fewer institutions and fewer works of civilization. "I shall feel refuted," Henry said, "only when we have produced (setting the present high company—yourself and me—for obvious reasons apart) a gentleman who strikes me as a novelist—as belonging to the company of Balzac and Thackeray." In the meantime it was futile to argue; Henry said he did agree with Howells that it was necessary to feel as he did about the possibilities of America as a scene for fiction; only in this way would the country ultimately produce such geniuses of the novel as had flourished and were flourishing in the older civilizations. But Henry doubted whether a Balzac or a Thackeray would agree with Howells. When he did, he, Henry, was prepared to "lie flat on my stomach and do him homage," even in the centre of the *Atlantic Monthly's* column "The Contributors' Club," or on the threshold of the magazine or in any public place.

Good-humoured as this reply was, Henry was first bewildered and then hurt by the storm he had raised in America and while he shrugged it off as "a very big tempest in a very small teapot," it nevertheless made a deep impression on him. "The hubbub produced by my poor little *Hawthorne* is most ridiculous," he wrote to Perry. "My father has sent me a great many notices, each one more abusive and more abject than the others. The vulgarity, ignorance, rabid vanity and general idiocy of them all is truly incredible. But I hold it a great piece of good luck to have stirred up such a clatter. The whole episode projects a lurid light upon the state of American 'culture,' and furnishes me with a hundred wonderful examples, where, before, I had only more or less vague impressions. Whatever might have been my own evidence for calling American taste 'provincial,' my successors at least will have no excuse for not doing it." He expressed this forcefully to his mother: "It is like turning up the underside of a stone in the country—full of interesting revelations concerning the states of mind of the too numerous race of the literary animalculae." And thanking his friend Perry for a favourable review, Henry wrote in April 1880: "What a public to write for!—what an inspiration in addressing them! But let us hope they are not the real American public. If I thought they were, I would give up the country."

In the end he shrugged the matter off as "the clucking of a brood of prairie hens." However, it is clear that this emotional ordeal could not be disposed of quite so easily. For America, like his brother, had suddenly turned upon him: he and his work had been spurned and abused at the very moment when he seemed to be harmoniously attaining all his aims. The tempest, to be sure, blew itself out; but the weight of fraternal and national disapproval, in which his friendly editor had joined, left a certain amount of wreckage in its wake. Superimposed upon the old wounds of his boyhood—the endless times when he had been pushed aside and relegated to a quiet corner—the reception of his *Hawthorne* brought Henry to a strange turning-point in his inner development which was reflected immediately in his work.

THE FRAIL VESSELS

THE change which occurred—and which led Henry to write certain of his masterpieces—had been quietly symbolized by the fact that the "Angel" was Angela in *Confidence*. From this moment Henry began to write novels about heroines instead of about heroes. Hitherto, in his larger works, he had recorded the adventures of the Rowland-Rodericks, or the Christopher Newmans; and even when he seemed to be studying American flirts abroad, like Daisy, it was through masculine eyes, such as Winterbourne's. Now, however, he found it necessary to create —and to show—how American women, "heiresses of all the ages," responded to their destinies in a world that jilted, denied, betrayed—that made them, for all their fine will to freedom and independence, into second-class citizens in the very society that bestowed their heritage upon them. There were, to be sure, certain later exceptions: as with Hyacinth Robinson in *The Princess Casamassima* or Lambert Strether in *The Ambassadors*; but from now on the female protagonist took over the Jamesian scene, and she was to range from the juvenile Maisie, through the adolescent Nanda, to the mature Milly and Maggie of the later novels, not to speak of the Miriam Rooths, Fleda Vetches, Rose Armigers and Isabel Archers of other works along the way.

In a sense, what this may be said to have reflected was Henry's deepest personal feelings during this time. Henry James, conquering London and its literary world, could be as assertive and as powerful as Christopher Newman; but, rejected like Newman —or pushed to the wall by his elder brother—told that he wasn't fit to play with rough boys, or that his writing was full of knots and bows and ribbons, found himself reminded forcibly that he was a perpetual "mere junior," that he seemed to have been doomed from the cradle to abasements and inferiorities. One has but to mention the titles of his succeeding works to recognize how this subterranean emotion must have welled up like a fountain in Henry's imagination. And out of it came a short and remarkable novel about a jilted heiress, and an even more remarkable novel about an American girl attempting to assert herself in the world. That these works should have been followed by a novel dedicated to the actual debate on feminism would seem, in these conditions, the most logical thing in the world. The circumstances of his emotional life had led Henry to his significant protagonists during the first great period of his writing life. They led him now to paint the portrait of a lady.

Years afterwards he was to ponder this matter and to attempt to explain what he had done. Contemplating his shelf of fiction, he asked himself why he had chosen to give the centre of his stage to his young heroines, rather than write stories of adventure and action, as other novelists did. "By what process of logical accretion," Henry wondered, "was this slight 'personality,' the mere slim shade of an intelligent but presumptuous girl, to find itself endowed with the high attributes of a Subject?—and indeed by what thinness, at the best, would such a subject not be vitiated? Millions of presumptuous girls, intelligent or not intelligent, daily affront their destiny, and what is it open to their destiny to *be*, at the most, that we should make an ado about it? The novel is of its very nature an 'ado,' an ado about something, and the larger the form it takes, the greater of course the ado."

Reasoning in this way, Henry was led to quote George Eliot's words, "In these frail vessels is borne onward through the ages the treasure of human affection." Eliot had had her heroines: Dickens, Walter Scott and even the subtle Robert Louis Stevenson had preferred to leave the task unattempted. Musing on this, Henry proceeded to justify his major studies of the female sensibility, his insistence, at the heart of his own work, upon the heroine rather than the hero.

"Frail vessel," however, was hardly applicable to Henry's strong and egotistical young women. They possess not a little of his own power, will and strength in imposing themselves upon the world. Henry, at any rate, argued that a novelist—a novelist like himself—did not necessarily have to deal with the life of action. He could, through characters such as Isabel, or Milly, record the fascination of mental and emotional experience —mild adventures, perhaps, certainly independent "of flood and field, of the moving accident, of battle and murder and sudden death." Thus Isabel Archer could sit quietly by her fire during the long and remarkable sequence of her thoughts in the *Portrait* while she reviewed in subtle detail the history of her life. "It is a representation," Henry was to say, "simply of her motionlessly *seeing*." The challenge for him as a novelist and narrator was to make of this act a matter as exciting "as the surprise of a caravan or the identification of a pirate."

I

Confidence was completed during the summer of 1879. Everyone seemed interested in what Henry James would do next. He had promised that he would write a "big" novel, and Quincy Street was constantly curious about it. Compared to his lighter works, he told his parents, this work would be "as wine unto water," and from this point the novel, destined to become *The Portrait of a Lady*, is spoken of in the family letters as the "wine-and-water novel." It was with the intention of starting this work in earnest that Henry had gone to Paris in the early autumn of 1879, on his way to Italy. On the eve of his departure from London he received a letter from his old Roman acquaintance, Matthew Arnold, congratulating him on *Roderick Hudson* which had recently appeared for the first time in England. "When will your Hawthorne be out?" Arnold queried genially. "That is a man I don't much care for, but I am sure to like what you say of him."

The study of Hawthorne had been completed that September at 42 Rue de Luxembourg, a few doors from the house in which he had passed his memorable winter, three years before. On the day the last sentences were written he had gone out to celebrate the occasion with Mrs Gardner. This was the time when the Henry Adamses were also in Paris on their way to Spain and Henry saw them almost daily. "It is the same old Paris," he wrote to T. S. Perry, "seeming transcendently civilized, after the grimy Babylon by the Thames, but a million times less interesting." Nevertheless Henry had a lively and enjoyable autumn. The English summer had been dreary and wet; the French capital was filled with sunshine. Certain of his English friends turned up and Henry acted as their cicerone. He found them quite as provincial as his American friends—the Andrew Langs for instance, who assumed they could post letters in Paris with English stamps. Hamilton Aidé the amiable dilettante arrived, and Henry took him to Bougival to see Turgenev. The Russian was "delectable as ever, though a little gouty." Later in the autumn Ivan Sergeyevich joined him in town for what had become their traditional *déjeuner*. Of his old Russian friends Henry re-encountered the Princess Ourousov and had some enjoyable meetings with her. Zhukovsky was in Naples, and Henry planned to see him there. However, early in December, as he was about to leave for Florence, a raging blizzard covered all Europe with snow. The tunnels to Italy were blocked; the drifts were waist-high in Paris. At the height of the storm Henry sat snugly in his hotel, in the Rue Neuve St Augustin, whither he had moved with the advent of the cold, and wrote in a single sitting his light tale of American and European manners, "A Bundle of Letters." This was the story, later pirated, which he allowed Theodore Child to publish in the *Parisian*.

For Child Henry reviewed the newly published *Nana*, and while in the French capital he seems also to have written the long reviews of the recently published correspondence of Sainte-Beuve and of Delacroix. This return to the writing of criticism was confined to these reviews, and they show how much authority he had gained in the three years since his Paris residence. They are not only vigorous in their close analysis of the qualities of the writers; they demonstrate how much more receptive he was to their nature as artists. With Sainte-Beuve, and with Delacroix, he is much more sensitive than hitherto to the admixture of the masculine and feminine in their make-up. "There is something feminine," he writes of the French critic, "in his tact, his penetration, his subtility and pliability, his rapidity of transition, his magical divinations, his sympathies and antipathies, his marvellous art of insinuation, of expressing himself by fine touches and of adding touch to touch." He then goes on to enumerate the faculties "of the masculine stamp" in Sainte-Beuve, "the completeness, the solid sense, the constant reason, the moderation, the copious knowledge, the passion for exactitude and for general considerations." He adds however that in any appreciation of the French critic "it is impossible to keep these things apart; they melt into each other like the elements of the atmosphere; there is scarcely a stroke of his pen that does not contain a little of each of them."

Henry had long mastered the art of generalization. There is now however a greater use of aphorism, of sharpened epigram. "In the arts," he writes, "feeling is always meaning." Or again, "Art is but a point of view and genius but a way of looking at things." If on the one hand James seems to toss these profundities at the reader with a light gesture, he seems to invite him on the other to give close attention to his seeded paragraphs. How accurate Henry's touch had become may be judged by a single sentence in which he summarizes Sainte-Beuve's idea of criticism. "The critic, in his conception, was not the narrow law-giver or the rigid censor that he is often assumed to be; he was the student, the inquirer, the observer, the interpreter, the active, indefatigable commentator, whose constant aim was to arrive at justness of characterization." And he speaks of Sainte-Beuve's search in his biographical studies for "the seam as it were between the talent and the soul."

The review of *Nana* remained buried for years in the *Parisian*; Henry never reprinted it. He complained, in the best Victorian manner, that the novel was simply "unclean," and he did not have as yet the interest he was to show later in *le naturalisme*. Nevertheless he has much praise for the solidity and the strength of Zola himself. He is prepared to allow him his subject: indeed his complaint is that *Nana* is not quite human and that there is an absence of humour in the book. Humour, he suggests, might have served as a disinfectant. "It is not his choice of subject that has shocked us; it is the melancholy dryness of his execution, which gives us all the bad taste of a disagreeable dish and none of the nourishment."

The cold winter and the heavy snows of 1879–80 caused Henry to change his plans. He postponed his trip to Italy and the beginning of his wine-and-water novel until spring. He recrossed the Channel amid heaving wintry seas, and was happy to find himself again by his Bolton Street fire. Moreover he was writing a new short novel, and was deeply absorbed by it. He called it *Washington Square.* It was while he worked on this that his *Hawthorne*, as we have seen, created its storm in the American press.

FATHERS AND DAUGHTERS

HE had apparently begun *Washington Square* while he was on the Continent, intending it to be a short story, and hoping to send it to the *Atlantic*. Early in 1880 he wrote to Howells that "I tried to squeeze it down for you, but it was no use." At first he offered it to *Scribner's*, judging it to be a rather thin tale; however, that magazine had just finished the serial of *Confidence*. *Washington Square*, on an accurate estimate of its length, turned out to be even longer than Henry supposed, requiring six instalments. He sold it finally to the *Cornhill*. *Harper's New Monthly Magazine* took it in America and both journals used illustrations by George du Maurier. This was the first time Henry had achieved simultaneous serialization on both sides of the ocean, and it enabled him to lay plans for an even longer stretch of leisure for the writing of his promised big novel.

I

Washington Square was based on an anecdote told him by Mrs Kemble, a small item of her family history. Her brother had jilted an heiress when he discovered that her father would disinherit the girl. This simple theme Henry transferred to a mansion in New York. In England, when it was published, it began with a sale double its predecessor's, and it has always been one of the most popular of James's works, even though its author depreciated it, feeling that it was too simple and unvarnished a narrative. He had, indeed, told it without varnish, and with an unsparing economy, in a structure wholly scenic; and while Henry began by focusing the story on the jilting of the girl, he ended up with a brilliant picture of a father's clumsiness in dealing with his daughter's love and his crude failure to spare her feelings. The father is understandably concerned; he wants to protect his daughter, a rather plain and altogether unpretentious girl.

He is a successful medical man and also a martinet, and his skills in diagnosis and doctoring seem to have ill-equipped him for the simple task of attending to his daughter's heart. He prevents the marriage, but he also alienates the girl. She is left in the end alone, in the great house fronting on the Square, middle-aged, an heiress, her life blighted by parental want of imagination. The tale could claim as its ancestor *Eugénie Grandet* or even, in some respects, Goncourt's *Chérie*, where a girl also lives in a fine house and suffers from a wounded sensibility. It is a perfect piece of psychological realism, and with its four characters, the father, the daughter, the lover and a romantic foolish meddlesome aunt, named Lavinia Penniman, achieves a considerable degree of intensity and pathos. Although he has made her rather simple and plain, Henry's sympathies are clearly with the daughter, Catherine Sloper. And in terms of his recent life she is an image of himself as victim of his brother's—and America's—failure to understand either his feelings or his career. Dr Sloper would appear to be still another of Henry's fictional recreations of his brother: the William who had treated him and his work with sarcasm and contempt—the William who could love him and also spurn him. He seems to be embodied in the personages of both the father and the jilting suitor. Striking indeed is the way in which Catherine tries to deal with her predicament: she duplicates Henry's well-known manœuvre of resistance. "She was simply patient . . . there was a great excitement in trying to be a good daughter . . . It was as if this other person, who was both herself and not herself, had suddenly sprung into being . . . She only had an idea that if she should be very good, the situation would in some mysterious manner improve. To be good, she must be patient, respectful, abstain from judging her father too harshly, and from committing any act of open defiance." This was the young Henry in his familiar disguise, trying to bide his time, avoiding all overt action and hoping, by a kind of dogged persistence, to triumph.

Catherine Sloper has her modest, if negative and painful triumph. She does not yield an inch to her father; in the end it is she who can spurn her lover, when he returns years after, still possessed of a faint glimmer of hope that he can acquire the benefits of her fortune. She, however, can neither forget nor forgive. Among the endings of James's novels there is none more poignant than when Catherine, her interview with the middle-aged Morris Townsend over, picks up her morsel of fancy-work and seats herself with it again, "for life, as it were." In the intensity of the narrative, the short scenes, the heightened dialogue, the clash of wills, Henry James showed the mastery he had now attained. Indeed the chasm between this novel and *Confidence*, which immediately preceded it, is extraordinary.

Washington Square is often criticized for having little to do with the Square and for reflecting almost nothing of the background of old New York. For the attentive reader this narrative, within its small compass, contains all the touches that are needed to evoke the old tight world of the city. If there is little direct scene-painting, we neverthelesss experience, by the time we have finished, its aspect, half-provincial, half-metropolis, and the doings of its genteel upper class—their parties, their marriages, their Sunday dinners, their rigid manners; and we are reminded of a New York that was—in brief allusions to the "grassy waysides of Canal Street," the striking detail of Mrs Montgomery's home in Second Avenue, or the picture of the Square itself with its ailantus trees and the summer heat hanging over its mansions. To a New Yorker, acquainted with the city, the location of Townsend's office in Duane Street, and the oyster-saloon on Seventh Avenue are touches as precise as they are atmospheric. Above all, however, the novel is concerned with a struggle for power, a will to freedom, and the refusal of a simple soul to bow before the domineering spirit of another. This is the very heart of Henry's subject. He was to treat again and again of the relationship between fathers and daughters, but *Washington Square* was to remain at once the simplest and most dramatic—and most American—handling of the subject, framing an eternal drama of a certain kind of family life in a Square that was both a personal and an historical symbol of American upper-class prosperity. The novel testified also to the destructive power of a materialism untouched by the imagination.

II

Washington Square was completed between his visit to Paris, during that rude winter, and his departure for Italy in the spring of 1880. In the same interval Henry gave himself up to the pleasures of London's social life. He dined out strenuously, visited friends, and laid his plans for the large novel which he had been wanting to write for the past three years. His negotiations for its serialization had begun long before, when *The American* was still appearing in the *Atlantic*. He had then outlined for Howells his plan to do "the portrait of the character and recital of the adventures of a woman—a great swell, psychologically a *grande nature* —accompanied with many 'developments.'" But Howells could not take a large novel on the heels of *The American*. He had preferred the shorter work, *The Europeans*. This had been followed by the increased demand for Henry's stories and he had been side-tracked into writing certain of his international tales. He had made a beginning of his novel, however, and he described it as an "aching fragment." Nevertheless the delay enabled him to conclude better arrangements for publication, and by the middle of 1879 it was agreed that he would start his *Atlantic* serial during 1880 and run it simultaneously in England in *Macmillan's Magazine*. The contracts must have been signed, for Henry felt free to tell G. W. Smalley of his plans, with the result that the London correspondent of the *New York Tribune*, conscious of Henry's popularity, announced the forthcoming production in his newspaper on 5 August 1879. It was to be, he said, what the French called "a *serious* work." This did not imply that it had a religious character, but that "Mr James will devote his powers seriously to the completion of a novel which shall represent him at his best." Smalley went on to say that the English edition of *Roderick Hudson* in the conventional three-volume circulating library form was proving a success, and that "the main objection to it is that it was written too long ago; in other words that Mr James has done nothing since which shows a sufficient advance in power upon that very original story."

This paragraph had been published before the appearance

of *Hawthorne* and *Washington Square*. In essence it reflected Henry's own feelings. The time had come for him to write a substantial work. "I must try and seek a larger success than I have yet obtained, doing something on a larger scale than I have yet done," he told Howells. "I am greatly in need of it—the larger success." He realized this acutely during his stay in Paris when his current royalty statement arrived from the Macmillans. He had had substantial advances against his royalties; nevertheless Macmillan now had six of his books in print, and the sum (which he did not mention) seemed pitifully small. On the day that he received the statement he wrote to Chatto & Windus offering them *Confidence*. If Macmillan could not do better, he would publish elsewhere. Chatto promptly accepted and paid him a good sum down for the rights to the novel during a three-year period. To Alexander Macmillan Henry wrote that it was a pity his novels were not doing better, since they had been favourably noticed on the whole "and apparently a good deal talked about." The Macmillans, fearing they might lose Henry, and disturbed by his move toward Chatto, responded by sending him an advance against future royalties. For the moment this mollified him.

Since he was negotiating from a position of advantage, he made stiff terms for his big novel. The *Atlantic* was to pay him $2500 and *Macmillan's* £250. He estimated that he would receive in all $5000 by the end of the serialization. *Confidence*, *Hawthorne* and *Washington Square* had yielded him about $4000. Early in 1880, when T. S. Perry offered to write an article on Henry's works to date, he told him to wait for the novel he would do that year. "It is from that I myself shall pretend to date—on that I shall take my stand." And to Howells he announced that he had his title. The novel would be called *The Portrait of a Lady*.

III

With the old fragment of his novel in his writing portfolio, and provided with ample funds, Henry left London for Italy on 17 March 1880. The memory of his winter crossing of the Channel the previous December was fresh in his mind. He cautiously waited at Folkestone for five days and took ship on a calm sea on 22 March, spent two or three days in Paris, and then, in a straight run *via* Turin and Bologna, arrived in Florence on the 28th. He put up at the Hôtel de l'Arno, in a room with a window on the river yellow in the spring sun; he spread his writing materials on his work-table—but he was not yet ready to start. He needed a holiday.

He lost no time in calling on the "gentle and pure-minded" Bootts. They had wintered in Florence proper but were in the process of re-installing themselves in the thick-walled Castellani; they had possession of the big rambling apartment on the ground floor, where Lizzie had her studio beside the rough terrace that led to a low parapet and a view of the towers of Florence, glittering in the Val d'Arno. Lizzie had been ill but was better. She now appeared to Henry rather elderly and plain, but happy in her indefatigable industry. "She seems to spend her life in learning, or rather in studying without learning, and in commencing afresh, to paint in someone's manner," Henry, who had tried to place certain of her panels in London, wrote to his father. His largest interest was reserved now for her painting-master, the burly Frank Duveneck, whom Lizzie had persuaded to move from Munich to Florence. To Henry, who had just written a novel about a stern father and a plain daughter, this image of the trio, Francis Boott, with his "indefatigable devotion" to Lizzie and her simple-hearted and simple-minded painting-master, struck Henry as strange and even weird. Duveneck was a son of the frontier, a rough-and-ready "child of nature and of freedom" from Kentucky, who had learned his craft decorating altars in Catholic churches all the way to Canada. He had been living in Munich, had studied at the Academy and carried off prize after prize. Henry considered his work strong and brilliant, "the most highly-developed phenomenon in the way of a painter that the U.S.A. has given birth to." It had about it a "completeness" he would not have suspected from some of his things he had seen earlier in Boston and New York.

Aside from his painting he seemed the strangest person in the world to be in the constant company of Lizzie Boott. Lizzie, in her thirties, was a product of a careful education and a sheltered life. Duveneck had what Henry termed an "almost *slovenly* modesty and want of pretension." He was uncouth, vigorous and good-natured. Lizzie seemed to Henry to stand to him in "a sort of double relation of pupil and adoptive mother—or at least adoptive sister. I hope," he wrote to his Aunt Kate, "she won't ever become his adoptive anything else, as, though an excellent fellow, he is terribly earthy and unlicked." They were a strange group, the father, the daughter and the painter, and Henry was to watch the evolution of Lizzie's love-affair with her Bohemian teacher with the interested eyes of a friend—who was also a novelist.

A NEAPOLITAN EPISODE

HENRY was restless and he decided, a few days after arriving in Florence, to take a ten days' run to Rome and Naples and fulfil his promise to Paul Zhukovsky. They had been, after all, great companions during the memorable winter in Paris and had sworn eternal brotherhood in their long walks after intimate dinners with Turgenev and the Princess Ourousov. On his way to Naples Henry paused for a few days in Rome and found the city much changed—new streets, horse-cars, a hideous iron bridge over the Tiber—all "so many death blows to the picturesque." He had an enjoyable dinner however with the Storys and was welcomed this time not as a young aspirant in letters, but as one of the celebrities Story liked to receive in the Barberini.

What happened at Posilippo, in the Naples environs, we can only guess, but Henry's disillusionment seems to have been complete. Zhukovsky had appeared to the novelist as a charming and romantic dilettante in Paris; now he saw him as a rather weak and dissolute hero-worshipper. His latest hero was Richard Wagner. He had met him recently at the Villa Ungri, where the composer was spending that year—at a short distance from Zhukovsky's villa. The Russian was all for Henry's meeting Wagner at once. The American, however, had had his fill of Wagner operas, played on the pianoforte in Parisian studios during the spring of 1876, and he demurred. He frankly told Zhukovsky he had no desire to meet "the musician of the future." He believed such a meeting would be futile—he spoke too little German, and Wagner spoke neither English nor French. Henry described Zhukovsky as the "same impracticable and indeed ridiculous mixture of Nihilism and bric-à-brac as before." He spoke almost simple-mindedly of Wagner—the "greatest and wisest of men," and confided to Henry that it was his ambition to go and live at Bayreuth so as "to take part in the great work."

Henry doubted whether Zhukovsky would do this, since he seemed such an eternal dabbler. To his sister Alice he wrote that the Russian was "always under somebody's influence, first (since I have known him) under Turgenev's, then under the Princess Ourousov's, whom he now detests, and who despises him, then under H. J. Jr. (!!) then under that of a certain disagreeable Onegin (the original of Turgenev's Neshdanov in *Virgin Soil*), now under that of Wagner, and apparently in the near future under that of Madame Wagner."

Henry left Posilippo after three days and drove from Castellammare to Sorrento. There, in a hotel on the edge of the sea, looking out on to the Bay of Naples, with Vesuvius "smoking his morning pipe," and in the clear air that etched the villas on the opposite side, with fishermen under his window in red caps sending up a murmur of lazy sounds, he felt himself again in tune with the world. The bay seemed like a vast pale-blue floor, streaked fantastically with currents of lighter and darker colour. The gentle-looking flanks of Vesuvius were covered with patches of pale purple; there were bunches of oranges in the trees that looked like small Chinese lanterns, and their colour mingled with the silvery dusk of the olives. Writing to Grace Norton with this scene under his eyes, he told her he had just been observing "the manners and customs of a little group of Russians." These, he said, "were about as opposed to those of Cambridge as anything could well be—but to describe them would carry me too far." He did go on to tell her of Wagner and of Madame Wagner, the daughter of Liszt and Madame d'Agoult, and the divorced wife of von Bülow—"a curious collection of attributes." He has found the Naples museum more interesting than the "vileness" of the humanity of Posilippo. In his letter to Alice he contrasted a day spent with English friends at Frascati near Rome and their "admirable, honest, reasonable, wholesome English nature" with the "fantastic immorality and aesthetics of the circle I had left in Naples."

Decidedly the group of Russo-German sensualists in the Wagner entourage had troubled Henry. There are no records of later meetings with Zhukovsky. The Russian carried out his plan. He followed Wagner to Bayreuth and became one of the inner circle of his intimates. The composer was so attached to him that he spoke of him as his "son by his first marriage"—thus avoiding making Cosima into Zhukovsky's mother. The friendship lasted only three years, for Wagner died in 1883, but Zhukovsky achieved his ambition. He painted the sets for *Parsifal*. A photograph of 1881 shows him on Wagner's right, with a fine curly beard, a high forehead, deep-set eyes and a balding dome. He contributed to the Wagner legend by painting the picture of the "Holy Family" at Wahnfried, into which he incorporated Wagner's daughters as angels, and the face of the author of *The Ring*, with himself as a figure in the background.

Late in life he and Henry established touch again and one of his letters is preserved among Henry's papers. It is long, effusive, affectionate. He had been, for his brief moment, one of those with whom the novelist had thought he might have founded a lifetime friendship, so happy had been their Parisian encounters. Henry had to recognize that he had been mistaken. He had misjudged Zhukovsky. The Russian had proved an object unworthy of his affection.

FENIMORE

DURING the stormy winter of 1870–80 there had come to Europe an American authoress who had published many sketches in the magazines, a narrative poem entitled *Two Women* and a volume of tales, *Castle Nowhere*. Her name was Constance Fenimore Woolson. Her middle name proclaimed her ancestral relationship to American literature: she was a grand-niece of James Fenimore Cooper. She had crossed the rough Atlantic during late November on the *Gallia*, serenely preparing a volume of tales of the South, *Rodman the Keeper*, for the press, and arriving in London had taken rooms in Clarges Street, adjoining Bolton Street. She was a trim and dainty figure of thirty-nine, with a clear complexion, an alert manner and the bearing of a gentlewoman. One of her treasured possessions was a letter of introduction to Henry James Jr which she promptly presented at No. 3 Bolton Street. "Henry James is in Paris," she wrote to a relative after she had been in London less than a week, "and will not be here before Christmas, so we shall not see him after all." The cold and damp made her seek the warmer climate to which she was accustomed. She had been living for some years in Florida. Miss Woolson crossed to the Continent at about the time that Henry was returning to London, after the big snow in Paris.

The letter of introduction had been given to Miss Woolson by Henry's cousin, Minny Temple's sister, Henrietta Pell-Clark, who lived in Cooperstown, New York. The authoress wanted to meet James because she had read him, admired him, studied him, and enthusiastically reviewed him in the anonymous "Contributors' Club" of the *Atlantic*. Miss Woolson had strong opinions, and a strong sense of her vocation. She had dedicated herself to literature before she had gone to her finishing-school in New York. New-England born, the sixth of nine children (eight of them daughters), she had grown up in the Lake Country on the shores of

Erie and she knew the flora and fauna of America; she had caught, in the lands of *The Pathfinder*, some distant emanation of her great-uncle's genius. She had travelled in her father's buggy to outlying areas, walked the Indian trails, visited islands and marshes of the lake-shore, experienced the deep fogs, the prairie silence, and met the early settlers. Distinctly "regional," her northern sketches imbibed both the tradition of her great-uncle and the spirit of Bret Harte and they had proved generally popular. Then circumstances had taken her to the South of the reconstruction. Her father had died and she had sought a mild climate for her mother. This marked the second phase of her still young career. Her imagination was captured by the society reconstituting itself after the fratricidal war, the garrison life, the run-down plantations, the wretched houses. She went to the war-cemeteries. "I used to go out of my way to visit them," she wrote to Thomas Bailey Aldrich. "I have stood in many of these southern cemeteries—'National' they call them—poor lonely unvisited spots, the very perfection of their order only increasing their solitariness." She was something of a solitary herself. She talked to negroes and made notes on their dialect. She took lonely walks at the end of hot days on the edge of rice-fields, skirting swamplands and observing the death-in-life of the South. She made the South hers as she had done the Lake Country, and the tiny brushstrokes with which she wrote the opening lines of one of her most celebrated sketches, "Rodman the Keeper," show her talent for precision and neatness, as well as her limitations. "The small town, a mile distant, stood turning its back on the cemetery; but the keeper could see the pleasant rambling old mansions, each with its rose-garden and neglected outlying fields, the empty Negro quarters falling into ruin, and everything just as it stood when on that April morning the first gun was fired on Sumter; apparently not a nail added, not a brushful of paint applied, not a fallen brick replaced, or latch or lock repaired . . . magnificence went hand in hand with neglect." She had perceived, as Henry James was to say, "that no social revolution of equal magnitude had ever reflected itself so little in literature, remained so unrecorded, so unpainted and unsung."

The newest phase was now beginning. Miss Woolson had discovered the works and the style of Henry James; she had come to know Europe through his writings. As she neared her forties she was in the typical predicament of devoted Victorian daughters—she had given her best years to her mother, who had now died. She faced the world unmarried and alone. She had sisters, nieces, nephews—but these were other lives and others' children. She had her power of lonely sustained work, and a sufficient income from her writings. She would go to Henry James's Europe. Her friends John Hay and William Dean Howells encouraged her.

Europe, when she reached it that winter, was as snowbound as her Lake Country. The cold drove her to the Riviera. Here in the dazzling sunshine she was happy. She settled into the Hôtel des Anglais at Mentone, a quarter of a mile from the Italian frontier. It wasn't as warm as Florida, but the scenery was more beautiful. The grandees of Europe were there, new facial types, new modes of life, the leisure class of England, France, Russia. The daughter of New England, and of the West and South, lingered until spring. She spent her mornings in her room writing a novel, *Anne*, that was to bring her a wider public still, and the afternoons in sightseeing and local excursions. She also wrote poems. She wrote a poem called "Mentone"—

> Upon this sunny shore
> A little space for rest. The care and sorrow,
> Sad memory's haunting pain that would not cease,
> Are left behind. It is not yet tomorrow.
> Today there falls the dear surprise of peace.

In the second stanza she spoke of "a little space for love."

I

Henry James returned to Florence at the end of April 1880 and re-installed himself in the Hôtel de l'Arno. There, "in a room in that deep recess, in the front," he began *The Portrait of a Lady*, or rather worked over the "aching fragment." He was late in getting started on his book and rather than crowd himself wrote to Howells and to Archibald Grove of *Macmillan's* asking permission to begin the serial in October instead of in August as had been arranged. He argued that with *Washington Square* appearing in England and the United States until November, it would not be wise to have the two stories overlap. But he confessed also that the loveliness of Italy was causing him to look too much out of his window instead of remaining at his writing-desk. To his sister Alice he wrote that he was at last leading a quiet life, although Florence was "a place where one is liable to tea-parties." He added: "I have to call, for instance, on Constance Fenimore Woolson, who has been pursuing me through Europe with a letter of introduction from (of all people in the world!) Henrietta Pell-Clark."

Miss Woolson was living at the *pension* of Madame Barbensi on the Lung' Arno. When Henry finally paid his respects he seems to have been pleasantly surprised. Instead of the dowdy literary females he had often encountered in London, he saw a trim woman, her hair carefully braided and piled in rings at the back of her head, leaving a pair of delicate ears to the view. A fringe of hair concealed a high forehead. Miss Woolson had an oval face, questioning eyes, a straight nose and a firm if a trifle wide mouth. Her face was expressive and she was obviously impressed. Henry represented for her a certain summit in American literature. She listened intently, and he noted that she seemed to be hard of hearing. "Constance is amiable," he wrote to Quincy Street, "but deaf, and asks me questions about my works to which she can't hear the answers." Actually he discovered that her deafness was confined to one ear, and it was a matter of being on the good side. Little that he said was lost upon her.

In ordinary circumstances Henry James would have limited his amenities to his countrywoman. However, her charm of manner, her interest in his work, her bearing, and her sense of her own literary position quite disarmed him. Perhaps, too, he was still hurt over the break in his friendship with Zhukovsky and it was pleasant to find a new admirer. Miss Woolson had in her something of the flirt, a very cautious one of forty; and a competitive sense. She could be ironic in the manner of the members of the

James family. She tended to pay high, if barbed, compliments. And then other forces were at work as well: Lizzie Boott, who always devoted much time to Henry when he was in Florence, was preoccupied with Duveneck. This combination of circumstances may have made him more attentive to Miss Woolson than he usually allowed himself to be to strange women. There seemed, after all, small danger of his becoming too interested in an earnest provincial, middle-aged, deaf woman who was trying very hard to learn the meaning of art and was clearly discomposed by the nudity of the statues. Henry quite forgot his usual reserve: he turned on the full power of his charm for Miss Woolson. She tended to exalt herself, and her Americanism, at the expense of his cosmopolitanism; this however touched familiar ground; Henry was accustomed to rougher mockery from Quincy Street, and he had had recently a rather large dose of it from the American press.

Presently the two were seeing each other with a frequency that elsewhere might have been considered indiscreet. They did much sightseeing in the mornings. In the afternoons, during the warm part of the day, Henry liked to remain in his room and write. At the end of the day he went to his usual tea-parties and dinners with friends, including visits to the Villa Castellani.

The novelist did not reckon with Miss Woolson's loneliness and her craving to be loved. If she had given up hope of marriage, she must have now begun to wonder a little about the prompt and assiduous attentions of the aloof bachelor, who was three years her junior. Henry was all decorum and distance: nevertheless he showed endless patience and kindness; and he seemed delighted to be her cicerone and escort. Their interest in one another seems to have served as a kind of mutual flattery. The record of this, we must recognize, stems largely from Miss Woolson: in letters to friends and relatives she speaks of Henry's kindnesses—and frequently enough to show that they were far from perfunctory. Thus in the ancient city of the Medici, against a background of old palaces and the glories of renaissance art, this son of New York whose adopted home had been New England, and this daughter of New England whose adopted home had been the frontier, came to form one of the strangest friendships in American literary history, and one of the most secretive. A long chain of evidence shows that Constance Fenimore Woolson—Fenimore as he was to call her—became one of those friends in his life whom he considered "a private resource," and to whom he was always to be loyal, in his distant way. And she, as the years advanced, clung to him in a kind of pathetic dependency as the one man who gave her a "disinterested" yet welcome attention. Gradually she would be absorbed into the little group on Bellosguardo and into the Italian experience of Henry James.

II

At first it was almost as if Fenimore were a kind of intellectual Daisy Miller in whom Henry, in the rôle of Winterbourne, was interested, without showing any willingness to let himself go. "Florence," Fenimore wrote to a friend shortly after meeting Henry, "is all that I have dreamed and more; here I have attained that old-world feeling I used to dream about, a sort of enthusiasm made up of history, mythology, old churches, pictures, statues, vineyards, the Italian sky, dark-eyed peasants, opera-music, Raphael and old Michael, and ever so many more ingredients—the whole having, I think, taken me pretty well off my feet! Perhaps I ought to add Henry James. He has been perfectly charming to me for the last three weeks."

The meaning is fairly clear: she had been swept "pretty well off my feet" by all this—and by Henry James. She described him. He was rather taller than John Hay and with a larger frame. He had a "beautiful regular profile," a brown beard and hair, and large light-grey eyes, from which, she wrote, "he banishes all expression." His manner was "very quiet, almost cold." His "style" was unpretending and unobtrusive. "Yet," said Fenimore, "I wouldn't like to be the person who should think from his unpretending quietness that he could not be incisive when he chose!" She had read her man well. "He has many acquaintances in Florence," she went on "and he was constantly invited out to lunch and dinner parties; yet with all this, he found time to come in the mornings and take me out; sometimes to the galleries or churches, and sometimes just for a walk in the beautiful green Cascine."

His criticisms were novel and remarkable for someone new to Europe. From this time on, in certain of Miss Woolson's tales a Henry James character makes his appearance, with Henry's style of beard and Henry's build, and always with grey *expressionless eyes*—eyes that refuse to commit themselves, one might say. By the end of that summer Miss Woolson had written and published a tale called "A Florentine Experiment," in which she incorporated a certain number of Henry's observations on Florentine art, and her sense also of his aloofness, as well as what she seems to have considered his self-assurance and conceit.

From her letters:

"At present, I confess, Giotto remains beyond me. And H. J. says calmly, 'Some day, you will see it.' May be."

"The Duomo is too vast and cold. I went there one rainy afternoon alone, and had the weirdest time! It was almost dark inside, and I was the only person in all the great gloomy space. I went there again with H. J. who admires it, and tried to make me admire it too."

"The statue of Lorenzo in the new Sacristy of San Lorenzo is the finest statue, a thousand times over, I have ever seen. But I confess frankly that it is going to take some time for me to appreciate 'the nude.' I have no objections to it, I look at it calmly, but I am not sufficiently acquainted with torsos, flanks, and the lines of anatomy, to know when they are 'supremely beautiful' and when not. Now 'Lorenzo' is clothed and therefore comes within my comprehension and oh! he is superb."

She goes on to say that the reclining statues by Michelangelo of Day, Night, Evening and Dawn "are rather beyond me." And she continues:

"In speaking of these statues, Henry James said—'Of course you admired those grand reclining figures?' 'No,' I replied honestly, 'I did not. They looked so distracted.' 'Ah yes,' he said, '*distracted.* But *then*!' Here words failed him and he walked off to look at a fresco, to recover from my horrible ignorance."

"Yesterday Mr James came to take me to one of the galleries, and, as he is a delightful companion, because he knows all about pictures, I went, although I knew we were going in the afternoon to Fiesole."

"I enjoyed being very much with Henry James . . . he knows the pictures as well as I know Florida. He is a very quiet fellow; and very (though in an unobtrusive way) English."

Sketchy these fragments from the letters may be, but when they are read beside their amplification in Miss Woolson's "A Florentine Experiment" they suggest that this was an instance in which the artist in Henry ran away with his usual discretion. Something in Fenimore must have put him at his ease. It was almost as if he were entertaining Quincy Street—his mother or Alice—rather than speaking to a woman he had recently met for the first time. "He delivered quite an epic upon Giotto's two little frescoes in the second cloister of Santa Maria Novella," Miss Woolson wrote in her Florentine tale, "and he openly preferred the third there—the little Virgin going up the impossible steps—to Titian's splendid picture of the same subject, in Venice. He grew didactic and mystic over the round Botticelli of the Uffizi and the one in the Prometheus room at the Pitti; he invented as he went along, and amused himself not a little with his own unusual flow of language." Henry could be an easy improviser. He lost sight of something of which he was only too well aware in his tales; that an eligible bachelor could be generous and kind to a lady "of a certain age" up to a point; and that beyond it she might feel that he should declare his intentions. He did have a certain awareness of Fenimore's feelings, for he wrote to his Aunt Kate on 3 May 1880—that is, early in his newly-formed friendship—"This morning I took an American authoress [on] a drive—Constance Fenimore Woolson, whose productions you may know, though I don't, and who was presented to me (by letter) by Henrietta Temple. Constance is old-maidish, deaf and 'intense,' but a good little woman and a perfect lady." He added to his aunt: "I hope your spring is genial, without being (like Miss Woolson) intense."

At another time Henry might have been more wary of such intensity. It is abundantly present in "A Florentine Experiment" in which a young American heiress, believing the Henry James character (whom she named Trafford Morgan) to be in love with another woman, trifles with his affections. The "experiment" is hers; it stems from her belief in his masculine arrogance and conceit, which she is quite prepared to deflate. What the tale overlooks, understandably, is the heroine's own large measure of conceit as well. The Henry character, however, is rejected by the woman he loves, and comes back to conduct his "experiment" in turn, and finally to win the heroine. In the tale, at least, Miss Woolson provided a happy ending.

There is another tale which is perhaps more significant in disclosing the deep literary ambition Miss Woolson nourished, and her feelings about a writer like Henry James. It was written just before the two met, for it appeared in *Lippincott's* in the May 1880 issue, that is during the very month of their sightseeing in Florence. The tale is set in Rome, which Miss Woolson had not yet visited when she wrote the story. Titled "Miss Grief" it reflects a close reading of Henry's work. It is told in the first person by a man, a writer, who mentions that he models himself on Balzac, and there is an allusion to a tale of a buried god which would resemble "The Last of the Valerii." "Miss Grief" is the author's nickname for a literary lady named Aarona Montcrief, which she has shortened to Crief. She is forty-three, and she tells the great author, "I have read every word that you have written," and then recites his favourite scene by heart. "She had understood me—understood me almost better than I had understood myself." She gives him the manuscript of her play to read. After he praises it, she tells him that his adverse criticism would have led to her suicide. The author however feels that one character in it is wrong. He tries to edit it. The character, nevertheless, is so closely woven into every part of the tale that "to take him out was like taking out one especial figure in a carpet; that is impossible unless you unravel the whole."

Miss Woolson, taking James's own tapestry imagery, had in this early story used a phrase that was to become the title of one of his celebrated tales—"The Figure in the Carpet." In "Miss Grief," however, it is not the phrase which is revelatory, so much as the literary lady's final declaration to the great author: "You had success—but I had the greater power." This he acknowledges after she is dead: "She, with the greater power, failed—I, with the less, succeeded." There is enough evidence to show, in what she was to write to Henry James, that Fenimore had a certain exalted notion of her own literary powers. She aspired to the style, the manner, the mastery of Henry James. In truth she could pretend to mastery only in such wish-fulfilling tales. As a story "Miss Grief" is better written than most of her discursive work. She was to try, during the ensuing decade—her final "phase"—to write international stories, after the manner of the man to whom she became attached, and with whom she now felt herself, on some strange deep level, to be competing. Henry must have sensed this. It would have given her, in that case, something of the status of his brother. It is to some such appeal to his constituted nature that we may attribute his long and persistent friendship with Fenimore, an attachment that was to lead to secret meetings and a liaison in Henry's life never suspected by his friends. The inevitable question may be asked at this point in the terminology of James's own novels; was it a "virtuous attachment?" There is no reason for believing that it wasn't. And there are significant later tales—among the greatest of Henry's stories—which offer us certain clues to one of the few relationships in Henry's life in which his eyes may be said to have been partially sealed. Insight was to come only in the long aftertime.

A BAND OF EGOTISTS

WHEN Henry bade farewell to Florence—and to Fenimore—late in May or early in June 1880, he had in his portfolio the first instalments of *The Portrait of a Lady*. This time his copyright would be safeguarded: the serial was to begin in October in England and a month later in America. Moreover he now had the advantage of working from proofs supplied by Macmillan, and would not be dispatching raw manuscript to Howells. At this stage Henry was still writing in longhand and dispatching usually a first draft; in the *Portrait*, nevertheless, he worked over each chapter, "every part being written twice," he later said.

In his journal-summary of this period he wrote: "I returned to London to meet William who came out in the early part of June, and spent a month with me in Bolton Street, before going to the Continent. That summer and autumn I worked, *tant bien que mal*, at my novel which began to appear in *Macmillan* in October (1880). I got away from London more or less—to Brighton, detestable in August, to Folkestone, Dover, St Leonard's, etc. I tried to work hard, and I paid very few visits. I had a plan of coming to America for the winter and even took my passage; but I gave it up. William came back from abroad and was with me again for a few days, before sailing for home. I spent November and December quietly in London, getting on with the *Portrait*, which went steadily, but very slowly."

I

Henry had had short notice of William's sudden trip. He engaged rooms for him under his own in Bolton Street and sought to offer him the amenities of London. William did not respond to Henry's hospitalities, arguing there was no point in meeting a great many persons whom he would never see again. The purpose of his trip abroad had been to obtain a change and a rest. He was still prone to nervous fatigue and eye-trouble, and after a while Henry left him pretty much to his own resources, since he was himself deeply preoccupied with his novel. William did not remain long, and he spent the rest of the summer on the Continent.

The brothers had not seen each other since Henry had come abroad in 1875. In the interval the novelist had found his place in life, and William had become a husband and a father. Henry reported to Quincy Street that he found him little changed, "with the same tendency to descant on his sensations—but with all his vivacity and brilliancy of mind undimmed." There remained in him, Henry felt, "more of nervousness and disability" than he had supposed, "and I can't get rid of the feeling that he takes himself, and his nerves, and his physical condition too hard and too consciously. As he takes himself however, so one must take him; but," Henry added, in a letter to his mother, "I wish he had a little more of this quiet British stoutness." The "angel, hero, martyr" associated himself with the maternal view of William.

Henry did, however, give a small dinner for his brother at the Reform Club. Otherwise his efforts to draw William into his own social orbit failed; even an evening arranged at the home of T. H. Huxley was cancelled when William suddenly decided to leave London. He found England, he said, "oppressively social." On reaching the Continent the elder brother wrote a letter to Quincy Street which shows that he was still using the problems of his own career as a measure for his brother. "I think as he grows older," William wrote, "that he is better suited by superficial contact with things at a great many points than by a deeper one at a few points." This was quite accurate in describing his own focused interests, psychological and philosophical, as against Henry's wide-ranging absorption in the ways of the world. But no one reading the fruits of Henry's contact with "things at many points" would today use the word "superficial." And then there was in William's letter the need to find grace in parental eyes as Henry had found it. It took the form of his saying that during his stay in London he had often thought of his parents and their early visits to England and their burdens of travel with their children and the sacrifices they had made. And then, William said, "when I went into St John's Wood and its monotony, and contrasted the life you led there with that which Harry is now leading in Bolton Street, it made me feel how few things you laid claim to, and how entirely at that time your lives were given up to us. There is a strange inability on the part of children to project themselves out of their egoistic standpoint, so far as their parents are concerned." And William added that now he was a husband and a father he understood better—"perhaps my own parental condition makes me now more able to do so than before." Read in the light of the fraternal power-play, we might say that Henry had never been called an egotist with greater subtlety.

His brother's visit this time was but a ripple in Henry's generally contented life and work in London. Nevertheless William had barely left for the Continent when Henry was reporting to his mother that he was recovering from "one of those wretched sieges of pain in my head which I have had so often and which are so unprofitable." Henry also informed Quincy Street that he would not be returning to America that autumn as he had planned. It seemed to him the wiser course to remain abroad until his novel should be complete, and then give himself a total holiday at home. He had actually taken passage for the end of August. He used the most practical arguments available to mollify his parents. He was to get a great deal of money for *The Portrait*, "and therefore I wish to carry it on quietly and comfortably—the more so as I have just been correcting the opening proofs and that they seem to me very good." He might also decide, he said, to do the study of Dickens, and this could better be written in London than in Cambridge. "My delay has nothing to do with my not wanting to go home; on the contrary, I wish to go keenly, and see a thousand uses and satisfactions in it; but I wish to do it in the best conditions and to return in a word with a little accumulation of opulence and honour." He added: "On this then I take your blessing and your embrace and assume that for the present you will philosophically cease to expect me." In a later letter he thanked his parents for "not reviling me for having disappointed you," and remarked that "for the present, William will take you plenty of news."

Henry resumed the usual course of his London life. During his concentrated work on his novel he dined out less, but allowed himself certain country visits, including one to the American banker Russell Sturgis and his wife, in their luxurious country house—a type of expatriate he incorporated in the Touchetts in his novel; and he also allowed himself many week-ends away from Bolton Street. At the end of 1880 he paid a round of Christmas and New Year visits, and in February he turned once again to Italy, there to complete his novel.

II

The Portrait of a Lady was the third of Henry James's large studies of the American abroad and twice as long as either of its predecessors. In *Roderick Hudson* he had posed the case of the artist, the limitations of his American background, and the frustration of his creative energy from the moment it was confronted by passion. In *The American* he had pictured an ambitious business man, bent on civilizing himself, proud enough to know his worth, and arrogant enough to think that the best of Europe was none too good for him. *The Portrait* was envisaged as a kind of feminine version of *The American*, and James began with the thought that his Isabel Archer would be a female Christopher Newman. Indeed this may be why he named her Isabel; there is a certain logic in moving from Christopher to the Queen who sent him faring across the ocean. And Isabel Archer deems herself good enough to be a Queen; she embodies a notion not unlike that of Isabella of Boston, whose motto was *C'est mon plaisir*.

In Isabel Archer Henry wished to draw "the character and aspect of a particular engaging young woman," and to show her in the act of "affronting her destiny." Like her male predecessors she goes abroad a thorough provincial, with her "meagre knowledge, her inflated ideals, her confidence at once innocent and dogmatic, her temper at once exacting and indulgent." A person who is dogmatic and exacting on the strength of meagre knowledge can only be characterized as presumptuous; and there is presumption in Isabel, for all the delicacy of her feeling: presumption suggests also a strong measure of egotism. James presents her to us as a young romantic with high notions of what life will bring her; and also as one who tends to see herself in a strong dramatic light. She pays the penalty of giving "undue encouragement to the faculty of seeing without judging;" she takes things for granted on scanty evidence. The author confesses that she was "probably very liable to the sin of self-esteem; she often surveyed with complacency the field of her own nature." He speaks of her "mixture of curiosity and fastidiousness, of vivacity and indifference, her determination to see, to try, to know, her combination of the desultory flame-like spirit and the eager and personal creature of her conditions." And he adds: "She treated herself to occasions of homage."

The allusion to her "flame-like spirit" suggests that Isabel images Henry's long-dead cousin Minny Temple, for he was to describe her in the same way. He was to confess that he had actually thought of Minny, in creating the eager imagination and the intellectual shortcomings of his heroine. But Minny, as he pointed out to Grace Norton, had been "incomplete." Death had deprived her of the trials—and the joys—of maturity. Henry, as artist, could imagine and "complete" that which had been left undone. Nevertheless, if Isabel has something of Henry's cousin in her make-up, she has much of Henry himself. He endows her, at any rate, with the background of his own Albany childhood and, as in *Washington Square*, he interpolates a section wholly autobiographical, depicting his grandmother's house, the Dutch school from which he himself had fled in rebellion (as Isabel does), the "capital peach trees," which he had always sampled and always remembered. The scene is re-evoked years later in the autobiographies.

The most Jamesian of Henry's heroines is thus closely linked by her background and early life to her creator. And when Henry sends Isabel to Europe and makes her into an heiress, he places her in a predicament somewhat analogous to his own. Henry was hardly an "heir;" but his pen had won him a measure of the freedom which others possess through wealth. In posing the questions: what would Isabel do with her new-found privileges? where would she turn? how behave? he was seeking answers for himself as well as for her. The questions are asked in the novel by Ralph Touchett, Isabel's cousin, a sensitive invalid who has silently transferred his inheritance to her. He knows he has not long to live, and he wishes to see how Isabel's large nature will profit by endowment. If this is a sign of his love for her, and the sole way in which he can be symbolically united to her, it is also Ralph's way of living vicariously in Isabel's life and participating in whatever fate her temperament may reserve for her. He, too, has a substantial fund of egotism.

Like her early predecessor in *Watch and Ward*, Isabel presently finds herself with three suitors. The first is a young man of very respectable fortune and family from the United States who has pursued her abroad. His name is Caspar Goodwood. He is an individual who has a "disagreeably strong push, a kind of hardness of presence, in his way of rising before her." He insists "with his whole weight and force." He is in short monotonously masculine; and if Isabel finds his sheer sexual force attractive it is also terrifying. Passion, or sex, as with *Roderick*, is not freedom. She rejects Goodwood several times during the novel and flees from him at the end when she finds his kiss to be like "white lightning." When "darkness returned she was free."

The second suitor is less dull and much less terrifying. He is a British Lord named Warburton, a fine upstanding liberal, without too much imagination, one of the types Henry has met at his club or in country houses, fortunate heir of a position in a hierarchical society and the means by which to sustain it. He inspires a different kind of fear in Isabel. "What she felt was that a territorial, a political, a social magnate had conceived the design of drawing her into the system in which he rather invidiously lived and moved. A certain instinct, not imperious, but persuasive, told her to resist—murmured to her that virtually she had a system and an orbit of her own." Social position in a word was also not freedom; moreover, social position in a hierarchical society represented a strong threat to a woman powerful enough and egotistical enough to believe that she had "an orbit of her own."

Isabel is romantic, and young. "I'm very fond of my liberty," she says early in the book, and she says also "I wish to choose my fate," quite as if the ultimate choice were hers. If we see this as containing a measure of the egotism of youth, we must recognize that in her it has its ingenuous charm. Nevertheless Henrietta Stackpole, an energetic and rather meddlesome newspaper-woman, recognizes it for what it is—for she is endowed with not a little egotism herself. She reminds Isabel: "You can't always please yourself; you must sometimes please other people."

At this stage Henry's heroine is still full of her hopes and dreams. Asked to define success—a matter of some interest to her author—she replies that it is to see "some dream of one's youth come true." And asked to define her idea of happiness she offers a vision of a journey into the unknown—"A swift carriage, of a dark night, rattling with four horses over roads that one can't see." The concept is largely that of a girl who reads novels. However the young lady from America does not really mean what she says. She tries very hard to see, at every turn, the roads before her—and in broad daylight. She is supremely cautious in action, for one so daring in her fancy. And what she discovers is that even in daylight on a clear highway it is possible to take a wrong turning.

III

Isabel's wrong turning occurs without her knowledge, when she meets a woman of a certain age, worldly-wise and accomplished, the last word in refinement, an American expatriate of long standing, who has absorbed Europe into her being and bestrides the Continent with that appearance of freedom and insouciance to which Isabel aspires. The charm she exhibits, the deep attraction Isabel feels for her, are founded in part on the girl's inexperience of people and her inability to recognize the treacheries of life. The woman's name is Madame Merle. The *merle* is a blackbird.

Serena Merle introduces Isabel to another American expatriate, who lives in a thick-walled villa in Florence on Bellosguardo, with his young daughter. At this point Henry places in his novel his early vision of Francis Boott and Lizzie recorded in his travel-sketch of 1877, when he had mused on the "tranquil, contented life" of the father and daughter, and the exquisite beauty that was a part of their daily existence. He had spoken of Frank and Lizzie as "figures in an ancient, noble landscape," and Gilbert Osmond and his daughter Pansy are such figures. Pansy, though pictured at a younger age than Henry had ever known Lizzie, is re-imagined as having the same cultivated qualities of the *jeune fille*, the *achieved* manners of an old civilization. Osmond, however, bears no resemblance to Boott, who was an open, generous, naïve and easy-laughing amateur of life. Osmond's sinister character derives from other sources, and in all critical speculation as to who was his "original" the principal original has been overlooked. To discover him we must compare him first with Catherine Sloper's father in *Washington Square*. He has the same intelligence and the same piercing sarcasm. As a father Osmond is capable of the same coldness to his daughter's feelings. But he is an infinitely more malign father, and his will to power is infinitely greater than Dr Sloper's self-aggrandizement in the Square.

"There were two or three people in the world I envied," Osmond tells Isabel shortly after meeting her "—the Emperor of Russia, for instance, and the Sultan of Turkey! There were even moments when I envied the Pope of Rome—for the consideration he enjoys." Nothing less than the Tsar of all the Russias, and the man who could claim to be holier than all others. We grant Osmond his fine irony, as he says this, but we must nevertheless recognize what it expresses. Since he cannot be Tsar or Sultan or Pope, Osmond has consoled himself with being "simply the most fastidious young gentleman living." By now he is no longer young; he is confirmed, however, in his own private domain of power, as the perfect collector of bric-à-brac and *objets d'art*, and a subtle manipulator of persons as well as things. Pansy has been made into one of these objects: and Isabel is to be added to the collection. Strange as it may seem, Osmond clearly expresses one side of Henry James—the hidden side—not as malignant as that of his creation, but nevertheless that of the individual who abjures power by clothing it in meekness and deceptive docility. In this sense Henry is the "original" of his villain. Osmond is what Henry might under some circumstances have become. He is what Henry could be on occasion when snobbery prevailed over humanity, and arrogance and egotism over his urbanity and his benign view of the human comedy. Perhaps the most accurate way of describing this identification with Osmond would be to say that in creating him Henry put into him his highest ambition and drive to power—the grandiose way in which he confronted his own destiny—while at the same time recognizing in his villain the dangers to which such inner absolutism might expose him. In the hands of a limited being, like Osmond, the drive to power ended in dilettantism and petty rages. In Henry's hands the same drive had given him unbounded creativity.

Isabel and Osmond are then, for all their differences, two sides of the same coin, two studies in egotism—and a kind of egotism which belonged to their author. For Isabel, generous high-minded creature though she is, in pursuit of an abstraction she calls "freedom," insists self-centredly (in spite of grim warnings from all her friends) that she has found it in Osmond. She sees "a quiet, clever, sensitive, distinguished man . . . a lovely studious life in a lovely land . . . a care for beauty and perfection." He is the "elegant complicated medal struck off for a special occasion" and she feels it to be her occasion. Has she not always felt she was rather "the special thing" herself—a subject of her personal homage? And now, possessed of her wealth, it is as if she could combine her own power with the quiet existence of this individual and his exquisite flower-like daughter. When she marries him she believes that it is she who brings powerful elements into the union; "she would launch his boat for him; she would be his providence." This is indeed an exalted notion of her rôle, and it suggests the rôle she assigned to Osmond. Thinking back on this later, she wonders at the "kind of maternal strain" she had possessed in her passion: she believes that her money had been her burden. But this is rationalized after the fact. Isabel and Osmond had been attracted to one another because each saw in the other a mirror-image of self. The two had experienced an irresistible need for each other and in the end they cannot suffer each other. Power may be attracted to power, but cannot endure it. Each insists on supremacy. Osmond tries to bend Isabel to his will. She cannot be bent. Her kind of power refuses to be subjugated: it exerts its own kind of subjugation. His, more devious, returns perpetually to the assault. The impasse is complete.

Henry had written into this work two aspects of himself: there was his legitimate aspiration to freedom, and his covert drive to power hidden behind his compliance, docility and industry. In the largest sense, egotism and power are the real subjects of *The Portrait of a Lady*, concealed behind a mask of free will and determinism. How was one to possess the power and arrogance of one's genius and still be on good terms with oneself and the world? How was one to establish relationships with people when one felt—and knew—one was superior to them? Yet how avoid loneliness and isolation? Above all, how enjoy one's freedom and not make mistakes in the exercise of it? Ralph watches Isabel make her mistakes: and it is he who in the end delivers the uncomfortable verdict that she has been "ground in the very mill of the conventional." Ralph thereby accepts Isabel at her own evaluation; he believes, as she did, that she was worthy of something more than the conventional. And beyond the unhappiness of Isabel's marriage lies the revelation that she has been the victim of a carefully-laid plot: that Madame Merle had been the mistress of Osmond; Pansy is their child; and the marriage had been arranged by the wily blackbird to endow Pansy with Isabel's fortune.

It is possible in this light to see that Isabel's rejection of Goodwood and Warburton went beyond the mere sense that they threatened her freedom. They would have inhibited her freedom to exercise her power. Goodwood would have imposed his masculinity and the power of his passion; Warburton would have involved Isabel in a society where the determinants of power had been fixed long before. She had looked upon one aspect of herself in Osmond and had fallen in love with it. He had done the same in looking at her. The other image, that of Osmond's selfishness, and his "demonic imagination," belong in all probability to Henry's "buried life," some part of which he concealed even from himself, but which emerged from the depths in the writing of this character.

In *The Portrait of a Lady* there is a kind of continuous endowment of the characters with aspects of their author and the questions arising in his life even as he was writing the book—as if he were putting on different hats and different neckties and looking at himself in a series of mirrors. Curiously enough this observation was made long before the biographical knowledge we possess today enabled us to identify this process of character-infiltration. James Herbert Morse, writing in the *Century Magazine* a year after the publication of the novel, observed that there was in nearly every personage of *The Portrait* "an observable infusion of the author's personality." He went on:

> The men and women are almost equally quick-witted, curt and sharp. While each has a certain amount of individuality, the sharpness is one of the elements in common, preventing a complete differentiation. It is not wit alone, and repartee, but a sub-acid quality which sets the persons to criticizing each other. One does not like to call it snarling. Mr James is too much of a gentleman to admit snarling among ladies and gentlemen; and yet every leading person in the book does, in a polite way, enter frequently into a form of personal criticism of somebody else.

Since Morse wrote these lines we have come to understand the technique by which James sought to cover up what he was doing; his method of using shifting angles of vision so as to make us feel the way in which people see one another. We see Osmond through the eyes of all the principal characters, and this dramatizes even more Isabel's blindness to his faults during the period when she is debating whether she will marry him. Morse was right, however, in feeling that in a certain sense the various speakers in the novel were "engaged in the business of helping the author develop his characters." On the level of technique, this was one of James's brilliant devices: and later he was even to boast that he created artificial characters for this purpose and managed to endow them with the attributes of life. For biography, however, this method has the unusual effect of throwing a personal shadow behind the impersonal puppets projected and fashioned by the artist's imagination. "We cannot escape the conviction," said Morse, "that he has at least so far written himself into his books that a shrewd critic could reconstruct him from them." And he went on to be the shrewd critic: "The person thus fashioned would be one of fine intellectual powers, incapable of meannesses; of fastidious tastes, and of limited sympathies; a man, in short, of passions refined away by the intellect."

This needs amendment today. The visage of the writer reflected in *The Portrait* is rather that of a man of large sympathies and powerful passions, which are in some degree inhibited, and are struggling to be set free, indeed are using all kinds of indirection to find some liberating channel. And it is in the relationship between Isabel and Osmond that we can best observe this at work.

In the end one feels that Isabel's disillusionment, the damage to her self-esteem and the crushing effect of her experience, resides in the shock she receives that so large a nature should have been capable of so great a mistake; and in her realization that instead of being able to manœuvre her environment, as her freedom allowed, she had been manœuvred by it. Christopher Newman had had a similar shock, in the Faubourg St Germain. But he could write it off as the corruption and deceit of the French nobility. The deeper illusion here resides in the fact that Serena Merle and Gilbert Osmond are Americans, and the implications are that as expatriates, long divorced from their native soil, they also have been corrupted: they conceal a world of evil unknown to Isabel. America had ill-prepared her for this. The American and the Americana in Henry's two novels represented—in the larger picture—the New World's concept of its own liberties, the admixture of freedom and of power contained in America's emerging philosophy, and in the doctrines of pragmatism of which Henry's brother William was to be a founder. In drawing his novel from the hidden forces of his own experience into the palpable world of his study and observation, Henry James had touched upon certain fundamental aspects of the American character.

IV

When he had sent off his early instalments, Henry received certain worried letters from Howells. The editor suggested that Isabel was being over-analysed; and that the figure of the American newspaper-woman, Henrietta Stackpole, was over-drawn. "In defence of the former fault," Henry replied, "I will say that I intended to make a young woman about whom there should be a great deal to tell and as to whom such telling should be interesting; and also that I think she is analysed once for all in the early part of the book and doesn't turn herself inside out quite so much afterwards." This in the end was not to be true; Henry was to consider the book's finest passage to be Isabel's self-analysis after she perceives the relationship between Madame Merle and Gilbert Osmond. As for Miss Stackpole, Henry told Howells that she was not "I think really exaggerated—but 99 readers out of a 100 will think her so: which amounts to the same thing. She is the result of an impression made upon me by a variety of encounters and acquaintances made during the last few years; an impression which I had often said to myself would not be exaggerated." Henry however added that perhaps it was an impression which "the home-staying American" would not receive as vividly as the expatriate. "It is over here that it offers itself in its utmost relief."

It is possible to discover one "original" for Miss Stackpole in Henry's letters. Shortly after he had moved to London, William sent to him a young woman from Cambridge, a Miss Hillard (probably the Katherine Hillard who edited her mother's journal and later an abridgement of Madame Blavatsky's doctrines). Writing to William on 28 June 1877 he says: "I have got to go and see your—excuse me but I must say—accursed friend Miss Hillard, who has turned up here and writes me a note every three days, appointing an interview. I do what I can; but she will certainly tell you that I neglect her horribly. Do you admire her, particularly? She is, I suppose, a very honourable specimen of her type; but the type—the literary spinster, sailing-into-your-intimacy-American-hotel-piazza type—doesn't bear somehow the mellow light of the old world. Miss H. announced her arrival here to me by writing to ask me to take her to the Grosvenor Gallery and Rembrandt etchings and then go out and dine with her—at Hammersmith, miles away!—at the Conways'! And this a maid whom I had never seen!" Henry then interrupted this letter to call on Miss Hillard and on returning added: "I have in the interval of my two sentences driven over to the remote region of Paddington and back, at an expense of three shillings, to see Miss H. whom I did not find. But she will nevertheless deem that I have neglected her."

On the back of this letter, in William's hand, are the following words: "Do you notice the demoniac way in which he speaks of the sweet Miss Hillard?" Decidedly Miss H. had impressed the brothers quite differently. In a letter a few days later Henry added to the chronicle of his adventures with Miss H. "I did what I could further about Miss Hillard, who has left London: called again upon her and saw her, and went to a party at the Boughtons' in order to meet her." He added: "She is a good girl: her faults are that she is herself too adhesive, too interrogative and too epistolary. I have received (I think) seven notes and letters from her, for two or three that I have written her." The final mention of her occurs in a letter some weeks later, when Henry says to his mother of William: "His silence has led me to fear that he is 'mad' at what I wrote touching poor dear Miss Hillard; if so I take it all back."

If he took it back, he nevertheless had found his type. And Henrietta Stackpole, her forthrightness, good humour, meddlesomeness, and hundred-per-cent Americanism, in *The Portrait* was to be but the first of a number of characterizations of the gossipy American journalist abroad. Miss Stackpole is able to say all the things Goodwood, in his supreme inarticulateness, does not utter. She is completely characterized in an interchange between Isabel and Ralph. "She's a kind of emanation of the great democracy—of the continent, the country, the nation," Isabel says. And Ralph replies: "She does smell of the Future—it almost knocks one down."

V

A great deal has been made of the resemblance of *The Portrait of a Lady* to *Daniel Deronda.* As *Roderick* had been his conception of the novel Hawthorne might have written about Rome, so *The Portrait* was Henry's way of making Isabel Archer the personality he felt George Eliot should have made of Gwendolen Harleth. His description of Gwendolen, in his paper on the Eliot novel, can be applied to Isabel. Henry had written that she "is a perfect picture of youthfulness—its eagerness, its presumption, its preoccupation with itself, its vanity and silliness, its sense of its own absoluteness. But," he added, "she is extremely intelligent and clever, and therefore tragedy *can* have a hold upon her." And again: "The universe forcing itself with a slow, inexorable pressure into a narrow, complacent, and yet after all extremely sensitive mind, and making it ache with the pain of the process—that is Gwendolen's story." It is Isabel's as well. She is indeed the victim of her own complacent temperament, and the real determinism of the novel is psychological determinism. If *The Portrait of a Lady* can be related to George Eliot's novel (and the character of Grandcourt related to Osmond)—the work Henry wrote is still pure James, and the distillation of his own experience: his fierce will to freedom as an artist, his hidden fear of his drive to power, his awareness that, no matter how careful one may be, one can still be betrayed by one's egotism.

Over and above its substance *The Portrait of a Lady* established itself, by degrees, as one of the best-written novels of its age. In a prose of high style, with a narrative unsurpassed for its rhythmic development, with a mastery of character and of all the threads of his complicated story, Henry had created a novel that could be placed among the supreme works of the century. It introduced into a Europe that was reading Turgenev and

Flaubert, and would soon be reading Tolstoy, a distinctly American heroine.

Her portrait hangs in the great gallery of the world's fiction. We can see Isabel as we saw her when she first stepped into the garden of the Touchetts, at Gardencourt; her clasped hands are in repose; they rest in the lap of her black dress. She looks at us with those light grey eyes of hers, and her face, framed by its black hair, possesses a distinctive American beauty. She holds her head high; she possesses a great pride, and there is something arrogant in her steady gaze. The gallery in which Henry placed her was remarkable. On its walls were the paintings of many other women who, like Isabel, had never literally "lived." All of them were tissued out of the minds of their authors, mere figments of the literary imagination, creatures of the printed word. And yet they all had taken on a life of their own—Becky Sharp, or Dorothea Brooke, the Lady of the Camellias or Jane Eyre, Anna Karenina or Emma Bovary. It was as if they had really lived. And Isabel Archer, who partakes of this reality, and who actually seems to have resided in Albany, and ultimately in a palace in Rome, retains her uniqueness among her European sisters. Theirs had been largely dramas of love, often of physical passion. Isabel's had been a drama of suppressed passion, passion converted into high ideals and driven by a need for power that reckoned little with the world's harsh realities.

The painting is exquisite. Every touch of the artist's brush has been lovingly applied to his subject who, though not a daughter of the Puritans, has something of their rigidity in her bearing, and not a little of their hardness of surface. She looks down at us always in the freshness of her youth—and the strength of her innocence and her egotism.

VENICE

EARLY in 1881, with *The Portrait* scheduled to run through the magazines until autumn, Henry found his novel so far advanced that he could seek once again the light and air of Italy. "I wished to get away from the London crowd, the London hubbub, all the entanglements and interruptions of London life; and to quietly bring my novel to a close," he said in his journal. This time he fixed his eye on Venice. He had often visited the water city, but he had never stayed there as long as in Florence or Rome. He waited only a day for a calm sea at Folkestone, and crossed on 10 February. As usual he gave up a few days to the Paris way-station—paying three longish calls, in particular, to Turgenev's gouty couch. "He seemed and looked a good deal older than when I saw him last; but he was as pleasant and *human* as ever. On the other hand, I can't get over the sense that the people he was with (the Viardot circle) are a rather poor lot and that to live with them is not living like a gentleman."

Aside from Turgenev, he saw Henrietta Reubell, now firmly fixed in the permanent circle of Parisian friendship, the Laugels, the other Turgenevs. The Edward Lee Childes gave a dinner in Henry's honour, and he was always to remember a remark made on this occasion by Guillaume Guizot, who had read his *Hawthorne*: "*Il sortait de toute espèce de petits trous—de Boston, de—comment appelez-vous cela?—de Salem?*" Once again Henry was struck by the "lightness and brightness of the French conversational tone." He greatly enjoyed his room at the Hôtel Continental, with his windows looking out on the Tuileries. He had planned to remain three weeks, but twelve days sufficed. "In Paris, I suspect, it is always the little Parisian horizon," he wrote to Quincy Street, and took his train southward.

I

He made leisurely progress. He was in Marseilles on 24 February eating a big bowl of *bouillabaisse*, "a formidable dish, demanding a French digestion," in a restaurant opposite the Château d'If. The carnival flourished in Nice, so Henry moved on to San Remo. Here he found the Lombards of Cambridge and spent three congenial weeks, working at his novel and using Miss Fanny and her mother as a social resource. "I worked there capitally," he was to remember, "and it made me very happy. I used in the morning to take a walk among the olives, over the hills behind the queer little black, steep town." The paved roads behind and above San Remo were of "an extraordinary sweetness," with the sea glittering through the grey foliage. Between a big yellow sun and the bright blue Mediterranean, he enjoyed his morning strolls, often with Miss Lombard, after which he would return to his inn, eat an enormous *déjeuner* and settle down to three or four hours of writing. In the fading light he would take another walk, dine, go to bed early and read until late. One day he went on an excursion with the Lombards to the mountain town of Ceriana—"the grand clear hills, among which we wound higher and higher; the long valley swimming seaward, far away beneath; the bright Mediterranean growing paler and paler as we rose above it; the splendid stillness, the infinite light, the clumps of olive, the brown villages, pierced by the carriage road, where the vehicle bumped against opposite doorposts."

On 16 March Henry was in Genoa for a day. In Milan he spent ten days. He worked industriously. The place was cold and he knew no one. He speaks of going to La Scala to see *Der Freischütz* and an "interminable ballet." Arriving in Venice he finds it cold and dreary and after a few days he leaves for Rome. On the way he stops in Florence for his customary visit to the Bootts. Lizzie was in Spain, travelling with a group of artists; she wrote asking Henry to join them. He was tempted. He had fallen into the habit of travelling a beaten path to Italy. It would have been "more original and enterprising." However he allowed the question to be settled by the fact that he had no time for new adventures: *The Portrait* had to be finished; and he had arranged to write an article on Venice for the new *Century* magazine, into which *Scribner's* was being merged.

In Rome he stops at the Hôtel de Russie. It is wet and cold, and he has a violent attack of lumbago and a bad headache. Here, after a year, he sees Fenimore again. She has settled in the Holy City for the time being. We know this through one of her letters to Henry which accidentally survived and in which she speaks, at a later date, of "a tea-table, with the same spluttering little kettle you saw in my sky-parlour at Rome." Fenimore was living in a fourth-floor apartment, and we have no record of how often they saw each other during this time. Given the brevity of his stay there could not have been much of a renewal of their old sightseeing together.

In his journal his account of his stay in Rome is sketchy and he seems to have been interested in another lady. "Toward the last part of April I went down to Rome and spent a fortnight—during part of which I was laid up with one of those terrible attacks in my head. But Rome was very lovely; I saw a great deal of Mrs V. R.: had (with her) several beautiful drives. One in particular I remember; out beyond the Ponte Nomentano, a splendid Sunday. We left the carriage and wandered in the fields, where we sat down for some time. The exquisite stillness, the divine horizon, brought back to me out of the buried past all that ineffable, incomparable impression of Rome (1869, 1873)."

Mrs V. R., is never identified in Henry's letters and is always alluded to by her initials, or as the "Rensallina" in his correspondence with the Bootts. This suggests that she was probably Mrs Philip Livingstone Van Rensselaer, who lived for many years abroad. A short, dumpy woman—a "pincushion of a woman" in her old age, with three double chins—she seems first to have charmed Henry by her energy and liveliness; and then for a period in London, when she moved much in English society, she bored him; and eventually she became one of his London friends to whose home, on occasion, he could come for tea and talk over old days and old friends. She seems to have been widowed early, and during her Italian years Henry believed her to be searching for a husband. Henry's Roman headache may have been a consequence of finding himself caught in a frustrating crossfire between Fenimore and Mrs V. R.

From Rome Henry went back to Venice, by way of Ancona, visiting Leopardi's birthplace at Racanati. He was in a hurry to return to his work. "Every day I lost was a misery, and I hurried back to Venice and to my manuscript." This too might have contributed to his headache, which seemed invariably to be the consequence of some personal frustration.

II

His stay on the Riviera and in Rome was the prelude to one of Henry's most memorable visits to Italy. As he had taken possession early of Rome, later of Paris and finally of London, so now he took possession of the city of the Doges—and for all his life—in its grandeur and decay. "You desire to embrace it, to caress it, to possess it; and, finally, a soft sense of possession grows up and your visit becomes a perpetual love-affair." Venice was to be one of the greatest love-affairs of Henry's life; it was a city to be visited, haunted and revisited, for the sake of piling memory upon memory. A dead city on the Adriatic, it was yet alive with every change of weather. As he was to say, "the place is as changeable as a nervous woman, and you know it only when you know all the aspects of its beauty. It has high spirits or low, it is pale, or red, grey or pink, cold or warm, fresh or wan, according to the weather or the hour. It is always interesting and almost always sad; but it has a thousand occasional graces and is always liable to happy accidents."

The city was not without its inconveniences. That spring there were hordes of Germans encamped in the Piazza; they filled the Ducal Palace and the Academy with their uproar. Later came the English and the Americans; and there were a great many French tourists too, but the latter were discreet enough to make very long repasts at the Caffè Quadri, during which they were out of the way. St Mark's, with its beggars and vendors, seemed like a booth in a bazaar. And yet for Henry all Venice had an endless charm—there was so much for his eyes to explore and study. He found rooms, "dirty apartments with a lovely view," on a fourth floor at 4161 Riva degli Schiavoni, near the passage leading off to San Zaccaria. He recalled that the niece of the landlady was a dancer at the Fenice theatre and that she hovered about the premises in a velvet jacket and a pair of black kid gloves with one little white button. Her face, a charming oval, was always smeared with powder; it had, however, a weak expression. His rooms looked out on the lagoon. Straight across, before his windows, rose the great pink mass of San Giorgio Maggiore, which Henry felt had a success beyond all reason for an ugly Palladian church. It was "a success of position, of colour, of the immense detached Campanile, tipped with a tall, gold angel." It stood suffused with its rosiness, "a faint, shimmering, airy, watery pink; the bright sea-light seems to flush with it, and the pale whiteish green of lagoon and canal to drink it in." This melting together of light and air and water—the harmony of the elements—enchanted Henry.

In his journal his account of this stay in Venice, written a few months afterwards, is perhaps the most lyrical passage in an otherwise long enumeration of English dinners and country visits. "I seemed to myself to grow young again," he wrote. He passed his thirty-eighth birthday there. "The lovely Venetian spring came and went, and brought with it an infinitude of impressions, of delightful hours. I became passionately fond of the place, of the life, of the people, of the habits." He asked himself then, and was to ask himself almost every time he came to Venice, whether he should not rent some small apartment, and have a permanent *pied-à-terre* in the city.

During the early part of his sojourn he stood hauntedly at the windows of his room, and with an opera-glass studied the gondolas and ships. No ballet was more beautiful than the rhythmical movement of arm and oar on every side. There was always the same silhouette—the long black slender skiff, moving yet seeming not to move, with the grotesquely-graceful figure on the poop. It stood like a dancing-master, but from the waist up it had a freedom of movement that did not belong to dancing. That mixture of grace and awkwardness was "the boldness of a plunging bird and the regularity of a pendulum." There was nothing elusive or reluctant about the gondoliers. For the most part they were excellent fellows, the very children of Venice, associated "with its idiosyncrasy, with its essence, with its silence, with its melancholy." And also with its sounds. The sounds were constantly in his ears. "The view from my windows was *una bellezza*; the far-shining lagoon, the pink walls of San Giorgio, the downward curve of the Riva, the distant islands, the movement of the quay, the gondolas in profile. Here I wrote diligently every day and finished, or virtually finished, my novel."

III

He would rise in the morning and have an early breakfast at Florian's. Then he would go to the Stabilimento Chitarin for his bath. Refreshed, he would stroll in the coolness looking at pictures, watching the street-life, idling away the hours until it was time for his real *déjeuner*, which he would take at the Caffè Quadri. After this he would return to his rooms and work—sometimes till five and sometimes until six o'clock. A quarter of a century later he was to remember how again and again in the "fruitless fidget of composition" he would respond to the human chatter coming up to his windows from the Riva, and would wander over to see whether "out in the blue channel, the ship of some right suggestion, of some better phrase, of the next happy twist of my subject, the next true touch for my canvas, mightn't come into sight." There were pages of *The Portrait*, when he reread them, which recalled to his memory the colour-spots of the balconied houses, the undulation of the hunch-backed bridges, and the clicking pedestrians—"the Venetian footfall and the Venetian cry—all talk there, wherever uttered, having the pitch of a call across the water;" coming up to him, it reminded him of his divided and frustrated mind. Venice was an invitation, constant and repeated, to idleness—and yet he worked.

His writing done, he would go out on the water in a gondola for a couple of hours. In the evenings he would stroll about, sit at Florian's, listening to the music in the Piazza; and two or three nights a week he would visit Mrs Bronson and sit on the balcony of Ca'Alvisi smoking cigarettes with her and watching the traffic of the Grand Canal. For he had renewed his acquaintance with Katherine De Kay Bronson, his fellow-passenger during the memorable crossing of the Atlantic when he had sailed out to embrace the Old World. Mrs Bronson, her husband and her daughter had gone out then, and she had fixed herself in this old Venetian house, as if America had never existed, and within it played, and was to play, hostess to a whole generation of visitors from her homeland and from England. She had a kind of water-side salon, whose most distinguished members were Robert Browning and Henry James. The poet's attachment to her was profound, and the novelist always said on his side that he was "extremely fond" of her. "She sat," he was to write, "for twenty years at the wide mouth, as it were, of the Grand Canal, holding out her hand, with endless good-nature, patience, charity, to all decently accredited petitioners, the incessant troop of those either bewilderedly making or fondly renewing acquaintance with the dazzling city." Casa Alvisi was directly opposite the Baroque church of Santa Maria della Salute. Henry used to say that from the balcony over the water-entrance one's eye, crossing the channel, seemed to find the keyhole of the great door right in line. In a city of palaces, it was a small house indeed: this is what Mrs Bronson liked about it. She preferred intimate rooms, and she made it "the friendliest house in all the wide world." Henry became attached to the stately balcony and its crimson cushions; he made friends with her big brown gondoliers; he was fond of her little yellow dogs. Everything seemed in the right proportion. She would have traded a Tintoretto or two, Henry said, for a cabinet of tiny gilded glasses, or a dinner-service of the right old silver. The De Kays had been Newport neighbours when Henry was a youth, and Katherine De Kay of New York had a vivid and lively personality. Less ambitious than Isabella of Boston, she preferred her quiet corner, her friends, her far-flung Venetian charities, and the life of Venice itself. If Isabella Gardner sought to annexe fragments of Europe and reshape them into her own haven in Boston, Mrs Bronson simply occupied her little terrain, bestowed in queenly fashion innumerable generosities among gondoliers and their families, cultivated the Venetian dialect, and held open house. "The old bright tradition, the wonderful Venetian legend had appealed to her from the first, closing round her house and her well-plashed water-steps, where the waiting gondolas were thick." Her affectionate portrait is sketched, one seems to see, as Mrs Prest in "The Aspern Papers." Mrs Bronson was to have only one set of rivals in Venice for Henry's affection, the Daniel Curtises, who in greater opulence forsook Boston once and for all and acquired the Palazzo Barbaro a short distance from Mrs Bronson's and diagonally opposite the Accadémia. Between this Palazzo, commemorated in *The Wings of the Dove*, and the Casa Alvisi, celebrated in *Italian Hours*, Henry had in later years his *pied-à-terre* in Venice—a very substantial one in each case.

The novelist complained during these early weeks that Mrs Bronson's *milieu* was too American for his taste. Nevertheless his testimony to its pleasantness is incorporated with great charm in the closing sentences of his Venetian essay: "If you are happy you will find yourself, after a June day in Venice (about ten o'clock), on a balcony that overhangs the Grand Canal, with your elbows on the broad ledge, a cigarette in your teeth and a little good company beside you. The gondolas pass beneath, the watery surface gleams here and there from their lamps, some of which are coloured lanterns that move mysteriously in the darkness." And if the serenading is overdone, he adds, "you needn't suffer from it, for in the apartment behind you—an accessible refuge—there is more good company, there are more cigarettes."

IV

Late in May Henry came upon an unexpected companion. He encountered in Venice an old Cambridge friend, in reality a friend of William's. William used to bring him to Quincy Street where he greatly amused Mary James with his pleasant talk, his songs and his guitar. Apparently a man of some means, he had

CASA ALVISI
Mrs Bronson's palazzetto in Venice

wandered far and wide, and he was to continue to do so during a long life. "Tell William," Henry wrote to his father, "his old friend Herbert Pratt has turned up here, and I have seen a good deal of him. He is a queer, but almost delightful, creature and entertaining through all the strange eastern lands he has seen. He is romantic, sentimental and naïf, and is redolent of Persia. He seems to think always of William."

They did not constitute a little Cambridge together. If Henry was cosmopolitan in the sense that he could alternately be a western European and an American, or both at the same time, Pratt was the embodiment of the graceful American wanderer, the perpetual poetic hobo. He was at ease in all lands and he seems to have carried his good nature and his guitar wherever he went. He had in him a loitering soul, superimposed upon the refinements of Cambridge. There was in him that part of New England that lived perpetually in whaling ships and sought distant horizons. William had met him at medical school, where Pratt was completing his studies interrupted by the Civil War, in which he had served as an "acting assistant surgeon." He had done a little post-graduate study in Vienna and Berlin, and had set up in practice at Denver. From 1874, and for the next forty years, however, he was a wanderer upon the face of the earth, travelling in remote corners, always with an eye for manners and customs, scenery and architecture. Henry would have liked to be as footloose, without responsibility, and taking life as it came. He achieved this dream rarely. But the forces that made him a disciplined writer militated against his ever being able to emulate Herbert Pratt. There was always another instalment to be written, always some deadline to be met.

"Herbert Pratt was there for a month, and I saw him tolerably often," Henry wrote in his journal. "He used to talk to me about Spain, about the East, about Tripoli, Persia, Damascus; till it seemed to me that life would be *manquée* altogether if one shouldn't have some of that knowledge. He was a most singular, most interesting type, and I shall certainly put him into a novel. I shall even make the portrait close and he won't mind. Seeing picturesque lands for their own sake, and without making any use of it—that, with him, is a passion—a passion of which if one lives with him a little (a little, I say; not too much) one feels the contagion." And James added: "He gave me the nostalgia of the sun, of the south, of colour, of freedom, of being one's own master, and doing absolutely what one pleases."

Pratt used to say to Henry: "I know such a sunny corner, under the south wall of old Toledo. There's a wild fig tree growing there; I have lain on the grass, with my guitar. There was a musical muleteer, etc." These words were put by Henry into the mouth of Gabriel Nash in *The Tragic Muse*, eight years later. The likeness is considerable, save that James endowed the fictional Pratt with a considerable degree of artistic aestheticism. But the easy, drifting quality of his "original" is in the book.

They drifted in Venice when Henry was free. One evening Pratt took him to a queer little wineshop, frequented largely by gondoliers and *facchini*, and located in an out-of-the-way corner. They drank some excellent muscat wine. Pratt had discovered the place and made himself at home in it. On another evening he took Henry to his rooms, far down the Grand Canal, overlooking the Rialto. The night was hot. The cry of the gondoliers came up from the Canal. Pratt took out some Persian books and read extracts from Firdusi and Saadi.

"A good deal might be done with Herbert Pratt," Henry said to himself in his journal.

V

Mrs V. R. came out from Rome, and Henry went with her one day to Torcello and Burano; they carried their lunch with them and ate it on the edge of a canal. At Burano the children assailed him for coppers and pursued the gondola into the sea. Henry took away an impression of bright-coloured hovels, stagnant canals, young girls with splendid heads of hair and complexions smeared with powder, fishermen mending their nets. It was altogether a happy time and Henry recaptured his old faculty for experiencing and enjoying the picturesque which had faded during his long months in Bolton Street. In June he took a brief recess for five days and wandered in Vicenza, Bassano, Padua. Three of these days were spent at Vicenza, and a letter to Grace Norton records his impressions. "It is a bright hot Sunday morning; I have closed the shutters of my smartly-frescoed apartment and only a stray sunbeam rests on the cool scagliola floor. I wish this rapid scrawl to carry a breath of the Italian summer, and of sweet Vicenza, into your New England hills." Henry had sat the previous evening in the city's square. The place was flooded with moonlight. He had been recalling his 1869 visit and "was pleased to find that on the whole I have not quite lost my 'sensibility.' " The Vicentini strolled on the big smooth slabs of the piazza, and the tall slim companile seemed to lose itself in the brightness of the night. Sitting at the café Henry found himself in conversation with an Italian officer, a captain of cavalry with a salary of $400 a year. He treated Henry to all the gossip of the place—and to generous complaints about the hardness of his life.

To Grace Henry confessed that he had "fallen deeply and desperately in love" with Venice, in spite of the fact that they had begun to run steamboats up and down the Canal. He added: "I have enjoyed extremely this year being away from London during the spring. I receive every now and then, forwarded from Bolton Street, a memento of lost opportunities chiefly in the shape of invitations to dinner a month ahead; but they do nothing to turn my heart against Venice. The rest, the leisure, the beauty, the sunsets, the pictures, are more than compensation. I go back to England, however, direct after July 1st, and it is PROBABLE that I go home in September." He added that he was expecting his sister in London but this would not seriously change his plans.

Before he left the Adriatic city the heat had become intense. The days and the nights were now impossible. "I left it at last and," Henry wrote in his journal, "closed a singularly happy episode—but I took much away with me."

From London he wrote to Mrs Bronson: "I can't tell you with what affection I think of Venice, and how at this distance my whole stay there takes on the semblance of a beautiful dream. Happy you to spend your life in such a dream."

When he consulted his memories he had, as Proust was to have after him, colours before his eyes, iridescence, little corners rather than images of the great Square. "I simply see a narrow canal in the heart of the city—a patch of green water and a surface of pink wall. The gondola moves slowly; it gives a great smooth swerve, passes under a bridge, and the gondolier's cry, carried over the quiet water, makes a kind of splash in the stillness." The old pink wall seemed to sink into the opaque water. Behind the wall was a garden, out of which the long arm of a June rose, one of the splendid roses of Venice, flung itself as a spontaneous ornament. On the other side of the small waterway was a great shabby façade of Gothic windows and balconies—on which dirty clothes were hanging—and there was a cavernous door opening from a low flight of slimy steps. It was hot and still. That garden, the rose, the gondola, the general Venetian colour and imagery—the memory of a girl crossing a bridge with an old shawl on her head seen against the sky as he floated beneath—were to melt together into "The Aspern Papers." Almost a decade would elapse, however, before he would be ready to write this story.

Book Nine

Terminations 1881–1883

★

HOMECOMING

THE DOME AND THE SHAFT

MARY JAMES

AN EXQUISITE STILLNESS

A LITTLE TOUR IN FRANCE

NOVEMBER PARTING

A WINTER SUMMONS

A BLESSED FAREWELL

SON AND BROTHER

HOMECOMING

In his room in the Brunswick Hotel in Boston, late in November of 1881, Henry James found himself seated one day in front of a rather pretentious little marble-topped table, writing with an indelible pencil, in a fat scribbler he had purchased some months before in London. The walls of his room were white and bare; they shone at night in the flaring gaslight from a chandelier of imitation bronze, which hung from the middle of the ceiling and emitted a hissing brightness, flinging a patch of shadow across his page. When he extinguished the lights, illumination poured in through the transom over the double doors, flooded his bed, beat at his closed eyelids. There was too much glare, too much scorching air from the heating-system, too much ice-water in the perpetual pitchers carried by waiters and bell-hops. The rooms in Bolton Street, as contrasted with these in Boylston Street, might have their English chill, but Henry had learned to accommodate himself to a fireplace and to candlelight; to adjust temperature and illumination to his needs. Nothing seemed adjustable in his hotel-room. Henry was lonely and homesick. Cambridge and Boston had enclosed him, as always, in a possessive embrace. This act of writing in the fat scribbler was in itself a way of transporting himself out of his immediate American environment back to London—or to Venice. For what Henry was indelibly setting down was a statement unique among his surviving papers. It was a long retrospective summary of his six years abroad; a survey of his travelled cities and country visits, his new friendships and his Continental resources. He wrote in his light, rapid, characterizing manner, mainly a catalogue of sociabilities and impressions, as if to remind himself of all that he had seen and done, all that had been precious to him on the other side of the Atlantic.

He had returned to the old horizons, the house in Quincy

Street, the Harvard Yard, with big square fresh buildings and slender elms reduced to spindles by the winter. Cambridge stretched away from the horizontal collegiate fence, low and flat, with vague featureless spaces. It looked like a clean encampment; the small wooden houses had a tent-like impermanence. There had been first a blaze of autumn; now the trees were profiles against high winter skies; the piled snow had come with Thanksgiving. In his two-sided Atlantic world there were these contrasts—the horse-car and the gondola, the cultivated parks of London and Boston Common, the hierarchic world of England and the "tepid bath of democracy" in America. These were perhaps extremes. They reflected, however, a solemn fact. Henry was now an expatriate in his own land.

I

"Here I am back in America after six years of absence," he wrote on his marble-topped table, "and likely while here to see and learn a great deal that ought not to become mere waste material. Here I am, *da vero*, and here I am likely to be for the next five months." He was glad that he had returned. He had needed to see his family, to revive the "sense of the consequences that these relations entail. Such relations, such consequences, are a part of one's life, and the best life, the most complete, is the one that takes full account of such things. One can only do this by seeing one's people from time to time." Thus Henry assured himself that his journey had not been in vain. He added however: "Apart from this I hold it was not necessary I should come to this country."

What follows is a passage justly celebrated, for in it Henry reflected upon the choice he had made and the consequences it entailed. "My choice," he wrote, "is the old world—my choice, my need, my life. There is no need for me today to argue about this; it is an inestimable blessing to me, and a rare good fortune, that the problem was settled long ago, and that I have now nothing to do but to act on the settlement.—My impressions here are exactly what I expected they would be, and I scarcely see the place, and feel the manners, the race, the tone of things, now that I am on the spot, more vividly than I did while I was still in Europe. My work lies there—and with this vast new world, *je n'ai que faire*. One can't do both—one must choose." He went on:

> No European writer is called upon to assume that terrible burden, and it seems hard that I should be. The burden is necessarily greater for an American—for he *must* deal, more or less, even if only by implication, with Europe; whereas no European is obliged to deal in the least with America. No one dreams of calling him less complete for not doing so. (I speak of course of people who do the sort of work that I do; not of economists, of social science people.) The painter of manners who neglects America is not thereby incomplete as yet; but a hundred years hence—fifty years hence perhaps—he will doubtless be accounted so.

The statement is not strange, but it is prophetic. Few Americans at the time would have understood it if they had been allowed to read it over Henry's shoulder. It was to remain unpublished for more than sixty years and thus was to be read in that future foreseen by the novelist. When it was written, most Americans were as oblivious of Europe as Europe was of them: the people on the great continent were preoccupied with their relations to their own land and each other, not their relations with the world. And Henry's statement was, as he himself saw, the statement of a novelist in search of subjects larger than those offered him by the scattered American scene. "My impressions of America I shall, after all, not write here. I don't need to write them (at least not *à propos* of Boston); I know too well what they are. In many ways they are extremely pleasant; but," he added, "Heaven forgive me! I feel as if my time were terribly wasted here!"

II

When he had left Venice five months earlier, he could not have foreseen that he would thus be sitting, homesick, in a Boston hotel, indulging in a long reminiscence, offering himself the solace of the past for the inconveniences and nostalgia of the present. He had gone to Lake Como and then to Switzerland. He had felt a great relief as the coach mounted the Splügen into the Alpine air, out of the stifling cauldron of Italy. He remembered a certain glass of fresh milk which he drank that evening far up in the gloaming—a woman at a wayside inn fetched it from the cow. It was "the most heavenly draft that ever passed my lips." He went to Lucerne to visit Mrs Kemble, but she had gone to Engelberg; he followed her to that "grim, ragged, rather vacuous, but by no means absolutely unbeautiful valley." One day he climbed the Trübsee toward the Joch pass. "The whole place was a wilderness of the alpine rose—and the alpine stillness;" the beauty of the high cool valley, whose "great silver-gleaming snows overhang it and light it up," revived for Henry his memories of his old Swiss days. "I hadn't believed they could revive even to that point."

After Switzerland he had returned to London to meet his sister. She had come abroad frail and convalescent from her long illness, accompanied by a Boston friend, Katherine Loring, a hearty woman who seemed to derive a genuine satisfaction from using her own vitality and strength to make life easier for her sickly friend. Henry recognized that Alice had become deeply attached to Miss Loring and seemed happy in her company and even dependent on her. The novelist spent a few days with his sister at Richmond, saw her afterwards at Kew and still later in Mayfair. It was quite clear that she was adequately companioned; she had her own itinerary and was scheduled to sail for Boston before Henry would be ready to leave. Henry accordingly departed to pay a series of visits while the final chapters of *The Portrait* were at the printer's. He visited the Anglicized Russell Sturgises at Leatherhead, he went twice to Lord Rosebery's Mentmore, and on one occasion had as fellow-guest Mr Gladstone; he also visited his publisher, Frederick Macmillan, at Walton-on-Thames. Above all he relished a visit to Somerset. "I think I have never been more *penetrated*—I have never more loved the land." He found a mellow and ancient feeling in the country and above all its houses—Montacute, Barrington, Ford Abbey and others. "These delicious old houses, in the long August days, in the south of England air, on the soil over which so much has passed and out of which so much has come, rose before me like a series of visions. I thought of a thousand things; what becomes of the things one thinks of at these times? They are not lost, we must hope; they drop back into the mind again, and they enrich and embellish it."

Then, as his sailing-date approached, he had gone to Scotland, to Tillypronie, Cortachy, Dalmeny, Laidlawstiel. He remembered the drive from Kirriemuir to Cortachy—a commonplace road by daylight, as he later discovered, but in the twilight it was romantic to ford the river at the entrance to Cortachy and to drive through the dim avenues up to the great lighted pile of the castle, where Lady Airlie, hearing the wheels of the vehicle on the gravel, "put her handsome head from a window in the clock-tower." She asked if this were indeed Henry James and wished him a bonny good-evening. Henry was in a Waverley novel.

II

Now, sitting in the uncomfortable hotel-room, writing and remembering, Henry was confronted by things far removed from romantic novels. He had crossed the October Atlantic on the steamer *Paris* by the St Lawrence route, so eager to get home that he disembarked with the mails at Rimouski and spent two days getting connections to Boston. He had gone directly to Quincy Street. His mother struck him as tired and shrunken: she had passed into old age while he had been away; his father was infirm and more lost than ever in his self-composed world. His Aunt Kate had come from New York to greet him. She found him "the same dear Harry who left us six years ago," but she also noted that he had become "a large, stout, vigorous looking man." Henry made friends at once with William's wife—the second Alice in Quincy Street—and saw his sister again: she had arrived but a few days ahead of him. There was also William's little boy, sufficiently articulate to boast shortly after Henry's arrival that he was "Uncle Harry's fascinating little nephew." He too had been named Henry—"the little Henri-trois" his uncle dubbed him. In the midst of so much "family" Henry passed almost a month before moving to the Boston hotel. He saw Howells almost immediately; his friend had just resigned the *Atlantic* editorship, and had been succeeded by the bland, sociable, gracefully-verbal Thomas Bailey Aldrich. He saw his old friend T. S. Perry. He began to pay calls on Mrs Gardner. He spent evenings with Grace Norton. He journeyed to Newport to see the Tweedys. Newport was charming: there were large light luxurious houses, planted with Dutch definiteness on the green of the cliff; the lawns touched each other without benefit of English hedge or fence; the ladies were brilliantly dressed and carried pretty parasols. The long lines of the far shore were soft and pure. All in all the effect was quite delicate, "and anything that is delicate counts immensely over here."

But he was restless. His removal from Quincy Street to a Boston hotel had been designed to give him a feeling of his Bolton Street privacy; he wanted to resume his work. He found the hotel incompatible with literature. Early in December he went to New York to see what threads he could pick up there after his five-year absence from that city.

In Manhattan he stayed at 115 East 25th Street with Edwin Godkin, his former editor at the *Nation*, in the same neighbourhood in which he had passed his long book-reviewing months of 1875. Manhattan was hospitable to its literary son—*The Portrait of a Lady* had just come out as a book and had proved immediately popular. "I have been three weeks in New York," Henry recorded in his journal, "and all my time has slipped away in mere movement. I try as usual to console myself with the reflection that I am getting impressions. This is very true; I have got a great many." To Grace Norton in Cambridge he wrote: "I have seen many persons—but no personages; have heard much talk—but no conversation. Nevertheless the sense one gets here of the increase of the various arts of life is—almost oppressive; especially as one is so often reminded of it. The arts of life flourish—but the art of living, simply, isn't among them."

Henry went back to Quincy Street for Christmas. His younger brother, Wilky, increasingly an invalid, came from Wisconsin to be with the family, and with the exception of Robertson, the youngest son, the James family was briefly reunited. But somehow it was all rather melancholy. One gets a sense of sadness from the way in which, on the day after Christmas, in the old back sitting-room, Henry gave himself over once again to his journal and to his memories—this time of his young manhood. "The freshness of impression and desire, the hope, the curiosity, the vivacity, the sense of the richness and mystery of the world that lies before us—there is an enchantment in all that which it takes a heavy dose of pain to quench and which in later hours, even if *success* have come to us, touches us less nearly. Some of my doses of pain were very heavy; very weary were some of my months and years. But all that is sacred; it is idle to write of it today."

In this passage he spoke of recovering "the vision of those untried years." Never, he wrote, was "an ingenuous youth more passionately and yet more patiently eager for what life might bring. Now that life has brought something, brought a measurable part of what I dreamed of then, it is touching enough to look back. I knew at least what I wanted then—to see something of the world. I have seen a good deal of it, and I look at the past in the light of this knowledge. What strikes me is the definiteness, the unerringness of those longings. I wanted to do very much what I have done, and success, if I may say so, now stretches back a tender hand to its younger brother, desire."

When Christmas was over Henry did not linger in Cambridge. He returned to New York to attend "a gorgeous flowery banquet" given by Whitelaw Reid, whose Paris correspondent he had been. Here he met the just-retired Secretary of State, James G. Blaine. From New York he went to Philadelphia to pay a visit to Mrs Wister and her husband. From Germantown he went on to Washington. He had never been there. In *The Bostonians* he was to make one of his ladies ask whether anyone had heard of "that little place," and to add that "they invented it" while she had been abroad. Henry seems to have had this feeling as he stepped from the train one morning early in January, in streets filled with slushy snow, and looked at the single Dome and the single Shaft of the Capitol which then dominated the scene.

THE DOME AND THE SHAFT

HENRY found the streets of Washington "enormous." They were lined with little red houses. Nothing seemed to pass save the tramway. Two sun-filled rooms were waiting for him at 720 Fifteenth street; Henry Adams had reserved them; and in the same street the novelist had access to the Metropolitan Club. The first thing he did was to take a solitary walk to the Capitol. With the critical eye that had many times studied St Peter's and the Florentine Duomo, surveyed the Invalides and the dome of St Paul's, he now appraised this great American dome, in the great democratic vista of a city that seemed to him still "too much of a village." False classic, white marble, iron, stucco. And yet it had a grand air. He went into the rotunda. It was a little like entering a railway station. There were no functionaries, no officers, no uniforms, no door-keepers—not the least spot of colour such as one found in the European seats of government. What was missing was some incarnation of the national conscience and the national dignity. He was to make a character remark that "this isn't government by livery;" however it is quite clear that Henry would have liked some livery in the vast expanse of marble, some relief from the labyrinth of spittoons.

He was to have later views of Washington, and to see the emergence of the designs over which Dome and Shaft now preside. His was the Washington which had just buried President Garfield and was trying the assassin, Guiteau; in which the new President, Chester A. Arthur, moved in an easy intimacy, almost as a private citizen. The spittoons would recede and works of art would take over; but this was not, in effect, to change the artistic complexion of the place; Henry was to feel simply that the rotunda resembled "a stonecutter's collection of priced sorts and sizes." His first feeling, which he concealed, was that the Capitol was "repulsive." Later he was willing to concede that it embodied a kind of New World concept of space and air, of dominion and of power created *de chic*. His final picture was built on analogy—"the Washington dome is indeed capable, in the Washington air, of admirable, of sublime, effects; and there are cases in which, seen at a distance above its yellow Potomac, it varies but by a shade from the sense—yes, absolutely the divine campagna-sense—of St Peter's and the like-coloured Tiber." Looking at it a quarter of a century after his first vision of it, he was to speak of the Capitol "as a compendium of all the national ideals, a museum, crammed full, even to overflowing, of all the national terms and standards, weights and measures and emblems of greatness and glory, and indeed as a builded record of half the collective vibrations of a people; their conscious spirit, their public faith, their bewildered taste, their ceaseless curiosity, their arduous and interrupted education."

This was a neat mixture of the flattering and the derogatory; for Henry had to reckon with American complacency. What he felt in 1882, and was to express no less succinctly in 1907, was that there wasn't in Washington "enough native history, recorded or current, to go round." He was also to echo a quarter of a century later Oscar Wilde's quip that "Washington has too many bronze generals." Describing the perpetual perspectives and converging avenues, the circles and crossways, the sense of great wide gardens, he was to have the feeling that given such ample measurements "the bronze generals and admirals, on their named pedestals, should have been great garden-gods, mossy mythological marble." The long vistas yearned for something more than the mere brief military or naval commemoration—they "waited for some bending nymph or some armless Hermes." Washington was an oddly scattered city, in which he got a general impression of high granite steps, light grey corniced colonnades, rather harmoniously low, contending for effect with slaty mansard roofs and masses of iron excrescences. It was all "a loose congregation of values." Much of the background seemed provisional, as if it could be unhooked and rolled up like canvas scenery.

The city had two faces for Henry. There was official Washington, "the democratic substitute for a court city," and there was social Washington, harbouring a society well organized, with its own tight codes and standards, that seemed to have little to do with politics. Henry marvelled at this; for in London he met parliamentarians and lords everywhere; while in Washington he encountered chance legislators in a society that seemed bent on excluding senators and congressmen from its houses rather than admitting them. There seemed to be passages of national life in which "the President himself was scarce thought to be in society."

Society seemed to operate in the foreground, and it used official Washington as its backdrop. It was a "City of Conversation"—and the conversation was mostly about itself. Moreover, elsewhere in America women were in control, and absentee husbands spent their days beside their ticker-tapes; but in Washington there was a "re-committal to masculine hands of some share at least in the interests of civilization, some part of the social property and social office." It was all strange, and rather entertaining; and looking upon it Henry wondered how the foreign diplomats, facing the phenomena of a capital that differed from, rather than resembled, the phenomena of other capitals and other societies, could cope with their task of "penetration and discretion." One supposes that Henry found it difficult to be discreet. He was hardly an "observant stranger" in his own capital. And the story which he began at this time and completed months later, "The Point of View," is indeed the most sharply critical of any which he ever wrote about his homeland. He may have concealed his opinions in it behind those of foreign visitors to New York and Washington, whose letters he created with craft and cunning, but his own "point of view" is unmistakable. One had to recognize, however, that much of Henry's vision of Washington was influenced by the spacious drawing-room of 1607 H Street, in the tart reflections of his friend, the "Voltaire in petticoats."

I

"Thursday, Henry James put in an appearance; that young emigrant has much to learn here," wrote Clover Adams to her father on 8 January 1882. "He is surprised to find that he can go to the Capitol and listen to debates without taking out a licence, as in London. He may in time get into the 'swim' here, but I doubt it. I think the real, live, vulgar, quick-paced world in America will fret him and that he prefers a quiet corner with a pen where he can create men and women who say neat things and have refined tastes and are not nasal or eccentric."

"I shouldn't wonder if the place were the most agreeable of our cities," Henry wrote to Grace Norton. "The Henry Adamses, who are my principal friends here, have a commodious and genial house and have been very kind to me. The pleasant thing here is the absence of business—the economy-empty streets, most of them rather pretty, with nothing going on in them. I am making the best of everything—so much so that I feel at moments as if I were rather holding my nose to the grindstone. It goes very well—but I will confide to you in strict privacy that in my heart of hearts I am woefully and wickedly *bored!* I am horribly homesick for the ancient world. *There* we needn't be always making the best of things. One may make the worst of them and they are still pretty good." To Henrietta Reubell he wrote: "Enormous spaces, hundreds of miles of asphalt, a charming climate and the most entertaining society in America." And to Godkin: "I have seen a good many people, chiefly under the influence of the Adamses, and find the social arrangements, and the tone of conversation, very easy and genial."

The Adamses constituted themselves Henry's guides and evaluators of all he reported to them from his social rounds. Mrs Adams paraphrased scripture to her father to describe the novelist's predicament—"And a certain man came down to Jerusalem and fell among thieves . . . and they sprang up and choked him."[1] To which she added "Henry James passed Sunday evening at Robeson's and dines tomorrow with Blaine." On his side

[1] Mrs Adams was quoting from memory Luke 10: 30: "A certain man went down from Jerusalem to Jericho, and fell among thieves, which stripped him of his raiment . . ."

Henry wrote to Godkin that the Adamses disapproved of the company he was keeping, "though I notice that they are eagerly anxious to hear what I have seen and heard at places which they decline to frequent. After I had been to Mrs Robeson's they mobbed me for revelations; and after I had dined with Blaine, to meet the president, they fairly hung upon my lips." In the Adams house he was a constant visitor; Mrs Adams seemed to have a perpetual tea-party under way—two or three times a day—and frequent dinners at a little round table. Here Henry dined, early in his stay, with the new British Minister, Sir Lionel Sackville-West, fresh from his post in Spain where he had contracted his since-much-publicized alliance with Pepita, commemorated both by his descendant and by Virginia Woolf. "A rather dull (though amiable) personage," was Henry's verdict; however, he liked his "delightful little foreign daughter, who is the most perfect *ingénue* ever seen in America."

The Robeson of whom the Adamses disapproved was Congressman George Maxwell Robeson of New Jersey, whose wife of fifty Henry thought something of a "personage" although she was "fundamentally coarse." The Robesons were about to attain much notoriety by their sponsorship of Oscar Wilde during his visit to the capital. Newly-arrived from England, trading on his Gilbert and Sullivan reputation, Oscar had brought his aestheticism to New York and Philadelphia and now to Washington. The press talked largely of Bunthorne-Wilde. "The newspapers haven't got scent of Henry James yet," Mrs Adams observed, and Henry managed to keep out of their way. However he called on Wilde as a matter of courtesy. "Oscar Wilde is here—an unclean beast," he wrote to Godkin. He told Mrs Adams he found him a "a fatuous cad." But then Henry had admitted to Oscar he was homesick for London, and Oscar adroitly implied that this was rather provincial of him. "Really! You care for *places*? The world is my home."

The Adamses approved of Henry's seeing Senator Thomas F. Bayard, member of an old Delaware family and brother of Mrs Lockwood. Senator Bayard promptly sent Henry two invitations to dinner and offered him the use of a private room at the

Capitol in which to entertain his friends. At Bayard's he met Horace Gray, a new associate Justice of the Supreme Court. He goes to a ball at the British legation; he dines with the Swedish Secretary; he chats with the Republican leader, Wayne MacVeagh, and pleases him by remembering that Matthew Arnold considered him quite the pleasantest American he had ever met. To Mrs Gardner Henry wrote that what he liked best in Washington society were certain girls, "very charming with a *désinvolture* rather rare *chez nous*." These included Miss Bayard and Miss Frelinghuysen, daughter of the new Secretary of State, "happy specimens of the *finished* American girl—the American girl who has profited by the sort of social education that Washington gives." The Bayard girls were (he told his mother) "such as one ought to marry, if one were marrying." For the rest he was seeing "plenty of men, more than elsewhere, and a good many energetic types; but few 'accomplished gentlemen.' "

II

James G. Blaine, after meeting Henry in New York, invited him to his home to meet the twenty-first President of the United States, Chester A. Arthur. It was an elaborate dinner attended also by the British Minister, the Governor of California, Generals Sherman and Hancock, Senator Hale, Murat Halstead, Andrew Carnegie, Hon. S. B. Elkins, and Allen Thorndyke Rice. The press called it a "small and noted company," and Henry James Jr was described as "that eminent novelist and anglicized American." Henry observed the President's "well-made coat and well-cut whiskers," and enjoyed an intimate chat with him after dinner. President Arthur had known various members of the James family in Albany; he had even been present at the suicidal deathbed of a distant relative, Johnny James; and he had known Smith Van Buren, son of President Martin Van Buren, who had married one of Henry's aunts. Henry wrote to his mother that he "evidently believed me to be the son of Uncle William [the Rev. William James, elder brother of Henry's father] and wouldn't be disillusioned. This illusion was indeed apparently so dear to him, that I felt that if I had any smartness in me, I ought, striking while the iron was hot, to apply for a foreign mission, which I should doubtless promptly get." To Mrs Gardner Henry wrote saying he thought the President "a good fellow—even attractive. He is a gentleman and evidently has that amiable quality, a desire to please."

At the end of January Henry was enjoying himself sufficiently to plan to remain until late February, and he had thoughts of visiting the South. He was finding the capital "genial and amusing." On 27 January, however, his brother Robertson wrote that his mother had suffered an attack of bronchial asthma. On Sunday morning the 29th Henry wrote to her saying that it was "impossible almost for me to think of you in this condition, as I have only seen you hovering about the bed of pain, on which others were stretched." Late that evening, while he was dressing to go to a party, he received a telegram from William's Alice: "Your mother exceedingly ill. Come at once." There was no train until the next morning. Distraught and anxious, Henry rang the bell of the Adamses at 11 p.m. to inform them of his impending departure. He took the morning train to New York, and by that time Clover Adams had received an answer to a telegram of inquiry she had sent to Boston. She knew—what he did not—that Henry's mother was no longer alive.

MARY JAMES

In a driving snowstorm Henry made his way from the Boston depot to Quincy Street. Thirty-six hours had elapsed since he had been summoned home. He had arrived in New York at five the previous evening; at his cousin's Alice's telegram was explained to him: Mary James had died quite suddenly the previous evening, as she sat in the closing dusk with her husband and her sister—Aunt Kate—in the Quincy Street house. She had been recovering from the attack of asthma. Her heart had simply stopped in her seventy-first year.

Henry went to the Hoffman House to rest until he could take the night train to Boston. Here he spent the first hours of his grief. "I shall never pass that place in future," he wrote in his journal, "without thinking of the wretched hours I spent there."

Now, in the early snow-reflected light, with the flakes swirling in the wind, Henry entered the north room of the house where his mother lay in her shroud. He found her "as sweet and tranquil and noble as in life." She seemed unchanged by death; there was much life—unendurably much—in her lifeless face. He later said he had never known how tenderly he loved her till he saw her lying there that morning. His death-vigil was lonely—and triumphant: lonely, in that he had always felt a special tie between himself and his mother, as her favourite son; triumphant, in that he seemed to feel that with her death he came into full possession of her. In life he had had to share her with his father, with William, with his younger brothers and sister. Now, in the depths of his memory and imagination, she belonged only to him. He had felt this long ago when his cousin Minny died—felt the way in which she had been translated from "this changing realm of fact to the steady realm of thought." And this was why, when he wrote the long elegiac passage in his journal, commemorating all that his mother meant to him, he spoke of these "hours of exquisite pain." He was ready to thank Heaven that "this particular pang comes to us but once."

His father and Alice, by the time he talked with them, had begun to reconcile themselves to this break in their lives. Alice, frail as she was, seemed to have sufficient strength and courage for the occasion; and the elder Henry, infirm and tired, had his own philosophical way of taking the sorrows of life. Both were "almost happy." His mother still seemed to be there, in the house in which she had lived so long, "so beautiful, so full of all that we loved in her, she looked in death." Wilky arrived the next morning a matter of hours before the funeral, from Wisconsin. Robertson had been in Quincy Street while Henry was in Washington. For the first time in fifteen years—and for the last—the four sons and the daughter of Mary James were together under the family roof.

Wednesday dawned clear and cold. The storm had spent itself during the night. The sky was blue, the snow-shroud was deep, the air brilliant and still. In the bright frosty sunshine the sons of Mary and the elder Henry carried their mother to her temporary resting-place in a vault in the Cambridge cemetery. In the spring a site would be chosen for the grave.

"She was the perfection of a mother—the sweetest, gentlest, most beneficent human being I have ever known," Henry wrote to his friends. " I was passionately attached to her," he told Mrs Gardner. "She was sweet, gentle, wise, patient, precious—a pure and exquisite soul. But now she is a memory as beneficent as her presence." In the depths of his being Henry possessed that memory.

AN EXQUISITE STILLNESS

A FEW days after his mother's funeral Henry James moved from Quincy Street into Boston. "I wish to remain near my father," he wrote to a friend. "I do not wish however to be in Cambridge." He found rooms at 102 Mount Vernon Street on Beacon Hill. They were bare and ugly, but comfortable. Here he reconstructed, as best as he could for this interim period, the conditions of Bolton Street. At first he felt that he should prolong his stay in America; his father was not well and Alice was not strong. William had his own family and his work. His other brothers were away. Of the sons of Mary James he alone was available. But as the weeks passed it became clear that Alice had for the time being found new strength in taking over her mother's rôle. She ministered to her father and ran the Quincy Street house without difficulty. The elder Henry insisted that his son return to his London tasks and to his own life. He therefore decided to maintain his original sailing-date in May.

I

On the day after he moved into his rooms—9 February 1882—he wrote the long passage in his journal on his mother's death, describing her as the "keystone" of the James family arch. The passage is eloquent in its subdued and self-conscious grief, and it reflects Henry's complete idealization of his mother. There is nothing comparable to it in the available writings of his brother; William, in all that he set down, said very little about Mary James, with whom he had had so often been at odds. Henry's worship of her contains within it no suggestion that he ever imagined his mother as other than a creature of angelic tissue.

She held us all together, and without her we are scattered reeds. She was patience, she was wisdom, she was exquisite maternity. Her sweetness, her mildness, her great natural beneficence were unspeakable, and it is infinitely touching to me to write about her here as one that *was*. When I think of all that she had been, for years—when I think of her hourly devotion to each and all of us—and that when I went to Washington the last of December I gave her my last kiss, I heard her voice for the last time—there seems not to be enough tenderness in my being to register the extinction of such a life.

There were consolations. His mother's work was after all done; the "weariness of age had come upon her." He preferred losing her forever to seeing her begin to suffer. He thought "with a kind of holy joy of her being lifted now above all our pains and anxieties." Her death had given him "a passionate belief in certain transcendent things—the immanence of being as nobly created as hers—the immortality of such a virtue as that—the reunion of spirits in better conditions than these. She is no more of an angel today than she had always been."

He felt as if an "eternal stillness" had settled around him. It was "but a form of her love. One can hear her voice in it—one can feel, forever, the inextinguishable vibration of her devotion." He rebuked himself for not having been tender enough with her at the end; he had been too blind to her sweetness and beneficence. He wished he had known what was coming "so that one might have enveloped her with the softest affection." And Henry went on to speak of her continued restlessness, her preoccupation with her children, her loyalty to her husband. "Summer after summer she never left Cambridge," he noted. His father was responsible for this—"it was impossible that Father should leave his own house." The passage is worth mentioning; under the guise of praising his mother's self-sacrifice he seems to criticize the elder Henry. "The country, the sea, the change of air and scene, were an exquisite enjoyment to her; but she bore with the deepest gentleness and patience the constant loss of such opportunities. She passed her nights and her days in that dry, flat, hot, stale and odious Cambridge, and had never a thought while she did so but for father and Alice. It was a perfect mother's life—the life of a perfect wife." It is difficult to see why Henry, in his sorrow, made this point; for there had been many summers spent away from

Cambridge—in New England coastal resorts and even in Canada. Henry also seemed to glide over the fact that Alice had been seriously ill in recent years, and this, as much as the father's increasing infirmities, had kept his parents in Cambridge. In death as in life Henry made himself his mother's champion against a kind of family oppression. His peroration has in it the note of triumph:

To bring her children into the world—to expend herself, for years, for their happiness and welfare—then, when they had reached a full maturity and were absorbed in the world and in their own interests—to lay herself down in her ebbing strength and yield up her pure soul to the celestial power that had given her this divine commission. Thank God one knows this loss but once.

It was inevitable that Henry should give to these words all the resonance of a funeral oration. In a touching manner he sought to pay his lifelong debt in the most precious coin he possessed: in the power of language, the strength of imagery, the emotion carried by his pen. Mary James had been the central figure of all his years, and so she would remain. The strange thing was that on a deeper level of feeling, which he inevitably concealed from himself, he must have seen his mother as she was, not as he imagined and wanted her to be. She is incarnated in all his fiction, not as the fragile self-effacing and self-denying woman he pictured in his filial piety, spending her last strength for her children. The mothers of Henry James, for all their maternal sweetness, are strong, determined, demanding, grasping women—Mrs Touchett or Mrs Gereth, Mrs Hudson or Mrs Newsome. Sometimes these mothers have great charm and strength; sometimes they become the frightening figures of the governess or of Mark Ambient's wife. It is perhaps strange to juxtapose the mothers of Henry James's novels and tales beside the ideal mother of the commemorative tribute. Only in life was Henry prepared to create such a mother; in his fiction she is neither ideal nor ethereal.

Mary James had reared a family of five children. The younger brothers and the daughter had been crushed by the irrationalities and contradictions of the familial environment over which Mary had presided. The elder sons had surmounted them. Out of these tensions and emotions generated by the mother, which played against the easy compliance of the father, there had emerged a novelist and a philosopher capable of expressing the very contradictions that had produced them—the one in brilliant fiction, the other in the lucid prose of rational thought.

II

"All those weeks after Mother's death," Henry was to write in his journal, "had an exquisite stillness and solemnity." He kept his London hours. In the mid-morning he would walk across the Common and have his breakfast at Parker's. Then he would return to his rooms and write until four or five o'clock. In the gathering winter twilight he would walk to Cambridge, "over that dreary bridge whose length I had measured so often in the past," a mile of wooden piles, supporting a brick pavement with its rough timber fence from which he looked at the frozen bay, the backs of many new houses and a big brown marsh. He had the horse-cars for company. And four or five times a week he would dine in Quincy Street with his father and sister. Then he would walk back to Boston in the clear American starlight. "It was a simple, serious, wholesome time. Mother's death appeared to have left behind it a soft beneficent hush in which we lived for weeks, for months, and which was full of rest and sweetness." Henry thought of her constantly as he walked to Boston "along those dark, vacant roads, where, in the winter air, one met nothing but the coloured lamps and the far-heard jingle of the Cambridge horse-cars."

His work interested him. He chose, during this period, to write not the fiction to which he was addicted, but a play, the harbinger of his later siege of the theatre. He had written, in his youth, three little skits or playlets, and published them; they had however relied neither on action nor on any particular characterization—had been simply little comediettas or farces sustained by a certain conversational charm. Now, however, he set to work to make a play of the least theatrical of his stories—"Daisy Miller." It seemed to him that its success in the magazines and as a book could be duplicated on the stage. In New York he had had some preliminary negotiations with the Mallory brothers, who owned the new Madison Square Theatre. They had encouraged Henry and it was for them that he converted his light and airy little tale into the concreteness of a dramatic action. To do this he had to invent new "business." In the first place Daisy had to survive; he could not kill her off; and she would marry Winterbourne. A villain was needed. Eugenio, the courier, was given this rôle, and the foreign lady in Geneva, whom we never meet in the tale, now emerged as an *intrigante*, a *demi-mondaine* such as Henry had witnessed often on the stage of the Théâtre Français. Daisy recovers from her malaria, while the Roman carnival is in full swing. The manager found it "beautifully written" but distinctly too literary. "It had too much talk and not enough action," he said. In his journal James speaks of the Mallorys as behaving "like asses and sharpers." To Howells he wrote: "When we meet, I will tell you how those gifted brothers led me on protesting over the same path you trod to the same flowery pitfall, and with another play." Thus ended his first struggle—the first of a series—with theatre-managers. Henry seems to have been naïve enough to think that in the world of the theatre managers were like magazine-editors; he was master of the latter, he knew exactly how to deal with them. In the theatre, however, where direct business negotiation was involved wholly without the amenities and courtesies of the publishing world, he was usually baffled—and defeated. He had his play privately printed; he made an effort to get it accepted by the Boston Museum Theatre, and he offered it to London managers. The verdict was always the same, and Henry finally sold it to Aldrich, for publication in the *Atlantic*, for $1000. During this period he also roughed out a first act for a drama founded on *The American*, planning here also to substitute a happy ending for Newman and Claire. The collapse of the "Daisy" negotiations led him to put it aside.

His preoccupation with play-writing during those snowy winter weeks may have betokened his inability, for the moment, to continue his fictional work. The story he had begun in

Washington lay unfinished in his portfolio, and play-writing filled in the time very well. It was like working out an elaborate puzzle. "My work interested me even more than the importance of it would explain—or than the success of it has justified," he noted. "I tried to write a little play and I wrote it; but my poor little play has not been an encouragement." It confirmed his convictions "as to the fascination of this sort of composition. But what it has brought [me] to know, both in New York and in London, about the manners and ideas of managers and actors and about the conditions of production on our unhappy English stage, is almost fatally disgusting and discouraging. I have learned, very vividly, that if one attempts to work for it one must be prepared for *disgust*, deep and unspeakable disgust."

The dramatic form seemed to him "the most beautiful thing possible," but "the misery of the thing is that the baseness of the English-speaking stage affords no setting for it." These reflections however belonged to a later time; at the moment he had only the joy of his creation, and when his play was written he carried his script to Mrs Gardner and read it to her, during two long evenings. She was a sympathetic listener. Thus Henry had long ago imagined Benvolio reading his plays to the irresistible Countess. He had, so to speak, had his private performance at the Court of Isabella.

III

The weeks passed; March came, and between bouts of homesickness and small Boston sociabilities Henry managed to decrease the distance to his 10 May sailing-date. How desperate he must have been we may gather from his writing a letter to William J. Hoppin, asking him for "a little parcel of London items." How was Mrs Duncan Stewart? What was the latest news of her daughter, Mrs Rogerson? He was homesick for London, "the full extent of my devotion to which I didn't know until I had put the ocean between us. My country pleases, in many ways, but it doesn't satisfy, and I sometimes wrap my head in my toga, to stifle (stoically) my groans." He told the First Secretary of

Legation that when he next arrived at Euston Station, "I shall fall down and kiss the platform."

Mr Hoppin dutifully pasted the letter into his diary; it is the only letter of any length he ever received from the novelist. On the same day that he wrote it, Henry also wrote to Henrietta Reubell, thanking her for her budget of news from Paris—"your little whiff of the great Parisian hubbub seems to me the carnival of dissipation." To Mrs Kemble he wrote that he smiled with derision at her suggestion that he might be "weaned" from "my London loves and longings by remaining over here." He was within a month of his sailing. "My father is much better than he was a month ago, and will not listen to my making any 'sacrifices' for his sake." He had heard from Mrs Wister; he had had a letter from Mrs Procter, "who writes as neatly as she talks, and from whose firm and brilliant surface the buffets of fate glance off." He was impatient to leave, "and you are for a great deal in it."

Some time before he sailed his father and Alice took a small house in Mount Vernon Street, not far from his rooms, at No. 131. This represented the final breaking-up of the house in Quincy Street, which had been the seat of the James family since the end of the Civil War. The house was too large for William's needs; and the elder Henry and Alice wanted something smaller and cosier. Henry saw them comfortably installed and was ready to sail with an easy conscience. Almost the last thing he did before his departure was to attend another funeral. On 27 April the bells of Concord had tolled the death of Ralph Waldo Emerson, and Henry made the familiar journey three days later to pay his respects to the old family friend, the benign figure of his childhood. The older generation was passing. Longfellow had died little more than a month before. It was a cool day in Concord and there was a threat of rain in the air. Regular and special trains brought a large congregation; others came in wagons and on foot to pay tribute to "the principal gentleman in the place." As a public funeral Henry found it "curious, sociable, cheerful," a popular manifestation, the most striking Henry had ever seen provoked by the death of a man of letters. He was to attend more elaborate burials; nevertheless he cherished this memory of an almost rustic occasion, beside the new grave, near the grave of Hawthorne.

On the day before he sailed, his father wrote a long letter to him, to speed him on his journey: "My darling boy, I must bid you farewell. How loving a farewell it is, I can't say, but only that it is most loving. I can't help feeling that you are the one that has cost us the least trouble, and given us always the most delight. Especially do I mind Mother's perfect joy in you the last few months of her life, and your perfect sweetness to her. I think in fact it is this which endears you so much to me now. I feel that I have fallen heir to all dear Mother's fondness for you, as well as my proper own, and bid you accordingly a distinctly widowed farewell."

Henry was now his father's "angel" as he had been his mother's. "Goodbye then again, my precious Harry. We shall each rejoice in you in our several ways as you plough through the ocean and attain to your old rooms, where it will be charming to think of you as once more settled and at work." And he repeated: "A lingering goodbye, then, dearest Harry, from all of us! and above all from your loving Father."

A LITTLE TOUR IN FRANCE

HENRY crossed the Atlantic on the *Gallia* in eight days and nine hours. He left the ship at Cork. Eager as he was to return to Bolton Street, he wanted a glimpse of the land of his father's father. He spent a week in Cork and Dublin and found both cities filled with constables and soldiers; otherwise he saw little but green fields and dirty cabins. He had no desire to become a sentimental tourist again, and if he had had any idea of turning his Irish visit into copy he abandoned it. On 22 May he was back in Bolton Street. Reclining on the sofa and awaiting him was an unexpected guest, his brother Robertson. On his desk was a pile of invitations. The London Season was on with a vengeance. The city seemed oppressive, big, black and "actual." It was "a brutal sort of a place," he wrote to Godkin, and while he reverted to it with "a kind of filial fondness" everything somehow seemed changed. He was restless, he was bored. The death of his mother had, for the moment, drained life of all interest. The American episode was already fading away, and while he looked back at it with "a great deal of tenderness," he knew that Boston meant "absolutely nothing to me—I don't even dislike it," he wrote in his journal. He added: "I like it, on the contrary; I only dislike to live there." Much of his visit to his homeland seemed like a dream—"a very painful dream."

Nevertheless the nostalgia for his London life seemed to have evaporated as well. He went through the motions of participating in the Season, yet the London social world, into which he had plunged with such eagerness three years before, seemed to him "a poor world, this time; I saw and did very little that was interesting." And at the end of a brief journal-note, he remarked: "I have gone in too much for society." To make matters worse he found himself invaded by editors and friends from the other side of the sea. At various times that summer Howells and his family, Osgood, Aldrich, Charles Dudley Warner, John Hay, Clarence King, whom he met at this time, were all in London, not to speak of certain ladies to whom he was indebted in various ways for hospitality, and whom he liked well enough in their own surroundings. Henrietta Reubell crossed from Paris; Mrs Boit and her "merry laugh" reappeared; Mrs V. R. arrived and took rooms a few doors away from Henry's lodgings and made great advances into London society; Mrs Wister came from Philadelphia to visit Fanny Kemble. In this "bewilderment of conflicting duties and pleasures" Henry was fretful. "All summer I had been trying to work," he wrote in his journal, "but my interruptions had been so numerous that it was only during the last weeks that I succeeded, even moderately, in doing something." This was when the Season abated and the visiting Americans crossed to the Continent. Nevertheless he also remarks: "Shall I confess, however, that the evenings had become dull." Even his election as an honorary member of the Athenaeum, where he had been proposed by Leslie Stephen, seemed now a routine matter. That he should possess two clubs in Pall Mall, side by side, and thus be on an equal footing as it were with England's political, literary and religious world, now seemed to him less than significant. A process of disenchantment had begun. Indeed he found his evenings so dull that he sought out William J. Hoppin for company. Hoppin's journal of Sunday, 25 August 1882, records:

"I had a long visit from Henry James last Sunday evening. He spoke of the neglect he had experienced in Boston when he was there last winter. One would have thought with the literary taste attributed to these people they would have fêted him. But he got the privilege of the Union Club with some difficulty and was invited once to dinner. He spoke of all this without bitterness. Perhaps one should remember that he had just lost his mother and the Bostonians may have thought he did not care to be invited to parties. But they might have given him the chance of refusing."

I

To make Henry's restless summer complete, William suddenly decided to apply for a year's leave from Harvard with the double purpose of having a vacation and meeting some of his fellow-psychologists in Europe. Early in September the novelist found himself on his way to Euston Station to meet his brother's boat-train. The strange thing was that William chose to take this leave a few months after the birth of his second son (who had been named William after his father and great grandfather). At this moment of renewed paternity he was planning to be away from his wife and infant for a year. He had done the same thing two years before after his firstborn had arrived; had rushed abroad for a summer's vacation, as if the presence of infancy in his house was more than he could bear. To be sure, his house, in which his mother-in-law and his wife's sister also lived, must at times have been a bedlam, and William could hardly have found peace there for the pursuit of his work. Perhaps the new child, like the first-born, may have also touched some chord of early memory in William and awakened an old anguish, that of little rivals invading *his* nursery—as Henry had done long ago. Shortly after arriving in Europe he wrote a letter to his wife which might have given her pause, were she not so preoccupied: he described the German peasant-women he had seen "striding like men through the streets, dragging their carts or lugging their baskets, minding their business, seeming to notice nothing in the stream of luxury and vice, but belonging far away, to something better and purer. . . . All the mystery of womanhood seems incarcerated in their ugly being—the Mothers! the Mothers! Ye are all one! Yes, Alice dear, what I love in you is only what these blessed creatures have." That sentence about "ugly being" and "ye are all one," if whimsical, nevertheless betrayed a singular state of feeling. And perhaps this was why William had, for the moment, put an ocean between himself and Cambridge. To Henry it seemed that William's timing was unfortunate. He used the word "abandoned" twice in writing to his sister-in-law. "With your husband in Venice and your eldest brother-in-law in these strange

French cities [he was writing, later, from Bordeaux] you must feel rather bewildered and abandoned." But clearly he did not think of himself as the abandoner. "Your situation seems to me most unnatural, but I hope you bear up under it, and that you derive some assistance in doing so from your little Harry and William." And Henry returned to the charge: "Abandoned by your husband, you seem to me, dear Alice, very greatly to be pitied, and I assure you that I think of you with tender sympathy."

As William descended from the train at Euston Station he gave high proof of his temper to his brother. It was a vigorous monologue: "My!—how cramped and inferior England seems! After all, it's poor old Europe, just as it used to be in our dreary boyhood! America may be raw and shrill, but I could never live with this as you do! I'm going to hurry down to Switzerland and then home again as soon as may be. It was a mistake to come over! I thought it would do me good. Hereafter I'll stay at home. You'll have to come to America if you want to see the family."

His eldest son, recording this many years later, remarked that William was always under the spell of Europe when he was in America—and was "most ardently American when on European soil." The account continues: "The effect on Henry can better be imagined than described. Time never accustomed him to these collisions, even though he learned to expect them." Henry usually ended by rushing William off to his continental destination—which was what he did this time, two days later—and, his nephew added, "he remained alone to ejaculate, to exclaim and to expatiate for weeks on the rude and exciting cyclone that had burst upon him and passed him by."

II

This season of malaise was reflected in Henry's fiction. In Bolton Street he completed the tale he had begun in Washington—"The Point of View"—and its picture of American life comes to us as in a series of folding mirrors, capturing in a bright critical light the glittering weaknesses of the American democracy. What he found was a country in which egalitarianism was diluting individuality; in which a thinness of history and a smallness of national experience had to be reconciled with a continental grandeur and a national sense of space and freedom. The repatriated American gentlewoman, who has spent years in European *pensions*, complains that "there is no respect for one's privacy, for one's preferences, for one's reserves." The lady at Newport remarks on the liberties given—and taken—by American youth and their deformation of the English language. "Of course, a people of fifty millions, who have invented a new civilization, have a right to a language of their own; that's what they tell me, and I can't quarrel with it. But I wish they had made it as pretty as the mother-tongue, from which, after all, it is more or less derived. We ought to have invented something as noble as our country." She finds the men "better than the women, who are very subtle, but rather hard." The men are simply professional and commercial, "there are very few gentlemen pure and simple."

> The girls are not shy, but I don't know why they should be, for there is really nothing here to be afraid of. Manners are very gentle, very humane; the democratic system deprives people of weapons that everyone doesn't equally possess. No one is formidable . . . I think there is not much wickedness, and there is certainly less cruelty than with you. Everyone can sit; no one is kept standing . . . The general good nature, the social equality, deprives them of triumphs on the one hand, and of grievances on the other . . . You will say I am describing a terrible society,—a society without great figures or great social prizes. You have hit it, my dear; there are no great figures . . . There are no brilliant types; the most important people seem to lack dignity. They are very *bourgeois*.

The emerging picture is of an easy democracy that breeds an easy mediocrity, in an atmosphere of advancing material civilization and chattering women. "The women listen very little—not enough. They interrupt; they talk too much; one feels their presence too much as sound. American women make too many vague exclamations—say too many indefinite things. In short, they have a great deal of nature. On the whole, I find very little affectation, though we shall probably have more as we improve."

This is one appraisal which America receives. The British M.P. surveys the same civilization good-naturedly, comments on the luxurious trains, and on the people, visits the schools and finds it extraordinary how many persons "are being educated in this country; and yet, at the same time, the tone of the people is less scholarly than one might expect." His impression is that children are better educated than adults. "The position of a child is, on the whole, one of great distinction."

Improved cooking-stoves, rosewood pianos, gas and hot water, aesthetic furniture, and complete sets of the British Essayists. A tramway through every street; every block of equal length; blocks and houses scientifically lettered and numbered. There is absolutely no loss of time, and no need of looking for anything, or, indeed, *at* anything.

The expatriated American aesthete complains at the absence of variety—"Everyone is Mr Jones, Mr Brown; and every one looks like Mr Jones and Mr Brown. They lack completeness of identity; they are quite without modelling." The French academician sees the women as engaged in a chase for a husband, and American literature contains "no form, no matter, no style, no general ideas." The books seem written for children and young ladies. The newspapers contain no news, only stories about marriages and divorces, "not in six lines, discreetly veiled, with an art of insinuation, as with us, but with all the facts (or the fictions), the letters, the dates, the places, the hours." His conclusion is that America is "the last word of democracy, and that word is—*flatness*." But Henry gives the last word to the Americans and largely to Marcellus Cockerell, who has had his fill of Europe. It is from his letter that Clover Adams culled the epigram most pleasing to herself, as it was to most Americans. "We are more analytic, more discriminating, more familiar with realities. As for manners, there are bad manners everywhere, but an aristocracy is bad manners organized."

The tale was published late in the year in the *Century* magazine. Henry had predicted to his father that it would "probably call down execration on my head," and it did. The reviews were peevish: Henry's readers liked neither the sharpness of his observation nor the pointedness of his criticism. He was accused of being too severe in his treatment of the American national character. The tale tended to confirm the public image of the novelist as a chronic critic of the land of the brave and the free. James knew how "to play the harp of fiction," said one reviewer, but, he added, his harp didn't have enough strings. These remarks inevitably made him feel that his people were thin-skinned. In the fullness of time it is possible to observe that Henry James was saying nothing more to Americans about their land than what his fellow-novelists in France or in Russia or in England were doing to their own countrymen, that is functioning as artists, and by this process functioning as critics of life.

His disenchantment with English Society emerged in a tale which was originally designed as a contrast between Anglo-American and French morality. It will be recalled that during his little journey of 1877 he had seen Dumas's *Le Demi-Monde* and had found it impossible to swallow the denunciation of the heroine "with a past" by a very moral young man who had been her lover. To "tell" on a woman, even if she were not the most moral creature in the world, seemed to Henry ungentlemanly; and he could not accept the high virtue made of this in the French play. In "The Siege of London," which he gave to Leslie Stephen for the *Cornhill*, he described the attempt of an American adventuress to obtain admission into London society. Nancy Headway wants to elbow her way to respectability in spite of her multiple divorces. She sets her cap at a stolid English baronet, Sir Arthur Demesne, under the observing eyes of a Secretary of Legation—a composite figure of Nadal and Hoppin, though somewhat more suave than either—as well as of a sophisticated American, rather like James himself. The society to which Mrs Headway aspires is certainly "bad manners organized," and the lengths to which the mother of the baronet, Lady Demesne, goes to find out about Nancy's past embarrasses and finally irritates the sophisticated American. The tale is written in a rich vein of high comedy and its morality is the reverse of the French. Nancy gets her nobleman, and the American "tells" only when he knows it is too late to change anything. But in reality this tale is James's farewell to London Society. He seemed to feel now that it was not much of an achievement to get into it—"poor world" that it was—indeed that anyone could do so with a little effort, as witness the case of Mrs Headway. Even New York would find her acceptable, once she became Lady Demesne.

The matter is put with some force by the Jamesian observer; his remarks show the road Henry had travelled since his talks with Nadal three years earlier. "I hate that phrase, 'getting into society.' I don't think one ought to attribute to one's self that sort of ambition. One ought to assume that one is in society—that one *is* society—and to hold that if one has good manners, one has, from the social point of view, achieved the great thing."

Perhaps Henry also felt the English had taken him up not because he had good manners and was a gentleman, but simply because they found him "entertaining." Nancy Headway proves to be a roaring success on the strength of her quaint Americanisms and her bold manner. "When she saw her audience in convulsions, she said to herself that this was success, and believed that, if she had only come to London five years sooner, she might have married a duke." This strong reaction to London Society may have had some part in Henry's writing, at this time, his essay on "Du Maurier and London Society" which he published a few months later in the *Century*. He praised du Maurier for holding up "a singularly polished and lucid mirror to the drama of English society." He showed with what closeness he had studied the cartoons in *Punch* ever since his boyhood. And in a final passage Henry wondered, it seems, whether the conquest of London had been really worth while after all. Philistines were philistines, on either side of the Atlantic, and the artist was doomed always to be a stranger and an outsider anywhere in the world. Pondering du Maurier's Mrs Cimabue Brown and his satire of aesthetes, Henry concludes that no revolution has occurred. The English were simply not an aesthetic people:

They have not a spontaneous artistic life; their taste is a matter of conscience, reflection, duty, and the writer who in our time has appealed to them most eloquently on behalf of art has rested his plea on moral standards—has talked exclusively of right and wrong. It is impossible to live much among them, to be a spectator of their habits, their manners, their arrangements, without perceiving that the artistic point of view is the last that they naturally take. The sense of manner is not part of their constitution. They arrive at it, as they have arrived at so many things, because they are ambitious, resolute, enlightened, fond of difficulties; but there is always a strange element either of undue apology or of exaggerated defiance in their attempts at the cultivation of beauty. They carry on their huge broad back a nameless mountain of conventions and prejudices, a dusky cloud of inaptitudes and fears, which casts a shadow upon the frank and confident practice of art. The consequence of all this is that their revivals of taste are even stranger than the abuses they are meant to correct. They are violent, voluntary, mechanical; wanting in grace, in tact, in the sense of humour and of proportion.

Art thus seemed to have no place, either in an industrially expanding America bent on equalizing everything, or in an England where the "conventions and prejudices," not to speak of "inaptitudes and fears," made him feel as if he were a freak of nature, or some curiosity, to be wined and dined and patted on the back without ever being truly appreciated or understood.

III

After Henry got William off to the Continent he paid a few country visits—this was one way of escaping from the London crowd and his fellow-countrymen—and crossed the Channel in mid-September to do a specific chore. A Harper editor had suggested to him that he write a travel-book about France; this seemed to him a profitable thing to do. In spite of his large professional experience by this time, he did it without obtaining a definite commitment and Harper later backed out. But Henry sold the book to Osgood and, as *A Little Tour in France*, it was to serve successive generations of tourists in the château country and the Midi. Before starting his tour he paid his customary visit to Turgenev at Bougival, and this time found him seriously ill. They had some good talk nevertheless, and Turgenev wrote to Ralston: "Henry James has paid me a visit. He is as amiable as ever. But he has grown enormously fat."

Henry devoted all October 1882 to his "little tour." He began it in the town of Tours, the birthplace of Balzac. Here he spent a week, joining Mrs Kemble and Mrs Wister who were holidaying there. Neither had the energy for much sight-seeing however. Mrs Wister had her young son Owen with her, later to be celebrated as the pioneer of the "western" novel. Henry found him "attractive and amiable," but felt he was "light and slight, both in character and in talent." Mrs Kemble was always her tragedienne self—"neither light nor slight," Henry remarked, and Mrs Wister was now "a tragic nature, so much worn, physically, that I am sorry for her."

He found the châteaux interesting, however, and the country around Tours "as charming as the essential meagreness of the French landscape will allow it to be." Leaving Tours and the Kemble–Wisters on 8 October, Henry first travelled a small circle—Angers, Nantes, La Rochelle and Poitiers; then he went to Bordeaux, Toulouse, Carcassone, Narbonne, and Montpellier, and finally into the heart of Daudet's Midi—Nîmes, Tarascon, Arles, Avignon; after which he curved northward to Orange, Mâcon, Beaune and Dijon. By mid-October, when he was in the Midi, he wrote to William, who was in Venice: "I pursue my pilgrimage through these rather dull French towns and through a good deal of bad weather, and all my desire now is to bring it to a prompt conclusion. It is rather dreary work, for most of the places, I am sorry to say, are much less rich in the picturesque than I had supposed they would be." Decidedly the French provinces were not Italy. To Howells he wrote: "There is no more to my purpose at Bordeaux than there would be at Fitchburg, and I am not even consoled by good claret, as what I am given here is very much what you would get at F." He felt that France had preserved the physiognomy of the past less than England or Italy—that Napoleon had erased much of the pictorial and the "quaint." He experienced a revival of interest however when he came to the Roman towns; and certain of the cathedrals, as always, deeply absorbed his attention. In Avignon the Rhône was in flood, and he was pleased to get out of its watery streets and make a straight line for Paris. He had kept a journal during his little tour (apparently later destroyed) and from it he wrote his book a few months after. It is much less personal than his other travel-writings, much more strictly a guide-book; and while it abounds in accurate and vivid descriptive passages, it leans a great deal on mere historic recital. The material was too architectural, and too historical; it lacked what he called the "human picturesque," and the book suffered accordingly. But it suffered too, one might add, from the lack of his former freshness and from his general mood of fatigue and depression.

NOVEMBER PARTING

NOVEMBER had come when Henry travelled from Dijon to Paris, his little tour accomplished. He had seen more of France than he had ever seen before, and "on the whole" liked it better. The autumn was uncommonly wet. He put up at the Grand Hotel and recognized once again that Paris had "a little corner of my complicated organism." He found the "same rather threadbare little circle of our sweet compatriots, who dine with each other in every possible combination of the alphabet—though none of their combinations spell the word satisfaction. That, however," he added to Mrs Gardner, "is the most difficult word in the language—even *I* am not sure I get it right."

The pleasantest coincidence was to find John Hay at the Grand Hotel. Henry had never known well the man who had been Lincoln's assistant secretary and who combined a love of letters with national duty in a way that was rare in Washington. But he respected him highly. With Hay was his friend Clarence King, author of the major governmental survey of the mineral resources of the United States, and friend of Henry Adams. Like Adams, James admired King's wit, his energy, his capacity for good talk, his ceaseless interest in the world around him. The three breakfasted together, roamed the boulevards, prowled in shops. "He is a delightful creature, and is selling silver mines and buying water-colours and old stuff by the millions," Henry wrote to Mrs Gardner. And to Howells he said; "King is a charmer. He charmed all the bric-à-brac out of the shops." After his solitary journey in the Midi it was a delight to come upon such congenial fellow-Americans in the French capital.

He had exchanged notes with Ivan Sergeyevich, who continued to be ill, and on 17 November went to see him at Bougival, where the Russian had remained much later than usual, attended by doctors, among them J. M. Charcot, who could not diagnose what was wrong with him. More recently they had recommended a milk diet, and when Henry found him he was astonished at the change in his friend. His towering figure was stooped. His great frame was shrunken. But he was as *accueuillant* as ever. "He had been ill, with strange, intolerable symptoms, but he was better," Henry later wrote, "and he had good hopes." Neither knew, when they saw each other that day in November, when the trees at Bougival were bare and the Seine was grey, what cruel months lay ahead. Ivan Sergeyevich had cancer of the spine.

After a period of complete immobility the Russian had begun to go out again, and on that afternoon he had to go into Paris. He did not want to take the suburban train because he feared he would find it uncomfortable; ordering a carriage, he asked Henry to ride with him into the city. It was just eight years since they had first met, when Turgenev used to mount with firm and powerful tread the endless stairs that led to Flaubert's perch. They rode through the thickening dusk and for an hour and a half Henry had his beloved friend to himself. Turgenev talked constantly, and never better. He talked in English and Henry was to quote from this occasion a certain sentence to illustrate the peculiar literary quality of Turgenev's use of that tongue—remembered phrases encountered in books. This gave a charming quaintness and an unexpected turn to what he said. "In Russia, in spring, if you enter a beechen grove"—these were the words that came back to Henry from their carriage-ride. What subjects they touched upon he never recorded; but it was the same rich, spontaneous talk which he had always cherished in his elder contemporary.

When they reached the city Henry left the carriage at an exterior boulevard. There was a little French fair going on in the chill November air, under the denuded trees. The nasal sound of a Punch and Judy show somehow became mixed with his farewell at the window of the carriage. Then the vehicle rolled away.

A WINTER SUMMONS

HENRY had hardly returned to London to settle down after his ramblings, when word came from his sister and aunt that his father was rapidly declining and had not long to live. Although he had left the United States barely six months before, he made immediate plans to return. William was in Paris attending Charcot's clinics at the Salpêtrière. They agreed that Henry should sail, and William would come to London and stay in Bolton Street while awaiting further news. Henry obtained passage on the *Werra*, from Liverpool, leaving on 12 December. The voyage was smooth and rapid. The ship reached New York on 21 December, and waiting for Henry at the dock was a letter from Alice written the day before, a Wednesday. "Darling Father's weary longings were all happily ended on Monday at 3 p.m. The last words on his lips were 'There is my Mary!' For the last two hours he had said perpetually 'My Mary.' He had no suffering but we were devotedly thankful when the rest came to him, he so longed to go, the last thing he said before he lost consciousness was 'I am going with great joy!' The end of life had come for him and he went and I am sure you will feel as thankful as I do that the weary burden of life is over for him. I have no terrors for the future for I know I shall have strength to meet all that is in store for me; with a heart full of love and counting the minutes till you get here always your devoted A—." She told him that the funeral would be on Thursday morning. "There seemed no use in waiting for you, the uncertainty was so great."

His father, then, had been buried that very morning while his steamer was pulling into New York harbour. Henry reached Boston at eleven that night and was met at the station by his brother Robertson, who had come from Milwaukee for the funeral, and was leaving in the morning. In Mount Vernon Street Alice was resting. Aunt Kate, however, was up; they talked into the morning.

The elder Henry had died as he had lived, with an unflagging moral optimism; although his physical strength had failed him, he had turned his sickroom into a place of joy. He announced that he had entered upon the "spiritual life" and thereafter refused all food. The doctors spoke of "softening of the brain," but all the evidence indicates that until his last hours he was in possession of his faculties. Francis Boott, who was in America that winter, came to see him a day or two before the end and they had a long talk. He lay facing the windows and refused to have them darkened. He slept a great deal. He was told that Henry was on his way. The news gave him pleasure, but he showed no signs of impatience—save to die. Toward the end Aunt Kate heard him say "Oh I have such good boys—*such* good boys!" Asked about funeral arrangements he said (Aunt Kate wrote this down):

> That here is a man who has always believed in the only true spiritual life, a direct intercourse with God—and who leaves it as his dying wish that men should know and understand that all the ceremonies usually observed in births, marriages and funerals are nonsense and untrue. The only true life is the spiritual one and this is only interfered with by these foolish words and doings that man has invented. [He further said] that he did not believe in individual salvation, but in the free personal intercourse of all men with God.

In long letters to William, conveying to him all the details as he gathered them, Henry said the father's passing had been "most strange, most characteristic above all, and as full of beauty as it was void of suffering. There was none of what we feared—no paralysis, no dementia, no violence." He had simply felt a great weakness; had swooned repeatedly; and after that had taken to his bed. Only the nurse and the loyal aunt were with him when he died. Alice had been increasingly ill and was being ministered to by Miss Loring. Thus ended the life of one of the most "original" of the earlier Americans, a strange, voluble, gifted man, who had led an unworldly life, out of the current of Transcendental thought. To an extraordinary degree he had given to his sons the vigorous qualities of his language, something of the bellicose Irishness of his nature, and the picturesqueness of his mind.

"A little fat, rosy, Swedenborgian amateur," Ellery Channing had called him, "with the look of a broker, and the brains and heart of a Pascal." He had been, as Ralph Barton Perry said, a man with a mission dogged by a sense of futility—a frustrated writer who never quite conveyed his message in spite of his lively prose. In the fullest way in which any man may hope to be represented by his progeny, William and Henry James accomplished what their father had failed to do. If the world had not listened to him, with all the life and intensity of his being and his own idiosyncrasies of style and speech, it was to listen to them. They were to write themselves—and him—into the memory of the civilized world.

In the house in Mount Vernon Street, so recently animated by the presence of the elder Henry, a great silence reigned that Christmas. Alice, in a state of collapse, had been taken by Katherine Loring on the day after Henry's arrival to the Loring home at Beverly. Henry, deprived of his last glimpse of his father, developed one of his debilitating migraines and was ill for four days. Aunt Kate, sole survivor of the paternal group, who had dedicated her life to her sister, and her sister's husband and children, sat in silent meditation in the parlour, "not only without a Christmas dinner but without any dinner, as she doesn't eat, according to her wont."

The suddenness of Henry's jump from London to Boston had left him in a daze. He wrote to his publisher that he could touch the red brick houses opposite with his pen-point and found himself wondering for the moment what had come over Bolton Street. "After I have been here two or three weeks I shall know pretty well where I am, and perhaps how long I shall be here."

"The house is so *empty*," he wrote to William. It was late in the evening and Henry had been down to the parlour to chat with his aunt. She repeated again and again that the father had "yearned unspeakably" to die. "I am too tired to write more, and my head is beginning to ache." He added: "All our wish here is that you should remain abroad the next six months."

A BLESSED FAREWELL

On the last day of the year 1882 Henry walked through the deep snow of the Cambridge cemetery where the previous spring a family plot had been selected on a small rise in the land. Here the mother had been committed to the earth. Now, in the silence of the Sunday morning, Henry looked at the new grave, cut in the cold ground ten days before. The elder Henry lay very close to his wife. At some point during this visit the son took a letter from his pocket and began to read it aloud into the wintry air, addressing it to the graves. There was no eyewitness, so far as we know, no one to record the quality of Henry's voice, or the way in which he stood in the performance of this act. But its very nature suggests a depth of feeling, a passion of tenderness. He seems to have stood there alone, under a blue winter sky, in the piled snow, within view of the distant field beyond the Charles.

What Henry read was a letter written by William to his father on 14 December, just after the elder son had arrived in Bolton Street. It had reached Cambridge the day before, too late by a fortnight for the man for whom it was destined. Substituting his own voice and presence for that of his brother, Henry now communicated it to the dead.

"Darling old Father," Henry read, "We have been so long accustomed to the hypothesis of your being taken away from us, that the thought that this may be your last illness conveys no very sudden shock. You are old enough, you've given your message to the world in many ways and will not be forgotten; you are here left alone, and on the other side, let us hope and pray, dear, dear old Mother is waiting for you to join her. If you go, it will not be an inharmonious thing. Only, if you are still in possession of your normal consciousness, I should like to see you once again before we part. I stayed here only in obedience to the last telegram, and am waiting now for Harry—who knows the exact state of my mind, and who will know yours—to telegraph again what I shall do." Henry read on: "Meanwhile, my blessed old Father, I scribble this line (which may reach you though I should come too late), just to tell you how full of the tenderest memories and feelings about you my heart has for the last few days been filled. In that mysterious gulf of the past into which the present soon will fall and go back and back, yours is still for me the central figure. All my intellectual life I derive from you; and though we have often seemed at odds in the expression thereof, I'm sure there's a harmony somewhere, and that our strivings will combine. What my debt to you is goes beyond all my power of estimating,—so early, so penetrating and so constant has been the influence. You need be in no anxiety about your literary remains. I will see them well taken care of, and that your words shall not suffer for being concealed."

William promised his father that he would compile a volume of extracts from the elder Henry's writings, after the manner of the extracts from Carlyle, Ruskin and others. "I have long thought such a volume would be the best monument to you."

"As for us [Henry continued to read]; we shall live on each in his way,—feeling somewhat unprotected, old as we are, for the absence of the parental bosoms as a refuge, but holding fast together in that common sacred memory. We will stand by each other and by Alice, try to transmit the torch in our offspring as you did in us." And so, after recognizing that he had at various times given his father trouble, and expressing the belief that in his own paternal rôle he would learn to understand his father's paternity, William ended:

"As for the other side, and Mother, and our all possibly meeting, I *can't* say anything. More than ever at this moment do I feel that if that *were* true, all would be solved and justified. And it comes strangely over me in bidding you good-bye how a life is but a day and expresses mainly but a single note. It is so much like the act of bidding an ordinary good-night. Good-night, my sacred old Father. If I don't see you again—Farewell! a blessed farewell!"

Henry had finished. He replaced the letter in his pocket. He had remained with his parents, in this solemn visit, a long time. He was certain, he told his brother, that the elder Henry had heard him "somewhere out of the depths of the still, bright winter air." And he also said: "As I stood there and looked at this last expression of so many years of mortal union, it was difficult not to believe that they were not united again in some consciousness of my belief."

The son and brother had performed his strange deeply-felt mystical act by the two graves. And now he could turn from the dead to the living. As he walked back, he stopped at William's house and sat with his brother's wife and her two children, admiring the infant William, "a most loving little mortal." Then he called on Francis J. Child, professor of English at Harvard, whom he had known from his own student days, and who had appeared to feel the elder Henry's death more than anyone outside the family. He received the condolences of Wendell Holmes, recently made a Judge of the State Supreme Court, and in writing all this to William he enjoined him not to come rushing home. Everything was being taken care of; moreover there was nothing William could do, since the elder Henry's last will and testament had named his second son to be the executor. For the time at least Henry, the quiet "angel," assumed legally the administration of the James family affairs. Jacob had indeed supplanted Esau—and Esau at this moment was in a far-away land.

SON AND BROTHER

William kept his word to his father. Within two years —in 1884—he brought out *The Literary Remains of the Late Henry James*, a substantial miscellany of his father's writings with a long introduction by himself. His father's last book was, in a sense, William's first. Henry, receiving it, wrote to his brother on 2 January 1885 that it gave him "great filial and fraternal joy." He spoke of the "extraordinarily individual (some of them magnificent)" utterances in the volume. His father's religious system seemed intensely original and personal. "I can't enter into it (much) myself—I can't be so theological, nor grant his extraordinary premises, nor throw myself into conceptions of heavens and hells, nor be sure that the keynote of nature is humanity, etc. But I can enjoy greatly the spirit, the feeling and the manner of the whole thing, (full as this last is of things that *dis*please me too,) and feel really that poor Father, struggling so alone all his life, and so destitute of every worldly or literary ambition, was yet a great writer." Henry did his utmost to get the book noticed in England. Few seemed interested. And when the *Nation* did inadequate justice to it, Henry scolded Godkin. "I have a tenderness for my poor Father's memory which is in direct proportion to the smallness of the recognition his work was destined to obtain here below and which fills me with a kind of pious melancholy in presence of the fact that so ardent an activity of thought, such a living, original, expression of spirit may have passed into darkness and silence forever." The volume, with his brother's introduction, he told Godkin, seemed to him to have "a real literary importance."

I

Henry James the elder left an estate valued at $95,000. It consisted of more than $80,000 worth of land, houses and stores, in

Syracuse, New York, yielding seven per cent after taxes and maintenance, or about $5000 a year. The remainder, largely money derived from the sale of the Quincy Street house, had been invested in prosperous railway stocks and bonds, with a yield per annum of $3500. These latter were willed to Alice and provided adequately for an invalid spinster of that time. The estate was to be divided among the three brothers, William, Henry and Robertson. Garth Wilkinson James, the improvident and happy-go-lucky son, was omitted from the will because he had received his inheritance in advance. For some years he had been a constant drain on his father. Only a short time before, on declaring himself bankrupt, he had been given $5000.

Wilky however was seriously ill; he had a rheumatic heart and other complications. He was crushed by his debts, and he had a wife and children in Milwaukee. Henry, from the outset, took the position that the will was "unfortunate," and proposed a redivision into four equal parts. Robertson, who had ample means, agreed; Alice, in so far as she was a party to the testament, also voted with Henry. William, thinking of his two sons, wrote from abroad that he was not at all certain a redivision would be equitable, given the large sums Wilky had squandered. He reminded Henry of the difference between the bachelor state and the responsibilities of paternity, and proposed redivision into fifths. He also worked out an elaborate breakdown into sixteenths, according to the population of the James family groups. Henry opposed this, and as a matter of fact had already moved for equal division, assuming William would agree. William's first impulse was to book passage for home early in February. What ensued was a strange and lively correspondence in which Henry threw all his weight into convincing William he must stay abroad—as if his very life depended on keeping his elder brother in Europe. In a 2000-word letter he pointed out that William would have no place to stay in Cambridge, since part of his house had been sub-let, and to live away from his family would engender gossip. He insisted that if William returned before his appointed time it would be "a melancholy confession of failure," a "sort of proclamation of want of continuity of purpose."

William had made a point of going abroad because he needed rest and had work to do, and "you were surely not altogether wrong." Cambridge itself was "barren" after London and Paris, Henry wrote, forgetting that this was his, not William's, feeling about the local scene. He peevishly said that William could be accommodated in Boston at the Mount Vernon Street house in the small guest-room, where Aunt Kate had stayed, but "I won't offer to give up Father's room, because I lately made you a present of my rooms in London." And he argued there would be "a painful want of *form*" in William's returning to Cambridge "prematurely"—especially after having remained away during his father's illness and death.

William replied that Henry was meddling in his affairs; that however much Henry considered Cambridge "barren," these were not his feelings; and he expressed the wish that his brother should cease treating him as if he were a baby. However he cancelled his passage, and after further negotiation certain adjustments were made. A portion of the estate was set aside for Wilky's family, in a trust fund, with the net consequence that William and Henry would each receive about $1300 a year.

Henry travelled to Milwaukee in a temperature of twenty below zero and a blinding blizzard for direct talks with the younger brothers, and later visited Syracuse to inspect the properties, which were located on James Street—the street named after the immigrant grandfather. William came home in March and Henry made over to him the general handling of the estate. His own income, he announced, was to go entirely to Alice—"this I desire always to be its regular destination. She assures me that she will have no occasion to use it—will save it and invest it for my benefit etc. But I wish her to have it, to cover all the contingencies of her new existence." Later, when William thought it his duty to keep Henry informed, he replied: "Never, I again beg you, take the trouble to tell *me* twice anything at all about my Syracuse dividend. I have made my income entirely over to Alice and take no further interest in it." Henry would continue to live by his pen.

II

He drove his pen on Beacon Hill during these months, and used to venture forth for walks in the snowy streets. He was to evoke, in a charming tale, "A New England Winter," written some months later, the familiar aspect of the long straight avenue airing its newness in the frosty day, with its individual façades, and their neat sharp ornaments, the large clear windows of the curved fronts facing each other "like candid, inevitable eyes." The picture of Beacon Street revives an earlier age of plate glass.

There was something almost terrible in the windows . . . how vast and clean they were, and how, in their sculptured frames, the New England air seemed, like a zealous housewife, to polish and preserve them. A great many ladies were looking out, and groups of children, in the drawing-rooms, were flattening their noses against the transparent plate. Here and there, behind it, the back of a statuette or the symmetry of a painted vase, erect on a pedestal, presented itself to the street, and enabled the passer to construct, more or less, the room within—its frescoed ceilings, its new silk sofas, its untarnished fixtures. This continuity of glass constituted a kind of exposure, within and without, and gave the street the appearance of an enormous corridor, in which the public and the private were familiar and intermingled. But it was all very cheerful and commodious, and seemed to speak of diffused wealth, of intimate family life, of comfort constantly renewed.

James became thoroughly familiar with the Boston winter-scene —"the denuded bushes, the solid pond, the plank-covered walks, the exaggerated bridge, the patriotic statues, the dry, hard texture of the Public Garden for its foreground, and for its middle distance the pale, frozen twigs, stiff in the windy sky that whistled over the Common, the domestic dome of the State House, familiar in the untinted air, and the competitive spires of a liberal faith." In Washington Street, on a winter's afternoon, Henry trod the slushy thoroughfare, past the crawling horse-cars, the thronging pedestrians, the "sisterhood of shoppers" laden with satchels and parcels, the snow which thudded to the street from the sloping house-tops, the mounds of pulverized, mud-coloured ice on the pavements. The houses offered a jagged line of tall and short buildings, and there were staring signs, labels, pictures, familiar advertisements, a tangle of telegraph-wires in the air.

Every fifty yards there was a candy-store. Behind the plate glass, behind counters, were pale, delicate, tired faces of women, with polished hair and glazed complexions. In Bolton Street, months later, Henry could recall it as vividly as if he had just seen it. He was struck by the "numerosity" of the womenfolk; there was a "deluge of petticoats." Henry felt he was in a city of women, a country of women, and it was this that determined him in the selection of the subject for his next novel. The talk, the social life—everything—seemed so completely in the hands of the opposite sex that he wondered whether he were not in a country stricken by war, with the men away on the battlefields.

"I feel strangely settled here for the present," he wrote to his publisher in London, "and shall probably remain for the summer. But after that—open thy bosom, London of my soul!" It was clear to him that he would not return again to America for a long time; there was no further reason for doing so. "My sister and I make an harmonious little ménage," he wrote, "and I feel a good deal as if I were married." He told Mrs Kemble he had suggested to Alice that she come to England with him to set up a common household in London. His sister had, however, "shrewdly declined," he said, "for we are really both much too fond of our individual independence, and she has a dread of exchanging the comfortable *known* of Boston for the vast unknown of London." It was true that he and Alice, during this period, seemed to derive pleasure from their brother-and-sister household; it was the last holding-together of the family, and Henry, in his father's room, and Alice, presiding over the house, must have felt a great deal as if they were re-embodying their parents. But if Henry spoke of Alice's "independence," he nevertheless noted the extent to which she leaned upon her powerful friend, Katherine Loring. Miss Loring had quite taken over the foreground of Alice's life; quite entered into her daily well-being and her nervous prostrations. Alice had described Miss Loring shortly after meeting her in terms that leave little doubt as to her rôle in their relationship: "She has all the mere brute superiority which distinguishes man from woman, combined with all the distinctively feminine virtues. There is nothing she cannot do from hewing wood and drawing water to driving runaway horses and educating all the women in North America." Even before Henry had met Miss Loring he had remarked that "her strength of wind and limb, to say nothing of her nobler qualities, must make her a valuable addition to the Quincy Street circle." This had been during Alice's long convalescence after her 1878 illness. He was to observe this relationship closely. One might say that the figure of Olive Chancellor in *The Bostonians* had appeared upon the novelist's very doorstep.

III

Henry's productivity during the months he spent in America—in spite of family preoccupations—was impressive. But, as after his mother's death, he did not do much new work. He saw through the press the dramatized *Daisy Miller* and he put together for J. R. Osgood a volume containing three tales, "The Siege of London," "The Pension Beaurepas" and "The Point of View." He assembled a volume of miscellaneous travel-papers to which he gave the title *Portraits of Places*, carefully editing those on England, so as not to offend his transatlantic readers, and reminding them, in a special prefatory note, that the papers had been written primarily for Americans. He included in this volume also his old papers on Saratoga, Newport and Quebec, and here he reminded both his American and English readers that these had "only the value of history." Thirteen years had brought many changes. He planned at this time to issue a volume of essays as well, to be titled *Studies and Sketches* or perhaps *Impressions of Art and Life*. However he abandoned this plan, feeling that he did not have a sufficient number of good essays. Four years later, when the volume came out as *Partial Portraits*, it contained an almost new table of contents. Henry reviewed all his American publishing arrangements and pledged himself to produce a novel and a series of tales, giving Osgood not only the serial and American book-rights but the English rights as well. This could only mean that he would receive more money from

Osgood than he could realize by direct sale to Macmillan. The English publishing house, on its side, at this time proposed to Henry the issue of a small inexpensive pocket edition of his principal fiction to date. Henry welcomed the idea. Over and above the pleasure of having a collective edition on the market, he felt that this would give him an opportunity to establish himself in his new identity on his title-page—to get rid of the Henry James "Jun. or Jr"—the "mere junior"—now that his father was dead.

The Macmillan edition was published late that year, in a series of attractive blue-bound volumes in small format. There were fourteen volumes in all. They sold for one and six apiece, and the full set for a guinea. Henry had written to Macmillan, "I should like them to be *charming*, and beg you to spare no effort to make them so." The first three volumes were devoted to *The Portrait of a Lady*; then followed *Roderick Hudson* and *The American* in two volumes each, after which came *Washington Square*, *The Europeans* and *Confidence*, one volume each; leaving four volumes for the miscellaneous tales. These consisted of "The Siege of London" and "Madame de Mauves" in the volume devoted to international marriages; "An International Episode," "The Pension Beaurepas" and "The Point of View"—tales contrasting American and European manners; "Daisy Miller," "Four Meetings," "Longstaff's Marriage," and "Benvolio"—representing a subtle mixture, stories in which the heroine is frustrated or dies, save for "Benvolio" which portrays the ambivalent hero of these tales; and finally "The Madonna of the Future," "A Bundle of Letters," "The Diary of a Man of Fifty," and "Eugene Pickering." The groupings were as close as James could come to achieving congruity of theme; he could not altogether carry out his plan, because some stories were shifted in the interest of uniform volume-size.

In addition to seeing this edition through the press, Henry completed the greater part of his French travel-sketches for Aldrich, and wrote the first of the series of tales he had promised Osgood. This was "The Impressions of a Cousin," a story set in New York. The "impressions" are recorded by the cousin in her diary, which contains her account of the way in which an executor defrauds a young heiress, who will not prosecute him since she loves him—and how justice is quietly done. Henry thus drew vaguely on his recent responsibilities in the family affairs. The tale is but half-heartedly written, a throwing together of miscellaneous observations of his American stay.

He was much more in the public eye during this winter than the previous year. This was due, in some measure, to a laudatory article about him which Howells had published the previous autumn in the *Century Magazine*, asserting that it was Henry who was "shaping and directing American fiction." Not many critics were prepared to accept this statement. With the article had appeared a rather neat engraving of Henry by Timothy Cole which suggests however his fine head, his clear-eyed gaze, and his general well-groomed and pleasant appearance. His lips are parted as if he is in the act of speaking, and beneath the picture is his large signature, full size, with the flourish that suggests but does not quite convey the about-to-be-withdrawn "Jr." Henry called it "a horrible effigy of my countenance." Howells's article was part reminiscence and part criticism. Now that he was no longer Henry's editor he could allow himself the liberty of expressing in public all the praise he had been obliged hitherto to bestow in private. He rightly recognized that the art—the technique—of fiction was becoming much more subtle than it had been in the era of Dickens and Thackeray, and he discussed in some detail Henry's gift for creating character. "Evidently it is the character, not the fate, of his people, which occupies him." Howells also said that a reader could find in Henry James's writings "a perpetual delight" in his way of saying things.

The effect of Howells's shrewd critical observations was not altogether what he expected. To some critics it seemed as if he were "puffing" the work of his friend; and in England certain journalists accused Howells and James of constituting an "American Mutual Admiration Society"—this in spite of the fact that Henry had never written about Howells save an anonymous review of an early novel. In a letter to Smalley, Henry referred to Howells's "ill-starred amiabilities to me." To Howells he remarked, a little ironically, that "articles about you and me are as thick as blackberries—we are daily immolated on the altar of Thackeray and Dickens."

Henry had been approached three times to give a reading in public, and finally he yielded. This was before a woman's "Saturday Morning Club," where he read from a section of his little tour in France. The newspapers of the time reported that the rooms were crowded "by people of taste and fashion." Henry was introduced as the "Thackeray of America," and (said the reporter) his "English er-er-er-" marred his utterance. He read in a monotonous manner, but the matter "more than made amends." At the conclusion of the reading he was given a bouquet of white daisies surrounded by leaves of the homely seaboard plant known as "dusty miller." "I have hundreds of Daisy Millers here," said Henry, in a statement the ambiguity of which must have been lost on his preponderantly young female audience.

He made one other appearance, this one unannounced, and the testimony of it is to be found in the accounts of a meeting of the American Copyright League in New York. Henry had good reason to be interested in the work of the League; he had been pirated all too often. At a given moment he asked for the floor. "For ten or fifteen minutes," wrote Lawrence Hutton, "the speaker, known to every man present by his work, unknown in a personal way to most of his hearers, talked of things à propos of the matter in hand, in a manner absolutely to the point and carrying much weight. He made as great an impression as a speaker as he had ever made as a writer; and for the first time, after a long residence abroad, he was brought into intimate contact with the men of his own guild in his own country."

IV

He was in New York on 15 April 1883, in the city of his birth—and it was his fortieth birthday. Ten years before, when he became thirty in Rome, he had felt how short a distance he had travelled in his career; and if, during the decade that had elapsed, he had achieved his ambition, he was still dissatisfied. If anyone had told him that he could cease writing at this moment and remain a major figure in American fiction, he would have scorned the suggestion. Contemplating the advent of his fortieth year, he had written in his journal the previous autumn—on one of the days when he was in the Grand Hotel in Paris: "I have hours of unspeakable reaction against my smallness of production; my wretched habits of work—or of unwork; my levity, my vagueness of mind, my perpetual failure to focus my attention, to absorb myself, to look things in the face, to invent, to produce, in a word. I shall be forty years old in April next: it's a horrible fact." The horrible fact had occurred. Having distinctly underestimated all his capacities, he had proceeded to offer himself some solace: "I believe however that I have learned how to work and that it is in moments of forced idleness, almost alone, that these melancholy reflections seize me. When I am really at work, I'm happy, I feel strong, I see many opportunities ahead. It is the only thing that makes life endurable. I must make some great efforts during the next few years, however, if I wish not to have been on the whole a failure. I shall have been a failure unless I do something *great*!"

These sentences may be taken as an accurate measure by Henry of himself. His first goal—success and a place in the world—had been solidly achieved. He had made himself into an author and a figure known on both sides of the Atlantic. The next step was to do more—"greatness" was a large word. In the meantime there remained almost half a year before he could see his way to returning to England, to his own habitation and the ground of his real work, since he wanted to remain for a while longer with Alice. The record of these months is filled with small detail. He visited Washington and was pleased by its aspect in the spring. He saw his friends the Adamses again. In New York he met and befriended the young Jewish poet, Emma Lazarus, whose verses were to be inscribed two years later on the Statue of Liberty. She was about to go to London and he gave her an introduction to Mrs Procter and to the Smalleys. He was much preoccupied with Wilky, whom he met in Washington on his return from Florida, and escorted back to Cambridge. His brother's health had taken a turn for the worse, and in Mount Vernon Street Henry sat up nights with him, giving him what aid he could during his heart-attacks. He paid calls as usual on Mrs Gardner, and he saw much of his old friend Grace Norton.

To this period belongs the forging of those links of emotional intimacy and attachment which were to make this one of the most valued of all his friendships. It did not resemble his friendship with Fenimore; Miss Norton was, after all, ten years older, and she was a woman who asked for the kind of philosophical comforting which Henry could give her to the full, as he might have given to his mother. She was going through a bad phase at this time, a certain strain with her brother, a sense of isolation in the separate home she had fashioned for herself in Kirkland Street away from Shady Hill, and Henry wrote to her always with great gentleness, good humour and much feeling. Since he could no longer write the letters of a son to his mother, he had found in Cambridge someone to whom he could offer his filial feeling—someone closer to him intellectually than his mother had been. Some of his greatest, his fullest and certainly his wisest letters were addressed to Grace Norton, with a richness of detail and with large pictures of himself in the great world which he had of old given to Quincy Street. To her he wrote a letter which embodies within it the very heart of his philosophy and his attachment to reality—a kind of simple stoicism based on looking neither backward nor forward:

> I don't know *why* we live—the gift of life comes to us from I don't know what source or for what purpose; but I believe we can go on living for the reason that . . . life is the most valuable thing we know anything about and it is therefore presumptively a great mistake to surrender it while there is any yet left in the cup. In other words consciousness is an illimitable power, and though at times it may seem to be all consciousness of misery, yet in the way it propagates itself from wave to wave, so that we never cease to feel, though at moments we appear to, try to, pray to, there is something that holds one in one's place, makes it a standpoint in the Universe which it is probably good not to forsake.

And then, recurring to his frequent warning to his correspondent not to give herself too much to the world's woes and to the grief of others, he tells her:

Don't, I beseech you, *generalize* too much in these sympathies and tendernesses—remember that every life is a special problem which is not yours but another's and content yourself with the terrible algebra of your own. Don't melt too much into the universe, but be as solid and dense and fixed as you can.

And with this, his admonition was that Miss Norton adopt his own kind of doggedness: "Don't think, don't feel, any more than you can help, don't conclude or decide—don't do anything but *wait.*"

We all live together, and those of us who love and know, live so most. We help each other—even unconsciously, each in our own effort . . . Sorrow comes in great waves—no one can know that better than you—but it rolls over us, and though it may almost smother us it leaves us on the spot and we know that if it is strong we are stronger, inasmuch as it passes and we remain. It wears us, uses us, but we wear it and use it in return; and it is blind, whereas we after a manner see.

A darkness, such as she was passing through, he said, was *only* a darkness—not an end, not *the* end. And so, arguing for acceptance of feeling, for opening oneself to it, James embodied here the concept of "living through" emotion until one has survived it. He argued equally for a certain kind of personal sovereignty in a world unfriendly to individualism.

Henry wrote this letter to Miss Norton within a month of his return to England. He took passage on the *Servia*, leaving Boston on 22 August; he filled in the intervening hot days by padding about in a state of undress in the Mount Vernon Street house and confining himself to lemonade and ice-cream. He kept reasonably cool, and he kept up his work. Wilky had left for Milwaukee to rejoin his family. Henry must have known that this was their final parting. Alice spent the summer in a rest-home, the Adams Nervous Asylum in Jamaica Plain, where Henry occasionally visited her. He saw little of William, who went off to the mountains with his family.

Some weeks before his departure he spent a friendly week-end at Marion, Cape Cod, visiting Richard Watson Gilder, of the *Century*, and his wife, who was a sister of Mrs Bronson's. His impressions are incorporated in *The Bostonians*, where Marion is renamed Marmion. In a later story, "The Patagonia," he describes what must have been his general feelings on the empty summery Beacon Hill. Like its narrator, Henry had gone shortly before for a brief visit to Mount Desert—escaped to coolness and greenness—but he found it "as beautiful as a place can be in which the details are mainly ugly," adding "I liked the whole thing extremely—and wish never to see it again." The Boston houses on the eve of his sailing were dark in the August night; Beacon Street seemed a desert. The club on the hill alone emitted light from its cylindrical front, and the sound of billiard-balls clicking within suggested the servants were passing the time in the empty place. The heat was insufferable. He thought with joy of the freshening breeze he would have on board ship. The crossing was uneventful, and on 29 August he arrived in Liverpool, where he stayed until 1 September. He had been but forty-eight hours in Bolton Street when word reached him that Ivan Turgenev had come to the end of his sufferings at Bougival.

V

This loss, now but one of the series Henry had experienced, plunged him into renewed grief for his dead. One by one the fixed landmarks of his life were vanishing. "I am greatly touched by his extinction—I wanted him to live—mainly, I am afraid, because I wanted to see him again: for he had done his work," he wrote to the editor of the *Atlantic*, promising an article on the Russian. He followed with intense emotion the newspaper accounts of the final rites: the ceremonial at the station in Paris when the Russia-bound coffin was placed on the train, and the farewell orations of Ernest Renan and Edmond About on behalf of the writers of France. It was with Renan's noble words that Henry began his own tribute, written little more than a month later, words which he himself rendered with great felicity from the French:

Turgenev received by the mysterious decree which marks out human vocations the gift which is noble beyond all others: he was born essentially impersonal. His conscience was not that of an individual to whom nature had been more or less generous; it was in some sort the conscience of a people. Before he was born he had lived for thousands of years; infinite successions of reveries had amassed themselves in the depths of his heart. No man has been as much as he the incarnation of a whole race: generations of ancestors, lost in the sleep of centuries, speechless, came through him to life and utterance.

But if Renan spoke of Turgenev as impersonal, and if now it seemed in Russia the grief of the nation and the funeral pomp lifted Ivan Sergeyevich out of the range of familiar recollection, Henry set down, in his long paper for the *Atlantic*, the "personal" Turgenev: a simple record of his meetings with the Russian writer, his many recollections of him, his whole-hearted devotion to his work. The paper is both a series of reminiscences and a moving elegy; it reads as if it had been written at a single sitting and as if Henry had poured out all that he could remember, clinging to certain moments as to personal treasures—the Sundays at Flaubert's, the little breakfast-lunches on the boulevards, the aspect of Bougival, Turgenev's manner of speech, the last ride in the carriage, when they had parted on the exterior boulevard in front of a Punch and Judy show. "Intolerable pain had been his portion for many months before he died," Henry wrote. "His end was not serene and propitious, but dark and almost violent. But of brightness, of the faculty of enjoyment, he had also the large allowance usually made to first-rate men, and he was a singularly complete human being." He brought his long and deeply-felt account to an end with these words—they were almost an epitaph: "He was the most generous, the most tender, the most delightful, of men; his large nature overflowed with the love of justice; but he was also a rare genius."[1]

At the request of the *Century* he translated for it Daudet's reminiscences of Turgenev: this he did anonymously and only the survival of the two manuscripts, Daudet's and his own, testifies to this silent act on behalf of his friend and his old acquaintance of the *cénacle*. Daudet's article appeared in the November 1883 issue titled "Turgenev in Paris." Thus in two leading monthlies

[1] James altered this, in revising the essay for *Partial Portraits*, to read "but he was also of the stuff of which glories are made."

of America the passing of the Russian genius was eulogized through the agency of Henry James.

VI

Henry had barely posted his tribute to the *Atlantic* when he found himself writing a private tribute of quite another sort to his father's old friend, the English Swedenborgian, Dr J. J. Garth Wilkinson. Wilky had been named after the doctor, and Wilky was now dead in Milwaukee at thirty-eight, the third member of the James family to die in two years, and the first of the children. He had been Henry's immediate junior; and if he had squandered his patrimony, it could be said that fate had squandered him. He had never had good health after his precocious service in the Civil War. When Henry got word that William had left for Milwaukee, summoned to Wilky's death-bed, he drew from among his possessions a little pencil-drawing William had made many years before, after Wilky had been carried home from the battle-field, wounded in the assault on Fort Wagner. It is one of the early vivid sketches made by Henry's elder brother, the head alone of the wounded, rough-bearded soldier. Sitting in Bolton Street Henry looked at this drawing a long time. The time of the war came back to him. "It was taken," he wrote to Lizzie Boott, "at a moment when he looked as if everything was over, and is a most touching, little vivid picture. I say to myself as I look at it that it probably represents the dear boy now." With the aid of the past Henry sought to visualize the present. He was to publish the drawing years later in his autobiographies. "Peace be to his spirit," he wrote to Lizzie, "one of the gentlest and kindest I have ever known."

And so Henry had buried his dead. And now he was once more in his lodgings in London and at his large work-table by the Bolton Street window, looking out on Lord Ashburton's big house across the way. He had lived through a period of terminations; but, as he had written to Grace Norton, one could not continue to be engulfed by sorrow. He had said good-bye to his parents in their graves on the Cambridge hillock, and to his younger brother, dead before his time. The house on Quincy Street was no longer fixed in the orbit of his days. And he had once more quit America. His return to Europe was almost like another beginning of the career he had begun almost a decade before.

NOTES AND ACKNOWLEDGMENTS

I WISH to express my indebtedness in the writing of this biography to the late William James, whose death in 1961 ended a friendship of more than a quarter of a century; to the President and Fellows of Harvard College for continued access to the James papers; to Prof. William A. Jackson, librarian of the Houghton Library, for many generosities, and to Dr W. H. Bond and Miss Carolyn E. Jakeman of his staff; to Mr Simon Nowell-Smith for researches kindly carried out on my behalf in England at times when I could not cross the sea to do them myself; to Miss Clare Benedict, niece of Miss Woolson, for the use of her privately published family memoirs and for personal reminiscences; to the late Mary James Vaux, daughter of Robertson James, for access to the Vaux papers; to Mr Norbert Heermann for generously allowing me to use a photograph intended for his biography of Frank Duveneck, as frontispiece to this volume, and to Mrs Andrew Dasburg for the photograph of her grandmother, Sarah Butler Wister. I wish to record again old as well as new debts to the late Allan Wade, to Mr Donald G. Brien, Mr Percy Lubbock, Mr Rupert Hart-Davis, Mr George Stevens, Prof. Kenneth B. Murdock, Mr John L. Sweeney, and to my wife, Dr Roberta R. Edel.

This volume benefited from a Bollingen Fellowship granted me to edit James's letters. I have also been helped by various grants from the Arts and Science Research Fund of New York University.

Mr C. Waller Barrett gave me generous access to his remarkable collection, now in the Alderman Library, University of Virginia. I have also, at various stages of my task, had access to materials in the following libraries: the British Museum; the Brotherton Library, University of Leeds; the Brown University Library; the Berg Collection of the New York Public Library; the Library of Congress; Duke University Library; the Isabella Stewart Gardner Museum; the Huntington Library; the New York Historical Society; the New York Public Library; the Pierpont Morgan Library; and the Yale University Library.

For assistance in various ways, either in furnishing documents or reminiscences or in furthering my researches, I wish to thank Mr Frederick B. Adams, Jr; Mrs Elizabeth Aldrich; Miss Alice Balfour; Dr Charles S. Blinderman; Mrs Norman Ballou; Lady Buxton; Mrs Alfred Castle; Mr Herbert Cahoon; Mr Alvin Langdon Coburn; Prof. Kathleen Coburn; Mr Ralph Curtis; Prof. Earl Daniels; Prof. Martin B. Duberman; Mr Donald Gallup; Prof. William M. Gibson; Mr James Gilvarry; Dr John D. Gordan; Prof.

Virginia Harlow; Dr Robert Halsband; Miss Mercede Huntington; Mr and Mrs Harold M. Landon; Rev. John LaFarge S.J.; Prof. Edward C. McAleer; Marchesa Nannina Fossi Rucellai; Dr Gordon N. Ray; Prof. A. J. M. Smith; the late Miss Ethel Sands; Miss Rosamond Sherwood; Mrs Ruth Simon; Mr Francis Steegmuller; Mrs Walter Stokes; Mr George L. Stout; Mrs Tamie Swett; Mr Robert H. Taylor; Miss Aileen Tone; Mr Edmund Wilson; Mr Owen J. Wister and Prof. Morton Dauwen Zabel.

I am indebted to Catherine Benjamin for her assistance in the difficult task of transcribing hundreds of James's letters, and to my former students Dr Viola Hopkins and Dr Gloria Glikin for helping with certain elusive and minute library work. My debt to others, when not indicated in the notes below, must await the publication of the remaining volumes.

In a work based on so many unpublished documents it is impossible to furnish annotation without sowing footnotes often after every phrase. Most of the letters to which I allude in the notes below, moreover, are unpublished —that is, not generally available. I have on occasion suppressed the usual three dots by which excerpting is indicated in the interest of a more readable text, but only where the phrases not used were of a parenthetical nature, or related to matters not under discussion. In some cases I have "telescoped" portions of published text for the same reasons. Although in the notes below I refer the reader usually to the collections of James's articles and stories, I have, where relevant, used the original magazine texts, which James often revised on including them in a book. I assume that scholars interested in my sources will consult *A Bibliography of Henry James* (revised edition 1961), which I compiled with Mr Dan H. Laurence. I wish to take this opportunity of thanking Mr Laurence for his valuable collaboration in a venture the usefulness of which I myself have now had ample opportunity to test. I am also grateful to him for other searches undertaken on my behalf during the course of his bibliographical work.

Unless otherwise indicated, the documents mentioned in the notes below are in the James collection or other collections in the Houghton Library at Harvard. In the interest of concision the following abbreviations are used in the notes:

AJ—Alice James
AK—Aunt Kate (Catherine Walsh)
Barrett—Barrett Collection
CEN—Charles Eliot Norton
CFW—Constance Fenimore Woolson
Curtis—Mr and Mrs D. S. Curtis
FB—Francis Boott
GN—Grace Norton

HJ—Henry James
HJ Sr—Henry James (father)
Hoppin—William J. Hoppin, *Journal of a Residence in London*
JF—F. O. Matthiessen, *The James Family* (1947)
LB—Elizabeth (Lizzie) Boott
Lubbock—*Letters of Henry James* (1920)
Mrs HJ Sr—Mrs Henry James (Mary Walsh, mother)
N—*The Notebooks of Henry James* (ed. Matthiessen and Murdock, 1947)
NSB—*Notes of a Son and Brother* (1914)
NY Ed—New York Edition of the Novels and Tales of Henry James (1907–9)
NYPL—New York Public Library
RJ—Robertson James (brother)
RBP—Ralph Barton Perry, *Thought and Character of William James* (1935)
SW—Sarah Butler Wister
SBO—*A Small Boy and Others* (1913)
TS—Typescript
TSP—Virginia Harlow, *Thomas Sergeant Perry* (1950)
WDH—William Dean Howells
WJ—William James (brother)
Vaux—Vaux Papers (Robertson James papers)

BOOK ONE: *A Season in Cambridge*

The Precious Wound: CEN, 16 Jan., 9 Aug. 1871; 4 Feb., 7 Mar. 1872; GN, 26 Sep., 27 Nov. 1870; 13 Apr., 16 July 1871; WJ, 19 Oct. 1893; NY Ed. XIII. *Transatlantic Sketches. The Bostonians. The Europeans.* Howells, "Novel-Writing and Novel Reading" (ed. W. M. Gibson, 1958). "I can smell it still," unpublished letter, courtesy James Gilvarry.

The Exquisite Provincials: GN, 26 Sept. 1870; "Emerson" in *Partial Portraits.* Carlyle-Emerson *Correspondence* (1883); "Occasional Paris" in *Portraits of Places.* NY Ed. XIII.

The Dispossessed: NY Ed. XIII. WJ, 24 Nov. 1872.

"*The Great American Novel*"*:* See my introduction to *Watch and Ward* (1960); Fields, TS, 15, 25 July, 24, 29 Sep., 15 Nov., 1870. CEN, 9 Aug. 1871. "Reader's flesh creep," WDH, 18 Dec. [1876]. HJ Sr, 19 Apr. 1878.

Alice: Alice James: Her Brothers: Her Journal (ed. Burr, 1934). The text of the published version is corrupt and there are omissions. I am indebted to Mr Henry James Vaux for access to the manuscript. Thackeray, crinoline, SBO VII; for other details of AJ childhood, see WJ *Letters* (1920), RBP, JF. WJ, 28 May 1894; also in Vaux, 31 May, 1 June, 14 Sep. 1878.

The Art of Seeing: The Painter's Eye (ed. Sweeney, 1956). Certain of

Henry's sketchbook drawings are reproduced in *Henry James: The Untried Years* (1953).

Escape: LB, 24 Jan. 1872.

BOOK TWO: *Transatlantic Sketches*

The material is drawn from *Transatlantic Sketches*, and the following letters of 1872: Parents 23, 29 May, 4, 28 June, 21, 24, 28 July, 11, 25 Aug., 9, 15, 29 Sep, 10 [?] Nov.; CEN, 1 June, 14 July, 11 Sept., 19 Nov.; GN, 8 Aug., 5 Nov.; WJ, 22 Sept., 31 Nov.; AJ, 16 Dec., WJ to HJ, 24 Aug., 10 Oct. Lowell, *Letters* (ed. Norton, 1894). *New Letters* (ed. Howe, 1932). Rusk, *Emerson* (1949).

BOOK THREE: *Roman Hours*

A Roman Winter: Parents, 29 Dec. [1872]; 8, 19, 26 Jan. 1873; TSP, 1, 24 Jan. 1873; AJ, 10 Feb. 1873; WJ, 8 Jan., HJ Sr to HJ, 14 Jan. 1873; Mrs HJ Sr to HJ, 21 Jan. 1873. *Transatlantic Sketches. Italian Hours. Roderick Hudson.*

The Two Palaces: Parents, 1, 17, 28 Feb. 1873; GN, 5 Mar. 1873; CEN, 13, 31 Mar. 1873; Jane Norton, 18 Feb. 1873; HJ Sr to HJ, 4 Mar. 1873; Mrs HJ Sr to HJ, 2 Feb., 21 Mar. 1873; CEN to HJ, 19 Jan., 13, 23 Mar. 1873; *William Wetmore Story and his Friends*. Maude Howe Elliott, *Three Generations* (1923), *My Cousin, F. Marion Crawford* (1934), *Uncle Sam Ward and His Circle* (1938); Mrs Winthrop Chanler, *Autumn in the Valley* (1936); Mrs Hugh Fraser, *Reminiscences of a Diplomat's Wife* (1912). Laura E. Richards, *Stepping Westward* (1912). Louise Hall Tharp, *Three Saints and a Sinner* (1956); Albert Ten Eyck Gardner, *Yankee Stonecutters* (1945).

Roman Rides: Parents, 4, 24 Mar. 1873. *Italian Hours.*

Six Women: Mr Owen J. Wister and Mrs Walter Stokes gave me access to HJ's letters to SW. Lady Buxton and Miss Alice Balfour gave me access to letters to Mrs Mason. GN, 5 Mar. 1873; Miss Julia Boit furnished certain details concerning her mother and Miss Reubell. Frank Duveneck Jr answered questions and provided the privately printed *Recollections of Francis Boott* (1912), a brief memoir written for his grandson. See also NSB XIII; *Foreign Parts*. Anna Lansens Dawes, *Charles Sumner* (1892).

A Study in Mauve: WJ, 9 Apr., 19 May, [?] June, 18 June 1873; Parents, 4 May 1873. Jane Norton, 18 Feb. 1873; AJ, 10 Feb. 1873.

The Monocle: AJ, 25 Apr. 1873; SW, 9 May 1873; CEN, 31 Mar. 1873; TSP, 25 Nov. 1883; WJ, 9 Apr. 1873. *William Wetmore Story and His Friends.*

A Roman Spring: CEN to HJ, 23 Mar. 1873; CEN, 31 Mar. 1873; GN, 5 Mar. 1873; Parents, 4 May 1873.

BOOK FOUR: *The Choice*

William: HJ Sr, 18 Mar. 1873; Mrs HJ Sr to HJ, 25 May, 12 Sept. 1873; WJ, 18 June 1873; WJ to AJ, 29 Oct. 1873. WJ *Letters:* RBP.

Angel and Brother: WJ to AJ, 23 Nov., 17 Dec. 1873; WJ to HJ Sr, 30 Nov. 1873; HJ Sr, 3, 22 Dec. 1873; AJ, 13 Jan. 1874; GN, 14 Jan. 1874; WJ to Mrs HJ Sr, 26 Jan. 1874; WJ, [?] Feb. 1874.

The Fork in the Path: WJ to HJ, 22 Mar., 18 Apr. 1874; Mrs HJ Sr, 17 May 1874; WDH, 9 Jan., 10 Mar., 3 May 1874; HJ Sr to Holland, 16 Feb. 1874; Parents, 15 Feb., 9 Mar. 1874.

The Palpable Present: "Tuscan Cities" (wrongly dated 1873 in *Transatlantic Sketches*, corrected to 1874 in *Italian Hours*). AJ, 18 Apr. 1874; NY Ed. I. Mrs HJ Sr, 4 Apr., 17 May, 3 June, 28 July 1874; LB, 7 Apr. 1874; CEN, 31 Mar. 1873. James on Turgenev: I had hoped to examine the manuscript of this essay in the Gluck Collection, Buffalo Public Library, to determine if possible the nature of the revisions made at the suggestion of HJ Sr, but I was informed the manuscript is "missing." SW, 29 July 1874. HJ Sr and Turgenev RPB. Turgenev's letters to HJ, *Comparative Literature* (ed. J. Seznac, Summer 1949); Mrs HJ Sr to RJ, 27 Sept. 1874 (Vaux); RJ, 13 Oct. 1874 (Vaux).

Roderick Hudson: NY Ed I. SW in *North American Review*, Apr. 1876. See my introduction to *Roderick Hudson* (1960).

A New York Winter: N 24–25. Quincy Street saved none of HJ's letters during this time. WDH, 13 Jan., 19 or 20 Mar. 1875; LB, 27 Jan., 8 Mar. 1875; SW, 23 Jan. 1875. NY Ed XII, XXIII. John Russell, *A Portrait of Logan Pearsall Smith* (1950). *Parisian Sketches* (ed. Edel and Lind, 1957) contains all the documents relating to HJ and the *Tribune*. Hay, 21 July 1875. HJ letters to Hay are in the Library of Congress and in the Brown University Library. "Trollope" in *Partial Portraits.*

BOOK FIVE: *The Siege of Paris*

Ivan Sergeyevich: NY Ed II. Parents, 9, 18 Nov. 1875; *Galaxy*, 1 Dec. 1875 (NYPL); AK, 3 Dec. 1875; Turgenev to Ralston: "Essayez de vous lier avec Henry James; c'est un homme tres aimable, qui a beacoup de talent, avec un certain penchant à la tristesse," in *Lettres Inédites de Tourguéneff à Ralston* (tr. J. W. Bienstock), *Revue Mondiale*, 1 Jan. 1925. Avrahm Yarmolinsky, *Turgenev* (1959); David Magarshack, *Turgenev* (1954).

The Lesson of the Master: In addition to his essays on Turgenev, see preface NY Ed III. WJ, 8 Feb. 1876; HJ Sr, 20 Dec. 1875; 11 Apr. 1876. Turgenev to HJ, 31 Jan. 1876: "La scène (avant le départ) entre Rowland, la mère de Roderick, Miss Garland et Striker—est fait de main de maître." Turgenev to HJ, 10 Aug. 1877: "Je me mettrai à vous lire aujourd'hui et je vous dirai mon avis sincèrement comme il convient à de la faire aux gens d'un talent pareil au vôtre."

Councils of the Gods: TSP, 3 Feb., 2 May 1876: "Tu vois que je suis dans les conseils des dieux—je suis lancé en plein Olympe." HJ "Flaubert," 1902; Francis Steegmuller, *Maupassant* (1949); WDH, 3 Feb., 4 Apr., 28 May 1876; Gosse, 15, 17 Oct. 1912 (Leeds). Mrs HJ Sr, 24 Jan. 1876; AJ, 22 Feb. 1876; CEN, 23 Mar. 1876.

Pastel: N26. LB, 31 Dec. 1875; HJ Sr, 20 Dec. 1875; 11 Apr. 1876. A. J. M. Smith generously rendered "Pastel" into English for this book.

Parisian Life: HJ on French hospitality, in his 1902 essay on Flaubert. I am grateful to Yvonne ffrench for details concerning Mme Mohl. Mrs HJ Sr, 11, 29 Jan. 1876; WJ, 14 Mar. [1876]; AJ, 24 May 1876. Mme Mohl quoted Mme Récamier: "Je ne voudrais pas avoir l'air pédant, mais je ne souhaite que la vertu." Childe: WJ, 14 Mar.; CEN, 25 Mar. 1876; AJ, 24 May 1876. Pierce: WJ, 14 Mar., 4 July 1876. Zhukovsky: Mrs HJ Sr, 8 May; AJ, 24 May; WJ, 22 June; LB, 11 Nov.; HJ Sr, 11 Nov. 1876. Princess Ourousov: Mrs HJ Sr, 8 May 1876. I am indebted to her granddaughter, Eugenie Lehovich, for access to the unpublished memoirs of Prince Serge Ourousov, *Noirs Oiseaux de l'Adversité.* The Princess is described also in André Gide, *Si le grain ne meurt* (1928).

Silk Purse and Sow's Ear: Parisian Sketches. I have here used portions of the preface to that volume, and am indebted to Ilse Dusoir Lind for her search of the *Tribune* archive.

The American: Letters to the *Galaxy* (NYPL). I am grateful to Alvin Langdon Coburn for the Faubourg St Germain streets as James outlined them to him for the photographic frontispieces of NY Ed. *The American* should be read in the original version to obtain the freshness of its writing. The revised version is much altered and softened. WDH, 3 Feb., 4 Apr. 1876; 30 Mar. 1877.

In the Provinces: NY Ed II. N 26–27. Mrs HJ Sr, 24 Aug. 1876; AJ, 6 Sep. 1876.

A Channel Crossing: HJ Sr, 16 Sep. 1876; WJ, 29 July 1876; Mrs HJ Sr, 27 Sep. 1876. N 27.

BOOK SIX: *The Conquest of London*

The Observant Stranger: See the never-reprinted "Suburbs of London," *Galaxy*, Dec. 1877. *Portraits of Places. English Hours.* N 27. NY Ed V, XIV. AJ, 13 Dec. 1876; Mrs HJ Sr, 24 Dec. 1876; prophetic letter WJ, 28 Jan. 1878.

London Clubs: N 28. WJ, 5 Feb. 1877; Mrs HJ Sr, 22 Mar. 1877.

The Bird of Paradox: WJ, 28 Feb., 29 Mar. 1877. The HJ letters to Lord Houghton are in the library of Trinity College, Cambridge, where Mr Simon Nowell-Smith kindly obtained copies for me. Houghton, 15 Apr., 6 Oct. [1878]. James Pope-Hennessy, *Monckton Milnes, The Years of Promise* (1950), *The Flight of Youth* (1951).

A Little Journey: Macmillan & Co. gave me access to HJ's letters in their archive. HJ Sr, 19 Sep., 21 Dec. 1877. NY Ed XIV. GN, 15 Dec. 1877; NY Ed XVIII. See also "Occasional Paris," "Florence Revisited;" "Very Modern Rome," a posthumous travel essay, Harvard Library Bulletin, Spring 1954.

Daisy: WJ, 28 Jan. 1878. NY Ed VIII, XVIII. George Somes Layard, *Mrs Lynn Linton* (1901). Mildred Howells, ed. *Life in Letters of William Dean Howells* (1928). Robert H. Taylor generously made available the letter from HJ to Mrs Hill, 21 Mar. 1879. Its full text is in *Selected Letters of HJ* (ed. Edel, 1956). Mrs HJ Sr, 18 Jan. 1879.

The Two Secretaries: Harold D. Cater, *Henry Adams and His Friends* (1937); G. W. Smalley, *London Letters* (1891). E. S. Nadal, *A Virginian Village* (1922). William Jones Hoppin, *Journal of a Residence in London*, 12 volumes in form of scrapbook and journal (unpublished) in the Houghton Library; HJ to Hoppin, 3 Mar. 1880. Yates on Hoppin, *World*, 3 Mar. 1880; Hoppin, 5 Mar. 1877, 6 Jan. 1878, 20 July 1879 (the essay on London Society), 18 Jan., 15 Feb., 4, 7 Mar. 1880. E. S. Nadal, "Personal Recollections of Henry James," *Scribner's*, July 1920. AJ, 19 Aug. 1879. CEN, 13 Nov. 1880.

A Position in Society: The Middle Years (1917). W. H. Mallock, *Memoirs of Life and Literature* (1920). N 28. Mrs HJ Sr, 31 Jan. 1877, 18 Jan. 1879. Browning: WDH, 30 Mar. 1877; AJ, 8 Apr. 1877; Curtis, 30 Oct. 1888. WJ on HJ, 13 July 1880; WJ, 25 Mar. 1878, 4 Mar. 1879; GN, 4 Jan., 15 June 1879; HJ Sr, 25 Mar. 1878; Sir John Pollock, *Time's Chariot* (1950). AJ, 5 June 1878. Justin McCarthy, *Reminiscences* (1899).

BOOK SEVEN: *A Reasonable Show of Fame*

The Objective Genius: TSP, 16 May 1879; WJ, 15 June 1879; WDH, 17 June 1879; Mrs HJ Sr, 11 Sept. 1880.

The Bachelor of Bolton Street: HJ's daily routine is here reconstructed from miscellaneous letters declining or accepting invitations and alluding to his working hours. AJ, 26 Mar. 1879; Hoppin, 7 Nov. 1880; GN, 28 Dec. 1880; LB, 11 Dec. 1883.

Three Old Women: GN, 7 July 1878; Parents, 19 Aug. 1880; Hoppin, 18 Jan., 20 Dec. 1880; Mrs HJ Sr, 13 Jan. 1878, 31 Jan. 1879, 31 Oct. 1880; Thomas Hardy, *The Early Life* (1928); Smalley, *op. cit.* HJ Sr, 20 May 1877. Mrs Kemble: Mrs HJ Sr, 4, 18, 31 Jan., 4, 14, 19 May 1879; AJ, 29 Dec. 1877, 9 Dec. 1878, 26 Mar. 1879. Mrs Procter: AJ, 29 Dec. 1877. Hoppin contains much documentation on Mrs Duncan Stewart. Frances Anne Kemble, *Records of a Later Life* (1882).

Visits: AJ, 15 Sept. 1878; Mrs HJ Sr, 28 Nov. 1880; N 29–30. GN, 28 Dec. 1880. HJ Sr, 27 Dec. 1880.

A Dinner at the Reform: WHJ, 15 June 1879; Mrs HJ Sr, 6 July 1879. Ethel F. Fiske ed. *Letters of John Fiske* (1949).

Cart Horse and Racer. The letters of HJ to W. E. Henley are in the Pierpont Morgan Library. Mrs HJ Sr, 12 Apr. 1878; WJ, 1 May 1878.

The Bard and Mr Browning: CEN, 17 Nov. 1878; GN, 26 July 1880. *The Middle Years* (1917).

Voltaire in Petticoats: WJ, 15 June 1879; Ward Thoron, *Letters of Mrs Henry Adams* (1936). The Massachusetts Historical Society gave me access to HJ's letters to Henry Adams. GN, 11 Oct. 1879; 20 Sept. 1880. W. C. Ford, *Letters of Henry Adams*, 1858–1891 (1930). LB, 26 May, 2 June, 19 Aug. 1879; 22 Feb. 1880; Mrs HJ Sr, 6 July 1879, 2 Feb. 1880. HJ Sr, 11 Oct. 1879; Mrs Gardner, 29 Jan. 1880; Hoppin, 4 Mar. 1880, TSP, 31 Aug. 1880.

C'est mon plaisir . . . : Mr George L. Stout, director of the Isabella Stewart Gardner Museum, gave me access to HJ's letters to Mrs Gardner. Morris Carter, *Isabella Stewart Gardner and Fenway Court* (1925). Curtis, 12 Feb. 1895. Gardner, 29 Jan. 1880.

BOOK EIGHT: *The Portrait of a Lady*

Provincial Storm: WJ, 15 July, 14 Nov. 1878; HJ Sr, 11 Jan., 15 Feb. 1880; WDH, 31 Jan. 1880; LB, 22 Feb. 1880; TSP, 22 Feb., 18 April 1880; CEN, 31 Mar. 1880. *Hawthorne.*

The Frail Vessels: NY Ed III. *Confidence.*

Fathers and Daughters: WDH, 3 Jan. 1880; N 29; CEN, 31 Mar. 1880; HJ Sr, 30 Mar. 1880. AK, 3 May 1880. *Washington Square.*

A Neapolitan Episode: GN, 9 Apr. 1880; AJ, 25 Apr. 1880. A search in the Richard Wagner Archive, Bayreuth, and the Liszt Museum, Weimar, where some of Zhukovsky's papers are preserved, yielded no HJ letters.

Fenimore: Clare Benedict, *Constance Fenimore Woolson* (privately printed, n.d.). This volume contains extracts from Miss Woolson's letters to relatives and friends, and from her notebooks and commonplace books. "Miss Woolson," in *Partial Portraits.* Grove, 18 Apr. 1880 (Macmillan); WDH, 18 Apr. 1880; AJ, 25 Apr. 1880; "At the Château of Corinne," *Harper's*, Oct. 1887; "Miss Grief," *Lippincott's*, May 1880; "A Florentine Experiment," *Atlantic*, Oct. 1880.

A Band of Egotists: The Portrait of a Lady. N 30. Mrs HJ Sr, 4, 20 July 1880; Mrs Huxley, 3 July [1880]; WJ to Parents, 13 July 1880 (Vaux); NY Ed III. James H. Morse, "The Native Element in American Fiction Since the War," *Century*, XXVI 362–375. WDH, 5 Dec. 1880; Hillard: WJ, 28 June, 10 July 1877; Mrs HJ Sr, 4 Sept. 1877.

Venice: N 30–32. HJ Sr, 24 Feb. 1881. Mrs Van Rensselaer is described in James Whitall, *English Years* (1935). "Venice" and "Ca'Alvisi" in *Italian Hours* (1841–1915): Mrs HJ Sr to AJ, Jan. 1867, 4 June 1872; WJ, 5 June

1881; also Harvard alumni records. E. B. Drew, *Harvard Memoirs*, June 1914 to March 1915. GN, 12 June 1881. Undated letter from 4161 Riva Schiavoni, also 19 July [1881] to Mrs Bronson.

BOOK NINE: *Terminations*

Homecoming: N 23–24, 32–36. "The Point of View," and "A Bundle of Letters." AK to Mrs RJ, 14 Nov. 1881 (Vaux); GN, 13 Dec. 1881.

The Dome and the Shaft: "The Point of View." *The American Scene.* NY Ed XIV. Thoron, *op. cit.*; GN, 10 Jan. 1882; R., 9 Jan. 1882; Godkin: 15, 22 Jan. 1882. Lewis and Smith, *Oscar Wilde Discovers America* (1936); *The Letters of Oscar Wilde* (ed. Hart-Davis, 1962). Gardner, 23 Jan. 1882; Mrs HJ Sr, 22 Jan. 1882.

Mary James: N 39–40. RJ, 27 Jan. 1882 (Vaux); Mrs HJ Sr, 29 Jan. 1882; Gardner, [3?] Feb. 1882; Mrs Francis Mathews, 13 Feb. 1882.

An Exquisite Stillness: N 40–42. Daniel Frohman, manager of the Madison Square Theatre, his comments on "Daisy" communicated to me. Hoppin, 9 Feb. 1882; R., 9 Feb. 1882; Mrs Kemble TS, 5 Apr. 1882; "Emerson" in *Partial Portraits.* HJ Sr to HJ, 9 May 1882.

A Little Tour in France: Godkin, 5 June 1882; N 42–43; WJ *Letters*, to his wife, 24 Sept. 1882; AJ, 6 Aug., 16 Oct. 1882. Account by WJ's son Henry, in WJ *Letters* I 209–10. Turgenev to Ralston, *Revue Mondiale*, Jan. 1925: "Henry James m'a fait une visite. Il est toujours aussi aimable. Il a beacoup grossi; il est presque aussi gros qu'Albert Turgenev, avec qui il est venu me voir." LB, 7 Oct. 1882; WDH, 15 Oct. 1882.

November Parting: "Turgenev" in *Partial Portraits.* Gardner, 12 Nov. 1882; Hay, 26 Nov. 1882 (Brown); WDH, 27 Nov. 1882.

A Winter Summons: WJ, 26, 28 Dec. 1882; RJ, 30 Dec. 1882 (Vaux); AK's notes on HJ Sr's last comments in Vaux. Macmillan, 26 Dec. 1882.

A Blessed Farewell: WJ *Letters* I 218–220. WJ, 1 Jan. 1883.

Son and Brother: Godkin, 3 Mar. 1885; WJ, 8, 11, 23 Jan., 5, 7, 11 Feb. 1883. "A New England Winter." Macmillan, 27 Jan., 9 Apr. 1883; Mrs Kemble TS, 1 Feb. 1882; letters of J. R. Osgood, Yale University Library, Barrett and Colby College. Osgood, 19 Apr. 1883 (Yale). Carl J. Weber, *The Rise and Fall of James Ripley Osgood* (1959). Prof. Weber kindly furnished typescript of two letters used in his book. Osgood, 5 Aug. 1887; C. F. Woolson, to Osgood, 30 Dec. [1887]. Reading in Boston: N.Y. *Tribune*, 9 May 1883. Laurence Hutton, *Talks in a Library* (1905). N 42–43. HJ's letters to Emma Lazarus in Columbia University Library, where I saw them through courtesy of Prof. Ralph L. Rusk. GN, 28 July 1883. "The Patagonia." Aldrich, 20 Sept. 1883. Daudet on Turgenev, and HJ translation: both manuscripts are in the Barrett Collection. LB, 14 Oct. 1883.

INDEX